Fix it
FAST

Fix it
RIGHT

Fix it FAST
Fix it RIGHT

Hundreds of Quick & Easy Home Improvement Projects

by Gene and Katie Hamilton

 Rodale Press, Emmaus, Pennsylvania

The authors and editors who compiled this book have tried to make all the contents as accurate and as correct as possible. Plans, illustrations, and text have all been carefully checked and cross-checked. However, due to the variability of local conditions, construction materials, personal skill, and so on, neither the authors nor Rodale Press assumes any responsibility for any injuries suffered, or for damages or other losses incurred that result from the material presented herein. All instructions and plans should be carefully studied and clearly understood before beginning construction.

Printed in the United States of America on acid-free ⬡, recycled paper ♻

Editor in Chief: William Gottlieb
Senior Managing Editor: Margaret Lydic Balitas
Editor: David Schiff
Editorial assistance: Stacy Brobst
Research Associate: Heidi A. Stonehill
Copy Editor: Louise Doucette
Indexer: Ed Yeager

Book design by Darlene Schneck
Cover design by Denise Mirabello
Illustrations by John Carlance

If you have any questions or comments concerning this book, please write:

> Rodale Press
> Book Reader Service
> 33 East Minor Street
> Emmaus, PA 18098

Library of Congress Cataloging-in-Publication Data

Hamilton, Gene.
    Fix it fast, fix it right : hundreds of quick and easy home remodeling and repair projects / by Gene and Katie Hamilton.
       p.   cm.
    Includes index.
    ISBN 0-87857-859-5   hardcover
    ISBN 0-87857-860-9   paperback
    1. Dwellings—Remodeling—Amateurs' manuals. 2. Dwellings—Maintenance and repair—Amateurs' manuals. I. Hamilton, Katie. II. Title.
TH4816.H286   1991
643.7—dc20   91-9700
                              CIP

Distributed in the book trade by St. Martin's Press

2 4 6 8 10 9 7 5 3   hardcover
2 4 6 8 10 9 7 5 3   paperback

Contents

Acknowledgments

We'd like to thank David Schiff, our editor, for his unwavering support and helpful suggestions. We jokingly refer to our good friend as "I have a few questions David" who helped to clarify and distill what we were trying to say. As always, our agent, Jane Jordan Browne, has seen us through another book with her steadfast direction and diligence. We sincerely appreciate her efforts.

Introduction

Thirteen houses and 23 years of marriage have taught us plenty about love, life, and lath and plaster. In each house we renovated, we learned more about the intricacies and idiosyncrasies of improving a house. In this book we've put together everything we've learned, with the hope that something you read here might help you to make your home a better place for you and your family to live in and enjoy.

One of the most important aspects of remodeling we've gleaned over the years is when not to do a project yourself. So we've set forth guidelines that suggest ways to work with professionals. For example, we feel that sanding hardwood floors should be left to a pro, but the grunt work is custom-made for homeowners wanting to save a few dollars. We'll share our inside information and the tricks and techniques we've developed, so that you can get the most out of your remodeling dollars and enjoy the good feeling and satisfaction of improving your home.

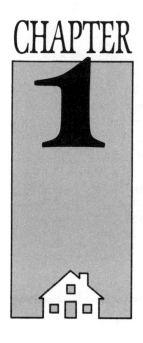

CHAPTER 1

Interior Painting

Painting is the least expensive way to improve a room, and it is one of the easiest remodeling jobs to tackle. The bonus is that it requires a very small investment in tools and equipment. It should come as no surprise then that painting is the most popular do-it-yourself project. What you possibly don't realize is that painting is strenuous work — so be prepared for some sore muscles from bending, reaching, and lifting. Here's inside information we've gleaned over the years that will help you get professional-looking results and make painting faster and *less* of a chore.

Sizing Up the Job

Ask any professional painter, and he'll tell you that the secret to a lasting paint job is preparation. In fact, you will probably spend more time getting ready to paint than actually painting. Here are the most important steps to follow.

Determine How Much Paint You Will Need

Generally speaking, a gallon of paint covers 300 square feet. If you're covering dark surfaces with a light color, two coats might be needed. If that's the case, or if you plan to paint over a color that is difficult to cover, such as bright yellow, it's more economical to paint the area with a latex primer first, then follow with your wall paint.

Estimating the amount of paint you need isn't difficult, but it sure isn't an exact science either. We like to err on the high side rather than run short at 9:30 some Saturday night with just one more wall to cover. Also, the new batch you buy may not exactly match the original. In fact, if you do find you have to buy more paint, it's a good idea to start the new batch at a corner so any slight color difference won't be noticeable.

To estimate the amount of paint

Paint Need Chart for Walls

WIDTH	8	9	10	11	12	13	14	15	16	17	18	19	20	21	22	23	24
20	1.5	1.6	1.7	1.7	1.8	1.8	1.9	2.0	2.0	2.1	2.1	2.2	2.3	2.3	2.4	2.4	2.5
19	1.5	1.5	1.6	1.7	1.7	1.8	1.8	1.9	2.0	2.0	2.1	2.1	2.2	2.3	2.3	2.4	2.4
18	1.4	1.5	1.5	1.6	1.7	1.7	1.8	1.8	1.9	2.0	2.0	2.1	2.1	2.2	2.3	2.3	2.4
17	1.4	1.4	1.5	1.5	1.6	1.7	1.7	1.8	1.8	1.9	2.0	2.0	2.1	2.1	2.2	2.3	2.3
16	1.3	1.4	1.4	1.5	1.5	1.6	1.7	1.7	1.8	1.8	1.9	2.0	2.0	2.1	2.1	2.2	2.3
15	1.2	1.3	1.4	1.4	1.5	1.5	1.6	1.7	1.7	1.8	1.8	1.9	2.0	2.0	2.1	2.1	2.2
14	1.2	1.2	1.3	1.4	1.4	1.5	1.5	1.6	1.7	1.7	1.8	1.8	1.9	2.0	2.0	2.1	2.1
13	1.1	1.2	1.2	1.3	1.4	1.4	1.5	1.5	1.6	1.7	1.7	1.8	1.8	1.9	2.0	2.0	2.1
12	1.1	1.1	1.2	1.2	1.3	1.4	1.4	1.5	1.5	1.6	1.7	1.7	1.8	1.8	1.9	2.0	2.0
11	1.0	1.1	1.1	1.2	1.2	1.3	1.4	1.4	1.5	1.5	1.6	1.7	1.7	1.8	1.8	1.9	2.0
10	0.9	1.0	1.1	1.1	1.2	1.2	1.3	1.4	1.4	1.5	1.5	1.6	1.7	1.7	1.8	1.8	1.9
9	0.9	0.9	1.0	1.1	1.1	1.2	1.2	1.3	1.4	1.4	1.5	1.5	1.6	1.7	1.7	1.8	1.8
8	0.8	0.9	0.9	1.0	1.1	1.1	1.2	1.2	1.3	1.4	1.4	1.5	1.5	1.6	1.7	1.7	1.8
7	0.8	0.8	0.9	0.9	1.0	1.1	1.1	1.2	1.2	1.3	1.4	1.4	1.5	1.5	1.6	1.7	1.7
6	0.7	0.8	0.8	0.9	0.9	1.0	1.1	1.1	1.2	1.2	1.3	1.4	1.4	1.5	1.5	1.6	1.7

LENGTH

Note: *Paint is in gallons; wall width and length are in feet.*

Paint Need Chart for Ceilings

WIDTH \ LENGTH	8	9	10	11	12	13	14	15	16	17	18	19	20	21	22	23	24
20	0.5	0.6	0.7	0.7	0.8	0.9	0.9	1.0	1.1	1.1	1.2	1.3	1.3	1.4	1.5	1.5	1.6
19	0.5	0.6	0.6	0.7	0.8	0.8	0.9	1.0	1.0	1.1	1.1	1.2	1.3	1.3	1.4	1.5	1.5
18	0.5	0.5	0.6	0.7	0.7	0.8	0.8	0.9	1.0	1.0	1.1	1.1	1.2	1.3	1.3	1.4	1.4
17	0.5	0.5	0.6	0.6	0.7	0.7	0.8	0.9	0.9	1.0	1.0	1.1	1.1	1.2	1.2	1.3	1.4
16	0.4	0.5	0.5	0.6	0.6	0.7	0.7	0.8	0.9	0.9	1.0	1.0	1.1	1.1	1.2	1.2	1.3
15	0.4	0.5	0.5	0.6	0.6	0.7	0.7	0.8	0.8	0.9	0.9	1.0	1.0	1.1	1.1	1.2	1.2
14	0.4	0.4	0.5	0.5	0.6	0.6	0.7	0.7	0.7	0.8	0.8	0.9	0.9	1.0	1.0	1.1	1.1
13	0.3	0.4	0.4	0.5	0.5	0.6	0.6	0.7	0.7	0.7	0.8	0.8	0.9	0.9	1.0	1.0	1.0
12	0.3	0.4	0.4	0.4	0.5	0.5	0.6	0.6	0.6	0.7	0.7	0.8	0.8	0.8	0.9	0.9	1.0
11	0.3	0.3	0.4	0.4	0.4	0.5	0.5	0.6	0.6	0.6	0.7	0.7	0.7	0.8	0.8	0.8	0.9
10	0.3	0.3	0.3	0.4	0.4	0.4	0.5	0.5	0.5	0.6	0.6	0.6	0.7	0.7	0.7	0.8	0.8
9	0.2	0.3	0.3	0.3	0.4	0.4	0.4	0.5	0.5	0.5	0.5	0.6	0.6	0.6	0.7	0.7	0.7
8	0.2	0.2	0.3	0.3	0.3	0.3	0.4	0.4	0.4	0.5	0.5	0.5	0.5	0.6	0.6	0.6	0.6
7	0.2	0.2	0.2	0.3	0.3	0.3	0.3	0.4	0.4	0.4	0.4	0.4	0.5	0.5	0.5	0.5	0.6
6	0.2	0.2	0.2	0.2	0.2	0.3	0.3	0.3	0.3	0.3	0.4	0.4	0.4	0.4	0.4	0.5	0.5

Note: *Paint is in gallons; ceiling width and length are in feet.*

needed, calculate the area of the walls and subtract the area of the doors and windows. To find the wall area, add the lengths of all the walls together to find the perimeter, then multiply this figure by your ceiling height. From this wall area subtract about 20 square feet for each door and 15 square feet for each average-size window, and you will have the area you actually have to cover with paint. Then divide this by 300 to find the number of gallons of paint you need.

The answer will be a decimal number. Remember wall paint comes only in quarts and gallons, so round the decimal to the nearest quart (1.4 = 1 gallon 2 quarts, or 0.78 = 3 quarts). Don't purchase 3 quarts; instead get a gallon. This gives you extra paint for touch-ups, and 3 quarts cost almost as much as a gallon.

If all this figuring boggles your mind, use our estimating charts. Find the width of your room along the left side of the table (vertical column). Then find the length of your room along the bottom (horizontal row). Read the number of decimal gallons from the table where the row and column intersect. Round off this number to gallons and quarts as we explained.

Choose a Type of Paint

You have two basic types of paint to choose from—latex and oil-based. These days, most oil-based paints use alkyd, which is composed of synthetically manufactured soybean resins, rather than linseed resins, which occur naturally in plants. Alkyd resins are less brittle and less expensive than natural resins, and they dry faster.

Oil-based paints are more durable and washable. But it is harder to get them to spread smoothly, and sometimes they have to be thinned with mineral spirits. You'll also need thinner to clean your brushes, rollers, and skin.

Latex paints are easier to apply and much easier to clean up. These paints are water-based, so water is all you need for cleanup. They also have much less odor than oil-based paints.

Both oil-based and latex paints can be purchased with enamel added. Enamel makes the paint dry to a hard, nonporous surface.

Oil-based paint is available in flat, semigloss, or high gloss. Latex comes in flat or semigloss. However, a flat oil will be glossier than a flat latex, and a semigloss oil will be glossier than a semigloss latex. Also, the addition of enamel makes each grade a little glossier than it would be without enamel.

Generally, we stick to latex paints for walls and ceilings. We use a flat paint for most interior walls, but in high-wear areas such as kitchens, bathrooms, halls, and stairways, we use a semigloss enamel latex because it is more washable. We use semigloss enamel in children's rooms, too—it makes it easier to get the crayon off the walls.

You may want to use oil-based paint in the bathroom, especially if you like to take long, steamy showers. Oil-based semigloss paint is good at resisting mildew. If mildew does appear, it's easily removed with a solution of bleach and soapy water. The paint will maintain its tough surface.

We still use oil-based paint on windows, doors, and woodwork trim. While latex semigloss and enamel have been around for a long time and are constantly being improved, we find them hard to work with because they dry so fast. Painting doors and woodwork without lap marks isn't easy, because you can't keep up with the paint. While latex paint's fast-drying quality is great for walls and ceilings, it's a problem when painting a five-panel door and its frame.

Another drawback we've found is that latex semigloss paint does not dry hard. We've had it stick to the bottom of things placed on windowsills and counters months after we thought the paint was dry.

Most good-quality paints offer one-coat coverage. Sometimes this works out and sometimes it doesn't. Let's say you are going to paint white walls a light blue. Under normal conditions you should be able to expect to get by with one coat, right? Sometimes. If you don't put the paint on very evenly, you will be disappointed with the results. The paint will cover in the areas where it is spread thickly enough, but in other areas you will be able to see the light background peeking through. So unless you work carefully and roll it evenly, there will be a slight difference in the wall color when you look at it closely.

Better-quality paints will give better coverage, but most of the time we find ourselves adding a second coat of even the best paints. More important reasons for buying top-quality paint are better washability and stain resistance. The cost difference between bargain paints and top-quality paints usually adds up to no more than $10 or $15 per room—not much of a savings when you consider the labor you are putting into the job.

When painting woodwork trim that has never been painted before, you have to prepare the wood properly. Sand it lightly and evenly, and use a primer coat followed by two finish coats. Primers are sold for latex and oil-based paints. Make sure the primer is compatible with the paint you're using.

We buy most of our paint at a paint store where we often find bargains on single gallons of paint, which we use for closets or small areas. Like most paint stores, the one we go to custom-mixes colors. Occasionally, someone goofs and adds a wrong tint. A delightful character named Max is the chief honcho at our paint store. Often we can pick up one of "Max's mistakes," a good-quality paint with a slightly different color from the color chart, which we use for painting the attic stairway or the laundry room. Before you buy a mistake, have the salesman machine-mix the paint for a few minutes before opening the can so you can take a look at it.

Choose Paint Colors

When deciding on a color or colors to paint a room, you'll naturally want to consider the color of the furnishings you'll use. One of the most important considerations is the color of the flooring or carpet. But there are other, less obvious considerations as well. Here are some points to remember when you're looking at paint charts:

▶ Colors tend to look much deeper and more intense when they are spread across a wall than they do in a 1-inch square on the paint chart. Consequently, choose a color you like and then buy a lighter shade. It's usually above the sample you like but looks paler and less intense.

▶ If you have something to hide or down-play in a room—a radiator, an odd-shaped window, or an exposed pipe—paint it with a pale color.

▶ To make a small room appear larger, choose a pale shade. Conversely, if your room is large and you want to create a more intimate atmosphere, use a deep, rich color, which will enclose the room.

▶ If there's an awkward built-in cabinet or protrusion in a small room, paint everything the same color. This will de-emphasize the awkward element and give the room a more harmonious and uniform look.

▶ Bring home color samples and look at them in the room at different times of the day to see how the light affects them.

▶ Red, yellow, and orange create a warm feeling within a room. Green, blue, and violet are cool colors.

▶ Consider the activity that takes place in a room and the mood you want to create when choosing a color scheme for it. For example, a combination of primary colors like red, yellow, and blue suggests energy. They're terrific colors in a busy contemporary kitchen or kids' playroom. For a soothing, spacious atmosphere, use a monochromatic scheme. This combines various shades and textures of one basic neutral color such as taupe.

Clean Up Before You Paint

Dust thoroughly, especially at ceiling corners and along baseboards and inside closets. Wrap a rag around a broom to get cobwebs out of the ceiling corners. A vacuum's crevice tool works well to suck out dust that is difficult to reach.

Remove grease, grime, and mildew from walls and woodwork with a solution of trisodium phosphate mixed with water. Spic and Span is one readily available brand. Use a strong household detergent if phosphate-based solvents are not allowed in your area. Rinse thoroughly with water and let everything dry.

Save preparation time and the drudgery of sanding enameled woodwork or kitchen cabinets by cleaning and etching the shiny surfaces with a paint deglosser. This strong solvent breaks down the hard enamel shine so your new paint will have a rough surface to stick to. It also removes all grease and dirt. The result is a clean surface ready to paint—and you don't have to sand it.

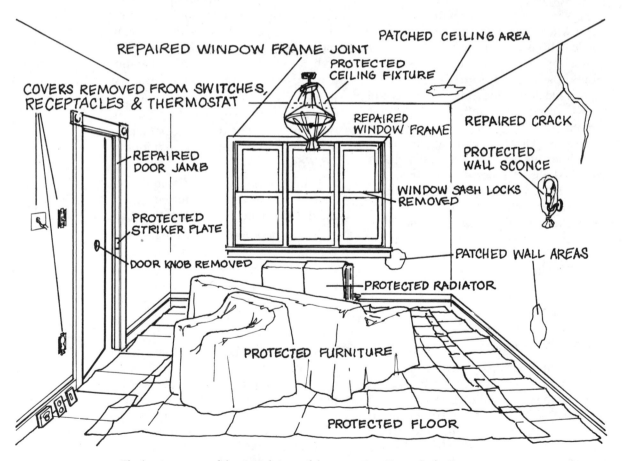

The key to a successful paint job is careful preparation. Here are the important areas to patch, prime, cover, or otherwise protect.

Apply the deglosser with a clean rag, wiping with good strong strokes. Be stingy with the stuff! You're using too much if it leaves a film. Don't put the rag soaked with deglosser into your back pocket and forget it. This is strong stuff, and in a little while you're sure to get a hot seat! Wear a pair of rubber gloves if the deglosser begins to bother your hands, and be sure you open a window or two to provide some added ventilation. When the surface is dry, you're ready to paint.

Cover Up to Protect Furnishings

The main reason a professional paint job looks so neat is that pros take the time to protect anything that is not going to be painted. At least half of a painter's time is spent in preparation. You should spend the time, too. Remove as much furniture as possible from the room, then cover the remaining furniture with plastic drop cloths taped closed. Remove all area rugs, and cover up wall-to-wall carpeting with a drop cloth.

If you plan to do all your own painting, it's worthwhile to purchase at least two 8 × 10-foot canvas drop cloths. These are not cheap (about $25 to $45 each), but the price beats replacing carpeting or refinishing the floors. To cover a large room, use canvas drop cloths, with disposable plastic drop cloths placed around the perimeter.

Plastic drop cloths are a good, inexpensive (about $3 to $5) alternative to canvas ones. Get the heaviest (highest mil number) plastic drop cloth you can find, because it will stay in place and probably won't stick to your feet as you walk across the room. It's also reusable.

You can put old blankets or draperies over the drop cloths to hold them down. This can be especially helpful in the winter, when dry air causes plastic drop cloths to become so charged with static electricity that they stick to almost anything. Stain won't soak through rubber-backed draperies, but otherwise make sure you clean up spills right away.

Also, if you place old blankets or drapes over plastic drops, make sure the combination isn't too slippery to work on. We found that some fabrics slip and slide on top of a plastic drop cloth. You also want to be careful not to allow any of your equipment, such as a brush or scraper, to get between the two layers. You won't find it until you trip on it or turn your ankle.

After you have covered the floor, moved the furniture to the center of the room, and covered these pieces, it's time to protect the trim. No matter how careful you are, the paint roller is going to give off a fine splatter that settles on areas below the roller. You might not notice it until you begin to paint the baseboard or try to clean the chandelier. Protect these areas by loosely applying 1-inch masking tape to the upper edge of all moldings and chair rails. Protect the tops of all door and window moldings in the same way. Press the tape down lightly. You don't have to be precise—just cover all surfaces where splatter might settle.

You can usually leave masking tape in place for a couple of days, especially if it is on a painted or varnished surface such as woodwork. But it's best to remove the tape as quickly as possible. Don't allow tape to sit for a long time if it gets strong sunshine. Either the sun heats up the mastic or there is a chemical reaction with the sunlight that results in a hard set. We did it only once and promptly learned not to do it again. We had to use a razor knife to remove the hard mastic from the glass, and in the process chipped some of the new paint, which of course called for touching up. Mineral spirits sometimes works to remove mastic from painted surfaces that cannot be scraped.

Paint has a way of splattering, even if you don't notice it. So protect hanging chandeliers or wall fixtures by wrapping them in clear plastic garbage bags taped closed.

Remove electrical switch plates and outlet covers with a screwdriver, and store all the hardware with screws in a plastic bag. Mask door and window hardware with tape. If the hardware has never been painted, it's worth the effort to remove it, because painting the door will go faster and be easier to do. If the hardware is already spotted with paint, don't bother to mask it. Paint over the areas that already have paint on them, otherwise some of the old color will be visible.

Patch and Repair

Today's paint will cover just about anything, but it still must be applied to a smooth surface to look good. Two products will come in handy here—spackling compound and joint compound. They can be used interchangeably in a pinch, but each is best at the task for which it was designed. Formulated for filling holes, spackling compound is thick and quick-drying. It usually is sold in small containers. Joint compound is soupier because it is formulated to spread easily in long strokes over drywall joints. It is most commonly sold in 5-gallon buckets. Here are a few quick solutions to common wall repair problems:

Bumps and high spots on walls: Knock off any bumps from the walls before painting. These include any debris (hair, dirt, tape) that may have been painted over in previous jobs. Use a wide-blade razor knife because it works faster than sandpaper. Keep the handle as close to the wall as possible, holding the blade angled so you don't gouge the wall. If you are scraping wallboard, be extra careful so that you don't cut the top layer of paper covering the wallboard.

Nail holes and hairline cracks: Use a razor knife to knock off any high spots around the hole, then clean out any loose plaster or dust that is in the hole. Use a swipe of spackling compound on a putty knife to fill in small hairline cracks and holes. Allow this to dry for a couple of hours, then recoat. Sand it smooth when dry. Many times we get by without sanding by applying the second coat of spackling compound and smoothing the area with a damp sponge after the second coat has dried. This works only if the crack you are filling is very shallow; otherwise you will have to apply a heavy layer of compound, which will shrink as it dries and will show the patch.

Small holes: Examples of these are the indentation a doorknob makes when bashed against a wall without a doorstop, and a hole in a hollow-core door. Use a putty knife with a wide, flexible blade and fast-setting patching plaster. Cut a piece of cardboard slightly larger than the hole. Then make a couple of holes in its center, and thread a piece of string through these holes. Knot the string so it can't pull out of the cardboard.

Check that the area around the hole is free of any high spots or bumps. Check this by pushing a putty knife blade over the gouge or hole. The blade will hang up at any high spots. Knock these spots level with the putty knife or sand them smooth. Then roll the cardboard or fold it in half so it will fit through the hole, and slip it into the wall cavity. Pull the string so the cardboard flattens against the back side of the wall. Use the cardboard as a form to keep the patching plaster from falling through the hole into the cavity behind the wall.

Mix up a batch of patching plaster according to the manufacturer's directions, and apply it to the hole with a putty knife. Make sure plaster goes behind the wall and between the cardboard and the back side of the wall. Fill the hole with patching plaster until it is about ⅛ inch below the wall surface. You can hold the string for a couple of minutes, or you can tie it to a pencil or some other object that is long enough to span the patched area.

When the plaster begins to set, you can release the string. When it is hard (usually in about 10 minutes or so), cut the string and score the surface of the patch. Then apply a top coat of spackling compound. When it's dry, apply a second, thin coat, feathering the compound beyond the edge of the repair.

Loose drywall tape: A small bulge in the corner or along a joint between two panels of drywall is usually caused by loose drywall tape. Use a razor or sharp utility knife to cut out the bubble, then fill the depression with joint compound. When it's dry, recoat, feathering the joint compound several inches past the edge of the bulge. Sand lightly when dry.

If the bubble is large and has occurred in the middle of the tape right over the drywall joint, you'll want to replace the section of tape, or your patch will eventually crack. Just cut through the tape on both sides of the bubble and lift it out. We like the self-sticking fiberglass mesh tape. It is easy to apply since it stays put by itself without drywall compound. This makes it easier to patch a small imperfection. It also eliminates the possibility of air bubbles, which probably caused the problem with the paper tape. Once the tape is in place, coat it with joint compound.

Persistent cracks: When cracks reopen after being filled with spackling or joint compound, use fiberglass mesh drywall tape for a permanent fix. This self-adhering mesh tape is easier to use than paper tape. Simply stick the tape over the crack, and use a wide putty knife to push joint or spackling compound through the tape into the crack.

When it's dry, sand lightly and add another coat. Spread the compound several inches past the edges of the tape, then smooth the compound, feathering the edges of the patch with your putty knife. When it's dry, sand it smooth.

Nail pops: A loose wallboard nail is impossible to cover up with just spackling compound. The wallboard vibrates with everyday movement, and the nail remains fixed in the stud, cracking the patch. We found the only cure for this problem is to place drywall screws about an inch above and below the popped nail head to secure the wallboard to the stud behind it. Screws are better than nails because they will not pop and they leave a much smaller depression to fill. The trick is to drive the screw far enough to make a depression in the drywall without breaking the paper surface. After the screws are in place, drive the loose nail into the stud with a hammer and nail set. Then fill all three depressions with joint or spackling compound, let it dry, sand, recoat and allow to dry again, and then sand smooth.

Cracks in the plaster: Through the years most plaster walls develop small cracks over doors, around windows, and in other stress areas. These cracks should be repaired before painting. You get a longer-lasting patch if you open the cracks into a shallow "V." You can use a putty knife with a stiff blade, an old screwdriver, or the point of a beverage can opener. Just open the hairline cracks a bit so the spackling compound can be worked deep into the crack. Then remove any dust or loose plaster with a hairbrush or a stiff, old paintbrush.

Wet the crack and surrounding area with water to prevent the dry plaster from absorbing water from the spackling compound before it has time to properly set. A spray bottle designed for wetting clothes for ironing is ideal, or use a damp rag to moisten the edges of the cracks.

Apply the spackling compound, using a putty knife with a flexible blade. To work the compound into the crack, hold the putty knife blade with compound on it at a slight angle to the wall as you draw it over the crack. Then remove the excess by dragging the blade across the patch again at a steeper angle, to scrape all the compound off the wall.

Check the crack in a couple of hours to see if the spackling compound has shrunk and caused a small dimple. If it has, apply a second coat. When it's dry, sand lightly with medium-grade sandpaper.

Holes in the plaster: Joint or spackling compounds are useless for replacing plaster that has come loose or fallen out of large areas. For this you need patching plaster. Structo-lite from U.S. Gypsum Company is one brand.

It's important to remove all the loose plaster from the area you are patching. Otherwise, your new patch will crack where it meets any old, loose plaster.

Use a hammer and a cold chisel (a chisel with an all-metal handle) or an old woodworking chisel to remove the stubborn pieces of plaster from around the hole. Undercut the edges of the hole with your chisel to provide a good joint between the new patch and the old plaster. Then dust the hole with an old, stiff paintbrush or hairbrush.

Remove any broken lath (the wood strips nailed to studs that the plaster is attached to). If the lath is loose, renail it to the studs with 6d common nails. You can also use drywall nails if you have some handy; they will hold a little better than common nails. If the lath is missing and the hole is small, use the cardboard trick already mentioned for small holes. Then wet the rough edges of the hole and the lath with water.

Mix and apply the patching plaster. Apply the first coat of plaster with a putty knife. Fill the hole with plaster to about ⅛ inch below the wall surface. When the patching plaster has set, scratch the surface of the patch with the edge of the putty knife. Mix up another batch of patching plaster, and apply a second coat, leveling it with the wall surface.

After the plaster is dry, use a putty knife with a wide, flexible blade to apply a third and final top coat of spackling compound. Feather this coat several inches beyond the edge of the patch.

Sagging plaster: See "Pulling the Old Wall Together" in chapter 3.

Gaps between woodwork: Fill gaps between the wall and base moldings or door and window trim with latex caulk. *Push* the caulk gun and cartridge along the crack instead of pulling it. This way the caulk is pushed deeper into the crack as you move the nozzle down the crack. Smooth irregularities with a wet finger, and remove excess caulk with a paper towel or damp rag.

Painting Like a Pro

Whether you are painting a single closet or the entire house, there is an efficient way to paint. We have outlined the steps for you:

Cut in the ceiling. Begin your work by outlining the room, painting at least a 2-inch band around the perimeter of the ceiling. You don't have to be too careful if the walls and ceiling will be painted the same color, because you can paint over any overlaps.

Use an extension pole for the ceiling. It's a lot easier and quicker to paint a ceiling with an extension handle and roller than it is to continually climb up and down a ladder. Unless you have an unusually high ceiling, a 4-foot extension handle is what you need. Work the paint roller back and forth parallel to the longest wall, working your way across the ceiling in 3 or 4-foot-square patches. When you reach the opposite wall, start back. This procedure allows you to spread paint into new areas but prevents you from losing your wet edge, which causes lap marks.

Cut in the walls. Cut in or outline one wall at a time. Be careful when you make the ceiling cut. (You can buy a "paint pad" that has wheels in one edge that roll on the ceiling to help make a clean cut.) Cut in only as much as you can paint in 20 minutes, or the paint will start to dry and you will get lap marks.

Paint the walls. An extension handle is also helpful when painting the walls. Paint the upper half of the wall with the aid of the extension pole. Remove the handle and finish the wall, overlapping your roller strokes in the center of the wall. This area takes most of the abuse, and it's the part of the wall that people look at most, so you want it to look nice.

If you don't like to bend over at all, you can use the pole to paint the whole wall. This method is a little slower but easier. Start applying the paint to the lower third of the wall — but not too close to the baseboard, or the paint will be hard to spread. Then work the roller up the wall. Stand a few feet from the wall, and apply light pressure to the roller. Step back a bit as you move the roller toward the center of the wall, and then step forward as you move further up. This method may take a little more time until you get the hang of it, but it sure is easier on the back.

Your first stroke after dipping the roller should be upward. This way, the paint will squeeze up the wall instead of dripping down. Don't try to spread the paint too far. Dip your roller in the pan often. Dry rolling is just a waste of time because you'll have to go over the area again.

Paint the woodwork. When the walls are dry, paint the woodwork at the windows, then the doors, and finally the baseboards. If the woodwork is to be a different color than the walls, and you are planning more than one coat, alternate between painting the walls and woodwork. This way you can get a more accurate cut-in with each coat.

Our painting operation has evolved over the years, with each of us developing our own specialties. Katie is the cut-in person, and Gene handles the roller. Katie begins cutting in first to get a head start. When she's completed cutting in a wall, then Gene starts rolling on that wall. We work around the room going from wall

1. Lower the outside sash and raise the inside sash. Paint as much of the outside sash as is exposed. Then paint the inside sash, except for the top edge.

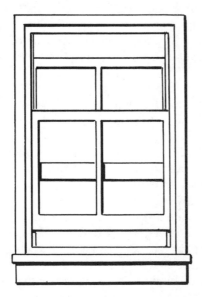

2. Reverse the position of the sashes, and paint the remaining portion of the outside sash. Then paint the inner sash, inner part of the window frame, and finally the casing, sill, and stool.

to wall. The cut-in person can usually keep ahead of the roller person.

Painting a Double-Hung Window

The trick to painting any window is to paint from the inside out and always paint to an edge. Don't drag your brush back across the edge, because the corner will scrape off some paint, causing a drip or run. Use a 1½-inch brush and follow this sequence:

Step 1: Reverse the position of the inner (lower) sash and the outer (upper) sash. Paint the lower half of the outer sash. Then paint the inner sash, except for the top edge where the lock is located.

Step 2: Move the sash back into their normal positions, but don't close the window. Paint the top half of the outer sash and the top edge of the inner sash.

Step 3: Paint the window frame, working out to the casing trim.

Painting a Panel Door

Painting a panel door without unsightly lap marks is easy if you begin at each panel and work out. Use a 2½-inch brush and follow this sequence:

Step 1: Paint the decorative edge molding surrounding the door panels.

Step 2: Paint the panels.

Step 3: Paint the vertical surfaces between the panels.

Step 4: Paint the central horizontal rail, stopping short of the outside vertical stiles.

Step 5: Paint the outside horizontal surfaces of the door, then paint the edges of the door.

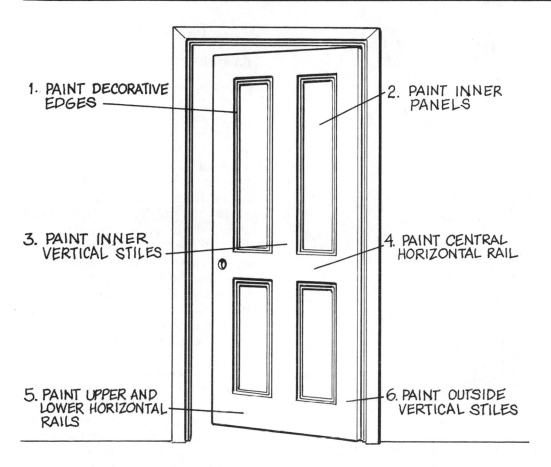

1. PAINT DECORATIVE EDGES

2. PAINT INNER PANELS

3. PAINT INNER VERTICAL STILES

4. PAINT CENTRAL HORIZONTAL RAIL

5. PAINT UPPER AND LOWER HORIZONTAL RAILS

6. PAINT OUTSIDE VERTICAL STILES

For best results, paint a door in this sequence.

Step 6: Paint the outside vertical surfaces of the door.

Katie and Gene's Man-Powered Painting System

We use a simple rig consisting of one empty 5-gallon paint bucket with a lid, a 5-gallon bucket of paint, a roller grate, and a paint roller. Empty half of the paint into the empty container, and save the rest until needed. The roller grate, which you can buy in any home center or paint supply store, hangs into the half-filled paint container. Dip the paint roller into the paint, and press it against the grate, working out excess paint. The 2½ gallons of paint keep you painting for a while without stopping to refill. The high sides of the hard plastic bucket make it stable and unlikely to be knocked over or stepped into by accident. When it's time for a break, just drop the grate into the bucket and snap on the lid.

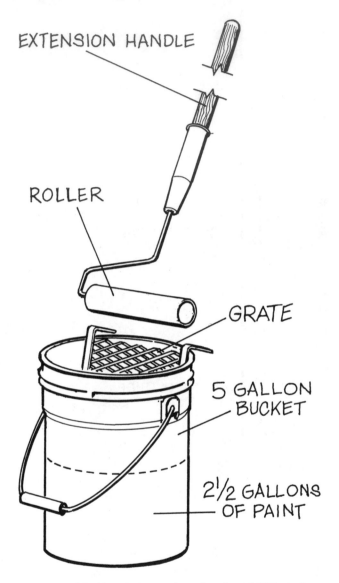

EXTENSION HANDLE

ROLLER

GRATE

5 GALLON BUCKET

2½ GALLONS OF PAINT

You can assemble this painting package for about $20, including the roller and extension handle. It's based around a 5-gallon paint bucket, which you might be able to get free from a paint store or scrounge from a construction site. Place a $2 roller grate inside the bucket. You can fill the bucket with 2½ gallons of paint for nonstop, no-stoop painting.

Power Painters: Time-Savers?

We've found that spray-painting equipment can make a job go faster, and in some cases produce better results, if you have a large area or several rooms to paint all the same color. Because spray equipment always sprays paint beyond where you want it, you need to factor in additional time to remove everything from a room and carefully protect all remaining furnishings, moldings, and so forth with drop cloths and masking tape.

All types of spray units must be carefully cleaned after each use and before a change in paint color. In many cases the extra time it takes to mask everything and clean up after power painting offsets the time saved compared with using a brush and roller.

On the other hand, small hand-held spray-type painters are invaluable for painting shutters, wicker furniture, and other intricate pieces that would be difficult to brush. Sprayers are also handy for painting acoustical ceiling tiles and other textured surfaces that are tedious and time-consuming to cover with a roller or brush.

Renting or Buying Equipment

The main reason you can save so much money doing your own painting is that it is so labor intensive. Playing on this fact, the marketplace is full of labor-saving devices. But before you invest too heavily in these gadgets, remember that one of your primary goals in producing a quality paint job is to avoid having to do it again for years.

Basic painting equipment is simple and rugged; if maintained, it will last for years. Scrapers, brushes, rollers, pans, extension poles, stepladders, and drop cloths are used in every type of painting operation and are therefore good investments.

Other specialized painting tools should be rented. Power washers, airless spray equipment, tall ladders, and scaffolding are expensive, and these will seldom be wise purchases for the average home painter. Be aware, too, that the equipment you rent is heavy-duty industrial quality. You might see a spray-painting outfit retailing for several hundred dollars, but you can rent an industrial unit with two or three times the capacity for $50 a

DECORATING WITH STENCILING

You can give any room instant architectural interest by adding a stencil design as a border or to accentuate a feature of the room. Your imagination is the only limit in deciding what to stencil. Stenciling looks great on baseboards, as a ceiling border, as a "chair rail," and as a way to frame a fireplace, window, or doorway. The key is to select a color to accentuate the best features in the room. Stenciling even helps to improve a room with less than perfect features.

Does a room have a high ceiling? Use a wide border stencil to visually "lower" it. To brighten up a small, dull room, use a narrow stencil around the ceiling, baseboard, doors, and windows to define the space. But remember—select a design that's in scale with the room.

First time stenciling? Use a stencil kit with a precut design. You can then focus your attention on learning how to dab the paint through the stencil cutout onto the surface beneath it.

Here are a few pointers for goofproof stenciling:

▶ Always do a few practice applications on newspaper or cardboard.

▶ Choose a design that is no closer than 1 inch from the stencil's outside edge, so you won't smudge paint on your walls.

▶ Use the registration holes on the stencil to help align it properly on the wall.

▶ Use any quick-drying paint. Artist's acrylics are easy to use and come in a wide variety of colors.

▶ To apply paint, use a stiff circular brush (available where stenciling supplies are sold), a small sponge, or a felt pad. Dab, don't brush, the paint into the cutout, working from the outside into the center.

▶ On a wall, use a chalk line to help position the stencil. Work from opposite corners toward the center when laying out your design.

▶ To hold the stencil firmly in place, use spray-mount adhesive on its back. You'll find this adhesive in photo and art supply stores.

▶ Use drafter's masking tape on the stencil front corners to hold it in place. (Regular masking tape works too, but it's stickier and might leave residue on your wall or lift the paint.)

▶ On vertical surfaces try using a stencil crayon (oil-based paint in stick form). It's easier to use than paint because it won't drip.

▶ Use automobile touch-up paint for a quick job. This paint dries very fast and is available in a wide variety of colors. It is more expensive, however, and requires more than one coat.

▶ Mask the surrounding area with plastic drop cloths to protect it from splattering or overspray.

day. If you use the sprayer only once every 5 years, it will be years before you can expect to recover the cost of purchasing one.

Some power tools, such as a wire brush attachment for your electric drill, a heat gun, and a pad sander, can be used to do other projects around the house and therefore may be good investments.

Professional Solutions to Tough Problems

If every paint job were easy, the pros would have a hard time keeping busy. Through the years a painter picks up little tips that help him do a professional job quickly. While we are not professional painters, we certainly have painted our share of houses and have had to solve a myriad of our own painting puzzles. Here are some quick fixes for problems you might face in a typical weekend painting project:

Mildew: This is a discoloration caused by a fungus. It is found where there is a persistent damp condition. To test for mildew, wipe the area with household bleach—if the discoloration can be wiped away, then it is mildew. To eliminate it, wash it thoroughly with trisodium phosphate, followed by household bleach. Then allow the area to dry thoroughly. Paint with mildew-resistant paint, or mix a mildewcide additive into your paint. Use a mildew-preventing primer to recoat areas where the paint has lifted or peeled. Prevent mildew from recurring by providing additional ventilation and light.

Stains: Water-soluble stains such as felt-tip marker ink, rust, or water-ring marks will bleed through latex paint unless blocked with a stain killer. Coat with a pigmented shellac-based primer/sealer (Bin and Kilz are two popular brands). The shellac dries quickly and can be painted in 10 to 15 minutes. This quick drying makes shellac-based primers tricky to work with. Apply a small amount of primer at a time, and brush it out well before it dries. Brush vigorously to work the primer into the surface. You want a good even coat, but you don't need to worry about long, continuous brush strokes, because the primer will be covered with two more coats.

Alligatoring: Alligatoring is a term used to describe paint that has cracked and looks like the hide of an alligator. It is caused by weather, aging, and excessive coats of paint. The solution is to scrape and sand the old finish off completely, apply a primer, then top-coat with latex or oil paint.

No-Cost Painting Aids

If you bought all the painting aids stocked in the local home center, you probably couldn't afford the paint. Here are some no-cost or low-cost tricks that will help you become more efficient and make the job a little easier:

Boil the hardware. To remove layers of old paint from brass door hardware and light-switch or outlet plates without using an expensive paint remover, just place them in an old pot and boil them in water for about 10 minutes. Remove them from the water and let them cool. Then rub off the paint with a mesh pot scrubber. Next, polish and add a few drops of oil to locking doorknobs or door hinges.

Wrap brushes and rollers. At coffee-break time, wrap your roller or

Great Gadgets & Gizmos

☞ **Glass Mask**   Cut down window-painting time by masking the glass with a coating of wax. Glass Mask is a nifty masking device that rolls out a thin waxy film on the windowpane next to the surface you will paint. It prevents paint from sticking to the glass. Later, you remove the paint and film with its built-in scraper. It is made by Wagner Spray Tech Corporation, 1770 Fernbrook Lane, Plymouth, MN 55447.

☞ **Tape 'n' Drape**   There's a new kind of drop cloth that is a combination of plastic sheeting and masking tape. Called Tape 'n' Drape, the drop cloth and tape rolls out of its dispenser just like plastic food wrap, ready to tape to woodwork or molding. A compatible product is **Easy Mask,** a painting tape that is a smooth brown paper with a special acrylic adhesive edge that is not affected by sunlight. It is sold in 50-foot rolls of various widths from 2 to 12 inches. Both products are from Daubert Coated Products, Inc., One Westbrook Corporate Center, Suite 1000, Westchester, IL 60154.

☞ **Pro-Finish rollers**   A solution to the problem of uneven coverage with standard paint rollers is the new Pro-Finish roller designed for applying paint with a well-balanced, even stroke. The roller is supported at both ends, so even pressure is applied across the entire roller. Standard wire roller handles support the roller at one end only, which can cause uneven spreading of paint. Pro-Finish rollers are made by Padco Inc., 2220 Elm Street SE, Minneapolis, MN 55414-2693.

☞ **Extension pole**   Don't try to paint ceilings and high walls without a roller handle extension pole. If you have a broom or mop handle with a screw-type end, try screwing it into the end of your paint roller handle. You might be able to save a couple of bucks if it fits. If not, buy a 4-foot pole to save you endless trips up and down a ladder. It's also handy for painting a floor or finishing a wooden deck.

☞ **Spinner**   No pro would be caught without a roller/paintbrush spinner to get brushes and rollers thoroughly clean. It works just like a kid's spinning top. First, wash the roller to remove as much paint as possible. Then place the roller on the spinner end, pump the handle, and the spinning action creates a centrifugal force that removes most of the water from the roller nap. It's just like a wet dog shaking himself dry! So use the spinner out of doors, in a bathtub, or in a 5-gallon bucket or container. The spinner also dries paint brushes. It has a clip grasp that secures the end of a brush handle for spinning.

☞ **Pad**   A paint pad makes short work of cutting in, or outlining, a room. Be sure that you feather-paint edges if the paint will dry before you continue to roll the wall.

paintbrush in plastic wrap or aluminum foil so the paint won't dry.

Store brushes in a can.   If you are using oil-based paint, it is not necessary to clean your brush at the end of each day. If you plan to resume painting with the same color within a few days, fill a coffee can about halfway with mineral spirits. Make a small slit in the can's plastic lid, and force your paintbrush handle through the bottom of the lid. Place the lid on the can, with the paintbrush suspended in the mineral spirits. Check that the mineral spirits covers all the bristles and that the brush can't touch the bottom of the can where the paint residue collects. When you are ready to paint again, just squeeze the excess paint and mineral spirits into the coffee can. You can't store brushes this way indefinitely. Eventually, the mineral spirits will evaporate and the brush will be ruined.

Store painting tools in a bucket.   If you are using a roller along with brushes for oil-based paint, get a 5-gallon bucket with a lid (the kind joint compound and paint come in) and pour a gallon of mineral spirits into it. Hang the brushes from their handles around the perimeter of the bucket with hooks made from coat hanger wire. Again, be sure all the bristles are submerged in the mineral spirits. Just toss the roller in the bottom of the bucket.

When you are ready to use the brushes or roller again, shake most of the mineral spirits out of a brush or roller, then spin it dry with a paintbrush spinner. Keep the brush or roller in the bucket when you spin, so the spirits the spinner throws off will be contained in the bucket. After the job is finished, put the lid on the bucket and let the paint settle for a couple of days. Then you can pour the clear spirits back into the gallon can with little loss. Scoop the paint crud from the bottom of the bucket and dispose of it. Remember paint residue is flammable and toxic.

Punch holes in the paint can lip. The holes allow paint trapped in the rim to drip back into the can instead of running down the side. The lid fits tightly into the valley, sealing off air that would dry the paint. In fact, the lid can seal better because the excess paint is not stopping up the valley where the paint lid wants to go.

Make sanding strips.   To properly prepare rounded surfaces, such as stair spindles or table legs, for painting, it's important to sand the surface smooth. This is not always easy. We make sanding strips by cutting strips of sandpaper to the width we need. Then we place masking tape on the backs of the strips for added strength. Use the sanding strips like dental floss, working them around and back and forth. These strips make a tedious job more bearable.

Sand with playing cards.   To sand curved areas such as crown ceiling molding, use a deck of playing cards. Wrap a piece of sandpaper around the deck, fit it into the curved area, and sand away.

Make a painter's tray.   An ordinary cardboard box can be converted into a painter's tray that is handy for holding a quart can of paint and a couple of rags. Cut the sides of the box down to about 2 inches. The short sides stiffen the tray and keep paint, brush, tack rag, and other items in place. The tray will also catch any drips from the brush as it comes out of the can.

Keep your fingernails paint free. Getting paint under our fingernails used to be part of the job. Then a painter suggested we rub some petroleum jelly around our fingernails, and then wipe our hands on a rag to remove most of the jelly. If you don't wipe too hard around the nails, the jelly sticks in the small crevices and prevents paint from sticking to your nails and cuticles. After painting, just wipe away the jelly, and the paint will come with it.

CHAPTER 2

Exterior Painting

Think carefully before you decide to tackle the job of painting the exterior of your house. It's a much more demanding job than interior painting. For one thing, exterior painting usually involves much more arduous preparation work, mostly in the form of scraping and sanding off weathered paint. On top of this, unless you have a single-story ranch house with very low eaves, you'll probably have to do a good portion of the work from a ladder or scaffolding. And if you have dormers, you'll have to climb onto the roof to paint them. The fact that you have to work high off the ground is enough to nix the job for some people, and it has caused us to carefully weigh the savings of doing the job ourselves against the cost of hiring a painter.

Even if you don't mind working in

SAFETY FIRST
WHEN ON A LADDER

You can minimize the risk involved in climbing ladders with a little planning and these tips:

▶ To raise a ladder against a structure, set its base firmly against the wall and walk it upright into position. Lift the base and move it outward into a position away from the wall.

▶ Adjust the base of the ladder until it is at least one-quarter of the ladder height from the wall. For example, a 12-foot ladder should be at least 3 feet away from the wall.

▶ Check to see that the base of the ladder is resting on level ground.

▶ Never climb a ladder with tools or materials in your hands. Put both hands on the rungs. Tie a rope to the handle of a bucket and the other end around your waist. Fill the bucket with what you need, climb the ladder, and pull the bucket up after you when you are in position. Once you have climbed the ladder, it's a real nuisance to have to climb down for something you forgot. It's helpful to have someone on the ground fill the bucket and be the go-for team member so the ladder person can concentrate on his job.

▶ Never lean to either side of the ladder. Move the ladder closer to the work area.

▶ Never climb past the third-from-the-top rung. For high work, heighten the ladder by extending the ladder if it is an extension type, and move the base further from the wall. Or get a longer ladder.

▶ Never overextend an extension ladder. The two sections must overlap at least three or four ladder rungs to be safe.

the air, chances are you don't own a scaffold or an extension ladder long enough to reach the peak of your roof. So you'll have to consider the cost of purchasing a ladder or scaffold or renting one for an extended time.

You can reach the entire exterior of your house from a single extension ladder, but you will be able to work much more quickly and safely if you set up scaffolding. This requires at least two ladders, ladder jacks, and a platform. If you decide to buy a ladder, consider one of several types of scaffolding ladders. These fold into various configurations that create a platform for painting.

Investing in a single good ladder may be worthwhile, but buying several ladders and scaffolding probably is a poor investment. On the other hand, you can rent this equipment very reasonably. The problem with renting is the length of time you will need the equipment. Since you probably will not be devoting full time to painting, it will take you several weeks or even months to finish the job. Keeping the equipment for a long period of time can get expensive, but taking it all down and returning it after each weekend can eat up a good portion of your precious weekend work time.

Are we conveying the impression that we don't relish exterior painting? Well then, you get the picture. Before you rush out and start this job, get bids from painters so you can compare what you will have to spend on materials and equipment rental. The savings will be substantial, but it may not be big enough to get you up on a ladder.

If you do decide to tackle this project yourself or if you have only part of the house to touch up, here are some tips and suggestions we have found useful.

Sizing Up the Job

Take a walk around your house. You'll probably notice that the southern side is in the worst shape. That's because the ultraviolet rays of the sun take a heavy toll on any paint. Meanwhile, the northern side may have moisture problems because it doesn't get enough sun to keep mildew from forming. If you have peeling paint in any area of your house, chances are it is caused by moisture. To help dry up excess moisture, keep trees and bushes trimmed and far enough away from the house. Any foliage close to the house increases the moisture, and the wet leaves and branches rubbing up against the siding do not do the paint any good. Trees, on the other hand, provide shade but allow free air movement around the house.

You can see that the condition of the paint on a house points out other potential trouble spots. For example, if there is peeling paint on the fascias (trim boards attached to the ends of the rafters) and on the underside of the roof overhang (eaves), the gutters probably are clogged or leaking, creating a moisture problem.

Biting Off What You Can Chew

A professional painting crew will scrape and sand your entire house, recaulk everything, and then prime the whole house. Then they will paint all the siding and finally all the windows and trim.

But if you are painting alone or with one helper, it's better to finish one sec-

This multiuse folding ladder can be set up as a traditional stepladder or as a scaffold.

tion of the house before moving to another. There are two advantages to this approach. First, it saves labor. You'll have to set up scaffolding only once for each area. More important, primer peels if exposed to the elements.

Choosing the Paint

Exterior paints are categorized in the same way as interior paints. They are oil-based or latex and come in grades of glossiness, with or without enamel. Generally, we use exterior latex paint for the wood siding and exterior oil-based enamel on the trim. Because exterior paint must protect your house from the weather, using good-quality paint is even more important on the exterior of your house than inside. See "Determine How Much Paint You Will Need" in chapter 1 as a guide for the right amount.

If the house has been painted before, flat latex house paint is the easiest to work with, and we have found that it holds up well. It's a good choice if you don't know what paint was used before, because it works well over old latex or oil. Latex paint breathes better than oil-based paint and therefore allows some of the moisture that collects in the walls in the winter to pass through. This lessens the chance of peeling. Of course, if you apply latex over an old oil-based paint, you won't have this advantage.

For trim, we use an oil-based exterior paint. The oil-based products don't dry as fast as the latex paints and therefore hold their wet edge a bit longer. You can keep up with these paints and not leave lap marks when you paint back into a section that has started to dry. These lap marks, or bumps, are formed where the top wet layer of paint meets

the bottom layer, which has already started to dry. With oil paints you can add a bit of thinner if the paint begins to drag. Better yet, add a few ounces of Penetrol, a paint conditioner, to help the paint flow better.

Using Stains

If you are lucky enough to be painting wood that has never been painted before, our advice is don't paint it. Instead, use exterior stain. These days, stain is not just for the natural wood look. You can choose a solid stain that covers the grain and looks very much like paint. Stains are not available in as many colors as paint, but you still have dozens to choose from. If you want the wood grain to show through, select a semitransparent stain.

Solid stains are similar to thinned paint. Like paint, they form a film on the wood, although the film is thinner and less prone to peeling than paint. Semitransparent stains soak into the wood and so will not peel and layers won't build up. You'll need to restain as often as you'd repaint, but you won't have to scrape or sand—a huge labor saver. Layers do build up with solid stains, but because the layers are thinner than paint, it's unlikely that scraping or sanding will become necessary in your lifetime.

Stains come in oil-based or latex form, but for exterior painting we recommend only oil-based stains. Because semitransparent stains never peel and solid stains very rarely peel, you don't have to worry about interior moisture coming through in the winter. The trouble with latex stains is that they are water-based and so allow water to soak into the wood from the outside, creating a potential for rot. Oil-based stains will provide much more protection simply because oil repels water.

The trick to working with stains is to stir them constantly. Because they are thin, the pigment settles quickly. Keep a stick in the can and stir after every two or three dips of the brush. Even if you mix frequently, pigment will tend to settle, making the stain thicker toward the bottom of each can. So, when you have used up half a gallon, open another can, stir it thoroughly, and pour half of it into the first can. Then stir the first can again before resuming staining.

Choosing House Colors

Choosing a house paint color can seem like a scary decision. After all, you're doing a tremendous amount of work and/or spending a bundle to paint your house. You'll be living with the results for a number of years. Here are some things to think about in making this momentous decision:

What style is your house? Old Victorian homes lend themselves to the use of several colors, maybe even pastels for a Queen Anne. A Cape Cod saltbox, on the other hand, looks better with gray siding and white trim. You might want to look in the library for books and magazines on the topic.

We found that one of the best ways to get ideas for house paint colors is to drive around neighborhoods. Sometimes we take a snapshot of a house painted in a color combination we like, so we'll remember what we saw. You might even knock on the door when you see a paint job you admire. Most people will be flattered and will gladly tell you what paint they used.

To experiment with color combinations, get out the kids' markers or crayons and a sketch pad. Initially, sketch out the basic shape of your house and use shades of colors to see what you like.

If you want to take this idea further, take a photograph of your house and then have it enlarged on a copy machine. Make several black-and-white copies of your house, and you have an instant coloring book to experiment with.

When choosing exterior paint colors, you have a few things to work around, namely the roof shingles and any brickwork or stonework on the house or its foundation. Choose colors that harmonize with those parts of the house.

Here's a rule of thumb that seems to work for us. We choose three colors that blend and contrast with each other. We paint the body of the house and the foundation one color—in most cases, it's the pale shade that works well. We paint the soffits and other trim, corner posts, and porches in the next deepest shade. We use the sharpest contrasting shade on the front door and window shutters.

Use color to highlight the best features of the house. That's why a more intense color is used on the front door or to accent roof peaks or brackets. Don't call attention to things like downspouts and gutters by painting them a bright color. Paint them the same shade as the siding or trim, so they don't stand out.

Doing the Prep Work

By the time you get done "prepping" (preparing to paint), the job of actually applying the paint will seem almost like a pleasure—like putting icing

PREPARING A HOUSE FOR PAINTING

Use a hook-type scraper to remove as much of the old, loose, flaking paint as possible from the siding, trim, and eaves.

Remove flaking paint from metal gutters, downspouts, or flashing with a wire brush. Save time by using an inexpensive wire brush attachment in your electric drill.

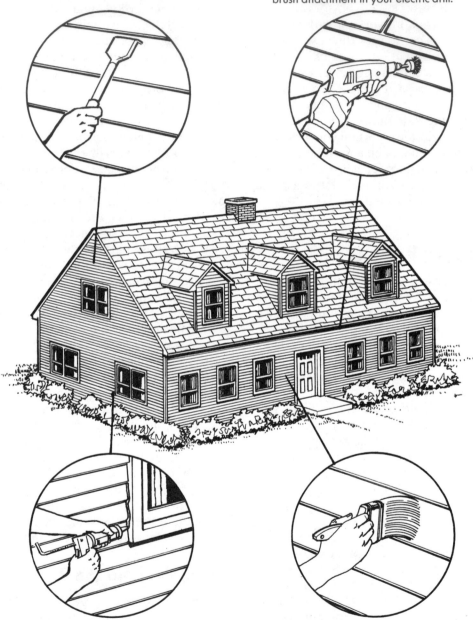

Caulk all joints in the siding, such as those at windows and doors.

Apply primer to all bare spots.

on a cake you have baked from scratch. Prep work is physically harder and takes much more time than painting, and when you're finished prepping, the house looks worse than before you started. But don't be tempted to skimp on the prep work. The quality of the prep will make the difference between a job that looks crummy for a year before it starts to peel and one that will still look great 10 years from now.

Here is a quick area-by-area run-down on what you have to do to get a lasting paint job for wood trim, windows, and metal gutters and downspouts:

Power-wash. Power washing is the quickest way to remove loose, peeling paint and at the same time clean the surface of wood siding. Rent a unit and use it with a strong cleaning solution (7 to 8 tablespoons of trisodium phosphate or household detergent per gallon of water) to remove all grime and to blast away the loose paint.

Feather bare spots. After power-washing the siding, you'll see bare areas where the old paint has been removed. If the siding has many coats of paint on it, there will be ridges around the bare spots. These ridges—which are caused by paint buildup—will show when you apply the primer and new paint. The easiest way to level these shallow craters is to sand the perimeter of the bare spot, feathering the edge of the old paint.

We found the easiest and quickest way to do this is to use an 80-grit paper disk and a rubber-backed sanding disk in our electric drill. If you work carefully and keep the sanding disk moving, you can feather the edges of the bare spots without gouging the siding. If you do leave some swirl marks from the disk, sand the areas smooth with a pad sander

or sandpaper wrapped around a block of wood.

Work carefully. The soft siding is easy to gouge with the disk. When all loose paint is removed, use a sanding block or pad sander to lightly sand the bare wood.

Caulk. Caulk all joints between the siding and windows, doors, and masonry. We like to use an acrylic latex caulk. It is a good-quality caulk and has given us good results, but there are many other types of caulk on the market. Except for sale or discount prices of caulk, the price of the caulk usually reflects its life expectancy. The more expensive caulks are usually rated for 15 to 25 years. More than likely, you'll be repainting and probably recaulking before then.

Applying caulk isn't hard, but it does take a little practice to lay down a smooth bead. Caulk is sold in cartridges that fit into inexpensive metal half-barrel caulk guns. To make the caulk stick in the joint, you do have to do some prep work. Here are some "have gun, will caulk" tricks to lay down a professional-looking bead of caulk.

One tube of caulk will fill about 25 feet of ¼-inch-wide cracks or seal two small windows. If you have the opportunity to buy caulk on sale, purchase more than you think you need. Caulk has a long shelf life if you don't open the tube. This way, you will always have a tube of matching caulk on hand to do touch-ups later.

Before you begin, check the label on the caulk so you will know what type of solvent is needed for cleanup. Keep a roll of paper towels handy. Then follow these steps:

Step 1: Caulk on a warm, dry day. The ideal temperature for caulking is

Choosing a Caulk

Type	Cost	Ease of Application	Durability	Paint-Holding Ability
Acrylic latex	Medium	Easy	Very good	Good
Butyl	Medium	Hard	Good	Good
Foam-in-place	Low	Hard	Good*	Good
Latex	Low	Easy	Poor	Good
Oil	Low	Easy	Poor	Good/prime
Paintable silicone	High	Moderate	Very good	Good/prime
Polyurethane	Medium	Moderate	Excellent	Good
Silicone	High	Moderate	Excellent	Poor
Synthetic rubber	Medium	Hard	Good	Good/prime

Use to fill large gaps and wall cavities; don't use outside without painting.

between 50° and 80°F.

Step 2: Clean old caulk from the joint with a scraper or chisel. Wisk away dirt with an old paintbrush, and wipe the joint with a damp rag. Allow the joint to dry before caulking.

Step 3: Cut the tip of the tube nozzle to a 45-degree angle with a utility knife or scissors. The nozzle is usually marked with several lines showing different-size openings; the size of the opening determines the size of the bead. Choose the first marking or make a ⅛-inch opening. Push a piece of wire coat hanger through the nozzle hole into the tube to break the seal.

Step 4: Load the caulk gun by pulling the L-shaped handle all the way back. Insert the cartridge into the gun so the cartridge nozzle faces opposite the handle.

Turn the caulk gun handle so the notches in the plunger face down, and pull the trigger until you feel resistance.

Step 5: Place the caulk tube nozzle in the joint, and squeeze the trigger while pushing the tube away from you to fill the gap. When you reach the end of the crack or joint, turn the handle so the notches on the plunger face up, to release pressure in the caulk tube. If you forget to do this, the caulk will leak out.

Step 6: As you lay in a bead of caulk, complete the joint by smoothing it with your index finger. Wet your finger with water if you are using latex caulk; use mineral spirits if you are using another type. Run your wet finger over the joint to straighten out any off-course caulking compound.

Step 7: Clean up any excess caulk

immediately, with water or mineral spirits, before it has a chance to skin over. Prevent the remaining caulk in the tube from hardening by putting a nail in the tube nozzle. This prevents the caulk from hardening for a couple of months.

Use oakum for deep crevices. Oakum is a treated hemp rope that unravels to make a strand of the diameter desired to pack into a crack or joint that is more than ½ inch deep. You'll find it in most hardware stores and home centers. Place the oakum on the crack, and push it tightly into the void with a putty knife or screwdriver. It's cheaper than caulk for filling large cracks. Then you can caulk over the oakum.

Painting the Siding

Prime bare spots. Use an exterior latex primer.

Paint the siding. Once the primer has dried, paint the siding with a flat latex house paint. It's best to paint on a dry, mild day. Definitely don't paint with latex paints if it looks like rain—remember these paints are water-based. The temperature should be at least in the mid-50s. Start on the shady side of the house and try to work around the house so you won't be painting in direct sunlight. This gives the paint time to dry properly. Besides, it's a good defense against sunburn and heat exhaustion. Use a good-quality 4-inch nylon or polyester brush. If you have rough-textured shingle or shake siding, use a painting pad.

Painting Windows and Trim

First remove loose or peeling paint with a hook-type scraper and putty knife. Wash the woodwork with a solution of

USING A CAULK GUN

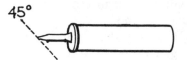

1. Cut off the tip of the caulk cartridge at a 45-degree angle. Poke a long nail or piece of wire through the tip hole to puncture the inner seal.

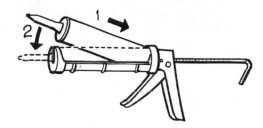

2. Pull the plunger handle all the way out, then insert the tube into the caulk gun. Push the plunger handle as far as it will go. Turn the handle until the ratchet faces down and engages the trigger.

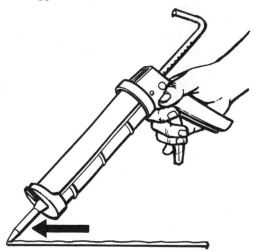

3. To apply caulk, place the nozzle in the crack, squeeze the trigger until the caulk flows, and then push the gun along as you hold it at a 45-degree angle.

water and trisodium phosphate or detergent to remove all dirt, grime, and chalking paint. You can use a power washer for this job, too.

Reglaze. Pry out the loose or crumbling glazing putty from your windows, and replace it with new putty. To keep the glazing putty from sticking to your blade, dip it into mineral spirits.

If the window has any broken panes, now is the time to replace them. It's worth the time to do the job, because you can paint the new glazing putty when you paint the window. If you reglaze and paint the putty later, there will be a mismatch between the old and new paint.

If you have a large window or door panel to replace, check with your local hardware store. Their charge to replace the glass in a window or door that you can carry to the store probably will be very reasonable. We have had storm windows and door panels reglazed this way, and it is inexpensive and allows us to concentrate on painting the house. Note that some building codes require you to replace broken glass door panels with shatterproof plastic or tempered glass.

On the other hand, we have found that it's not worth the trouble to remove a small window from its frame. Glass is inexpensive and reglazing a window isn't hard. Here's how we do it:

Step 1: Protect your hands by wearing work gloves. Most of the splintered glass will come out of the frame easily. If it is stuck, work the pieces back and forth to loosen the putty. If it is really stuck, pry the small pieces out one at a time with pliers.

Step 2: Clear away the old, hard glazing putty and glazier points (small triangular-shaped pieces of steel) with an old screwdriver, putty knife, or chisel.

Chip away everything, right down to the bare wood. You can soften the putty by heating it with a heat gun or, if you are very careful, a propane torch. Be careful not to scorch the wood or set the putty on fire. Then remove all the metal glazier points in the sash with pliers, and scrape the wood clean.

Step 3: Coat the raw wood of the window frame with an exterior primer. You can also use linseed oil or an exterior alkyd-based paint thinned slightly with mineral spirits. This prevents the dry raw wood from sucking the oil out of the glazing putty.

Step 4: Measure the height and width of the opening. Remember that the glass pane is larger than the opening you look through. Be sure to measure the inside of the window so the pane fits into the recess in the sash. Few older windows are perfectly square, so take these measurements in several places and use the smallest of the measurements.

Take the measurements to the hardware store, where the clerk will cut the pane to the proper size, allowing for glass expansion. If you have an odd-shaped window, make a pattern that fits snugly into the sash and bring it with you to the store.

Step 5: Putty is pliable and easy to work if it is the right temperature. In cold weather keep the can inside until you are ready to use it; on hot days don't set the can in direct sunlight.

Work the putty into a thin rope by rolling a ball between your hands. Put the rope into the frame, and push it into place with a putty knife. Cover the entire inside of the frame with a 1/8-inch-wide bead.

Step 6: Put the glass into the opening, and then gently rock it back and

REPAIRING A BROKEN PANE
IN A WOODEN WINDOW SASH

1. Wearing gloves, carefully remove broken glass.

2. Scrape out the old putty and prime the raw wood.

3. Put a bed of putty into the groove, and set the new glass in place. Secure the new glass with glazier points.

4. Dip the putty knife into mineral spirits, and smooth a layer of putty over the glazier points. Smooth putty on the inside of the window, also.

forth to seat it against the putty. Most of the putty should squeeze out between the glass and the front of the frame. Push the glass firmly around the edges only; you run the risk of cracking the pane if you push in the center. While holding the glass in place, use the tip of the

screwdriver to push the glazier points into the sash. Use at least three per side.

Step 7: Knead another rope of putty and push it into place around the inside perimeter of the sash. Push hard on the putty knife to direct the putty into the triangular gap between the glass and sash.

The putty does not have to be smooth but should fill the area, eliminating gaps or voids.

Step 8: Remove the excess putty and smooth it with the blade of your putty knife. Dip the blade of the putty knife into mineral spirits. Hold the knife at a 45-degree angle while pushing one corner of the knife tight against the glass. Drag the blade over the putty to cut off the excess at the glass and sash. Go back and peel off the excess putty. If the putty sticks to the face of the sash, dampen a rag in mineral spirits to remove it. Wait a few days for the putty to harden and cure before cleaning the window, so the putty doesn't smear on the glass.

Prime bare wood and new glazing. Use an oil-based primer unless there is a moisture problem causing previous paint to peel off. If there is a moisture problem, use a latex primer because it allows water vapor to pass.

Caulk joints. Fill all joints or cracks between the window and the siding or in the window frame with an acrylic latex caulk. Allow the caulk to set up according to the manufacturer's directions before you paint.

Select paint carefully. If you primed the window with an exterior oil-based primer, apply exterior oil-based enamel or house trim paint. Otherwise, use a flat latex house paint or an exterior latex semigloss or gloss enamel.

Painting Metal Gutters and Downspouts

Leaky gutters and downspouts are a major cause of peeling paint. It is a waste of time to paint eaves or walls under a badly leaking gutter or downspout with-out first correcting the source of water damage. Gutters also help keep the perimeter earth around the foundation and your basement dry. Here are several quick fixes for a bad gutter system:

Clean annually. Cleaning gutters is an easy but messy job. The easiest way we've found is to wear work gloves and use a garden trowel to scoop out the debris. Standing on a secured ladder, use a bucket to dump the debris into. It's tempting to just scoop the messy stuff out onto the ground, but then you'll have more work picking it up. Gardeners might find the debris useful as compost. When gutters are free of leaves and dirt, use a garden hose to flush them clean. While you've got the ladder out, trim tree or shrubbery branches that overhang the house, to keep leaves and twigs from accumulating in gutters.

Inspect gutters. Four conditions (all repairable) cause gutters to leak. The first is obvious—the gutters are filled with debris and can no longer function properly. Loose joints, pinholes or holes in the gutters, and sagging gutters caused by broken hangers are conditions that require mending.

Install anticlog screens and downspout guards. If your house is surrounded by trees, fit plastic or wire mesh screening over the gutters. The screening is very easy to install. Also, insert bird cage-type guards in downspouts to keep them clog free.

Caulk leaking joints. Use a silicone caulking compound and apply it to the inside of the joint. Smooth the caulk around the joint with your finger to prevent it from making a dam that will stop the free flow of water.

Patch holes. Use a wire brush to remove loose or scaling rust from the area around the hole. Wipe away all dust, then paint with rusty-metal primer to prevent rust from spreading. Rusty-metal primer is specially formulated for use over rust. Products labeled as metal primers are for priming new metal. Use roofing cement to patch small holes. The type that contains small cut fibers is the best type to cover holes.

For larger holes, embed fiberglass drywall tape into the roofing cement to help it span the gap. Apply a second coat of cement a couple of hours later, after the cement has had a chance to set up.

Check gutter hangers. Often gutters sag from the weight of ice and snow. Water collects and spills out at these low spots. Your gutters may be supported by several types of gutter hangers. Sometimes all that is necessary is to bend the gutter hanger back into shape or reattach the hanging strap with a few aluminum or galvanized nails. Don't use common nails—they will rust and streak your new paint job.

The easiest hanger to use to repair a sagging gutter is a spike-and-tube hanger. This is a long aluminum spike with an aluminum tube around it. This type of hanger requires a sound fascia board behind the gutter. To install a spike-and-tube hanger, drill a ¼-inch hole in the front gutter lip where you want the hanger. Remove the spike from the tube, and place the tube inside the gutter directly behind the hole you drilled. Hammer the spike through the gutter and into the tube. Lift the gutter into proper alignment, and drive the spike through the back of the gutter into the wood fascia. The aluminum tube keeps the gutter from bending.

Age before painting. Allow new galvanized metal gutters and downspouts to age for at least 6 months before you paint them. This aging removes the oil film left by the manufacturing process. If you can't wait, scrub the new parts with mineral spirits, followed by a strong trisodium phosphate solution.

Remove loose or peeling paint. Use a wire wheel in your electric drill or a wire brush to loosen any flaking paint on your gutters. The power washer also is very effective in blasting off loose paint.

Degloss oil paint. Use a liquid deglosser to clean and dull the surface of old paint that still has a good bond to the metal. This will allow the new coat to adhere.

Prime bare spots. Use a latex metal primer on all bare metal that is not rusty. Clean rusty metal with a wire brush, and then use a primer especially prepared for rusty metal before painting the surface.

Paint gutters and downspouts. Use the same paint that you use on the trim or siding. The tricky part is getting paint to stick to gutters and downspouts, and that involves prep work. If the metal is primed correctly, then either oil or latex paint will hold up pretty well. Oil paints are more impervious to moisture, so they protect the metal from rust a little better than latex, but holding back the moisture is the chief job of a primer. If you have primed the area with either a latex or oil metal primer, paint will not peel and the gutters will not rust for quite a while.

Professional Solutions to Exterior Problems

Blistering: This condition can be caused by excessive heat, by dirt, oil, or other contaminants, by moisture trapped behind the paint film, or by a combina-

HOW PAINT FAILS

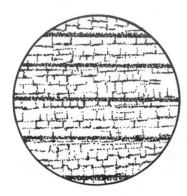

Alligatoring occurs when many coats of paint crack and peel. It can also indicate rotted wood. Remove all loose paint, then prime the area.

Paint that is old and has been oxidized by the sun will come off when you rub it. You will also see signs of this problem when white streaks appear on the siding under windows. Remove chalk residue with a water hose and wire brush.

Rust stains in siding or trim are usually caused by rusting nails. The best cure for this problem is to remove the nail and replace it with an aluminum or galvanized nail. If that is not possible, then coat the nail head with a metal primer. Kill the stain with a shellac-based stain killer.

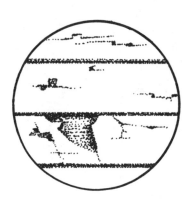

Peeling paint usually is caused by moisture coming through the siding. Eliminate the source of moisture. Then scrape off flaking paint and sand the wood smooth.

If paint is applied too thickly, it will dry on the surface but not underneath, causing wrinkles. Smooth the area with sandpaper or a hook-type scraper.

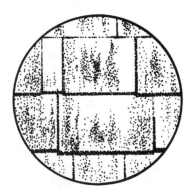

Stains and mildew will bleed through some paints. Kill mold with a bleach solution, and apply a stain killer before priming.

Great Gadgets & Gizmos

☞ **Practice board** First time with a caulk gun? Make a practice board by nailing two pieces of scrap wood together to form a corner. Practice laying a bead, using a tube of inexpensive caulk.

☞ **Dust masks** When sanding old paint off exterior siding, you want to protect your lungs from possibly harmful dust and particles. Pick up a pack of inexpensive paper dust masks found in the painting supply sections of hardware stores or home centers. Get in the habit of wearing a mask when you're doing any similar projects that might be harmful to your lungs.

☞ **Respirator** For protection against dust and paint fumes, invest in a rubber mask called a respirator, which fits comfortably on your face. A respirator has two replaceable filters and is designed to protect you from breathing organic vapors by filtering them out. Always use a respirator whenever you are working with paints or solvents in a confined area, to prevent inhaling the high concentration of fumes.

Remember, a dust mask will protect you only from dust, not from harmful vapors.

☞ **Wood repair systems** To repair damaged exterior wood such as a weather-beaten fence stringer or windowsill, use a wood repair system. One system includes a "High Performance" wood hardener and a filler (sold separately). The liquid hardener is poured into place and gives its companion product, the filler, a solid base to adhere to. It's made by Minwax Company, 102 Chestnut Ridge Plaza, Montvale, NJ 07645.

☞ **Adjustable ladders** If you don't own a ladder, consider investing in an adjustable one as opposed to the traditional type. A professional adjustable ladder opens and locks easily and securely and can be configured into several different positions (that is, one-piece scaffold, worktable, overhang ladder, and two-level staircase ladder). It is made by WestWay Products Corporation, 31878 Camino Capistrano, Suite 270, San Juan Capistrano, CA 92675.

---

tion of incompatible products. To determine the probable cause, burst a blister and look inside. If the bubble is caused by heat or poor adhesion between coats, you will see another layer of paint. If the blistering is caused by moisture, you'll most likely see bare wood. If the cause seems to be poor adhesion between coats, scrape all blistered areas to remove the loose paint, then sand the area, dust, and prime.

If the cause is moisture, remove the source of the moisture. Cut back bushes, trees, and other greenery so the area can dry after rainfalls. If the peeling is in an area outside a bathroom or kitchen, the moisture might be coming through the wall. Install a vapor barrier inside, paint the interior walls with an oil-based paint, or increase the ventilation, especially in the bathroom. After you have attempted to reduce the moisture, sand the blistered area, prime with an exterior latex primer, and then recoat with a flat latex house paint.

Chalking: This problem has any number of causes—inadequate priming and sealing of a porous surface, over-thinning of paint, or spreading paint too thin. To fix an area where this occurs, remove all chalk residue with a wire brush and water (it's easiest to use a garden hose). Let the area dry, then apply primer and repaint.

Cracking and flaking: These eye-sores are caused by numerous coats of paint that have lost elasticity, possibly during intense heat. The solution is to scrape and sand, then use exterior spackling compound to level the material that cannot be removed. If flaking has exposed bare wood, remove the paint completely. Then prime and repaint.

Peeling: Multiple coats of old paint, moisture, or an improperly prepared surface can cause paint to peel. You must first remove the source of moisture, then scrape and sand, prime and repaint.

CHAPTER
3

Walls

The walls of your home can serve as a giant canvas for creating the mood and style of each room. They are the backdrop that holds your decorating scheme together because they are the largest surface that meets the eye. With today's materials, it's never been easier to transform plain-Jane walls into just about any decor you might choose.

Wallpapering is a relatively simple way to give a room a new look. As in painting, preparation plays an important part. There are certain procedures that make the whole process easier, and we've outlined them for you in this chapter. There are other ways to transform walls— hanging wall fabrics and installing cork or fabric panels—and we will tell you how to go about them. Since we've often faced the tedious task of removing old adhesives from walls, we'll tell you what we've discovered. No discussion about walls would be complete without telling you how to add decorative moldings and how to hang decorative objects on walls —both are really quick fixes for tired-looking walls.

Removing Wallpaper

Some newer wallpapers are designed to be pulled right off the wall. But usually you are not so lucky. In most cases removing wallpaper makes a mess of the entire room, but the results are worth it. Here's the fastest method we've devised to get down to the bare walls (this works on even the worst condition—painted wallpaper):

Wet it down.   To remove wallpaper from a wall, you have to wet it down. So before you even think about starting this project, give some serious thought to protecting the floor. We have used drop cloths and newspapers, but picking up wet wallpaper from a drop cloth can be difficult because the wallpaper sticks to the drop cloth. The best method we've found is to use a combination of newspaper and plastic drop cloths. Put several layers of newspaper around the perimeter of the room. Over the newspaper, place a heavy plastic drop cloth. The newspaper will blot up any water that might leak through the plastic. Use masking tape to attach the edges of the drop cloth to the baseboard.

Apply remover.   Mix wallpaper remover in a clean garden sprayer, being sure that any pesticide has been thoroughly washed out. If you don't have a garden sprayer, use a bucket and a floor sponge mop or paint roller. The remover contains wetting agents that penetrate the paper and soften the glue.

For unpainted paper, apply the remover directly to the paper. Spray on or spread as much remover as the paper will soak up. When water starts to run down the walls, stop spraying and allow it to soak in.

Abrade painted paper.   If the paper is painted, you have to abrade the painted surface so the water can soak behind the paint. Use a razor knife or the edge of a putty knife to score the paper. Plaster is a hard surface which you can't damage too easily, but drywall has a paper facing that is easily cut. Go easy on the walls until you have some of the wallpaper removed and can see if you are damaging them.

You'll be well served to rent a wallpaper steamer if you are faced with several coats of painted wallpaper. This machine is not expensive to rent (about $20 a day) and does help force moisture behind the paper so it can be scraped off. If you have many rooms full of wallpaper to remove, consider buying a self-contained steamer (Black & Decker makes one for about $50). If you can remove all the wallpaper in one day, then renting a steamer is the way to go; if your work will be spread out, having your own tool on hand when you need it may be worth the money.

On the down side, a steamer is always a potential hazard because it's basically a boiler that emits a fine mist of boiling water. We've found that most of the time a steamer makes the job of removing several layers of painted wallpaper a little easier, but the job is still a tedious, time-consuming one.

Scrape the paper.   In either case, wait for the water to soak through the paper and soften the glue. This can take up to a half hour or more for several

REMOVING WALLPAPER

The key to removing wallpaper is to thoroughly wet the old glue behind the paper. You can do this with a paint roller, a steamer, a garden sprayer, or a squirt bottle. Once the paper is thoroughly saturated, you can remove it with a wallpaper razor knife if you have plaster walls, or a putty knife if your walls are drywall.

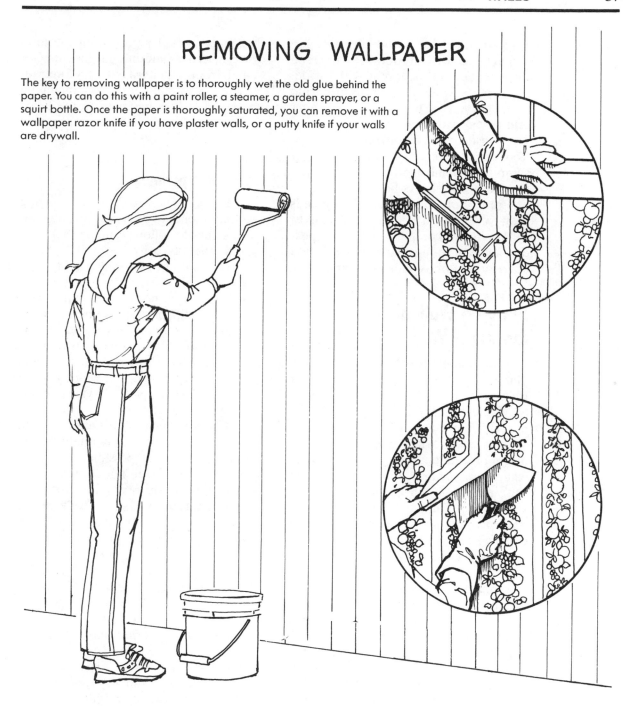

coats of paper or with painted paper. When the glue finally does soften, scrape the wet paper off of drywall with a wide-blade putty knife. If the walls are made of plaster, you can use a wallpaper scraper that takes a razor blade.

Wash with trisodium phosphate. You can get most of the glue off by scraping, but no matter how hard you try, there will always be some glue residue remaining on the wall. This glue is easy to remove if you get to it quickly. Before the wall completely dries, wipe it down with a sponge damp with solution of trisodium phosphate and water.

Hanging Wallpaper the Right Way

Wallpaper probably is the most popular wall covering. Hanging wallpaper isn't hard, and in most cases, you need only a few inexpensive tools to do the job. But there are at least two circumstances under which you may want to hire a pro: One is that you are going to wallpaper a stairway or other location that requires a high ladder and/or scaffolding. This can be dangerous work without the proper equipment and experience. Handling long runs of paper is also difficult, and a wrong cut can be costly.

Another reason you may want to hire a pro is that you have selected an expensive foil, flocked, or textured paper. These wall coverings are tricky for a beginner to hang, and since they are expensive, you have a sizable investment in materials at stake if you botch the job.

Remember that the cost of professional installation stays almost the same regardless of the type of paper, but it

becomes a smaller portion of the total job cost as the materials bill goes up. Get a bid from a paperhanger before you attempt a difficult job. You might be surprised at how inexpensive the labor is, compared with the cost of the wall covering.

Painless Paperhanging

If you are new to the art of hanging wallpaper or if you need to brush up on your skills, the following advice will help you do the job easily:

Do not be intimidated by the selection. The most staggering part of wallpapering is choosing the paper! Volumes of wallpaper books line the walls of paint stores. Plan to invest lots of time perusing those books to help narrow down your selection. Many wallpaper outlets have take-home samples, which can be quite helpful when you're trying to coordinate a color scheme.

Choose a paper that's easy to work with. Begin with a moderately priced pretrimmed paper. If possible, use a vinyl-backed paper; it will not stretch out of shape even if you reposition it several times, and it is easy to strip. Don't choose a foil, flocked, or embossed paper. Try to choose a paper with a pattern repeat or "drop" of 10 inches or less. The pattern repeat is the distance a pattern travels before it begins to repeat itself. The longer the repeat, the more extra length you'll have to allow on each strip so that you can align the pattern of each strip with the strip next to it. This, of course, means more waste and more expense. Also, papers with large repeats are harder to install, because a small misalignment will stand out. The pattern repeat is indicated on the back of each roll of paper and in the wallpaper books.

Begin in a hassle-free room. Begin your paperhanging career in a small bedroom or other area with wide walls and no obstacles to paper around. Don't tackle papering the kitchen, bath, or other rooms with lots of cabinets, soffits, or other protrusions that will make the work tricky.

Paint before you paper. It might seem obvious, but sometimes we overlook what's common sense. Complete all trim painting before you paper. Remember, too, that worn, chipped trim looks even worse when it is next to new paper.

Calculating How Much to Buy

When you choose your wallpaper, the back of the sample in the wallpaper book will tell you how much area each roll will cover—usually about 36 square feet for a single roll of American wallpaper or about 28 square feet for a single European role.

As we mentioned, the sample will also tell you the repeat or drop for a pattern. This tells you how often the pattern repeats itself and affects how much paper you will have to waste. If, for example, your paper is simply vertical stripes, there will be no drop. If it is a large design, you may have to throw away up to 18 inches of each strip to make the repeats line up.

To calculate how much paper you will need, multiply the length of all the walls by the ceiling height. Now multiply the height of each door and window by its width, and add up these areas. Subtract the window and door areas from the wall area to get the total surface area you'll be covering with wallpaper. Divide this surface area by coverage area of a roll. This will give you the number of rolls you need before adding in for waste.

To calculate the waste, note the width of the wallpaper you have chosen. Take a tape measure and go around the room marking out where each new strip will begin. Add up the strips and multiply this number by the drop. Remember, even if a strip is only a foot or two long over a door, it still needs a drop. Now add in 2 inches for each strip. This is for trim waste on the nondrop end of each strip. Of course, if the paper has no drop, you'll need to add a total of 4 inches for each strip—2 inches of trim for each end of each strip. The wallpaper book will tell you how long each roll is, so it's an easy matter to add up how many rolls you'll need for drop and trim waste.

When you have calculated how much wallpaper you will need, add 10 percent for waste. If this is your first wallpaper job, add in another roll after the 10 percent—you are likely to make more mistakes than an experienced paperhanger. It's a good idea to make sure you buy enough paper in one batch. If you buy more later, it may not match exactly, even if you order the same pattern from the same store.

Hanging It Yourself

If you have decided to hang your own wallpaper, you'll have a greater chance for success if you are patient and methodical and follow these procedures:

Prepare the wall surface. Walls and ceilings that are to be papered need to be clean and free of structural damage. It is easier to remove light switch plates and outlet covers and wall and ceiling fixtures than to paper around them. It also gives the job a professional look. Before you remove the fixtures and covers, turn off the electricity to that room and leave it off while you hang the paper. Otherwise, if you misdirect a knife while trimming paper around an outlet or switch, you might be in for a shock. Plan wallpapering for daylight hours, or use lamps plugged into outlets in another room.

If the walls are covered with several coats of paint, you generally can get by without applying sizing. But sizing does seal the walls and provide an ideal surface for the new wallpaper to stick to. Finally, it makes the wallpaper easier to remove. So, if this is your first papering job, consider sizing the walls. Sizing makes it easier to slide the paper around on the wall without stretching or tearing it.

Whether you size the walls or not, use a vinyl paste. We think this type of paste gives the best results, no matter what type of paper we hang. This paste is stronger and resists mildew better than the older wheat pastes, but it is more expensive.

If you have had a problem with mildew in the room, purchase a mildewcide additive and mix it into the paste. Otherwise, most vinyl pastes are sufficiently mildew resistant.

Another trick is to give a dark-colored wall a coat of inexpensive white latex primer. This will prevent the dark-colored wall from showing through the background of the wallpaper. You don't have to do this if you are hanging a very heavy or vinyl paper. There are products on the market that combine a white primer with a sizing for a one-step operation that works well for this situation.

Hang it straight.   Few walls are truly square, so you have to lay out vertical guidelines to help keep the paper straight. Even with these aids, by the time you work your way around the room, there will be some mismatch between the first and last strip of paper you hung. To help hide this inevitable mismatch, plan your job so the final seam falls over a door or window, in an inconspicuous corner, or at a built-in bookcase.

Use a chalk line or 4-foot level and pencil to make a vertical line where you plan to start papering. Put a roll of paper in position about ½ inch from the line, and make a pencil mark on the wall. Start hanging your first roll at this mark. Hanging the paper ½ inch away from the layout line that you snap or draw on the wall will prevent the line from showing through the seam.

Cut the paper.   Holding the paper in position against the wall, decide where you want the pattern to break at the ceiling, and lightly mark this spot on the paper. Remove the paper from the wall and set it on the floor. You should cut each strip of wallpaper at least 4 inches longer than necessary to allow a 2-inch trim area at the top and bottom. You'll want more than 4 inches extra if the paper has a long repeat. Hold it in place against the wall and check that the pattern is where you want it and that the paper reaches from the ceiling to the floor with enough extra paper for easy trimming.

To cut the second and third strips, lay the first strip on a clean floor and unroll the paper next to it to align patterns. If there is a lot of waste at the top, open another roll and check the match —there might be less waste. Then cut the second strip from the roll with the least waste. Don't cut more than a few strips at a time, at least until you have several strips up and are sure of all measurements.

TIPS FOR EASY WALLPAPER HANGING

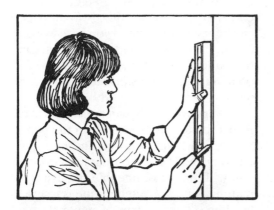

For your first strip on each wall, subtract about 2 inches from the width of your wallpaper and measure that distance from a corner. Strike a plumb line from that point.

Align the first strip to the plumb line before smoothing the wallpaper.

The only way to cut paper around windows, doors, and other obstructions is to hang the paper right over the obstruction and trim it in place.

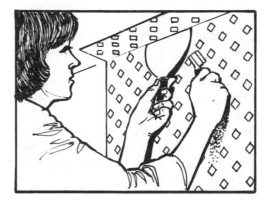

To avoid ripping wallpaper when cutting at the ceiling or baseboard, hold the paper firmly in place with a broad knife and then run a sharp razor blade along the knife.

Paste up the paper. Apply wallpaper adhesive smoothly and evenly to the back of the wallpaper with a wallpaper brush or a small paint roller, making sure all the edges are coated. Then fold the paper back on itself so the ends meet in the center of the strip and the pasted sides are in contact with one another. This keeps the adhesive from drying while the paper soaks up some moisture from the adhesive and swells up. To save time, apply adhesive to a couple of strips at a time so one strip can soak while you work with the other.

Hang it on the wall. Carry the folded wallpaper up the ladder, unfold the top flap, and let the paper fall with the bottom still folded. Put the paper in position, then slide it around until it is aligned with your plumb line. Remember you have planned for 2 inches of excess at the top and bottom. Push, don't pull the paper on the wall, to avoid stretching it. When it is aligned with the plumb line, unfold the lower section and complete alignment. Using a brush or sponge, smooth the paper, working from the center toward the edges, to remove air bubbles and wrinkles. Wipe off excess glue with your sponge. After you have hung several strips, go back over the seams with a seam roller. Use light pressure to secure any openings, and sponge away glue oozing out of the seam.

Trim the tops and bottoms. After you have hung several strips, trim the paper at the top and bottom. Hold a 6-inch-wide scraper (called a broad knife) tight against the wall, then push its blade into the joint between the ceiling or molding and wall. With a fresh razor blade in your razor knife, trim the paper by drawing the razor along the straight metal edge of the broad knife. As you reach the end of the broad knife, move the knife and repeat the process. Don't skimp on razor blades. Change them frequently to avoid tearing the paper.

Trim around objects. Sooner or later you will have to paper around a door or window. Don't try to precut the paper; it is easier to trim it in place.

Hang the paper as you normally would, aligning it with the last strip, but don't try to smooth the paper close to where it bulges or you will stretch it. Use scissors or a razor to cut away all but a 2-inch overlapping strip around the open-ing. Next, make a 45-degree cut at each corner around the opening. Now the paper can be smoothed. When you have worked out all the wrinkles and air bubbles, trim the paper flush against the edge of the opening, using the same technique you used to trim the tops and bottoms.

Negotiate inside and outside corners. Resist the temptation to wrap the paper around an inside corner and continue hanging. Seldom are corners square, and you will have a noticeable pattern mismatch. The easiest technique is to use a lap joint. Trim a strip of paper ½ inch wider than the distance from the last panel to the corner, and hang it. This will allow the strip to wrap around an inside or outside corner. If the waste strip you trimmed off is more than 6 inches wide, use it as the starter strip on the new wall. If it's less, start with a new full-width strip. On the wall that hasn't been papered yet, measure out from the corner the width of your next strip and draw a plumb line there; don't use the corner as a guide. The new strip will overlap the ½ inch of the strip from the other wall. The extra ½ inch will cover any slight gaps between the new plumb strip and the other wall. If you are using vinyl paper, use a bead of vinyl-on-vinyl adhesive between the overlapped sheets.

If you are using a heavy vinyl paper, the extra paper underneath may create a noticeable bump. If this is the case, you can double-cut the overlapping paper in the corner. To do this, cut the first strip of paper and install it with a 2-inch wrap at the corner just like a lap joint. Use a putty knife with a wide blade to push the paper into the corner. It should be tight in the corner without any air pockets. Install the strip on the new wall so it overlaps the other strip 2 inches and wraps around the corner. Check to see that it is tight in the corner.

To make the double cut, carefully run your razor knife down the center of the corner so you cut through both pieces of paper at the same time. Apply firm pressure to the blade, but don't push too hard if your walls are made of wallboard. You want to avoid cutting through the seaming tape used to cover the joint.

Remove the cut-off strip from the first wall; it is loose and you can peel it off. Then lift the strip of paper on the new wall and peel off the 2-inch cut-off piece from underneath it. Press the strip back in place, and smooth both sides of the corner with a seam roller for a perfect butt joint of the wallpaper.

Tips for a Professional Look

▶ Wait at least 5 minutes after you brush adhesive onto a strip of wallpaper for it to "wet out" before you hang it. Wallpaper expands when wet and contracts as it dries, so this wetting out lets it reach its maximum expansion and eliminates the development of bubbles.

▶ Reverse every other strip when hanging plain wall coverings, to avoid having slight discrepancies in the texture and color—a problem known as shading—show at the seams. Hang one strip with the arrow going up and the next strip with the arrow going down.

▶ Use small pointed scissors for cutting diagonal slots to allow the paper to lie flat next to small openings and tight corners.

▶ Use an adhesive even if the paper is prepasted, because the sticking power is that much greater.

Papering Switch Plates and Outlet Covers

To give a wallpaper job that final touch of distinction, paper the electrical switch plates and outlet covers. Wash and dry the covers and then apply a vinyl-to-vinyl primer (the same wall prep used for adding a border to a wallpaper) to all the plates and covers in a room. While the primer is drying, wallpaper the room.

Look for a piece of leftover paper that matches the pattern around the outlet and switch openings. If there are no suitable scraps, cut paper from the roll. Then follow these steps:

Step 1: Hold the scrap piece against the opening to match the pattern on the wall. Then position the wallpaper on the cover to see that it matches the pattern on the wall. You want the pattern on the cover to match the pattern on the wall so you actually don't notice that there's a cover.

Step 2: Cut the matched scrap about ½ inch larger on all sides of the cover. Fold the wallpaper over the top of the cover and align it with the pattern on the wall. Adjust the wallpaper and fold it firmly on the cover about ½ inch across the top and bottom. Repeat this on the two sides and you should have four neatly folded corners.

Step 3: Spread adhesive on the wallpaper and center the cover evenly within the folded lines. Cut away the corners and press firmly. When the paper is dry, cut the outlet and switch openings with a pin or narrow razor knife (such as an artist's X-acto knife).

If you want to, you can paint the heads of cover screws to match the new wallpaper. Be careful not to fill the screw slots with paint.

Wallpapering over Wallpaper

Don't do it. We have found that hanging new wallpaper over several layers of old paper rarely works. What's more, it's a nasty thing to do to the next people who decorate those walls! One problem is that pen marks or stains on the old stuff bleed through to the new paper. Another problem is that a vibrant pattern on the old paper sometimes shows through on a new paper with lightly colored, small print.

There's one possible exception to this rule. If you run into wallpaper hung directly on wallboard that was not properly primed or sized, you may find that removing the wallpaper can cause so much damage to the paper surface of the wallboard that you are better off papering over it. If we find we are wrecking the wall when removing old paper, then we reluctantly paper or paint over it. But it's something we do as a last-ditch effort and don't recommend it unless there's no alternative.

Before you apply more paper, prepare the wall for priming by first dusting the wall thoroughly, then remove grease and grime with trisodium phosphate or a strong detergent. Apply an oil-based primer/sealer, which will not loosen the water-soluble adhesive holding the paper in place. There are primer/sealers formulated especially for painting wallpaper. Check with the experts at the paint store.

Decorating the Easy Way— Hanging Border Paper

Adding a wallpaper border to a painted wall or on top of wallpaper is a nifty face-lift for a plain room. You'll find border paper available in yard rolls in a wide variety of sizes, designs, and color schemes. Most of these borders are 2 to 8 inches wide.

Use border paper in a room to give it some punch, to perk it up. Add a border of cheerful alphabet letters at the ceiling around the perimeter of a child's bedroom, in colors that match the bedspread and curtains. Use border paper to call attention to architectural details by outlining a fireplace or built-in bookcase.

In a small bathroom with a high ceiling, visually lower the ceiling by using a border paper coordinated with the bathroom's decor. Add pizzazz to an ordinary door or window frame, or create a chair rail in a dining alcove with border paper compatible with its furnishings.

Try outlining the tops of walls at the ceiling, or trace the eaves of a dormer window. Outline a staircase or create a formal frieze. If you have a wooden chair rail, you can accentuate it by using border paper above or below it.

A walk through a wallpaper store or the wallpaper department of a large home center will show you the variety of border paper that is available. Many designers of bedspreads and linens offer border paper, as well as wall coverings, to coordinate with many of their lines. To freshen up a nursery for a new baby, you can use border paper that coordinates with the baby's new quilt and furnishings. It's an economical way to get a designer look without wallpapering an entire room. Also, redecorating will be easier, when baby gets older.

Hanging Borders

Apply paste.   Border paper comes prepasted and ready to hang, just like

USING BORDER PAPER TO DRESS UP A ROOM

DOORWAYS AND WINDOWS

WALLS NEAR THE CEILING

SOFFITS AND CHAIR RAILS

CHILDREN'S ROOMS

conventional wallpaper. Use vinyl adhesive when applying border paper to a painted wall, and vinyl-to-vinyl adhesive when putting it over wallpaper. A 2-inch roller is handy for applying the adhesive to the paper.

Hang the paper. Border paper usually is hung tight against the ceiling or ceiling molding. You can drop the border several inches below the ceiling or molding to visually lower a high ceiling. If you are using the border paper as a chair rail, hang it about 36 inches from the floor. But that's just a guideline. Adjust border paper to the way you think it looks best.

A FOOLPROOF MITER FOR BORDER PAPER

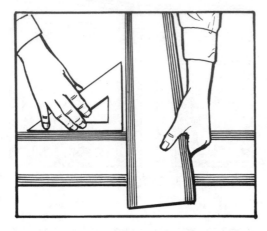

1. Use a square to lay one strip across the other at 90 degrees.

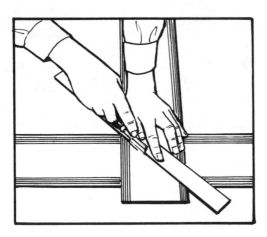

2. Cut diagonally through both strips, using a straightedge and a single stroke with a sharp blade.

Hang border paper so it butts tightly against the ceiling molding. If you don't have molding for a guide, hang the paper against the ceiling. If you plan to drop the border several inches from the ceiling or install it as a chair rail, snap a level chalk line or lightly mark a straight level line with a carpenter's level as a guide.

Overlap at corners. Working border papers around corners is the same as hanging regular wallpaper. Use a lap joint on an inside corner. Cut border paper slightly longer than the wall and hang it, working toward the most inconspicuous corner. Run paper around the corner, and then cut it off, leaving about ½ inch overlapping the adjoining wall. Cut the end of the next piece with a square and a utility knife. Butt it into the corner, matching the pattern. You can also use the double-cut technique that we mentioned in "Hanging Wallpaper the Right Way."

To negotiate an outside corner, just wrap the paper around the corner. If the walls are badly out of plumb, cut the paper so it turns the corner with a 2-inch overlap. Then start the paper run again, realigning the paper with the ceiling.

Miter the corners. Use a miter cut to hang a border around window or door frames. The easiest way to do this is to overlap the border strips at the corner. Each strip should extend past the other about an inch. Then use a razor knife to make a 45-degree miter cut through both border papers at the same time. Peel off the top piece of waste, then lift the other side of the border and remove the piece of waste from beneath it. Smooth it back in place and you have a perfectly mated cut. Since both papers are cut at the same time, even a wavy line will not show.

Hanging Embossed Wallpaper

Heavy, embossed wallpaper has been a popular cover-up for problem walls since Victorian times. First developed in England in the 1880s, these wall coverings were designed to lend an air of elegance to any room while concealing nonstructural defects. They came in various patterns and were designed to be painted. They absorbed the paint and became hard and durable. Today a lighter-weight version of this embossed wall covering is available, not only in Victorian patterns, but also in a wide variety of textures and designs.

Embossed wallpaper is more difficult to hang than conventional paper, but it is within the reach of most experienced home paperhangers. Supaglypta and Anaglypta Luxury Vinyl are two well-known brands.

While hanging these wall coverings is not too different from hanging conventional papers, you must use a wallpaper adhesive designed to hold heavyweight papers. Because the papers are very heavy, they must soak for at least 15 minutes before hanging.

Smooth the embossed wall coverings with a soft wallpaper brush, not a roller, to avoid crushing their relief pattern. Because the paper is thick, you won't want to leave overlaps at corners. Instead, use the double-cut method described in "Hanging Wallpaper the Right Way." Try wrapping full sheets around outside corners, but check the pattern alignment.

Once the paper is hung, you should wait a few days before painting it. You can wait and paint the trim and ceiling at the same time.

Painting Old Plastic Tile

Colorful plastic tiles became a popular bathroom and kitchen adornment back in the late 1940s. Compared with ceramic tile, the plastic variety doesn't age well. The finish dulls and the tiles frequently dent and damage more easily than the more durable ceramic tiles. So whenever we run across plastic, or even metal, tiles, we pop them off the walls. The tiles usually pop right off when you shove a putty knife behind them. In fact, sometimes we've found sections of plastic tiles that have popped off the wall by themselves, the result of excessive moisture localized in a bathtub corner area or above a kitchen sink. However, a few may be stubborn, splintering and breaking before you get them off the wall. So make sure you wear eye protection.

To remove the old dried mastic from the wall, follow the suggestions later in this chapter under "Removing Old Adhesives from Walls."

If you hate the color of the plastic tiles but you don't want to bother removing them, you can paint them. We've found that any interior paint will stick to tiles if you thoroughly clean them first.

Bring a sample of the tile to your local paint supplier and ask for his recommendation for a primer and compatible paint. We found that a pigmented shellac or latex primer sticks to plastic tiles. Either latex or alkyd paint works. But if you will be leaving any mastic exposed, for example if a tile is missing, don't use alkyd paint directly on the mastic. The mastic will bleed through. Prime it first with a stain-killing paint such as Bin or Kilz. Prep work and paint-

PAINTING PLASTIC TILES

1. Thoroughly clean the tile with trisodium phosphate. A pot scrubber pad is perfect for removing built-up soap scum.

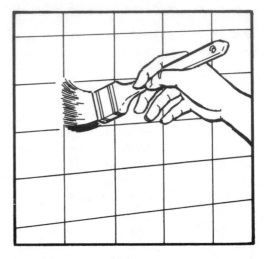

2. Use a paintbrush to work paint into the joints between tiles.

3. Roll paint onto the tiles.

ing is easy, but remember it's only a temporary cover-up. Here's how:

Wash the tiles. Use a solution of trisodium phosphate and hot water to remove any soap scum, dirt, or oil from the tile. An old toothbrush is handy to get grime out of the corners and from the joints between the tiles. A good tool to use to remove a tough buildup of scum is a pot scrubber pad. The cleaner the tile, the better the paint will adhere.

Prime the tiles. Apply primer to the tiles. There is no grout between plastic tiles, so seal the joints between the tiles completely with primer. Apply several coats of primer to any bare mastic. Work the primer into the grooves with a paintbrush, then apply the primer to the face of the tiles, using a roller with a fine nap cover.

Paint the tiles. When the primer is dry, paint the tiles with a latex or alkyd enamel. A high-gloss enamel will produce the best results since it resists water and cleans up easily. Use the same brush-roller combination to apply the paint as you used for the primer.

Removing Old Adhesives from Walls

Often when you buy a fixer-upper house, you're amazed at the "ingenuity" of its former owners. We've dealt with a few challenges ourselves. The dusty, dark cork wall tiles that we anticipated popping off the dining room walls turned out to be glued on with cement mastic. We've had the challenge of removing plastic and ceramic tile, cork panels and wood paneling, even floor tiles and carpeting glued to walls.

The common denominator these coverings share is that they are glued in place with some sort of mastic or adhesive. The black or brown mastic does a good job of holding things in place—such a good job, in fact, that it's a real hassle to remove. Once the tiles are chipped or pried off the wall, you will be left with a rough, uneven surface covered with old adhesive. To paint the walls, you must first remove all of the old adhesive. Not only is the adhesive rough, it will bleed through and stain most paints. The adhesive also is too rough to wallpaper over and will bleed through and stain most papers.

If the adhesive or mastic is old and hard, then it can be chipped off with a razor scraper. Use quick jabbing motions and work on a small area at a time.

The newer mastics do not get hard and brittle and consequently are much more difficult to remove. We have tried just about everything and have found that a heat gun and putty knife are the most effective weapons to use against this stubborn stuff. Use the wide heat-spreader nozzle attachment on the end of the gun. Wear heavy leather work gloves and eye protection, and be sure to provide plenty of ventilation. Use a putty knife with a wood or plastic handle if

you have one (the handle doesn't get as hot). Have a fire extinguisher handy.

Using the heat gun: Hold the heat gun about 3 or 4 inches from the mastic, and work it back and forth over a small area. The goal is to heat and soften the mastic *without* setting it on fire or melting the paint underneath. This takes practice to perfect.

Try different combinations of heat and putty knife action until you discover the best heating and scraping combination. Sometimes moving the gun slowly just in front of the putty knife works best. Be careful, though, not to set the mastic residue hanging from the putty knife on fire.

This job is one of the best upper-arm muscle builders known to man. Work in a small area and allow plenty of time. It's *not* a quick and easy job.

Hiding That Nasty Mastic Stain

Mastic leaves a stain on the walls that bleeds through just about any type of paint. To kill the stain, prime the wall with a white-pigmented shellac. You might have to apply several coats of this stain killer before the bleeding stops. You might also try aluminum paint if the stain continues to bleed through even the shellac.

Other Easy Wall Cover-Ups

Instead of paint or paper, you can try one of these attractive disguises to hide a problem wall or to create a totally new atmosphere. These suggestions are heavy-duty cover-ups, but they will not solve structural problems. Water leaks, the cause of many wall problems, must be cured, and loose or damaged wall material should be removed or reattached to the framing.

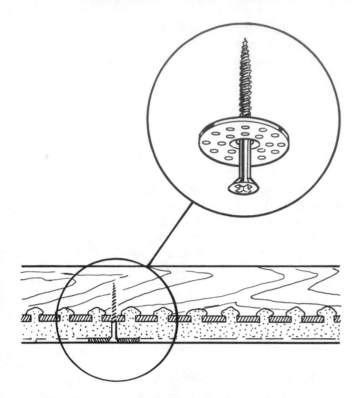

Use a long drywall screw and a plaster button to pull a loose plaster ceiling or wall tight against joists or studs. Drill a pilot hole through the plaster, then insert the drywall screw into the plaster button and screw it into the wall. Use your hand to push the ceiling or wall hard against the framing; then tighten the screw to hold the plaster in place.

Many times, after you have struggled to remove old paneling, tile, or other wall coverings, you are still faced with the problem of removing the mastic. Veneering a new wall surface over this mess is easier and, in some cases, less expensive than refinishing the old wall.

Plaster walls that look like road maps and drywall that has open seams or many popped nails can be resurfaced, but it is usually easier, and your job will last longer, if you apply a totally new surface. Besides traditional paneling, you have the choice of applying a thin drywall veneer or heavy

plaster-impregnated fabric to large areas. For a quick cover-up, choose sound-deadening cork panels or hide the wall with fabric-covered panels.

Pulling the Old Wall Together

The first job you face when resurfacing a wall is to correct any structural problems. If you have seriously damaged plaster walls that are loose, not just cracked, you should seek professional help. Generally, plaster that is cracked can be patched. If plaster moves when you push on it, then it has come loose from the lath, or the lath has come loose from the studs. Either way, no minor repair you can make will prevent the cracks from returning.

Keep in mind that loose plaster can be a safety hazard, especially on a ceiling. The material is very heavy, and if it pulls away from the lath or if the lath pulls away from the ceiling joist, a large section of the ceiling can come crashing down.

If the plaster is sagging from the ceiling or loose on the wall but is not badly cracked, you can reanchor it by using plaster buttons. These are washers that give extra holding power to drywall screws. As a substitute, you can use large galvanized washers that you countersink into the plaster. Top-coat the buttons with joint compound or finishing plaster to hide them.

Repairing loose drywall, on the other hand, is not hard. Drywall is a lot lighter than plaster and can usually be pulled tight against the stud with drywall screws. Push the drywall tight against the studs, and drive each drywall screw through the old wall into a stud. Put the screw in until it's just below the surface of the drywall but not far enough to break the paper on the drywall surface. Space screws about every foot or so in loose areas. Place a screw next to every loose or popped drywall nail. Then pull out all the loose drywall nails, or drive them completely through the drywall with a hammer and nail set so they are tight against the wall studs.

Gypsum Wall Fabrics

Plaster or gypsum-impregnated wall fabrics go up like wallpaper, but they have a more durable surface and a greater hiding ability. Available in 48-inch-wide rolls, this type of wall cover-up is basically a woven jute fabric coated with uncured gypsum plaster. The glue used to install the fabric activates the plaster so it cures and hardens in place. This covering can be applied over cracked plaster, old paneling, or concrete block walls, and it can be painted.

These fabrics are available in several finishes, but all are lightly textured and meant to be painted. If you don't like the textured look, trowel on a light coat of drywall joint compound to fill in the texture. Use a wide taping knife or a plaster trowel to apply a thin coat of taping compound to a 3 or 4-foot-square area. After the compound is on the wall, clean off the trowel blade and use it to skim as much of the compound off the wall as possible. Some compound will be left in the weave of the fabric. When the compound is dry and hard, check the surface to see if you can still see the pattern. If there are small areas that you missed, apply another thin coat. When the joint compound is dry, give the wall a light sanding to make it smooth. After the first coat of paint, you might still see

some imperfections, so apply a little compound to any craters or low spots between coats of paint. This technique yields a smooth, plaster-hard surface.

These gypsum wall fabrics also are available with the jute fabric exposed, which has the look of burlap or grass-cloth wallpaper. They are finished and do not require painting.

Cork Panels

For rooms where noise is a problem, we use sound-deadening panels made by the Homasote Company. These are panels covered with cork or burlap that come in various sizes up to full 4×8-foot sheets. These panels are $\frac{1}{2}$ inch thick with a $\frac{1}{16}$-inch veneer of cork or burlap. They can be hung on a wall with construction adhesive or nailed to furring strips that are nailed through the drywall to the wall studs. These panels are ideal for a teenager's room, where hanging up posters is a must. Also, they make sense as a one-wall treatment in a hobby or sewing room where hanging up patterns (sewing room) or directions and parts (hobby room) is important.

Cork panels also make nifty wainscoting for a little kid's room. Small artists can hang their work right on the panels, which are close to the floor so they can see them. The cork also makes a good bumper and will stand up to abuse from riding toys and other objects that might come into contact with the walls.

If you use the cork panels as wainscoting with a chair rail, make up the difference in thickness between the cork panel and chair rail molding by gluing two pieces of $\frac{1}{4}$-inch-thick lattice to the back of the molding. This makes it flush with the face of the panel.

Fabric Panels

Fabric-covered sound-deadening panels, sometimes called soundboard, are not only a good cover-up for bad walls but can also solve a noise problem. These panels work well in a variety of rooms, such as a home office with a noisy typewriter or computer printer, the den where a television plays nonstop, or the bedroom of a budding musician who has long practice sessions. These easy-to-make panels can be glued in place or nailed to furring strips. Here is how to make one:

Step 1: Cut panels of ½-inch-thick soundboard (available in sizes up to 4 × 8 feet) to 1 inch less than the height of your room.

Step 2: Cut ¼-inch-thick foam sheeting so that it overlaps the panel by 2 inches on all sides. Fold the sheeting over the panel edges and staple it to the back.

Step 3: Cut the fabric with the same overlap, wrap it over the foam sheeting, and pull it tight while you staple it to the panel back.

Step 4: To mount panels, use construction adhesive and drywall screws to attach ¼ × 1⅝-inch lattice strips to your wall at the ceiling, floor, and midwall. Glue the panels to the lattice strips with construction adhesive. Use finishing nails to hold the panels in place until the adhesive sets.

Decorative Moldings

There's no quicker way to add "instant architecture" to a room than with decorative molding. From plain to fancy, inexpensive to handcrafted, you'll find an amazing variety of moldings to suit your taste and budget. At lumberyards you'll find wooden molding that ranges from narrow screen molding and base shoe to elaborate crown molding and baseboard. It is primarily pine or fir and available in varying degrees of quality. At specialty millwork suppliers, you'll find moldings made of oak and other hardwoods. A millwork operation is where to look if you're trying to match and replace a piece of molding in an older house. When doing this, don't rely on memory—take a section with you.

At large home centers you'll find new molding systems made of polystyrene and other synthetic materials that are designed to fit together. As a system, this eliminates the need for miter cuts, because straight, long sections of molding fit between corner blocks and pieces. While wood molding can be stained or painted, these moldings must be painted.

Where to Use Moldings

The molding in a room acts like a picture frame to define boundaries and add depth to the space. Determining the size of molding appropriate for your room depends on its size and ceiling height. Take a look in older homes with high ceilings and you'll see high baseboard moldings teamed with various-size ceiling moldings, from heavy cornices to narrower, cove-type moldings. These ceiling moldings are ornamental, but they also are a practical way of concealing the joint between ceiling and wall. Some are installed flush on the wall, while others, called hollow crown moldings, bridge the gap by hanging diagonally out from the ceiling and wall. In Victorian-era homes you'll often find a picture rail placed about a foot below a crown ceiling molding. Its purpose is to support wire for hanging artwork and eliminate holes in the wall. Casing is the woodwork you see installed around windows and doorways. Baseboard conceals the gap between the floor and wall and acts to protect the wall from bumps and thumps. A chair rail is another type of protective molding, usually placed 32 to 36 inches above the floor.

Make-Believe with Moldings

Not sure what kind of molding will look right in your rooms? Here's a little trick to find out. Loosely tack various widths of masking tape to the walls to give you an idea of what molding will look like in a room. Leave one half of the room as it is and tape the other side, to show what the room looks like before and after molding is installed. Spend some time playing around with it. For a heavier molding such as a cornice, use several strips of tape that measure the width of the cornice you're considering. When you think you know what you want, buy scrap sections of molding and use them with double-stick tape to help you visualize how your room will look.

Here are some general guidelines for choosing molding:

▶ A molding at the ceiling draws your eye to it, making the ceiling seem higher and the walls wider at the top.

▶ A chair rail suggests wainscoting, making the room appear wider. Also, it helps prevent chair nicks and wall bumps if placed in the dining room. In a small room, place the chair rail about 30 inches above the floor. This will make the space seem wider and longer.

▶ In a room with only a patio door for architectural interest, add molding on the wall directly above the door frame

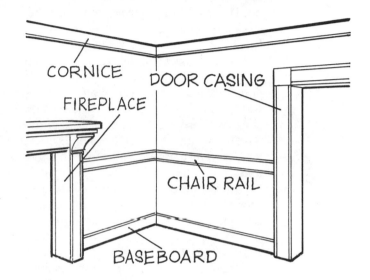

SOME TYPICAL APPLICATIONS FOR MOLDING

CORNICE
DOOR CASING
FIREPLACE
CHAIR RAIL
BASEBOARD

and carry it around the room. This creates a false ceiling height and visually deepens and widens the room.

▶ You can soften the tunnel look of a narrow hallway by adding a chair rail to deepen the perspective, making it appear wider.

▶ Avoid placing molding in the middle of the wall in a small room, because it cuts the room in half, making it look smaller.

Tips for Buying and Installing Wood Moldings

Choose a molding grade. If you plan to finish the molding with stain showing the grain of the wood, choose a clear or select grade of molding. If you're painting it, you can buy a less expensive grade, which has clearly visible signs of mismatched finger-jointed wood. The flaws don't matter if you can't see them.

Use construction adhesive.   You need to use only a few finishing nails to hold the molding in place while the adhesive sets. With fewer nail holes to fill, finishing or painting goes faster.

Prime or stain first.   It is much quicker to prime or stain molding before you install it. Plus, you won't have to worry about dripping on the floor or walls.

Work around the room.   Work clockwise if you are left-handed, counterclockwise if right-handed. This makes cutting and nailing less awkward.

Miter outside corners.   Wherever two pieces of molding join at an outside corner, make a 45-degree cut on the end of each piece so the moldings come together to form a finished corner. A backsaw and a miter box are the easiest, most economical tools to use. Sometimes it's confusing to know which way the miter angle should be cut. We always hold the molding in place and mark the direction of the miter on the end of the piece. Remember the cut must angle back toward the corner with the exposed wood facing the joint. You can form only one joint per cut. You cannot use the cutoff piece, because the miter is on the wrong side of the molding.

We also found it easier to cut the molding a little long, then cut the miter on the end. Check its fit, then trim the straight end so the molding fits. It's easier to trim the square end than to try to trim the miter.

Cope inside corners.   You can wrap molding around inside corners by using miter joints, but a coped joint works better because it prevents shrinkage of the wood from opening obvious cracks. In a coped joint, one piece of molding is butted into the wall while the other piece is cut to the contour of the molding to meet the first piece. To make this joint, you'll need a coping saw, which is specially designed to accurately cut tight curves. The saw has a thin blade held taut in a frame. Here's how we make a coped joint:

Step 1: Use a backsaw and a miter box to make a 45-degree cut with the point of the angle at the back of the molding. This is the opposite of the angle direction you would use for an outside corner.

Step 2: Cope-cut along the contour of the molding. The point on the face of the molding where the miter angle begins will act as your guide. Theoretically, your cope cut should be perpendicular to the back of the molding, but it is a good idea to undercut a little to ensure a tight joint.

Step 3: If your next joint also is an inside corner, measure the length of the wall, subtract the thickness of your molding, and cut the uncoped end square to that length. The advantage of the coped joint is that the butt cut on the other end does not have to be precise. The next coped joint will cover it, so you have the thickness of the molding as a margin of error. Butt the coped edge tightly into the molding running into the corner, and fasten it to the wall.

If the other end of the coped piece is to form an outside miter joint, butt the coped end tightly in place and then mark the inside of the molding at the corner. This will show you exactly where to start the outside miter cut.

Polystyrene Moldings

If you can't find it in wood, it's available in plastic! Many of the decora-

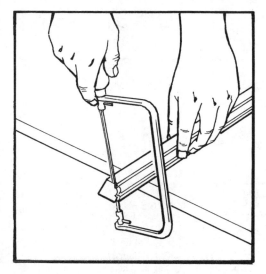

1. To cut a coped joint, place the back of the molding against the miter box fence. Then cut the molding end off at 45 degrees. This cut will reveal the molding contour, which is outlined along the front edge of the cut.

2. Use a coping saw to cut along the contour outlined on the edge of the molding face. Hold the saw at a slight angle so you will undercut the face of the molding. Have the saw blade angle toward the back of the molding so it will remove more wood from the back.

tive moldings found in older homes have not been made for years, and even if they were, they would be so expensive that few people could afford them. Now some of these two-part and three-part moldings are being made in polystyrene. This material is light and can be worked with standard tools.

These moldings are available in a wide range of sizes. Where the polystyrene moldings are most useful is in the more intricate larger sizes. Large crown moldings that were either wood or plaster can now be replaced or duplicated by the do-it-yourselfer. Polystyrene moldings are new to the marketplace, so you'll find a greater selection from mail-order sources than in home centers or lumberyards. There are even metal-wrapped moldings for a streamlined, high-tech look.

Tips for Installing Polystyrene Moldings

Use a fine-toothed saw. Cut polystyrene moldings to length with a fine-toothed saw that has ten or more teeth per inch.

Use construction adhesive. Use construction adhesive and finishing nails to install chair rails and moldings less than 3 inches wide. Use construction adhesive and drywall screws to install heavier crown moldings.

Fill cracks and holes. Fill all cracks between the molding pieces with latex acrylic caulk. Also fill any gaps between the molding and the wall or ceiling with this caulk. For a professional-looking job, smooth the caulk along the joints with a wet finger and clean up any excess caulk

POLYSTYRENE MOLDINGS

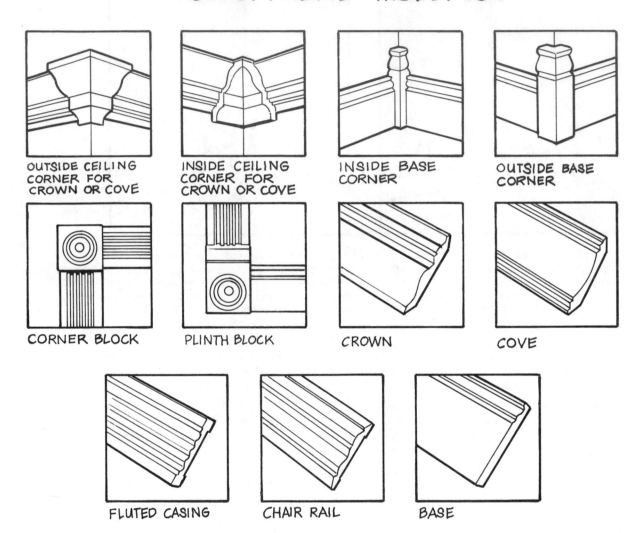

OUTSIDE CEILING CORNER FOR CROWN OR COVE

INSIDE CEILING CORNER FOR CROWN OR COVE

INSIDE BASE CORNER

OUTSIDE BASE CORNER

CORNER BLOCK

PLINTH BLOCK

CROWN

COVE

FLUTED CASING

CHAIR RAIL

BASE

with a wet rag. Fill nail holes or other imperfections with a wood filler or spackling compound.

Metal-Wrapped Moldings

Brass, copper, aluminum, and other thin sheets of metal are laminated to or wrapped around wood molding to create an interesting effect. Metal-wrapped moldings were first used in restaurants and hotel lobbies. But now they're available for consumers who want to try their hand at using moldings in even more dramatic ways.

While unconventional in appearance,

these moldings are installed in basically the same way as wooden moldings. Since the wood is covered with soft metal, you can cut the moldings with regular woodworking tools, but you will get better results if you use tools equipped with carbide-tipped cutters.

Construction adhesive is the best way to attach these moldings to the wall, since finishing nails can't be countersunk and filled with wood putty. These moldings are prefinished, so you have to be careful when working with them. Most have a clear plastic coating on them to protect the finish. Be sure to remove this wrapping from the back of the molding when you glue it in place, so you don't glue the plastic film to the wall.

Hanging Up Your Hang-Ups

Hanging pictures and decorative items on walls is easy if you follow certain procedures and use the right hardware. The goals are to not damage the wall and to ensure that the object won't fall off.

Picture Hooks

The easiest way to hang a picture on plaster or drywall is to use a picture hook. This is a hook with a brad passing through it at a downward angle. These hooks come in several sizes, rated for different weights. If "no nails" is the rule, then use a gummed cloth hanger. This device will not carry the weight of a heavy picture. One advantage is that it can be removed after being moistened with warm water.

Wall Anchors

Another way to hang light objects is to use plastic wall anchors. These are

WALL FASTENERS

Plastic wall anchors are for very light loads on hollow or masonry walls. Use with a sheet-metal screw or roundhead screw.

Hollow-wall anchors are for light loads on hollow walls. They come with their own bolts.

Lag bolts are for heavy loads on walls with wooden studs. They screw directly into studs.

Toggle bolts are for light loads on hollow walls or heavy loads on cinder block walls. They come with their own bolts.

Masonry nails are for light loads on masonry walls. They go through boards into the wall.

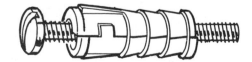

Expansion shields are for heavy loads on masonry walls. They come with their own bolts.

plastic plugs that are forced to expand as you drive screws into them. They are easy to install:

Step 1: Drill a hole slightly smaller than the anchor, and tap the anchor into the wall with your hammer.

Step 2: Drive a screw into the hole in the center of the anchor. The anchor expands in the wall and locks itself, and the screw, in place.

Molly Bolts

To hold objects of up to about 20 pounds, use a Molly bolt. A Molly bolt is a slotted cylinder of thin metal with a screw inside it. The end of the cylinder expands inside the wall when the screw is tightened.

Follow these simple steps to install:

Step 1: Drill a hole in the wall—the package will tell you what diameter—and fit the Molly into the hole.

Step 2: Tighten the screw until it will no longer turn.

Step 3: The screw can be removed completely and reinserted, or simply loosened enough to catch a picture wire.

Toggle Bolts

A toggle bolt is another anchor designed for loads up to 20 pounds. It is similar to the Molly bolt in effect, but unlike the Molly, you can't remove the screw if you want to use the bolt again, because the toggle will fall behind the wall. The toggle bolt consists of a long, thin bolt with a pair of folding "wings" (the toggle) that spring open behind the wall. Here's how to hang something from a toggle bolt:

Step 1: Drill a hole in the wall large enough to pass the folded toggle through.

Step 2: Insert the screw through

whatever you want to secure against the wall, then thread on the toggle. Close the toggle's wings flat against the screw, and push it through the hole. The wings will spring open behind the wall. Tighten the bolt. You can keep the toggle from turning inside the wall by pulling back on the bolt while you tighten it.

How to Remove a Wall Anchor or Toggle Bolt

To remove a plastic wall anchor, loosen the screw and pull out the anchor. If it is stuck, drive it through the hole into the wall cavity. Then patch the hole.

To remove a toggle bolt, unscrew the bolt until the toggle falls off behind the wall. Then patch the hole.

Nails or Screws

If you want to hang something that weighs more than 20 pounds, the only alternative is to find a wall stud and drive a nail or screw into it.

Special Hang-Ups

We all have special things to showcase on our walls. Here are some tricks for hanging the not so usual:

A quilt: This method insures that you don't damage the quilt. Hand-stitch a casing made of muslin across the top edge of the quilt's back. Insert a sturdy curtain rod, and hang it on hooks positioned so that they'll be concealed by the quilt.

A heavy quilt or tapestry: Sew Velcro tape at the top of its back. Staple a mating piece of Velcro to a board, and mount the board on the wall. Hang the quilt by pushing the Velcro strips together.

A picture on a brick wall: Using a

Great Gadgets & Gizmos

☞ **Paper Tiger** Another way to get paper off the wall is to use a roller wheel with two serrated blades. The Paper Tiger is designed to prevent damaging the face of the wallboard, because the blades are only slightly raised. It is manufactured by Wm. Zinsser & Company, 39 Belmont Drive, Somerset, NJ 08875.

☞ **Shieldz** Also made by Wm. Zinsser & Company, this white-pigmented prewall covering primer hides the old wallpaper and assures you of easy paperhanging. You paint it on the wall with a roller, wait a few hours, and then hang the wallpaper.

☞ **Cork panels and soundboard** These products are ideal for covering up walls. They're made by the Homasote Company, P.O. Box 7240, Lower Ferry Road, West Trenton, NJ 08628-0240.

☞ **Brass-wrapped moldings** These are sold by CMF/Colonial Moulding, 17-25 Camden Street, Paterson, NJ 07503.

☞ **Canterbury Moldings** A molding system called Canterbury Moldings is made of paintable synthetic material and sold in home centers. It is made by Abitibi-Price Corporation, 3250 West Big Beaver Road, Troy, MI 48084.

☞ **Picnic table** Applying paste to wallpaper is easy, but messy. Rather than mess up a good table, we use a lightweight, folding aluminum picnic table that we found in the sporting goods section of a discount store. The table is a snap to set up and is wide enough to hold a roll of paper. We set it up on a plastic drop cloth to catch any paste that drips from the table. When we are finished papering, we dispose of the mess by rolling up the drop cloth and taking it and the table outside. Then we dispose of the plastic drop and wash down the table with a garden hose.

☞ **Knife holder** To avoid being a one-armed paperhanger, purchase an inexpensive plastic razor knife holder that pins onto your work shirt or overalls. It has a magnet to keep the knife always ready and safely stowed.

☞ **Adhesive roller** Instead of a wallpaper brush to smooth adhesive on border paper, use a 3-inch paint roller designed to work in corners.

☞ **Crayons** To save time finishing molding and trim, fill the nail holes after you have applied the stain and installed the molding. Use a colored wax crayon made especially for this job. They come in various shades to match finishes and are sold at all hardware and paint stores.

☞ **Plaster buttons** These are available by mail order from Charles Street Supply Company, 54 Charles Street, Boston, MA 02114.

carbide-tipped masonry bit, drill a ¼-inch hole about 1 inch deep. Make sure you drill into the brick, not the mortar. The mortar will crumble. Use a small wad of steel wool as a "nail anchor." Pack the steel wool into the hole with a nail set or large nail and hammer. Then drive a 4d finishing nail into the packed steel wool. The steel wool will grip the nail and act as an anchor. Don't use this trick outside or in a damp area, because the steel wool will rust and can stain the wall.

An unframed mirror: Use inexpensive plastic clips to install an unframed mirror on a wall or the back of a door. These clips come with screws for mounting on wooden doors. If you want to mount the mirror on a wall, use plastic wall anchors, then follow these simple steps:

Step 1: With a pencil and a carpenter's level, mark where you want the bottom of the mirror to be.

Step 2: Install two clips (three if the mirror is over 24 inches wide or is very tall) on this line.

Step 3: Rest the mirror in the bottom clips and install the top clips. Use the top of the mirror as a guide when placing these clips.

Step 4: Install a couple of clips on each side of the mirror for added security.

4 Doors and Windows

The windows of a home are an integral part of its design, and the front door is often its focal point. In our neighborhood, we're seeing an increasing emphasis on upgrading and improving doors and windows. It used to be that a building supply center had only a few examples of wooden entry doors with differently designed panels, and a basic aluminum storm/screen door combination. Today, consumers have a variety of choices in materials and designs, and there are even doors especially designed for security. And added to this array is a staggering selection of door hardware and locks.

Window manufacturers have taken the lead from custom kitchen cabinet shops and created design centers for displaying their vast array of windows in various settings. There will always be fast-talking sales pitches for replacement windows, but even they seem to appeal to a more informed audience. Replacing or repairing windows and doors is an important investment in both time and money, and the payoff is real in conserving energy dollars. Here's what we've learned.

Doors

Most of the time, interior doors do their job for many years without problems. But occasionally they demand attention. For example, if you have beautiful new carpeting or flooring installed, you might discover the doors no longer "work." They won't clear the new, higher-level flooring. Perhaps many years of use have left a door with a large hole, or warped, or delaminated. Or maybe you just want a better door or one in a different style.

Unless an exterior door is especially well built and unique in some way, it is probably easier and more economical to replace the door with a newer, more energy-efficient type. Fortunately, it usually isn't difficult to replace or repair a door.

Working with Interior Doors

We have found that most of the time, interior doors can be saved and are easily repaired. Fixing an old paneled or even a flush door is well worth the effort, since finding a replacement can be a challenge. Doors are one of the most used and abused parts of any house. Most of the older homes we have worked on have had at least one sticking door, but because the doors are often beautiful paneled ones, repairing them is most satisfying. Fixing a door can go a long way toward improving a room, not to

mention the privacy it provides. Here are a few projects that are well worth doing.

Cutting Down a Door to Clear Carpet or Flooring

The addition of new carpeting or flooring material can make a dramatic difference in a room. Often it's not until after all the furniture's back in place that you realize a problem—the new flooring is wonderful, but your doors don't open or close. What you've actually done is raise the level of the floor by the thickness of the new material. To compensate for this, you have to shave off the bottoms of doors. Trimming down a door isn't a hard job, but it's one that requires careful planning so you don't hack off too much.

Sometimes if you cut the door off a little shorter than needed, the added clearance between the door and floor helps air circulation if you have a forced-air heating system.

Here's what is involved in trimming a door:

Decide how much to trim.   Depending on the type of carpeting and padding or flooring you've chosen, you can be faced with trimming anywhere from ¼ inch to a couple inches from the bottom of the door. Once the doors are removed, there's a chance you won't get them back on the hinges to check for clearance. You can discover how much needs to be trimmed by setting the door next to the jamb and measuring the misalignment between the door and jamb parts of the hinges. The door will sink into the carpet, so place it on a thin piece of plywood or other firm surface before you take your measurements.

Doors that can be rehung but still

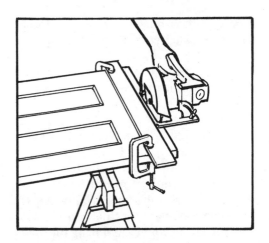

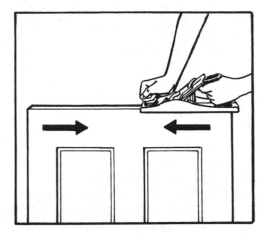

If you need to remove ¼ inch or more from the bottom of a door, clamp a straightedge to the door as a guide for your circular saw. Score the cut line with a utility knife to prevent splintering, and remember to put a scrap of wood under each C-clamp to avoid marring the door.

If you need to trim a door slightly, use a plane. Plane from the sides toward the middle. You will split the stile if you plane toward the end.

rub on the carpet or floor should also be cut down. Place a scrap of ¼-inch plywood on the carpet so it butts up to the bottom of the door. Mark the cut line on the door by running a pencil along the piece of plywood. The plywood will sit on top of the carpet, and its thickness will provide adequate clearance.

If you find you have less than ¼ inch to remove from the bottom of the door, use a hand plane. Make sure you plane from the sides into the middle. If you plane all the way across the end grain of the stiles, you will almost certainly split the ends of the door.

Here's how to trim the bottom of a door with a saw:

Lay out the cut. Place the door on a set of saw horses. Decide which side of the door will be most seen, the prominent side where you don't want any signs of splintered or shaved wood. Place the door with the prominent side down if

you are going to cut it with a power saw. Both circular and saber saws cut on the up stroke, so they tend to splinter the upper side. Place the prominent side up if you use a hand saw, because it cuts on the down stroke and will splinter the lower side.

Set up a guide. Clamp a straight piece of wood to the door as a guide for your saw. Place it on the cut line if you use a hand saw. For a power saw, measure the distance from the blade to the edge of the saw base, and then clamp the strip that distance from the cut line.

Trim the bottom. Before you make the cut, check the saw. You want the saw blade aligned with the cut while the side of the saw base rests against the guide strip.

Trim the door and check its fit. When you are satisfied with the clearance, seal the door bottom with varnish or paint to keep it from warping.

Replacing an Interior Door

Replacing an interior door isn't hard as long as you can find a door that fits into the existing jamb. Cutting a door down can be tricky, because some doors, especially hollow-core flush doors, have rather thin side rails. If you trim off too much, you can weaken the door, or end up with the rails being too thin to hold the hinge screws. Also, keep in mind that if you replace a door with a used door, the hole for the lockset in the replacement door has to be in the same side as the door you are replacing. Sometimes the hinge mortises of a used door will align with the hinges of the jamb, but most of the time new mortises will have to be cut in the door so the hinges will align. If you are installing a new door, of course, you will have to cut new hinge mortises. Here's how to hang a door:

Mark the hinge locations. This is easy if you begin by placing the door in the jamb. Don't let the door rest flat on the floor. Shim it up so it will be in the position you want it in when in use. It helps to have a partner to hold the door in place. There must be clearance at the bottom. Don't position the door tight against the top of the jamb, because there should be at least $1/16$-inch clearance all around, and more at the bottom. Carefully transfer the hinge location from the jamb to the door, then remove the door.

Cut the hinge mortises. We usually remove a hinge from the jamb and use it as a template to scribe (trace around it with a sharp knife) its shape in the edge of the door. Use the edge of the hinge to scribe its depth. Then use a sharp 1-inch chisel to make cuts along the scribe lines. Place the beveled side of the chisel toward the area you will

remove. Then make a series of closely spaced parallel cuts down the length of the mortise.

Next cut out the small pieces of wood raised in the mortise by working the chisel perpendicular to the first cuts with the flat side of the chisel down. Start this side cut at the depth of the mortise, usually equal to the thickness of the hinge, or about $1/8$ inch. Remove all the wood, and smooth the bottom of the mortise with the chisel. Then test fit the hinge and make any final adjustments.

Install the hinges and hang the door. Place the hinges in the mortise, then drill pilot holes for the screws and install them. Hang the door and check for clearance. If there is some binding, loosen the hinges and try placing some shims behind the hinges. Some experimentation will be necessary. You also might check to see if one of the hinges is in a mortise that is too shallow, causing the hinge to protrude and misalign the door. If this is the case, remove the door and hinge and cut the mortise deeper.

If it continues to bind, plane the door. If the door is sticking along the lock side, plane the front edge (edge that first contacts the jamb). This edge of the door should have a slight bevel that allows the front edge to clear the jamb. A door that sticks at the top or bottom can be cut down. See "Cutting Down a Door to Clear Carpet or Flooring."

Installing a Rim Lockset

Most likely your exterior door is secured with either a tubular or cylinder lock. To beef up security, you might want to consider adding a dead-bolt lock, particularly if the existing lock isn't a heavy-duty one. Seeing this lock on your door

MAKING A HINGE MORTISE

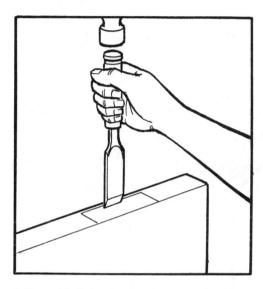

1. Use a 1-inch chisel with its beveled side toward the hinge area you will remove. Make cuts along the scribe lines outlining the hinge to the depth of the hinge plate.

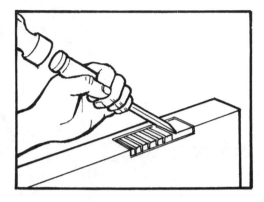

2. Make a series of closely spaced parallel cuts down the length of the hinge outline to the depth of the hinge plate.

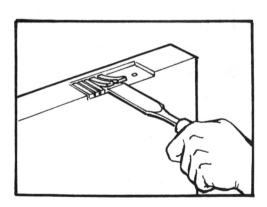

3. Remove the small pieces of wood raised in the mortise by cutting in from the side with the chisel, with the flat side of the chisel down. Start this side cut at the depth of the mortise.

could act as a deterrent and send a would-be intruder away.

A rim lock is a type of dead-bolt lock that is easy to install above the existing lock. Most of the mechanism of a rim lock is mounted on the inside of the door, so you have to bore a single hole through your door. There are many manufacturers of these locks designed for do-it-yourself installation, and they provide templates and step-by-step directions. Follow these instructions exactly. Here's an overall look at what's involved in the installation of a rim lock:

Lay out the position. Use the template supplied by the manufacturer to locate the position of the cylinder hole and the mounting screws for the lock body. Most locks require a 2⅛-inch hole. A hole saw that fits into an electric drill is probably the easiest tool to use to cut the hole.

EXPLODED VIEW OF A RIM LOCKSET

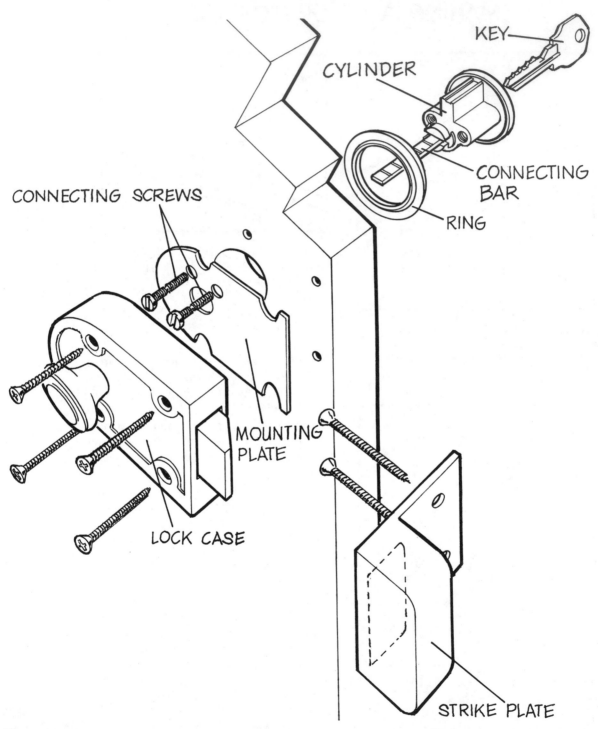

KEY

CYLINDER

CONNECTING BAR

RING

CONNECTING SCREWS

MOUNTING PLATE

LOCK CASE

STRIKE PLATE

Install the mounting plate. Most locks have a mounting plate that is screwed to the door. Install this plate and then insert the lock cylinder into the hole in the door. Secure the cylinder to the mounting plate with the screws provided. Before you tighten the screws, check the cylinder alignment to see that the lock works smoothly. Assemble the rest of the lock mechanism.

Hang the strike plate on the jamb. Mark the location of the strike plate on the jamb opposite the lock. Some require that a shallow recess be made in the face of the jamb. If this is the case, mark the outline of the strike plate on the jamb with a pencil and use a wood chisel to remove the wood from this area. (The manufacturer will specify whether a recess is required and, if so, how deep it should be.)

Check the strike plate for final alignment, and then mark the location of the mounting screws on the jamb. Drill pilot holes for the screws, and then install the strike plate.

Replacing an Exterior Door

No door takes more use and abuse than an exterior door. It takes a beating and can become warped and cracked. If the door is in bad shape, you're better off replacing it with a newer, more energy-efficient door. Most of the replacement doors on the market today are not too difficult to install.

The easiest approach is to purchase a new door that fits directly into your existing jamb. Since most doors are now manufactured in standard sizes, you will probably be able to find a replacement door the same size as your existing door.

We have found we can purchase a wood door that is a little larger than the existing jamb and cut it down to fit the jamb. Unless your door is very unusual in size, you should be able to find a door close enough to your existing door. You can trim only about an inch or so off the door's width and 3 or 4 inches from its height before you weaken the door or cause problems when installing the locks. See the sections of this chapter on tips for trimming a door and installing hinges.

Installing a Prehung Door

It is not possible to cut down a steel, aluminum, or fiberglass-clad door, so if you are thinking about upgrading to one of these doors, you should look for a prehung door. Easiest to install are doors that come prehung in weather-stripped frames that can be inserted directly into your old doorjamb. They are nailed or screwed to the old jamb. All you have to do is insulate the cracks between the jambs and reinstall the old trim or purchase new trim and install it. This is not a difficult project, but care must be taken to get everything square and see that the new jamb is properly attached to the old jamb for the door to function properly over the long haul.

You should be aware that installing a new jamb over your old takes up a bit of the door opening. So the replacement door will be slightly smaller than the original door.

Since manufacturers are trying to sell these doors to the do-it-yourselfer, they provide installation instructions that are very complete and clear. When you are shopping for a door, ask to see the installation booklet. Most prehung doors are installed in the same general way. Here's what's involved, but be sure to follow the specific directions provided by the manufacturer:

INSTALLING A PREHUNG DOOR

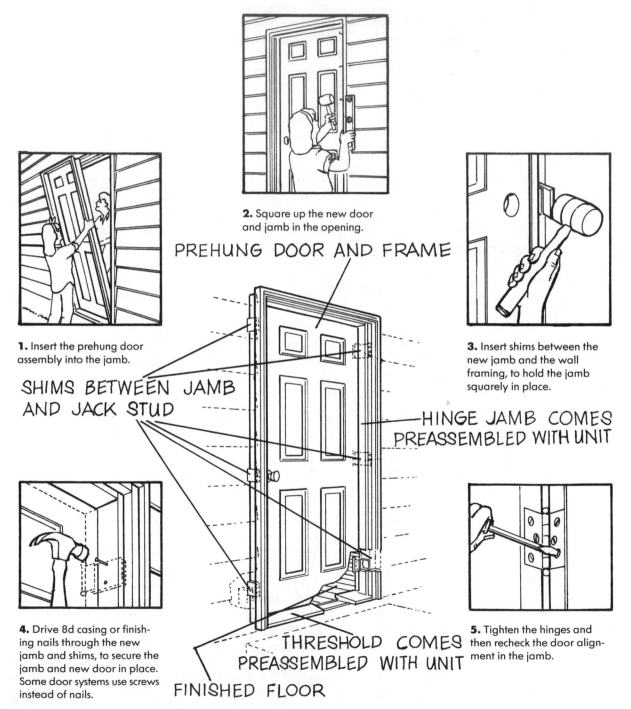

2. Square up the new door and jamb in the opening.

PREHUNG DOOR AND FRAME

1. Insert the prehung door assembly into the jamb.

SHIMS BETWEEN JAMB AND JACK STUD

3. Insert shims between the new jamb and the wall framing, to hold the jamb squarely in place.

HINGE JAMB COMES PREASSEMBLED WITH UNIT

4. Drive 8d casing or finishing nails through the new jamb and shims, to secure the jamb and new door in place. Some door systems use screws instead of nails.

THRESHOLD COMES PREASSEMBLED WITH UNIT

FINISHED FLOOR

5. Tighten the hinges and then recheck the door alignment in the jamb.

Step 1: Measure your existing jamb carefully. Take measurements in several places to determine the height, then use the smallest of these measurements. Do the same for the width. You can place wood shims behind the new jamb if the old opening is large, but there is not much you can do if the opening is too small. Most replacement doors give you an inch or so of adjustment, but that is all.

Know the swing of the door you need to order. Viewed from inside, doors that have hinges on the left side are right-hand doors, those with hinges on the right are left-hand doors.

Step 2: Remove the old door. Then carefully remove the inside and outside trim. We have found that driving the finishing nails through the trim with a nail set is easier than trying to pull the nails out. Some doors require you to remove the threshold.

Step 3: Place the new door frame in the opening and square it up. Then place shims between the new jamb and the old frame. Use the recommended screws to fasten the new jamb in place. Constantly check that everything stays square as you tighten the screws. Open and close the door to see if there is any binding. It will get worse over time, not better, so take your time and get it right.

Step 4: The threshold, weather stripping, and insulation go on next. Be sure to fill any gaps between the jambs with insulation, and carefully caulk up any cracks. It's easiest to weather-strip and caulk before the trim goes on.

Step 5: Reinstall the interior and exterior trim and caulk any cracks. Then install the door locksets. Most of these doors come predrilled; if your door is not predrilled, see "Installing a Rim

Lockset" earlier in this chapter. The procedure is the same for tubular locksets or dead bolts.

Some replacement doors require you to remove the old jamb. This is a major job, and you should hire a carpenter to hang this type of door unless you have had some experience working with exterior doors. The one advantage to this type of door is that you will get a door that is at least as wide as your old door.

Replacing a Storm/Screen Door

A storm/screen door is the first door someone sees when approaching your house, and it's your first line of defense against the elements. Storm doors are also a lot less expensive and easier to replace than exterior doors. We have replaced several old, worn doors and found this job to be a straightforward project that involves only minimal carpentry skills. It is a good project even for the first-timer.

A good storm door earns its keep winter and summer. In winter it prevents cold air from entering, and in summer it allows you to open up and enjoy a breeze without being eaten alive by the bugs. An attractive new storm door also goes a long way to dressing up the entrance to your house.

One option while shopping for a storm door is to consider the new security doors that come with dead-bolt locks. These are sturdy, top-of-the-line doors with strong grilles over the glass or screen areas. The decorative grilles are designed to be strong enough to prevent entry but still look attractive.

Installing a security door is no more difficult than installing a standard aluminum storm/screen door. In some cases, it's even easier. Ready-made storm/screen doors are available in several standard sizes to fit typical door openings. Most of the better doors come with three-piece jambs with Z-bars that allow you to install the doors to swing to either the right or left. Be sure to carefully follow the specific manufacturer's directions that will come with any door you order. Here are some general tips to help you install any storm/screen door:

Measure the doorjamb. Do this before you buy any door. You probably will find your door is about 32 or 36 inches wide and 80 inches high. Measure the widest opening, that is, from the inside face to the latch on the opposite jamb face. Take a measurement at the top of the door, in the center, and at the bottom. Use the smallest of these numbers when ordering. Also measure the height of the doorjamb, from the face of the top jamb to the threshold.

If your jamb is slightly larger than 32 or 36 inches by 80 inches, you can shim down the opening for a good fit. But if your jamb is more than 1/4 inch smaller than either of these standard dimensions, you probably will have to have a custom door manufactured to fit the jamb.

Decide on the swing. Decide how you want the door to open. Usually you would install the storm door so the latch is on the same side as the latch on the entry door. Temporarily place the door in the jamb as you want it to open.

There are three parts to the door frame: a header frame for the top, and side frames for the hinge and latch. This allows for hanging the door to swing either to the left or to the right.

Cut the side frames. Use a hacksaw with a fine-toothed blade (32 teeth per inch) to cut the hinge and latch side frames to length. To provide clearance at the top of the door for the header frame, cut these frames about 1/4 inch less than the door height (or as specified by the directions).

Install the hinges. Remove the door and set it on edge with the hinge side up. Position the hinge frame on the door so that it is almost flush with the top of the door and so that the weather stripping is in contact with the inside of the door when it is closed. The long end of the frame should extend beyond the bottom of the door.

Align the hinges with the predrilled holes for the center of each hinge, and attach them with the screws provided. Then drill pilot holes for the remaining hinge-mounting screws, and install these self-tapping screws.

Hang the door. Put the door and hinge frame into the doorjamb, and hold it there while you mark the location of the top predrilled hole on the jamb with a pencil. Drill a 1/8-inch pilot hole through the mark and install a screw, but don't tighten it all the way.

Before you install the other screws, square up the door and check its alignment in the doorjamb. Place shims between the hinge frame and the jamb if there is a gap of more than 1/8 inch between the frame and inside face of the jamb.

When the door is square and will open and close without binding, install another screw at the bottom of the hinge frame. Recheck the door alignment. Then install the rest of the screws in the face of the hinge frame.

Make the latch bolt mortise. Use the latch frame as a template to mark the location of the latch bolt mortise on the jamb. Use a 1/2-inch wood chisel to cut the mortise in the jamb. Make the latch bolt mortise at least ½ inch deep.

Install the rest of the frame. Place the lock side frame in the doorjamb, and check that there is no more than ⅛-inch clearance between the frame and door. If there is more of a gap, place shims behind the side frame, and nail and glue them to the doorjamb. Be sure the nails are not in the mortise area. Then screw the frame to the jamb, starting with the top screw. Next, install the bottom screw, then recheck alignment and install the remaining screws. Finally, install the top frame.

Adjust the door fit. The last adjustment is at the bottom of the door. Close the door, then push down the adjustable expander at the bottom of the door until the vinyl sweeps come into firm contact with the threshold. Open and close the door to check for binding, then drill pilot holes and install the screws locking the expander in place. Before you put the glass or screen in place, install the door closer and safety chain.

Replacing a Sliding Door with a French Door

A popular replacement for sliding doors is a swinging patio, or French, door. This type of door has one stationary glass panel with a second panel hinged like a standard door. A French door can be weather-stripped and is more secure than some sliding doors that can be pried off their tracks. There are several manufacturers and variations available. Most can be installed in the same opening as the old sliding door. Measure the opening of your old door and its dimensions to determine the size needed.

If you can't find one that will drop into the old opening, it is not much of a job for a carpenter to adjust the rough opening to fit the requirements of the new door. Unless you have experience installing an exterior door, leave this part of the project to the professionals. The unit is heavy, and if the jamb is not properly installed, the door will be a constant problem. Save some money on this project by removing the old door yourself and cleaning up the rough opening, so when the carpenter arrives, all he has to do is install the new door.

Choosing Weather Stripping for Doors

Installing weather stripping is one of the most cost-effective improvements you can make to your house. It is the only way to seal cracks and crevices around your doors and windows. Weather stripping comes in various forms—from inexpensive felt-and-adhesive-backed foam tape to strips made of rigid metal, vinyl, or tubular gasket material. It is applied to doorjambs or door bottoms and around the perimeter of windows.

We think spring-brass weather stripping is the most durable type for both doors and windows, but it is not easy to install. A newer vinyl version of this type of seal is available in a self-sticking adhesive-backed strip. This vinyl version is effective and will last at least 3 or 4 years. There also are several types of door sweeps and replacement thresholds that act as weather stripping for the bottom of a door.

Take the Drafty House Test

To make your own draft detector, tape a tissue to a pencil, or use a lighted candle, and hold it in front of doors and windows. If the tissue or candle flutters, you've found a candidate for weather stripping.

Use your draft detector or just your hand to check your house for air leaks. On a windy day, Mother Nature will lend some help, since the drafts will be more noticeable. Look at all doors and windows, and these often-overlooked places:

▶ around an attic door or disappearing attic stairs

▶ around a door leading to an unheated garage or porch

▶ around the garage door

▶ around a window air conditioner

Seal a Doorjamb

If snooping with the draft detector shows your door's weather stripping needs replacing, here's how to do it with quick-to-install V-strip or tubular vinyl weather stripping. If you plan to paint the door or jamb, do it before you install the weather stripping. But don't put off this job until you get around to painting; do the weather stripping now!

If your door fits the jamb, use V-strip or spring-brass weather stripping. If there are large gaps between the jamb and the door, use tubular-gasket-type weather stripping.

V-Strip or Spring-Brass Weather Stripping

Sealing a door with V-strip or spring-brass weather stripping is not hard, so don't put it off. This improvement will give you a double benefit: You can enjoy a draft-free house and save heating and cooling dollars. In fact, your investment in materials will be repaid in a couple of years. Just follow these steps for installing the vinyl V-strip weather stripping (The spring-brass type is installed in

exactly the same way, only you have to tack it in place since it has no adhesive backing):

Step 1: Prepare the doorjamb. Thoroughly clean the jamb in the area where you plan to install the weather stripping. Use trisodium phosphate or a paint deglosser. The deglosser not only removes dirt, grease, and oil, it etches the paint so the weather stripping adhesive gets a good grip.

Step 2: Use scissors to cut the V-strips to exact length. Beginning at the top of the jamb, measure and cut a strip to fit. Test the fit before you peel off the backing, because the adhesive will grab on first contact. It is better to have the strip fit perfectly or be slightly short. If it is too long, the strip will tend to bow and eventually the adhesive will let go.

Step 3: Press the weather stripping into place. The strip should be placed on the inside of the jamb against the stop (the piece of molding the door closes against) with the point of the V facing away from the stop toward the door. Peel off several inches of backing, and place the weather stripping in position, starting at the top of the jamb. Then, as you hold the weather stripping in place, pull off the backing as you press the strip in place. Work down, peeling off the backing as you go. After you have installed the piece for the top of the jamb, repeat the procedure, fitting and cutting a piece for the hinge side.

Step 4: Open and close the door to test the action. The door should close easily. You will hear a scraping sound as you open the door. This is caused by the friction of the weather stripping and the door.

Step 5: Having cut and fit the strip on the hinge side of the jamb, fit the strip on the latch side. You might have to cut

TYPES OF DOOR WEATHER STRIPPING

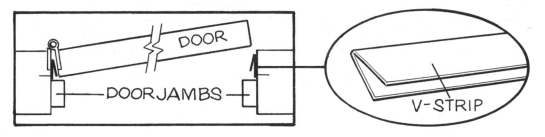

Vinyl V-strip weather stripping has adhesive on one edge.

Spring-brass weather stripping is tacked in place.

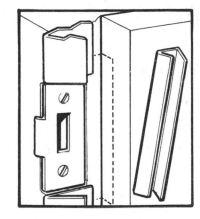

With spring-brass weather stripping, you'll need to cut a small piece to fit around the door strike plate.

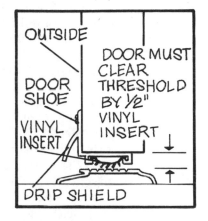

An aluminum threshold has a replaceable vinyl insert.

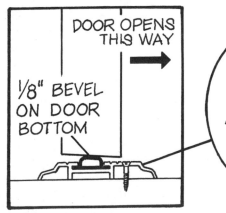

Door sweeps are easy to install but less effective than other threshold weather stripping.

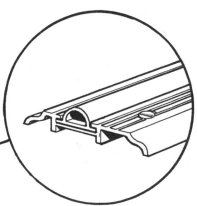

A door shoe has a heavy vinyl gasket that forms a seal.

the strip to fit around the latch. If you do cut this strip, place a short piece of weather stripping in front of the latch, but check that it does not interfere with the latch bolt action.

Tubular Gasket Weather Stripping

Tubular gasket weather stripping consists of compressible tubing attached to a mounting strip. It is mounted on the stop (the piece of molding that the door closes against) and provides a seal by pressing against the outside face of the door. It is available in self-stick or tack-in-place versions. Here's how to install either type:

Step 1: Prepare the doorjamb. Thoroughly clean the doorstop in the area where you plan to install the weather stripping, as already described.

Step 2: Cut the tubular gasket strips to length. Gasket-type strips are installed with the door closed. Push the tubular part tightly against the door so you know exactly where to attach the mounting strip on the stop for a tight seal. Cut the tubular gasket to exact length. Begin at the top of the jamb on the hinge side; measure and cut a strip to fit. If you use the press-in-place type, test the fit before you peel off the backing, because the adhesive will grab on first contact. Don't force into place a strip that is too long, because it will tend to bulge and eventually the adhesive will let go.

Step 3: Press or tack the weather stripping in place. Place the strip on the stop (the piece of molding that the door closes against) with the gasket pressing against the door. Tack the weather stripping in place with the brads provided.

If you are installing the press-in-place type, peel off several inches of backing and place the weather stripping in posi-tion. Then, as you hold the weather stripping in place, pull off the backing and press the strip. Work down the strip, peeling off the backing as you go.

Step 4: After you cut and fit the gasket on the hinge side of the jamb, fit the gasket on the latch side. Do the strip across the top last.

Door Sweeps, Shoes, and Thresholds

Gaps at the bottom of your doors develop as the house settles or the threshold wears down. Door sweeps, door shoes, or aluminum thresholds are the best solutions to close this gap. Here is what you should know about these draft fighters:

Door sweep: The easiest to install, but least efficient, weather stripping for the bottom of the door is a door sweep. It is an aluminum strip with a rubber flap that is screwed to the door at its bottom.

There are several variations available, but the type that installs on the outside of the door and is pushed down as the door closes is the most effective. This style of sweep is the best to use if you have carpet next to the threshold, because as you open the door, the sweep rises and clears the carpet.

Door sweeps are easy to install because most types don't require you to remove the door from its frame, and the door does not have to be cut down. If you have a draft at the bottom of your door in the winter months, consider a sweep as a temporary fix. Then, during the following summer, install a new threshold or door shoe. If the threshold is worn down, you can trim the rubber strip to fit the dip in the center of the threshold so it effectively seals off the gap.

Door shoe: A door shoe is attached to the bottom of the door. It has a heavy vinyl gasket that forms a seal between the door and an irregular or worn-down threshold. The door has to be removed for the shoe to be installed, and in most cases the bottom of the door has to be trimmed. The best features of the shoe are that it is hidden under the door and that the gasket is not worn down by traffic walking on it.

To install a door shoe, check the gap between the door and the threshold before you remove the door from its hinges. Then follow the manufacturer's directions for installation. Most of the time you will have to trim the bottom of the door. See "Working with Interior Doors" in this chapter for tips on making this cut. Be sure to seal the bottom of the door with paint or varnish to prevent it from warping. Also, apply a generous bead of caulk to the bottom of the door when you install the shoe, to prevent air infiltration between door bottom and metal shoe.

Threshold: An aluminum threshold with a replaceable vinyl insert is the best choice if the old threshold is worn. Depending on the height of the original threshold, you may have to remove it to install the new one. The door must be removed, and most doors will have to be trimmed to fit over the new thicker vinyl gasket.

Removing the old threshold can be challenging, because you do not want to damage the floor boards. We found the easiest method is to drill a series of large holes in the center of the old threshold. Be careful to drill through the threshold only. Try not to drill into the flooring below, but don't worry if you do, because it will be covered by the new threshold. Then use a chisel to cut the old threshold in half. Pry it up from the center,

being careful not to damage the door frame.

Put fiberglass insulation under the new threshold to prevent air from sneaking under the threshold. Also caulk the joints between the threshold and the floor. Don't forget to caulk the joint between the threshold and the side of the doorjamb.

After the threshold is installed, check the door clearance. You will probably have to cut an inch or so from the bottom of the door so it will clear the threshold. Most manufacturers suggest that you cut the bottom edge of the door at a slight angle. Adjust your saw a couple of degrees so the angle of the cut makes the inside edge of the door slightly lower than the front outside edge. This allows the door to close easily but still come into firm contact with the threshold seal.

Repairing or Replacing Windows

Unlike doors, we seldom come across an old window that can be economically rebuilt. The possible exception would be a window in a truly historic house. Otherwise, it's so expensive and labor-intensive that we replace, or have someone else replace, an old window. In some instances we get away with reusing the window sash and glass and just replacing the side jambs or sash channels.

This does not mean that we don't tune up an old window if it needs glass and hardware replaced and a good scrape, paint, and caulk job. We can't afford not to do these improvements, because they're not difficult and they do pay off. Here's how we deal with windows.

PARTS OF A WINDOW

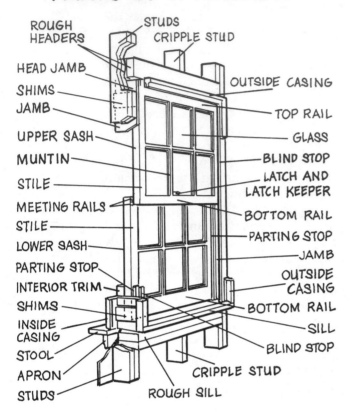

ROUGH HEADERS
STUDS
CRIPPLE STUD
HEAD JAMB
OUTSIDE CASING
SHIMS
JAMB
TOP RAIL
UPPER SASH
GLASS
MUNTIN
BLIND STOP
STILE
LATCH AND LATCH KEEPER
MEETING RAILS
BOTTOM RAIL
STILE
PARTING STOP
LOWER SASH
JAMB
PARTING STOP
OUTSIDE CASING
INTERIOR TRIM
BOTTOM RAIL
SHIMS
INSIDE CASING
SILL
STOOL
BLIND STOP
APRON
STUDS
CRIPPLE STUD
ROUGH SILL

Giving New Life to a Worn-Out Window

Neglected or badly worn double-hung windows are an eyesore, and even weather stripping can't completely stop the energy loss. Unless you have odd-size or custom-built windows, you can install new side jambs or sash channels. If the sash are worn, then you can replace both the side jambs and sash by purchasing a window-rebuilding kit. Some sash replacement kits have tilt-out sash that make window washing easier. You can wash both sides of the window from inside the house.

The kits come with complete directions and are not difficult to install. Replacement side jambs and total sash replacement kits are installed in the same way. You can rebuild the average window in less than an hour by following the kit directions and these general guidelines:

Remove the inner sash, then the outer sash. Remove the inside window stops that hold the lower sash in place. Use a stiff putty knife or chisel, being careful not to damage the stops so you can reinstall them later. Pry each stop up and off the jamb. If you can't pull the nails out easily, prevent splitting the stop by using a nail set to drive the finishing nails through the stop. Then pull the nail out of the side jamb with a claw hammer, and remove the inside window sash.

Remove the parting stop. Use a chisel to remove the parting stop (the strip of wood between the sash), and then remove the upper sash. You don't have to be careful with the parting stop, since it will be discarded.

Remove the counterweights and pulleys. Cut the old chain or counterweight cords, and allow the counterweights to fall behind the jambs. If you want to, you can remove the counterweights by prying out a small removable panel usually located in the channel for the lower sash. While the window frame is open, consider adding insulation around its perimeter.

Install new side jambs and possibly the head jamb. Screw or nail the new side jambs into place according to the manufacturer's directions. Some types have to be trimmed, others are precut. This is a good time to prime and paint them, since the window sash are removed.

Install the upper and then lower sash. Some installations require the sash to be cut to fit the new, slightly narrower window. Other window-rebuilding kits provide new, slightly narrower sash.

Replace the trim.   Check the sash movement. It will be stiffer than with the counterweight system, since the sash are now held in position by friction. After final adjustment, replace the inside window stops and any trim pieces you removed.

Replacing Windows

Replacing a window can be done by just about anyone with some carpentry experience under his belt. But we have found that windows are expensive, and therefore the cost of having the window professionally installed is not the major portion of the bill. When we consider the problems of transporting a large, cumbersome window and lifting it into place without damaging it or us, we usually opt to have a carpenter take on the job. To save money, we remove the old window and carefully shop for the appropriate replacement unit.

Window Styles

Few of us can afford to replace all the windows in the house in a single swoop. Most of the time, if a significant number of the windows will eventually have to be replaced, we try to choose a style that matches the existing windows as closely as possible.

This is especially important if the window is on the front of the house or on a prominent side visible from the street. We want the replacement window to fit the style of the house, not stand out as an obvious newcomer. This means that we usually end up choosing a double-hung or casement-style window.

There are other styles, such as sliding, awning, and hopper styles, but these are not as popular and therefore we usually are not trying to match these styles when choosing a replacement. However, awning and hopper windows are good choices for basement or small bath windows.

If you were to design a window to leak air, we don't think you could do a better job than the originators of the traditional double-hung window. Since both sash move, there is a potential air leak at every joint. Modern window designs deal with this problem by building in interlocking weather stripping.

TYPES OF WINDOWS

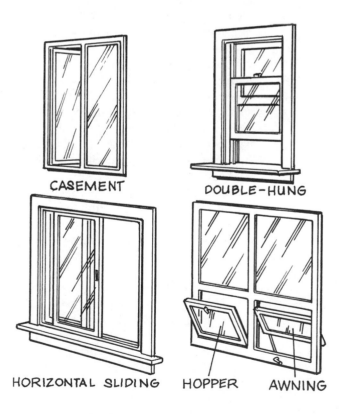

CASEMENT   DOUBLE-HUNG

HORIZONTAL SLIDING   HOPPER   AWNING

Most new double-hung windows are tight when they are first installed. But unless they are particularly well designed, the weather stripping quickly wears and allows air to pass. Look carefully at the weather stripping of any replacement window you plan to purchase. Look for interlocking channels and metal or vinyl weather stripping that will stand up to the friction and wear of repeated opening and closing. Also check the seal between the upper and lower sash where there should be an interlocking joint, not just a strip of weather stripping.

There are many features to weigh when you shop for a double-hung window, but the weather stripping is the most important. Other features, such as tilt-out sash or removable muntins (thin strips between glass panes) to make window cleaning easier, are nice to have but do not increase the performance of the window.

Casement windows, on the other hand, are easier to make airtight because there are fewer joints and no sliding surfaces. Casement windows also provide excellent ventilation since the whole window opens. Also, the sash swings away from the house when the window is open, so it can catch and direct even the slightest breeze into an otherwise stuffy room. We usually replace a double-hung window with a casement window whenever this style is not in conflict with the existing architecture.

Window Materials

Whatever the style you plan to install, don't purchase a window unless it bears the seal of approval from one of the major trade or manufacturing associations. Wood or vinyl-clad wood windows should bear a seal from the National Woodwork Manufacturers Association.

Wood windows are probably the most readily available. They are manufactured in all types, with a wide variety of finishes. Some top-of-the-line wood windows are clad with vinyl or aluminum. Wood is a better insulator than metal or vinyl, but metal and vinyl are virtually maintenance free. These vinyl-clad or aluminum-clad wood windows offer both advantages.

When looking at the different features of each of these types of windows, keep in mind that the construction and weather stripping are more important to the overall performance of the window than the finish is. If you are on a tight budget, purchase the best unclad wooden window you can afford. If it is well made and seals properly, it will do the job, but it will have to be maintained and painted.

Windows with frames made totally of vinyl or aluminum are popular as replacement windows. We've never installed this type of window, but the manufacturers of the top-of-the-line models claim they insulate as well as wooden windows. If you are considering an aluminum window, make sure that there is a thermal break between the inside part of the window and the outside surfaces. A thermal break is a non-heat-conducting material that connects the inside and outside of the window and prevents heat or cold from passing through the very conductible aluminum.

Thermal Glass

Another option worth considering is thermal glass. This is a window that is glazed with two or three panes of glass. The double and triple glazing increase the efficiency of the window considerably. Of course, the same effect is achieved by adding a storm window.

This option can be a significant energy saver if you are replacing a large window. Most of the more expensive vinyl-clad wood windows come with double or triple glazing. With the increased popularity of central air-conditioning, an energy-efficient window will save money all year long.

Another option some window manufacturers offer is low-E glass. This low-emissive glass has a transparent metal film on one side that reflects radiant heat back into the house in the winter and prevents radiant heat from entering during the summer months. This type of glass is about twice as efficient as regular glass at stopping energy loss, and when teamed with double or triple glazing, it represents the most energy-efficient window currently on the market. Low-E glass prevents ultraviolet light from passing through, so fabrics in drapes, carpet, and furniture won't fade or deteriorate as rapidly.

These options are all worth considering, but remember that if you are replacing a single window in an older house, you probably will not notice any savings. The increased efficiency from a single window will save only a small fraction of your total energy bill. A good-quality, tight-fitting, double-glazed window will probably be your best bet.

Plugging Up Energy Leaks at Windows

If you've ever looked at pictures of life in the good old days, you've probably noticed that when there's a hearty fire roaring in the hearth, all the chairs are pulled up close to it. Never do you see the furniture arranged beneath the windows in the wintertime. The reason, of course, is that their windows leaked like sieves and everyone avoided being near them, and instead clustered around the only heat source in the room. Windows in our homes today are better, but most of them are not entirely draft free. Here are some hints for plugging up the leaks in various types of windows, to better insulate your house against winter cold and, if you use air-conditioning, summer heat.

Tips for Weather-Stripping Double-Hung Windows

As we already mentioned (see "Window Styles"), double-hung windows will begin to wear and to develop costly air leaks. Storm windows help, but weather stripping still is needed. Spring-brass weather stripping is the most durable and is not hard to install in this type of window. The brass V-strips are installed with the brads provided. Refer to the illustration on page 80 for the location of each strip, then follow these steps:

Step 1: Cut two sets of V-strips the height of the inner and outer sash plus 2 inches. Then raise the inner sash to the top of its track, and slip the top end of a strip between the sash and side channel on each side. The edges with the nail holes should be to the inside, away from the central parting stop (the wood strip between inner and outer sash). Check that the strip is straight, then tack it into the side panels below the sash.

Step 2: Lower both sash. Slip the bottom 2 inches of the remaining strips between the outside sash and its side channels, again with the nailing edge toward the inside. Make sure these strips are straight and tack them in place.

Step 3: With both sash still lowered,

WEATHER-STRIPPING A DOUBLE-HUNG WINDOW

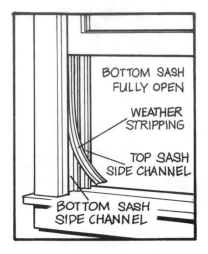

1. Raise the bottom sash and install V-strip in both inner side channels.

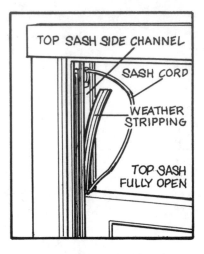

2. Lower both sashes and install V-strip in both outer side channels.

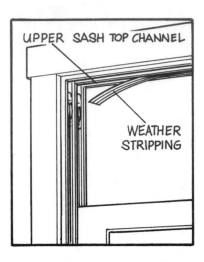

3. Install V-strip in the upper sash channel.

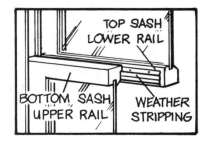

4. Install V-strip on the inside of the top sash lower rail and, if necessary, the bottom sash upper rail.

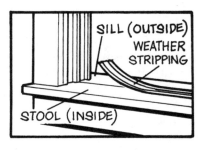

5. Install V-strip on the windowsill.

cut and install strips in the upper sash top channel, with the nailing flange toward the inside of the room.

Step 4: Raise the inside sash all the way, and pull the outside sash about halfway down to give you access to its bottom rail. Install weather stripping on the inside of the lower rail of the top sash. Make sure the nails are at the top and the V spreads down, so the bottom sash can close without getting hung up on the strip. If your window is really bad, you can also install a strip on the top rail of the inside sash. If you do this, install the strip with the nails down and the V spreading up, so the two pieces of strip wedge together. Before you install the strip, check the lock to make sure you won't be spreading the sash so far apart that the lock won't work.

Step 5: Raise both sash. Cut and install a strip on the sill so the bottom sash will close on it. The nailing flange should be toward the inside.

Tips for Weather-Stripping Casement Windows

Most casement windows have some sort of weather stripping. If your windows are not weather-stripped or the weather stripping is worn and ineffective, replace it with spring-brass or self-stick vinyl V-strip weather stripping. A casement window is sealed up much like a doorjamb. Refer to the accompanying illustration for the location of the weather stripping and follow these steps:

Step 1: Cut strips to fit the top and bottom of the window frame, and install them with the nailed edge toward the open window.

Step 2: Cut and install strips on the unhinged side of the frame.

Tips for Weather-Stripping Sliding Windows

This type of window usually seals well along its tracks but leaks air along the sides, where the window butts against the frame. Spring-brass is the best choice to seal off this area, but the self-stick vinyl V-strip is easier to install and, since there is little wear in this area, it will last.

Step 1: Open the window. Measure and then cut spring-brass or vinyl V-strips to fit the end of the window frame against which the movable sash butts.

Step 2: Tack or press the weather stripping into place, and check that the window will slide closed and that the lock will work properly.

Concealing Weather Stripping

If you can remove a window sash from its frame, you can install the weather stripping on the edge of the sash. This way the weather stripping will not be visible when the window is open. In this case the nailed edge or the point of the V should align with the inner edge of the sash.

WEATHER-STRIPPING A CASEMENT OR SLIDING WINDOW

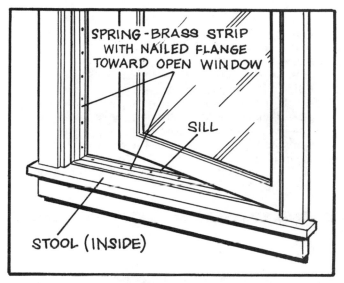

SPRING-BRASS STRIP WITH NAILED FLANGE TOWARD OPEN WINDOW

SILL

STOOL (INSIDE)

For a casement window, use spring-brass weather stripping on the top, bottom, and unhinged side.

For a sliding window, use spring-brass or vinyl V-strip on the sides only.

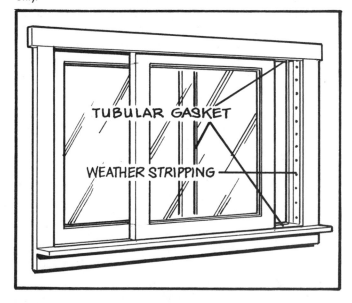

TUBULAR GASKET

WEATHER STRIPPING

CONDENSATION PROBLEMS?

Condensation (moisture that forms on the inside of a storm window) often can be eliminated by weather-stripping the window. Warm, moist air is prevented from escaping into the cold space between the window and the storm window and condensing on the inside of the storm window.

If the condensation is on the inside window glass, then add weather stripping to the storm window. In this situation, cold air is leaking past the storm into the space between the windows, making the inside window glass almost as cold as the outside air. This causes the warm inside air to condense on the panes.

Tips on Selecting a New Window Treatment

Covering the windows in a room is one of those personal choices that can be as frivolous or frugal as you decide. The basic function of a window treatment is to provide privacy and protection from the sun. Beyond that, you have an amazing array of choices because of the selection of shades, blinds, curtains, draperies, and shutters available for do-it-yourself installation. Here are some guidelines to help you decide what's right for your room:

▶ A blind or shade mounted between window jambs will call attention to the size and shape of the window.

▶ A blind or shade mounted outside the jambs, concealing the casing, can change or disguise the appearance of a window.

This look is more contemporary and goes well in a room with clean, straight lines. For example, you can use a blind that is larger than the window to provide a backdrop for furniture or to cover an entire wall.

▶ Always make certain that a new window treatment won't obstruct the window's normal operation. Check that the window opens and closes easily, and that pulls and handles remain accessible.

Measuring Guidelines

There are two basic drapery mountings: curtain rods and drapery devices. Simple curtain rods are the easier to install but support only stationary drapery panels. Drapery devices provide patented suspension systems that can mechanically open and close drapery panels.

Before you order a mounting system, check the manufacturer's directions or consult with the store where you order draperies or shades, to determine if your choice must be mounted inside or outside the window jambs. Then measure your windows in accordance with the directions from the manufacturer of the mounting hardware. Generally, here is how to measure your windows for either type of mounting; this is also how you measure for blinds or shades:

Inside mounts: Drapery or shade hardware mounted on the window jambs is referred to as an inside mount. Such a setup is difficult to install, because it requires exact measurements.

To find the width of the window opening, measure the distance from one window jamb to the other. Most windows are not exactly square, so take measurements at the top, at the midpoint, and again at the bottom. Use the small-

INSIDE-MOUNTED BLIND

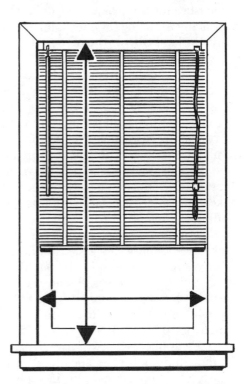

Measure the distance from the windowsill to the top of the window opening in several places and use the shortest measurement. To find the width, measure from the inside face of the frame to the other side of the frame. Take this measurement in several places and use the smallest.

OUTSIDE-MOUNTED BLIND

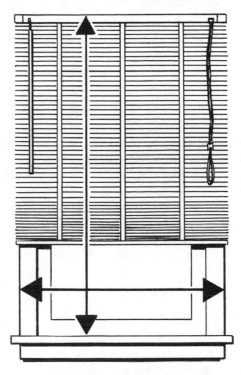

Check the manufacturer's literature to see how wide the brackets are, then add this amount to the width of your blind. Decide how wide you want your blinds, add in the width of the brackets, and then mark this measurement on the wall or window frame. Check that your marks are centered around the frame.

est of these measurements.

Outside mounts: Drapery or shade hardware mounted on the window casing or on the wall on either side of the window is referred to as an outside mount. This type of installation is easier to figure and install, because the measurements can be less precise. You have the full width of the window casing or the wall to work with. This type of mount requires that measurements be taken from the outside edges of the window casing, both the height and width.

Installing Drapery or Shade Hardware

▶ Keep screw holes at least ¼ inch from the end of the molding or trim, to avoid splitting.

▶ Check that the blind or shade will not disrupt the action of the window hardware. Open and close the window to check clearance.

▶ Make sure a shade or blind installed at a patio door clears the doorway completely when in its raised, stacked position.

▶ For an inside mount in a double-hung window, slide the window open to check for clearance.

▶ Most hardware includes wood screws for use on woodwork or wood paneling. If you're installing on drywall or plaster, use plastic wall anchors or, for heavy treatments, Molly or toggle bolts. See "Hanging Up Your Hang-Ups" in chapter 3. Use lead expansion shields for a brick or cement wall.

Installing Miniblinds or Microblinds

You'll find miniblinds with slats about 1 inch wide and microblinds with slats that are even smaller in standard, ready-made sizes. They can also be custom-cut to fit your windows. And they're sold in every color known to man! Before measuring, decide if you want the blind mounted inside your window frame or outside the frame, on the casing or wall.

We love microblinds and have them in every room in our house. But, here's a drawback to consider before investing in them. If you have a hyperactive cat that likes to chase bugs, you can expect to have the metal blinds dented quite easily. When Pete and Repeat, our ferocious felines, attack a fly, they have no regard for the blinds. Consequently, we have some dented blinds that we've reshaped, but they're not good as new.

Before you order, check with the manufacturer, who usually supplies a specification sheet that tells you exactly how to measure for the product. Installation is basically the same for microblinds and miniblinds. Follow these tips for a professional-looking installation:

Inside mounts: For an inside mounting, measure the width between the insides of the window jambs at the top and bottom. Use the smallest measurement for ordering. Also measure the height from the windowsill to the top of the jamb. For custom-made blinds, the manufacturer uses these measurements and makes the necessary adjustments for clearance.

If you buy ready-made blinds, the stock sizes cannot be wider than the width of your window jamb, but they can be slightly narrower. Because each mounting bracket is about 1 inch wide, they will support the blind even if it is ½ inch or so short. If in doubt, check with the supplier, who will usually supply the manufacturer's specifications. Some ready-made blinds come in a specific length that you can shorten by removing some of the slats.

Outside mounts: If you choose to mount the blind outside the window frame, measure the length and width of the window or area to be covered by the blind. Remember, if you plan to mount the blinds on the window casing, the brackets should be positioned so they are not too close to either the inside or outside edges of the casing, or the mounting screws can split the wood. If you plan to attach the brackets to the wall, make sure the shade or blind is long enough so the brackets are positioned outside the window casing.

Projection brackets: You can use projection brackets to hold the blind several inches away from the wall or window casings. These brackets allow you to mount the blind completely outside the window casing.

To mount the blind on the back of a door or in a window where the wind or door movement might cause the blind to bang around, use brackets designed to hold the bottom of the blind in place.

Mounting Blinds on the Wall

The manufacturer provides screws to mount the blinds on a wooden window frame. These screws will also hold in a vinyl or vinyl-clad window frame, but they will not hold in plaster or drywall. Use plastic wall anchors instead.

If you are mounting the brackets on the wall, follow these steps to determine what screws to use:

Step 1: Mark the location of the brackets on the wall with a pencil.

Step 2: Drill a pilot hole for a mounting screw and see if you hit the stud. There is a wall stud on each side of the window. If you hit a stud, then use the screws provided, but be sure they are long enough to bite deep into the stud.

Step 3: If the hole is at a cavity between wall studs, use plastic wall anchors for blinds up to about 4 or 5 feet wide. If the blinds are wider, or over 10 feet tall, use Molly or toggle bolts.

Installing Pleated Shades

A lightweight pleated shade that diffuses light and complements most windows is a high-style window treatment. Such shades are sold in standard sizes, and they can be custom-made. Like miniblinds or microblinds, they can be mounted inside or outside the window frame or on the wall, or hung from the ceiling.

If you have an odd-size window or skylight, pleated shades might be the solution. They make efficient use of space because, when folded, they compress to 1 inch for every 2 feet of drop, and they can be locked in any position. Pleated shades are easy to install. Here are some tips to make the job even easier:

▶ For an inside mount, measure the distance between the window jambs at the top and bottom. Use the smallest measurement for ordering. Also measure from the windowsill to the top jamb. Given these measurements, the manufacturer will make the necessary adjustments for clearance.

▶ If you choose to mount the shade on the woodwork or wall (outside mount), measure the length and width of the window or area to be covered by the shade. If you plan to mount the shade on the window casing, the brackets should be positioned so they are not too close to either the inside or outside edges of the casing, to prevent the mounting screws from splitting the wood. If you plan to attach the brackets to the wall, make sure the shade is long enough so the brackets are positioned outside the window casing.

▶ To hold the shade several inches away from the wall or window casing, use projection brackets. There also are brackets to hold the bottom of the shade in place. You can mount these on the backs of doors, but it is not advisable to secure the bottom of the shade against the wind. On a breezy day there will be considerable force against the shade and it could be damaged.

▶ Use the screws provided by the manufacturer to mount the shade on a wood window or door frame or on vinyl or vinyl-clad frames. If you are mounting the brackets on the wall, drill a pilot hole for a mounting screw and see if you hit a stud. If you don't, then use plastic wall anchors for shades up to about 4 or 5 feet wide, and Molly or toggle bolts for larger shades.

Installing Vertical Blinds

While vertical blinds are the traditional treatment for a sliding patio door, there are many other places where they can be used. Their main advantage at doors is that they open to the side, instead of pulling up, as horizontal blinds do. One pull of a cord, and the blinds move completely out of the way. You can partially open vertical blinds to allow passage through the door, while still covering the fixed portion of a sliding door. The vertical slats rotate, closing completely for privacy or partially to block the direct sun.

Measuring for and mounting the hardware for vertical blinds is similar to that for pleated shades and miniblinds. The brackets are slightly heavier since they must support a head box that contains the rotating and closing mechanism.

Vertical blinds usually are mounted on the wall above the door or window frame, but they can be mounted on the casing. If you plan to mount the blinds on a wall, first measure the length and width of the door or window, then add at least 6 inches to your width measurement to provide a slat overlap at each end of the opening. If you plan to mount the blind on the window or door casing, check that the brackets are positioned so they are not too close to either the

inside or outside edges of the casing, or the mounting screws can split the wood.

Use the screws provided by the manufacturer to mount the vertical blind on a wooden window or door frame. If you are mounting the brackets on the wall, drill a pilot hole for a mounting screw and see if you hit a stud. If you don't, then use large plastic wall anchors or Molly or toggle bolts to secure the brackets to the wall.

Installing Interior Wooden Shutters

Here's a tried-and-true way to take the tedium out of installing wooden shutters. The tricky part—even for a professional carpenter—is dealing with the window frame that is not absolutely square.

To get the job done right, build a frame to assemble the shutters in. Install the entire unit in the window jamb, and finish it off with molding to hide the joint between the jamb and shutter frame. Here are the basic steps involved:

Step 1: Measure the height and width of the window frame in several places.

Step 2: Cut two side frame pieces from ¾ × 1-inch wood to the shortest vertical measurement. Test the fit; you should be able to place these pieces against the vertical sides of the frame without binding. If your window is not square, one will fit more loosely than the other, but that's okay.

Step 3: Subtract 1½ inches (the thickness of the two side pieces) from the shortest width measurement, and cut two horizontal frame pieces to that size.

Step 4: Assemble the frame by attaching the sides to the upper and lower horizontal frame pieces with glue and 4d

INSTALLING WOODEN SHUTTERS

2. Use a circular saw to trim each side of the shutters so they fit into the frame.

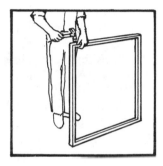

1. Measure the inside dimensions of your window frame, then construct a frame to hold the shutters.

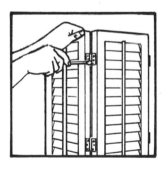

4. Install the hinges.

3. Clamp the shutters together under a straightedge set up as a guide to trim the bottom of all the shutters in one pass. Do the same for the top.

6. Install the frame in the window.

5. Hang the shutters in the frame.

finishing nails. Align the frame with a carpenter's square, and set it aside until the glue dries.

Note: The frame is assembled so the ¾-inch-wide edges form the face of the frame.

Step 5: Measure the inside dimensions of the frame. Divide the width measurement by the number of shutters you plan to install in the frame (usually two or four). Shop for shutters that are close to these dimensions. You may have to buy shutters that are larger than needed and trim them to fit.

Step 6: Trim equal amounts from both the top and bottom of each shutter, then trim off equal amounts from both sides of each shutter, to adjust them to fit inside the frame. Make these cuts on a table saw, or use a circular saw guided by a straightedge clamped to the shutter.

Step 7: Mount the shutters in the frame with the hinges provided. To help position the hinges accurately, clamp the shutters together, and mark the hinge locations on all the shutters at the same time.

Step 8: Mount the shutter frame in the window jamb. Use a carpenter's level to plumb up the frame. Then use shims to hold it in place while you nail it to the window jamb with 6d finishing nails. The important thing is to keep the frame square.

Step 9: Hide any gaps between the jamb and shutter frame with a strip of glass-bead molding. Or, if you plan to paint the frame to match the window jamb, fill the gap with a latex caulk, and paint.

CHAPTER
5

Ceilings

A good recipe is a careful blend of ingredients that work together to make it a family favorite. Family members may not be aware of each nuance of seasoning as they eat, but if one spice were missing, they'd know something was wrong.

The decor of a room is like that recipe. Some ingredients are obvious: the color and texture of walls and floors, for example. The ceiling, on the other hand, is more like a dash of seasoning. We don't pay much attention to it when we enter a room, but it can be a very important part of making the entire decor of the room harmonious.

In this section we offer techniques for repairing ceilings, and we tell you how to decorate and adorn them. We suggest options for covering up a ceiling and how to hang things from it.

Bringing a High Ceiling Down with a Wallpaper Medallion

Here's a simple wallpaper project that will create a dramatic effect in a room with a high ceiling. You'll need two 3-foot strips of wallpaper. The strips must have matching pattern repeats. You'll also need about 20 feet of a border paper with a design that coordinates with your wall treatment. See "Decorating the Easy Way—Hanging Border Paper" in chapter 3, then follow these easy steps:

Step 1: If you are papering around a fixture, it's usually easiest to turn off the electrical power to the room and remove the fixture you will be papering around.

Step 2: Make a light pencil line on the ceiling 2 feet from the fixture or center of the room and parallel to one wall.

Step 3: Match up the pattern on the two wallpaper strips, then rough-cut the strips into a 4-foot square.

Step 4: Apply paste to the paper, and with one edge of the paper against the pencil line, paper right over the fixture box and use a sharp knife or razor to cut out the paper over the box.

Step 5: Cut four pieces of border paper. Make each piece 4 feet long plus twice the width of the border paper. The

A wallpaper ceiling medallion is an easy way to dress up a room.

extra length allows the border to overlap at all four corners. Paste the pieces and apply them to the perimeter of the wallpapered area.

Step 6: Miter the ends of the border pieces by making 45-degree diagonal cuts from the inside corner outward with a sharp utility knife. Use a metal straightedge as a guide. Then remove the loose triangular border piece that you just trimmed off. Peel back the top flap of the corner, and remove the second triangular cutoff. Smooth both flaps and roll the miter seam. This procedure gives you a perfect miter corner.

Adding a Polystyrene Medallion around a Light Fixture

Draw attention to your ceiling by installing a decorative medallion around an overhead light fixture. In times past, this decoration was available only in expensive custom-molded plaster or carved wood. Today you can purchase a lightweight, easy-to-install medallion made of polystyrene. These molded plastic pieces are made to look like plaster.

A medallion is particularly appropriate in a formal setting in a room with a high ceiling and chandelier. The units come in a variety of sizes and designs and are light enough to be installed directly on the ceiling using construction adhesive. See the illustration on page 92 and be sure to consult the directions provided by the manufacturer. Here are some tips to guide you through the installation:

Remove the light fixture. Turn off the electricity to the light fixture at the fuse box or circuit breaker and remove the fixture from the ceiling.

Hold the medallion in place. Have a helper hold the new medallion in position while you stand back and see how it will look.

Cut the medallion to fit the fixture, then prime. Trim the center of the medallion to fit around the light fixture. You can use sandpaper to smooth any rough edges. To repair the medallion, use spackling compound or a wood filler. After cutting, prime the medallion with a primer recommended by the manufacturer.

Glue the medallion in place. Apply a construction adhesive (recommended by the manufacturer) to the back of the medallion, and then carefully place it in position around the light fixture. The medallion can be held in place with masking tape while the glue sets. Check that the medallion is tight to the ceiling around the perimeter; if it sags, you will see the gap. If the medallion is large, use four or five long drywall screws to hold it tight against the ceiling. You can remove the screws and fill the holes with spackling compound later.

Paint the medallion. After the adhesive has set, you can paint the medallion. You may want to paint the ceiling as well, since there probably will be fingerprints or scuff marks on the ceiling.

Making the Most of the Ceiling You Have

Some ceilings need a little more than a coat of paint and a wallpaper medallion to look good. Old plaster that looks like a road map will take considerable time to repair. If plaster is loose, consider using the plaster buttons mentioned in chapter 3, "Pulling the Old Wall Together." If your ceiling is structurally sound

INSTALLING A PLASTIC CEILING MEDALLION

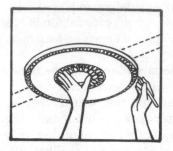

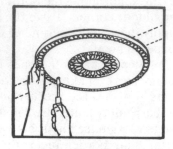

1. Remove the light fixture and place the medallion in position. When you get it centered, mark its location lightly with a pencil.

2. Apply mastic to the back of the medallion. Then carefully position it over the layout marks and push it into place.

3. Hold the medallion in place with a couple of drywall screws while the glue sets up. These screws can be removed or left in place and hidden with spackling compound.

but has lots of cracks, the quickest method we have found to cover up this mess is to give the large cracks a quick coat of joint compound (see chapter 1), but skip the sanding; then apply a coat of textured paint.

This thick paint fills in the small cracks and imperfections in the ceiling, and since the finish is bumpy, it deemphasizes the unevenness of the ceiling. Textured paint is more expensive than regular paint but is a lot cheaper than having a ceiling replastered. Its main drawback is that it will eventually crack as the ceiling cracks begin to open up. Cracked and peeling textured paint is a worse problem to deal with than the original cracks. We have found that if you apply textured paint just heavy enough to hide most of the imperfections, you will have less of a chance of it peeling or cracking later.

Keep in mind that textured ceilings don't always fit in with the decor. For example, in a room with southwestern furnishings, a textured ceiling can appropriately suggest stucco. But a smooth ceiling is more appropriate for a formal Chippendale or French provincial look.

The easiest way to apply this textured paint is with a roller with a heavy ¾-inch nap designed for painting rough surfaces. There are rollers designed specifically for textured paint, but we prefer the less expensive ¾-inch nap.

Even though textured paint is very thick, it doesn't cover dirty or colored ceilings very well because of the dimpling. So make sure you prime the ceiling with a white latex paint before using the textured paint. If you plan to install moldings on the walls, do this before applying textured paint. Otherwise the texture will prevent the molding from fitting tightly against the ceiling.

Face-Lifting a Suspended Ceiling

When we run into a suspended ceiling in a living or dining room, our first inclination is to remove it and restore the ceiling to its original condition. But in a home office or recreation area, an acoustical "dropped" ceiling is an ideal choice. The tiles absorb sound and it's a viable cover-up for a problem ceiling.

If you are faced with a not-so-perfect suspended ceiling in a room, do not make any rash decisions. First, remove a couple of tiles in various locations in the room, to take a look at the original ceiling. Whoever installed the suspended ceiling might have done so to conceal a ceiling needing extensive repair. Your choices are to remove the suspended tiles and grid and restore the original ceiling or to rejuvenate the suspended ceiling. If the original ceiling is in good shape and you want to remove the suspended ceiling, you'll have to patch several dozen holes left in the ceiling by the anchor hooks of the suspension grid.

If you decide to leave the old suspended ceiling in place, then it isn't a difficult project to give it a face-lift. We have gotten good results by sprucing up the suspension grid and painting the old tiles. Sagging or damaged tiles are impossible to repair, so replacing them with new tiles is the solution.

Remove the tiles. Most botched paint jobs on suspended ceilings occur because someone tries to take a shortcut by not removing the tiles to paint them separately. The metal grid should be painted with a semigloss or enamel paint, and the tiles should be painted with a flat latex.

Remove the tiles from the grid one at a time. Push up on the tile until it is clear of the grid. Turn the tile on edge, and lower it through the grid. Stack the tiles on a flat surface, being careful not to damage the corners of the tiles.

Clean and paint the grid. Use the crevice tool of a vacuum cleaner to remove dust and debris along the inside tracks of the grid. Then wash the grid with a solution of trisodium phosphate and water. If the paint is dull or chipped or there are signs of rust, wipe the grid down with a paint deglosser to prepare the surface for a new coat of paint. See the chapter 1 section "Professional Solutions to Tough Problems."

An alkyd-based enamel will give the best results because it dries to a hard finish. Alkyd paints also offer good resistance to rust. If the grid is small, you might consider using spray paint, but we use a small 3-inch roller with a foam or short-nap sleeve cover. Make sure you paint the edges of the grid, not just the flat surfaces.

Paint the tiles. Use a vacuum cleaner to remove dust from all sides of the tiles. Then wipe the faces of the tiles clean with a damp sponge and a solution of trisodium phosphate and water. Don't get the tiles too wet; just remove the surface grime. If there is any mildew on the tiles, wash them with a mild solution of two parts water to one part chlorine laundry bleach. Allow the tiles to dry overnight.

Before you paint, kill any stains or spots with a pigmented shellac, described in chapter 1, "Professional Solutions to Tough Problems." Then apply flat latex paint with a roller equipped with a medium-nap sleeve cover.

Adding a Ceiling Fan

Create the sultry mood of Casablanca (well, sort of) and enjoy the benefits of reduced energy bills with this simple project. In hot weather, a fan pulls air up, moving it throughout and cooling the space. Most fans have a reverse switch, so during the heating season they can push warm air down and recirculate it throughout the room. Here are some points to keep in mind when shopping for and installing a ceiling fan:

Ceiling height: A minimum ceiling height of $7\frac{1}{2}$ to 8 feet is needed to install a ceiling fan. Most electrical codes specify a minimum distance between the fan and the floor. Be sure to check your local code.

Fan location: For most practical purposes, the fan should be mounted in the center of the room. The blades should be 8 to 9 feet above the floor for best cooling, and a foot below the ceiling if you plan to recycle warm air. The fan should not be mounted closer than 8 inches to the ceiling.

Secure mounting: Ceiling fans are heavy and should be suspended directly from a ceiling joist or 2×4 securely nailed between the ceiling joists. You can purchase a fan-mounting kit that has an adjustable metal bar that is nailed between the ceiling joists and includes all necessary hanging hardware.

Fan wobble: If your fan wobbles when operating, check it for loose and misaligned blades. If the blades are tight, swap the position of two adjacent blades to see if this cures the imbalance. If swapping both sets of adjacent blades doesn't solve the problem, experiment with balancing the blades by taping some large washers to the back of one blade, and observe the action. If the wobble increases, try another blade; if it improves, add more weight until the wobble is reduced. Then glue the washers in place. If you have to add more than a couple of washers, you'll probably want to return the fan for one that is not defective.

Selecting a Cover-Up Ceiling

There are many ceiling systems, but they all fall into two categories: ceilings that attach directly to the ceiling joists in one way or another or suspended ceilings. Both have their advantages and some disadvantages. Here are a few general guidelines we have found useful in selecting a ceiling system.

High Ceilings

If you have at least 7½ feet of headroom, then you can consider a suspended ceiling. Suspended ceiling systems are often used to finish basements because they are great at hiding plumbing and heating ducts. The large ceiling panels can be removed easily from the suspension grid, so you have access to electrical, telephone, television, cable TV, and water lines. There is a wide variety of styles to choose from, and lights are easy to incorporate into the grid system.

In order for the tiles to be inserted into the suspended grid, there must be at least 3 inches of clearance between the grid and the old ceiling or ceiling joists. If you plan to incorporate light fixtures into the system, allow at least 6 inches. You should never install a suspended ceiling below an existing ceiling that contains embedded radiant heat coils.

Generally, a suspended ceiling is a good cover-up for a troubled ceiling. But before the suspended ceiling can be installed, any bad ceiling structure must be restored. At times, this is almost as much work as totally repairing the old ceiling.

Low Ceilings

If you have less than 7½ feet of headroom, a ceiling system that attaches directly to the ceiling joists is your best choice. Here are some alternatives:

Acoustical tile: This is a popular choice that can be glued to an existing ceiling or stapled to metal or wood furring strips that are nailed or screwed to ceiling joists. This is a good choice to install over an old ceiling in need of structural repair, since the furring strips will support any loose plaster or drywall. If you attach furring directly to joists, use nails. If you attach furring through old plaster, use drywall screws to draw the furring tight without breaking up the plaster.

Drywall: Another possibility is to install a ⅜-inch drywall ceiling over the old ceiling. The drywall mimics the look of plaster, so this is a good choice in an old house where you want to preserve the original look. Long drywall screws secured into the ceiling joists hold the old, loose drywall or plaster and the new drywall ceiling securely in place. The job will be even more sound if you use construction adhesive between the drywall and old plaster. The adhesive comes in tubes that fit into a caulk gun.

Decorative ceilings: Strips of embossed tin are another good cover-up for structural ceiling problems because they mount on furring strips.

Installing Acoustical Tiles

Step 1: Make an accurate layout. Get a planning sheet, available from most ceiling system manufacturers, or use a piece of graph paper with ¼-inch squares and let each square equal 1 foot. Make a scale drawing of the ceiling, and include the locations of obstructions such as heating ducts and water pipes. Also draw in the ceiling joists.

Step 2: Draw a 12-inch grid on a piece of tracing paper at least as large as your ceiling layout. Place this grid, which represents the ceiling tiles, over the ceil-ing plan, and move the grid around until the border tiles are as large as possible. Some compromises have to be made, but you should try for a layout where all border tiles are at least 4 to 6 inches wide.

INSTALLING ACOUSTICAL CEILING TILE ON WOODEN FURRING

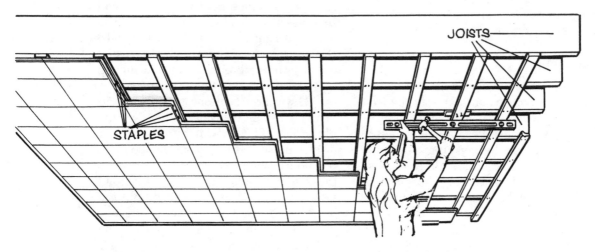

1. Nail furring strips to ceiling joists on 12-inch centers. Use a 4-foot level to check that the furring strips are level. Place wedges behind the furring strips where they don't touch the joists.

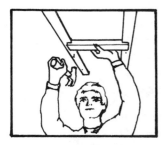

2. Cut a section of furring and use it as a spacer to maintain the spacing between furring strips as you nail them in place.

3. Staple the wide flange on the grooved side to the furring strips.

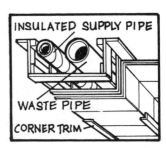

4. Use furring to construct a soffit around pipes or other protrusions.

Step 3: Tape the tracing paper to the ceiling plan, then trace the ceiling layout and erase all lines outside the layout lines. You now have the basic layout for your ceiling on the top sheet.

Usually, the 1 × 3 furring strips are spaced on 12-inch centers under the grid lines on the layout that run perpendicular to the ceiling joists. Use this layout to estimate the tiles and furring strips needed. The plan will also give you a good idea of how many tricky cuts you will have to make when installing the tiles.

You can make several plans and try tiles of different sizes and different placements on separate sheets of tracing paper. Before you finalize your plan, take it to the store where you plan to purchase your ceiling, and have it reviewed.

You can also glue the tiles directly to the ceiling. But we don't advise it. Your ceiling has to be in good shape, with no loose or flaking paint and in good structural condition. The adhesive is very difficult to remove later, if you ever decide to change things. If your ceiling is in such good shape—just paint it!

Tips for Working with Acoustical Tiles

Clean the old ceiling. Scrape away any loose paint on the ceiling and thoroughly vacuum any ducts, piping, or joists to remove dust and dirt before installing tiles.

Drive nail heads flush. If you're using nails to install the furring strips, make sure all nail heads are driven flush, so the tile can be stapled onto a flat surface.

Handle acoustical tiles carefully. Wash your hands and handle the tiles carefully. Corners can be damaged easily,

and you don't want oily dirt to smudge them.

Purchase extra tiles. Buy a few extra tiles to have on hand in case some are damaged—and to have on hand later if you have to open the ceiling to make a repair or to hide electrical or plumbing lines.

Allow the tiles to acclimate. Before installation, let the ceiling tiles or panels adjust to their new environment for at least a day. Ideally, the temperature should be between 60° and 80°F, with a relative humidity not above 70 percent. But few areas have those conditions all year long. Just allow the tiles to settle for a while, so they can expand or contract after they are moved from the warehouse to your house.

Wear protective clothing. Ceiling materials can cause a skin rash on some people. Avoid scratching or rubbing your eyes or skin if they become irritated. After using the materials, wash with a mild soap and warm water. Always wear safety glasses.

Installing a Suspended Ceiling

Suspended ceilings have tiles that are similar to the acoustical ceiling tiles but come in larger 24-inch-square or 24 × 48-inch sizes. The tiles are suspended from the ceiling in a metal grid system. There are many tile patterns, textures, and materials to choose from. Grid systems come in white or brown, and some are hidden and allow for a smooth ceiling.

As with installing acoustical tiles, it is important to prepare an accurate layout plan, using ¼-inch-square graph paper and tracing paper. See the previous sec-

INSTALLING A SUSPENDED CEILING

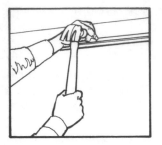

1. Install the L-shaped wall molding.

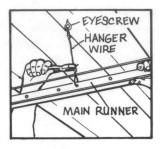

2. Hang the rails from wires attached to the ceiling joists.

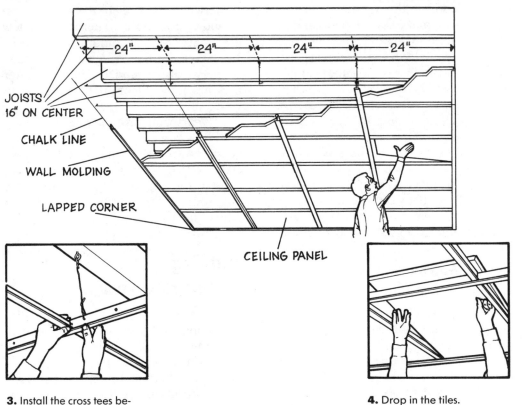

JOISTS 16" ON CENTER

CHALK LINE

WALL MOLDING

LAPPED CORNER

EYESCREW

HANGER WIRE

MAIN RUNNER

24" 24" 24" 24"

CEILING PANEL

3. Install the cross tees between the rails.

4. Drop in the tiles.

WALL MOLDING

MAIN RUNNER SPLICE

CROSS TEES

CEILING PANEL

This is how the parts of a suspended ceiling connect.

tion on installing acoustical tiles. The trickiest part of this job is figuring out the size of the border tiles, but all manufacturers supply complete step-by-step directions. Follow their directions carefully. Here are some tips we have learned about hanging a ceiling:

Install the main runners. For most installations, the main runners are installed so they run across the ceiling joists and parallel to the longest walls.

Use small panels for small rooms. The smaller 2 × 2-foot panels are easier to plan and will look more in scale in a very small room. You also might consider a system with a hidden grid.

Find the low point. Because your suspended ceiling must clear the lowest pipe, electrical box, or other obstruction, find this point. The easiest way to do this is to stand on a ladder with your head as close to the ceiling joists as possible. Look around; you should be able to "eyeball" the lowest spot. If it's a basement, you probably will still have to build soffits around large pipes and beams. Just find the lowest spot most of the ceiling can clear. Starting from this spot, use a straight piece of wood and a level to transfer this height to a side wall. Carry this line around the room according to the installation instructions.

Use sharp blades. Tiles are easy to cut with a utility knife, but the mineral or wood fibers quickly dull the blade. Have a pack of extra blades on hand. Use a straightedge when you cut.

Fit the tiles loosely. Cut the border tiles for a loose fit. The grid provides a ½-inch lip that the tiles sit on, so measure and cut accurately. If a tile is tight, trim it down. Forcing a tight tile into the grid system will push the grid out of alignment.

Installing a Plank Ceiling

Now you can create the look of a wood ceiling using an acoustical plank ceiling system. These planks are made of the same material as acoustical ceiling tiles but are manufactured into board-size tiles. The planks are 4 feet long and come in three different widths. Several finishes are available that simulate wood planking.

This ceiling system is installed like a standard acoustical tile ceiling. The planks are stapled to 1 × 3 wood furring strips or clipped to a metal track. They can also be glued up, but we don't recommend it.

Layout is the same as for a standard acoustical ceiling. Use ¼-inch-square graph paper and tracing paper as described in the section on installing acoustical tiles. The joint between the ceiling and the walls should be concealed by wood molding.

Installing a Metal Ceiling

During Victorian times, the metal ceiling was all the rage, and it has made a big comeback today. You can add character to any room and, if need be, cover up an old cracked or damaged ceiling with a metal ceiling system. Metal ceilings are available in 2-foot-wide sheets measuring 4 feet or 8 feet long.

The metal ceiling strips can be cumbersome to work with, compared with other ceiling systems. Basically, installation is similar to hanging an acoustical tile ceiling. The old ceiling does not have to be removed, since the new furring strips can be installed with long screws and will support the old ceiling. A decorative cornice molding (also metal) is

INSTALLING A METAL CEILING

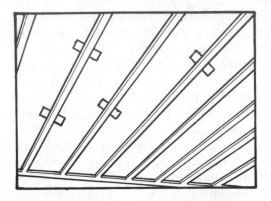

1. Install furring strips perpendicular to the joists. Nail them to the joists.

2. The metal sheets are light but flexible, so support them with a piece of furring as they are lifted into position. Nail the sheets to the furring.

3. Lightly tap the tip of a nail so the head crimps the joint between the sheets. This process is called caulking because it closes the seam between the sheets.

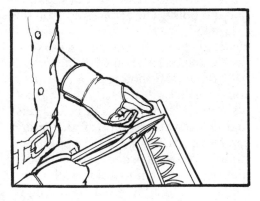

4. Use tin snips or aviation shears to cut the panels and trim pieces. Wear gloves since the pieces have sharp corners.

used to conceal the joints along the walls. The cornice is available in several sizes from 1½ inches to 10 inches.

Once the ceiling panels are installed, paint them with any oil-based paint. If you like the bright metal finish, apply a coat of lacquer or polyurethane to prevent tarnish.

If you think you can handle installing an acoustical ceiling, you should not be intimidated by this project. With each order the manufacturer furnishes installation instructions. If you follow those instructions and these tips, you will have a new "old" ceiling in no time:

Wear gloves: Wear heavy work

gloves when handling the metal ceiling panels, especially the cut edges; it's sharp stuff.

Wash the panels: Before you install the panels, wash off the mill oil with a liberal amount of denatured alcohol. Take extra care to do this, because paint or polyurethane won't stick to an oily surface.

Support the panels: The 8-foot-long panels can be difficult to position and nail in place without bending and kinking. Make a support from scrap furring. Cut a piece of furring about an inch longer than the height of the finished ceiling, to make the support post. Nail a 2-foot piece of furring to the top of the post, to form a "T." Then nail a couple of scrap pieces of furring between the T and the post to stiffen the support.

To use this support to hold the panels in place, push the metal panel up against the furring strips with the T, and wedge the bottom of the post against the floor by giving it a light kick. If you can't get a helper, make several of these supports.

Budget Face-Lifting a Ceiling

Drywall does it! Drywall is inexpensive compared with other ceiling materials, and it comes in standard 4×8-foot sheets as well as 4×12 and 4×14-foot sheets. If your ceiling is in relatively good structural repair, use lightweight $\frac{1}{4}$-inch-thick drywall. These sheets are light and easy to work with. The pros use the longest sheets possible, but we have found that transporting and handling the 14-foot sheets is too much of a hassle. Also, few lumberyards or home centers stock these larger sheets.

If you don't have a pickup truck or a van, the best way to get drywall home is to have the lumberyard deliver it. But if you must use a cartop carrier, be careful, because the thin sheets crack easily. Be sure to tie the drywall down securely in the front and back, so the wind doesn't catch it; if the wind gets under and lifts these thin sheets, they will break off.

When you're lifting and moving drywall, be careful to put it down gently. Its corners are easily crushed if dropped harshly to the floor. A banged-up corner makes taping harder.

Hanging a drywall ceiling is a two-person job. Even with a helper, it's a good idea to build a T-jack. Cut a 2×4 about an inch or two longer than the height of the ceiling. Then nail a 3 or 4-foot piece of 2×4 or 1×4 to one end to form a "T." This jack can then be wedged between the floor and ceiling to hold one end of the drywall sheet tight against the ceiling joists. This way, one worker can hold up one end while his partner runs screws through the drywall. Even a thin sheet of drywall is hard to hold overhead for any length of time, especially if you are trying to drive screws while you hold it.

Two people can drywall a good-size ceiling in a day or a weekend, so you may find it is worth your while to rent a rolling scaffold—much more convenient than climbing up and down a ladder. Here's the procedure and some tips we've learned about installing a drywall ceiling:

Find the joists. This is easier to do than in most situations, because you don't care how many holes you put in the old ceiling. So get up on the ladder with a hammer and a common nail, and poke through until you find a joist. Keep poking until you know for sure which way the joists run. Then tap a nail into the first joist at one end of the room. Hook a chalk line on the nail, and go find the same joist on the other side of the room. When you find it, snap a line showing where the joist runs. Do this for every

FINISHING A DRYWALL JOINT

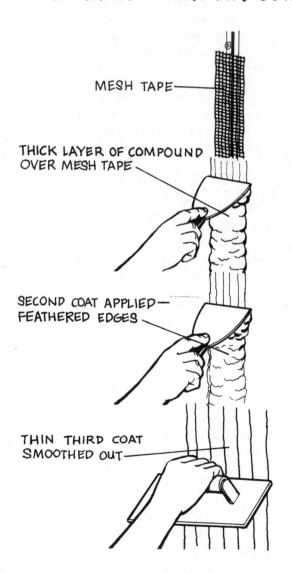

MESH TAPE

THICK LAYER OF COMPOUND OVER MESH TAPE

SECOND COAT APPLIED— FEATHERED EDGES

THIN THIRD COAT SMOOTHED OUT

joist and you'll have a guide for finding the joists when you hang each sheet. As the sheets go up, the line of screws will replace the chalk line as your guide.

Cut with a knife.   For straight, clean cuts in drywall, use a utility knife and a metal straightedge—a framing square works well. Pros use a 4-foot T square to keep cuts running at 90 degrees, but you probably won't want to buy one unless you have a lot of drywall to put up. Instead, measure along each end of the drywall and snap a chalk line between. Score the sheet on its face side with the utility knife. Run the utility knife in the score a couple of times, until it's at least halfway through the drywall.

Then go behind the sheet and hold the board firmly on each side of your cut. Hit the area behind your cut with your knee to snap the piece along the score. Next cut through the backing paper with the utility knife to separate the pieces. Drywall quickly dulls the utility knife blade, so change it often.

"Butter" the boards.   Buttering is carpenter's slang for applying glue to a surface. Use the type of construction adhesive that comes in caulk gun tubes. Get about one tube per two sheets of drywall, and squirt it all over the back of each sheet just before you put it up.

Butt your tapers.   Most drywall comes with tapered edges to make finishing easier. When you have to cut a sheet to meet the wall, make sure the cut edge is at the wall, not against another sheet.

Use drywall screws.   Drywall nails are not an option for a veneering job. If you try to nail through old plaster, you'll just break it up. Buy or rent an electric screw gun that allows you to automatically set the screws to the proper depth.

Set it so that the screwheads are below the surface of the drywall but don't go in so far that they break the paper surface. These screw guns can zip a screw in in about a second, and they usually have magnetic bits to hold a screw—both very handy features when you are trying to hold a sheet tight with one hand and screw with the other.

Make sure you push the drywall tight against the ceiling before putting a screw in, otherwise the screw will rip through. Use 2½-inch drywall screws placed about 8 inches apart. When drywall is being installed directly to studs in new construction, 12-inch spacing is adequate, but because you're pulling the old ceiling together with the new one, use more screws, especially in areas where the old ceiling is sagging.

Use fiberglass mesh tape. Our choice for joint tape is the fiberglass mesh type that sticks directly to the joint. It's a little more expensive than the perforated paper, but it speeds the job considerably because you don't have to lay it in a bed of joint compound. You just stick the tape up and put compound right over it. Also, mesh tape eliminates the possibility of air bubbles that sometimes form under paper tape.

Build up the joint compound. The most common mistake in finishing joints is trying to make the joints flat. This just won't work; the tape will show through. Instead, joints should be mounds that taper so gradually you don't notice they are there. To accomplish this, start with a 6-inch drywall knife and lay down a healthy 6-inch-wide layer of joint compound. Try not to leave big ridges. When it dries, knock off the ridges with your taping knife, or use 80-grit sandpaper if you have to. Then feather the edges out

a bit with a fat wet sponge. A sponge, as opposed to sandpaper, creates no dust and won't rip the paper surface of the drywall.

After sponging, use a wider knife to add a thinner swath of joint compound. This will cover the other layer and extend out a couple of inches more on each side of the joint. Sponge when it's dry. Repeat the process a third time, and you'll have a joint that is thickest in the middle and about a foot wide.

Fill the screw dents. Joint compound shrinks, so apply a swipe of compound over the screws during each of the three finishing rounds.

Hanging Objects from a Plaster or Drywall Ceiling

Want to hang a pot rack in the kitchen, an old-fashioned swing on the front porch, or a lush fern in the corner of the living room? Here are some tips that will help you hang just about anything from your ceiling.

Most light (under 10 pounds) objects can be suspended from anchors, but anything heavier should be directly attached to a ceiling joist.

Before you start a project that involves hanging something from the ceiling, check the condition of your ceiling. Cracked or loose plaster or water-damaged drywall will not hold wall anchors and may not be strong enough to support even light objects.

Hanging Light Objects

Here are three easy tips for a successful lightweight hang-up:

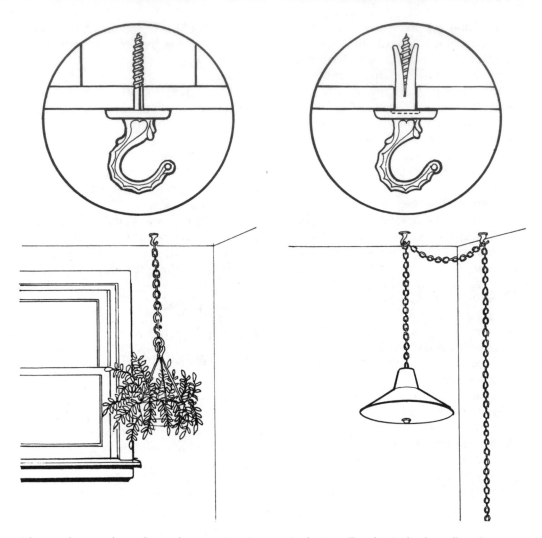

A heavy object, such as a large plant, requires a hook screwed directly into a ceiling joist.

A plastic wall anchor in the drywall or plaster can be used to hang a lighter object such as a lamp.

Check for a joist. No matter what you plan to hang, your first choice should be to secure it to a ceiling joist. But that's not always possible. Hold the object in position and mark the location where you want the object to hang from. If you have difficulty visualizing where the object should go, have someone hold it in place while you direct its placement. Then drill a small hole through the ceiling to check if there is a stud under the mark.

Use a ceiling hook for joist mounting. If there is a ceiling joist under the mark, use a simple screw hook or a decorative ceiling hook. Both can be screwed right into the joist.

Use a plastic wall anchor if there's no joist. If there is no joist behind the mark, use a plastic anchor to hang a lightweight object (mobile, wind chimes, and so forth) from a plaster or plasterboard ceiling that is in good condition. You also can use a decorative ceiling hook screwed into the anchor, or purchase one with a built-in toggle bolt.

Hanging Medium-Weight Objects

To hang an object weighing up to 20 pounds, such as a small flower pot or a swag lamp, use a ceiling hook screwed into a ceiling joist. If a joist isn't convenient, then use a large Molly or toggle bolt. Here are three easy tips for hanging medium-weight objects:

Check for a joist. Hold the object in position, or have someone else hold it in place while you direct its placement, and mark the ceiling. Then drill a small hole through the ceiling mark to check if there is a stud under the mark.

Use a ceiling hook for joist mounting. If there is a ceiling joist under the mark, then use a large decorative ceiling hook or a plant hook. Both should be screwed directly into the ceiling joist.

Use a large toggle bolt or Molly if there's no joist. If there is no joist behind the mark, then use a large ceiling hook with a built-in toggle bolt. You can also use a Molly bolt to secure a bracket ceiling hook in a plaster or drywall ceiling that is in good condition.

Great Gadgets & Gizmos

☞ **Stud finder** For less than $15, this device takes the guesswork out of finding a stud or joist. Some stud finders use a magnet to find the nails or screws. Better ones use an electronic circuit. A needle moves or a tone sounds when you hold the device over the stud or joist. You'll find several models available at hardware stores and home centers.

☞ **Water level** Drawing an accurate level line around the perimeter of a large room for the wall molding isn't easy. Professional ceiling contractors use a rotation laser light, hung in the center of the room, which shoots a beam of light on the walls for reference. The suspension wires are also bent to length using the light.

You can rent the next best thing to a laser, a water level. This simple device is nothing more than two calibrated tubes connected by a long plastic hose. Water seeks it own level, therefore the water in both tubes will always be aligned. If one tube is lower than the other, the water rises in the lower tube.

Hang one end of the level at the lowest point of your ceiling, and take the other end to any point in the room. When the water is aligned to the same mark as the suspended tube, both tubes are level. Use the level to mark the walls and check the main runners.

☞ **Pry bar** This is the tool you'll need if you decide to remove a damaged ceiling. Also called a rip bar, wrecking bar, or pull/pry bar, its two ends work to give you leverage when pulling off heavy materials, like sections of ceiling plaster. You'll use it for many other projects, such as removing baseboard from walls or taking a window apart. We have a couple, because they come in different sizes. For under $10, this is an indispensable tool to have around the house.

Hanging Heavy Objects

Heavy objects must be suspended from the ceiling joists. Most ceiling joists are installed on 16-inch centers and run across the width of the house or in the same direction as the floor joists. Occasionally, joists are 24 inches on-center. A quick trip to the attic or basement will tell you what that direction and spacing is. Even though there are many joists, one is seldom in the place you want to hang something. Here are some tips on how to find that elusive ceiling joist and what to do when it is not in the "right" place:

Locate the joist.   Look for clues to joist location. A loose drywall nail causes a small moon-shaped crack. Overhead light fixtures are either attached to or suspended between joists, so look on either side of a light fixture to find one. If you have drywall, not plaster, try tapping the ceiling; the sound changes in the area of the joist.

After you have located a joist, measure over to find a joist in the area you want to hang your heavy object. Drill a small test hole, or hammer in a small finishing nail where you think the joist is; many joists are not placed accurately on-center.

Use a heavy hook.   Once you have found the joist, use a large eyescrew or screw hook. Drill a pilot hole through the ceiling into the joist, and coat the threads of the hook or eye with soap to make it easier to thread into the joist.

Check the joist for a swing.   A two or three-person porch swing needs a sturdy ceiling to hang from. Many porch ceiling joists are made from 2×4s. Unless the joist you plan to use spans a very short distance (less than 10 feet), you should reinforce it by nailing a new 2×6 joist next to the old one.

Hanging Objects from Other Types of Ceilings

It's harder to hang something from an acoustical tile ceiling, especially if it is suspended from the original ceiling. But no matter what the ceiling is, there is a way to safely hang up that wind chime or favorite fern. Here are some solutions we have worked out. They cover a wide range of situations; if yours isn't exactly the same, then combine several methods. Just remember to always attach your hang-up to a structure that is strong enough to support it.

Suspended Ceilings

The easiest way to hang something light from a suspended ceiling is to use the grid for support. The tiles are not strong enough to support any weight without sagging. Here are some ways to do it:

Use a hanger kit.   Ceiling manufacturers make a two-part clip that snaps onto both sides of a grid rail and provides a tab with a hole in it. You can attach a hook or tie a cord to the hole in the tab. You can attach the clip to any grid rail, but if you want to hang a plant or other heavy object, use a short rail. These rails are attached to the suspension wires leading from the ceiling; long rails are not supported by wires.

Make a hanger.   Most of the time the "just right" location for what you want to hang up will not be under a grid rail. The easiest solution for this is to

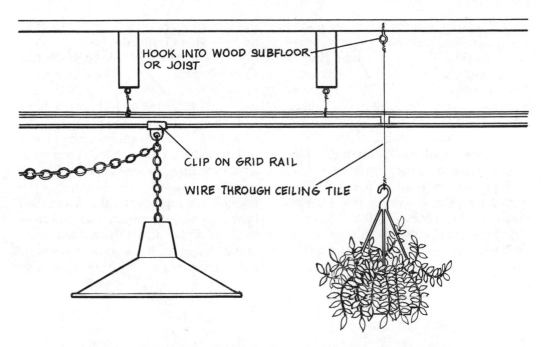

HOOK INTO WOOD SUBFLOOR OR JOIST

CLIP ON GRID RAIL

WIRE THROUGH CEILING TILE

To hang a light object, such as a drop lamp, from a suspended ceiling, use a metal clip that slips over the ceiling grid track. The clip can be positioned anywhere on the grid. The short rail sections, made of heavier metal, can support more weight. Hang no more than 2 pounds from long, lighter sections. A heavy object, such as a potted plant, must be suspended on a wire run through the tiles and attached to a hook screwed directly into a joist or wooden subfloor.

mark the tile where you want to hang the object. Remove the tile and place a piece of wood long enough to reach between two grid rails across the area. Then make a small hole in the tile and run your suspension wire or cord through the tile. Attach it to the board with an eyescrew. Replace the tile. You will have to lift the board up temporarily to work the tile back into the grid. This is good only for an object weighing less than 10 pounds.

Hang heavy objects from the rafters. For heavy objects you'll have to go through the suspended ceiling to find support from rafters. If the joists are exposed under the ceiling, then just run a heavy screw hook or eyescrew into the joist, tie a wire or cord to the hook, and run the wire or cord through a hole in the tile. If the joists are not exposed, then use the techniques already described to find the joist before installing a hook.

Acoustical Tile

An acoustical tile ceiling is not strong enough to support even light objects, so you should not attach anything directly to it. The tiles eventually will sag under the weight and pull away from the mastic or furring. The strategy here should be the same as trying to hang something from a suspended ceiling. That is, attach whatever you are hanging to the ceiling above the tile. Here are some suggestions on how to do this:

Screw a hook into the furring. The easiest method to hang medium-weight or light objects is to use a screw hook with a long shank screwed into the furring strip directly behind the tile joints. The furring strips usually run across the ceiling joists and are under only half the joints. Use an ice pick or awl to probe the joints; the point will go in less than an inch where it hits the furring.

Run wire or cord through the tile. Carefully remove a tile. Then use a screw hook secured into a ceiling joist if one is nearby. You can use a Molly bolt to hang something that is not too heavy (see the section on hanging things from plaster and drywall) from the ceiling. Then make a hole in the tile, pass wire or cord through it, and secure the wire or cord to the hook. Then replace the tile. You might have to remove some tile material from the back of the tile to form a small crater in the area of the hook so the tile will lie flat. Replace the tile with ceiling mastic.

CHAPTER
6
Floors

Installing a new floor can dramatically transform a room. But choosing the material, style, and color for a room's floor is more challenging than selecting wallpaper, because there are extenuating circumstances to consider and many more dollars involved.

You'll find a huge number of choices in materials, and various ways to install them. For example, vinyl sheet goods (large seamless sheets) can be installed with adhesive, laid loose, or attached at the room's edge with staples concealed by molding. Ceramic tile is available in sizes ranging from sheets of 1-inch-square tiles to foot-square quarry tiles. These tiles can be laid in cement, epoxy, or organic mastic. Carpeting and hardwood flooring also can be installed in various ways.

Long before shopping for new flooring, let your fingers do the walking through the pages of home magazines for ideas.

DECORATOR IDEAS FOR NEW FLOORING

Here are some simple ideas we have used to get the most mileage from our floor renovations:

▶ To make a small room look larger, use one solid color in a light shade, or a geometric pattern.

▶ To define a specific area within a room, such as the dining table in the kitchen, use an area rug over the new flooring.

▶ Outline a room with contrasting floor tiles by placing them around the perimeter.

▶ Widen the appearance of a long, narrow hallway with two contrasting tile colors (black and white, for example) run in a diagonal or diamond pattern.

▶ Coordinate flooring from room to room so space seems to flow naturally from one to another; this is especially noticeable in hallways where doors to rooms are often left open.

Clip and save ideas that you like and think might work well in your room. If you have furnishings, wall coverings, or window treatments that you want to coordinate, gather together some samples to take with you when you go browsing. Also, make a rough sketch of the room with dimensions, so you'll be able to calculate the amount of flooring material needed and have it checked by the salesperson where you eventually make your flooring purchase.

We have successfully installed vinyl tile and sheet goods, ceramic tile, hardwood parquet, prefinished wood plank flooring, and carpeting. Some jobs turned out easier to do than others, and some jobs were so tricky that we have come to the conclusion that "we won't do that again!" After sweating through most of the mistakes you can make, here's what we've learned, so you can decide whether you want to do it yourself or call in the professionals.

Knowing Your Old Floor

No matter what type of flooring you decide to use, you first need to learn what's underneath the floor you have if the original floor is not exposed. Begin the investigation by peeling back the floor (it may be several layers) and discovering what's really down there.

You might be surprised at what you find hiding under your old floor. Worn and stained carpet could be hiding old tired linoleum, which is sitting on a beautiful, if somewhat scruffy, hardwood floor just waiting to be liberated.

You are likely to find this multiple cover-up in kitchens, which in many cases started out with a maple or oak floor. In several houses we have happily found our "new floor" was just waiting to be uncovered. Here are some tips to help you evaluate your old floor and make a game plan. Also, this should help you decide what work to do yourself and when to call in the professionals.

Search for Your Original Floor

Unless you are just replacing existing carpeting, what's under the present flooring is significant. This is especially true if your floor has more than one layer. What you find should temper your choice in flooring materials. You can have just about any type of floor you want, but at times the extra work or expense becomes prohibitive. Here are the easiest places to search for your bottom-line floor:

Register or grate: The easiest way to get a look at the different layers of your floor is to pry up a hot-air heating register or cold-air return grate. Under the grate or register you can usually see the edge of each layer as it was cut to fit around the opening.

Pipe trim: If you have radiators, remove the metal trim ring around the radiator pipe; you can usually see the layers of flooring around it.

Threshold: Another location to investigate is the door threshold. Unscrew it or pull it up.

Baseboard: Expose the gap between the old floor and wall by removing a section of baseboard. Use a wide putty knife and a thin screwdriver, and work carefully so you can reuse the trim.

Choosing a Do-It-Yourself Floor

Once you have a handle on what's under your old floor, you're ready to consider what you want to put over it. You probably have a new floor in mind. But before you rush out and purchase 20 square yards of carpet and pad or a roll of sheet goods, let's run through each of the major categories of flooring. As we said earlier, some we install ourselves and some we don't.

Carpet

Installing carpet isn't difficult, but we don't recommend it as a do-it-yourself job. That's because installation is a rela-

tively small percentage of the cost—usually less than 30 percent, unless you are using inexpensive foam-backed or indoor/outdoor carpet. Of course, the more expensive the carpet, the smaller part the installation cost becomes of the total bill. To cover several rooms with a good-quality carpet, you will have to invest $15 to $30 or more per square yard, a considerable investment in materials. Therefore, your relative savings shrink while your investment in materials grows. And that investment is at risk if *you* botch the installation.

That's the main reason we don't recommend installing your own carpet. In addition, we found that by the time we finished the job, we were just getting used to the tools. But even if you don't install the carpet, you can still save a portion of the installation cost by doing the "grunt work" yourself. Make sure that your installation estimate does not include this work, or better yet, find out how much a complete job will cost with and without your efforts. Then you'll know how much you can pocket for your labor.

Begin by moving all the furniture out of the room, and then follow these steps for pulling up the carpeting:

Step 1: Starting in a corner, use a pry bar or large screwdriver to pry the carpet up.

Step 2: Grab the corner (be careful of tacks or staples) and pull it up. Use a short jerking motion.

Step 3: When you have pulled back the corner as far as it will go, work along the walls. Stand close to (but not on) the area you are pulling on. It is easier and you get better leverage if you pull the carpet straight.

Step 4: If you are going to discard

the carpet, use a utility knife to cut it into 4-foot-wide strips. Many disposal companies will take carpet if it is in small, neat packages that can easily be loaded onto the truck.

Step 5: Use a claw hammer and pry bar to remove wood tackless strips. A large pair of pliers can be used to pry up floor tacks.

While we hire an installer for most carpeting jobs, the exceptions are foam-backed and indoor/outdoor carpet. These types of carpet make good do-it-yourself projects because they usually are glued directly to the floor or held in place with double-stick tape. They are easy to cut with a utility knife and are installed like sheet goods. Foam-backed carpet is also available as adhesive-backed tiles. The foam backing allows the carpet to bridge minor floor defects. It can also be installed over a highly embossed floor without the pattern showing through. Follow the general guidelines for floor preparation and the tips in the sections on installing vinyl tiles or sheet goods; the techniques of installation are the same.

Carpet Cleaning

Sometimes all that's needed to transform a room is to clean the carpeting, a job made much easier with the advent of steam cleaning machines. You'll find these units for rent for about $20 a day at most large grocery stores and at rental equipment outlets.

The cleaning equipment does a good job because it extracts the loosened dirt from the carpet fibers. Most of these units are called steam cleaners, but they actually use hot water. Water and a cleaning solution is sprayed on the carpet, which loosens the dirt and holds it in suspension in the water. Then the dirty water is vacuumed up.

Check the cost of purchasing the cleaning solutions and renting the equipment. Then check with your local professional cleaner. If they are having a promotion and you have a large area to clean, you might be surprised how competitive their prices are compared with renting the equipment and doing it yourself.

All rental units come with detailed instructions, which should be followed exactly. Most of the units we've used operate basically in the same way. Here's what's involved:

Remove the furniture.   Move all the furniture out of the room. The carpet will be wet for several hours, longer in humid weather. If you cannot remove all the furniture, slide pieces of aluminum foil under the furniture legs to prevent furniture stain from bleeding onto the carpeting or to prevent metal parts from rusting. This is important especially if the bottoms of the legs have metal glides that will rust from the moisture in the carpet and cause a stain.

Vacuum the carpet.   Before you clean the carpet, give it a good vacuuming to remove as much dirt as possible from the surface. Go around the perimeter of the room with the crevice tool to pull dirt out of corners and along the walls.

Fill the machine.   Mix up the cleaning solutions according to the directions, and fill the dispensing tank.

Clean the carpet.   Most units have a lever that you press to spray the carpet with cleaner solution. When you release the lever or move it to the suction position, the unit vacuums up the liquid.

Begin in the far corner of the room, and apply the cleaner on the out stroke and vacuum it up on the return. Work on a small area and don't clean yourself into a corner. Apply the cleaning solution sparingly; don't go over an area more than a couple of times with the spray, or you will get the carpet too wet. You can vacuum all you want, just go lightly on the spray.

Allow the carpet to dry.　Good ventilation will speed drying. Under ideal drying conditions, you can walk on the carpet in a couple of hours. If possible, allow it to dry overnight. During a humid spell, the carpet might take a week to dry without air conditioning.

Replace the furniture.　When the carpet is dry, go over it quickly with the vacuum cleaner and then replace the furniture. Place small pieces of plastic wrap or aluminum foil under each leg of furniture to prevent stains to the carpet or damage to the bottom of the leg, and leave them in place for another 24 hours.

Installing Ceramic Tile

Ceramic tile has moved out of the bathroom and kitchen and is popular in all areas of the house. Tile is a versatile flooring material, but successfully installing floor tile presents a challenge for the average do-it-yourselfer. Our experience in laying floor tile has led us to the conclusion that installing a room full of expensive custom or high-quality tile should be left to the tile man. As with good-quality carpet, your investment in material is very high and the installation cost is usually less than 25 percent of the total tab.

We still install standard-grade tile in small areas like bathrooms or foyers. The installation costs are relatively high for a small job, and we haven't invested the family savings on materials. Also, we feel we can adequately deal with any of the floor's structural problems in a smaller area. Actually, laying tile in a small area is straightforward. Here are some tips that should make the job go smoother:

Don't lay tile in cement mortar.　We advise that you lay tile only with organic mastic (thinset method) or with epoxy adhesive. In cement mortar, it's difficult to get tiles level and maintain levelness throughout the floor. So leave that method to the professionals.

Remove the old flooring.　Even though it is possible to tile over just about any surface, you will get better results if you get down to the subflooring. The most frequent cause of tile floor problems is a subfloor that is uneven or too flexible. The subfloor movement causes tile joints to constantly open up and admit water. If the flex occurs directly under a large tile, it will break.

Install underlayment.　Unless you are laying tile directly on an old tile floor that is in good structural shape, install underlayment. Use construction adhesive to glue it, and nail it in place with 8d cement-coated nails. The adhesive will bond to the subfloor to create a stiffer base. Tile underlayment in the bathroom should be ½-inch exterior-grade plywood with the good face up. In dry areas of the house, you can use hardboard or particleboard. Underlayment comes in 4 × 8-foot panels and provides a smooth, level surface to install new tile on.

Tips for Laying Tile

If ½-inch underlayment plus the thickness of the tile (usually ⅜ to ½ inch) creates a problem with thresholds or other areas where floors meet, use ⅜ or ¼-inch

INSTALLING A TILE FLOOR

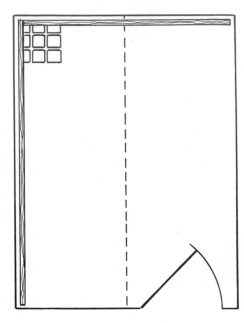

1. Lay out tiles so that border tiles are as close to a half width as possible. Since most rooms are not perfectly square, tile can run parallel to one wall only.

2. Spread adhesive with a notched trowel over a 3 or 4-square-foot area at a time, to prevent it from skinning over.

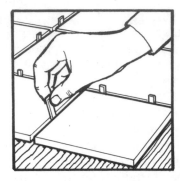

3. Use inexpensive plastic spacers to maintain even spacing if tiles do not have spacer knobs cast in their sides.

4. After all tiles are set in the main field, go back and set the border tiles. Walk carefully on the tiles after the mastic sets up. If the tiles move when you walk on them, place a sheet of ¼-inch plywood over them.

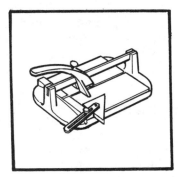

5. A tile cutter can be rented where you buy tiles.

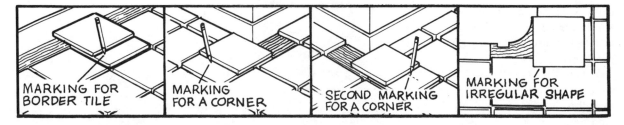

MARKING FOR BORDER TILE

MARKING FOR A CORNER

SECOND MARKING FOR A CORNER

MARKING FOR IRREGULAR SHAPE

6. Mark tiles for cutting.

plywood. Hardboard and particleboard can be used in dry areas, but don't use them in the bath. If these materials get wet, they swell.

Use small tiles in small areas. One-inch-square tiles, glued to a 1-foot-square mesh backing, are the easiest tiles to install in a small bath or confined area. These require less tile cutting, and most of the cuts can be done with a tile nipper.

Lay tile on tile with an epoxy adhesive. New tile can be laid over old tile. If the old floor is in bad shape, remove all loose tiles and fill the void with a floor-patching compound. Minor cracks can be filled with the epoxy adhesive when you are installing the new tiles. Follow the manufacturer's directions—the adhesive has a pot life, and once mixed, it will begin to set. Don't mix more adhesive than you can use in the recommended time.

Follow layout directions. Don't start laying full tiles along one wall, assuming you will save some cutting. The walls are not square to one another, and when you get to the far corner, the differences will become only too apparent. A professional-looking job has grout lines that appear to be parallel to all walls, with evenly spaced tiles. It is easier to cut a tile in half than try to trim ⅛ inch off a side, so plan your layout to have border tiles that will be easy to cut.

Borrow a tile cutter, nipper, and grout float. Most tile outlets and home centers selling tile will lend you all the necessary tools. Have the salesperson show you how to use the tile cutter, and even if you have to purchase a couple of cheap tiles, try it out in the store. Rental tools take a beating, and many times the cutter wheel is so dull that no matter how hard you try, you won't get a clean cut. Find out *in* the store if the tools are in good shape.

Hardwood Flooring

For years in many parts of the country, hardwood floors were a standard feature. Many older homes have hardwood floors that are covered with carpet, tile, or sheet goods. If you are one of those fortunate homeowners who have hardwood floors hiding under layers of cover-up, or just a tired hardwood floor waiting for some tender loving care, here is advice about floor renovation projects you should do and those jobs we found best left to the professional floor sanders and installers.

Rejuvenating a Wood Floor

Run-down hardwood floors can be rejuvenated with surprising ease. This is the type of work we always do with excellent results. Floor rejuvenators are easy to work with, and you can rent a floor polisher for very little money.

Many times, all a hardwood floor needs is a face-lift. This is the case when the floor is worn in high-traffic areas or if it is dull with an accumulation of wax and dirt. Use a floor rejuvenator that cleans and restores its finish; it removes dirt while it softens and dissolves some of the top layer of finish. The rejuvenator also contains a sealer that reseals the old finish and prepares it for wax or buffing. Here is the quickest way we found to give a face-lift to a troubled floor (the most difficult part of this job is removing all the furniture from the room):

Step 1: Rent a floor polisher and purchase four or five extra-coarse #3 steel wool polishing pads from the rental agency. Purchase a gallon of a commercial hardwood floor rejuvenator. Remodeling contractors use these products frequently, and you'll most likely find them sold in building supply outlets as well as at paint and flooring stores that cater to the professional trade.

Step 2: Read the directions for the particular brand of renovator. Heed the safety precautions: Provide plenty of ventilation, and remember most of these products are flammable.

Step 3: Remove all surface dirt with a vacuum or dust mop. Check the floor for loose boards, especially cracked boards and splinters or protruding nails, which can snag the steel wool pad.

Step 4: Apply the renovator to the floor, working in areas of about 100 square feet, using a rag, brush, or sprayer. Wait a few minutes, and then scrub the area with steel wool pads and the polisher. The pads pick up the dirt and old finish, so you'll have to replace them periodically.

Step 5: Let the floor dry overnight and then use the floor polisher to apply a top coat of a compatible finish or paste wax for protection.

If you have a home floor polisher, you can use it to renovate your floor. First check to see if steel wool pads are available for your machine. If not, purchase standard rectangular #3 (extra-coarse) steel wool pads, and place four or five equally spaced pads (depending on the diameter of the pad) on the bottom of the floor polisher's scrubbing-brush pads. The pads stick to the brushes and can be easily changed when full of old finish.

To clean the brushes after your renovation, wash them in a strong solution of household detergent.

Working with a Professional Hardwood Floor Refinisher

If your hardwood floors are deeply scratched or have dark, stained areas, they usually can't be salvaged with a rejuvenator. Refinishing is the only way you can bring them back to life. To refinish a hardwood floor, the old finish has to be removed (usually by sanding) and a new finish applied.

We're convinced that the floor-sanding part of refinishing is not a job for a homeowner to tackle. Renting the sander and purchasing the sanding belts is expensive. The sander is hard to transport and difficult to operate without gouging the floor. You can save about half the cost of a professional job, but the potential damage you can inflict on the floor with just one slip of the sander drum outweighs the money you might save. So, do the preparatory work, let the professional come in to sand the floor, and then you can apply the finish.

Here's how we save money by preparing the floor before the floor man comes in:

Seal off the area. Drum and edge sanders have dust pickup bags, but they miss the fine dust. Tape plastic drop cloths over the doors and heating registers. If you have floor registers, remove the grilles and stuff the registers with newspaper.

Remove the floor molding. Remove the small floor molding, called shoe molding, with a pry bar. Don't pull on the shoe molding, or you will break it. Place the pry bar as close to the nails as possible. Drive any stuck nails through the shoe molding into the wall with a nail set.

Sweep and inspect. Sweep the floor clean, then get down on your hands and knees to look for any nail heads, carpet staples, or other metal objects that can tear the sandpaper or damage the sander drum. Pull all staples and reset any nail heads with a nail set.

Nail loose boards tight. Use 8d finishing nails to face-nail all loose boards tight. Drive the nails in at an angle, to prevent splitting the floorboard. Set the nail heads deep.

Here's what we do after the floor man leaves:

Apply penetrating sealer.   Prevent your new floor from absorbing excess moisture by applying a penetrating sealer soon after sanding. Don't use a lacquer sealer; the fumes are explosive and they dry so fast that you will get lap marks. Choose a slow-drying sealer to avoid these marks. Penetrating sealers come in natural and many attractive shades. Check that the sealer is compatible with any surface finish (varnish or polyurethane) you plan to use. All finishes give off fumes and some are flammable, so open the windows for plenty of ventilation. Close off the cold-air return if there is one in the room, to prevent the fumes from being spread through the house by the heating or air-conditioning system. Apply the penetrating sealer with a pad applicator, roller, or old brush. Spread the sealer on about a quarter of the floor at a time.

Use a floor buffer.   For best results, use a floor buffer with steel wool pads to work the sealer into the floor. Change pads when they spit out sealer. If you don't have a buffer, use steel wool pads to wipe up the excess sealer. Work the steel wool in a circular motion, changing pads when they are full of sealer. Wipe up the excess with a clean rag. Move to the next section of floor and repeat the process.

After the sealer is buffed up, you can walk on the floor, but keep heavy traffic off until the sealer hardens overnight. When the sealer is dry, wax or surface-coat with polyurethane or varnish.

Top-coat with wax.   We recommend that you top-coat the floor with a good-quality floor wax. This is the easiest job for the do-it-yourselfer. A floor that has been sealed with a penetrating sealer and then waxed can be easily rejuvenated and is likely not to need sanding.

The Varnish Option

If you want more spill protection and wear resistance, you can apply varnish instead of wax after the sealer. Apply at least two coats of an alkyd (standard floor) varnish or polyurethane varnish. These finishes are more difficult to apply than the sealer because they dry faster and can show lap marks and grit if the floor is not clean. Do not varnish or apply polyurethane on a hot, humid day. Good lighting in the room is essential; it will help you avoid missing areas and help you spot drip marks. Here's what's involved in varnishing your floor:

Sand or buff.   Don't skip this step, since the sealer has raised the grain of the floorboards. Use 120-grit sandpaper or lightly buff with #2 steel wool.

Sweep carefully.   After sanding or buffing, sweep up all sawdust, then vacuum the floor and all areas where dust can settle, especially along the baseboards and in corners.

Apply the finish.   Use a brush, pad, or roller to apply the finish to a row of four or five floorboards, working from one side of the room to the other. Begin along the wall farthest from the door, and work on as wide a strip as possible. Keep a wet edge or you will create lap marks. Don't go back and start the next row until you have finished the first.

Check for holidays.   As you finish each row, look across the floor to see if it is uniformly shiny. The dull spots, or "holidays," are areas without enough finish. But don't apply more finish to an area that has become tacky and where the brush or roller drags over. Wait until the next coat, and be sure you hit the dull spot.

Recoat. Allow the finish to dry overnight, then sand lightly and recoat. In sanding between coats, remember, you are not trying to sand the wood, just rough up the finish enough to get good adhesion of the next coat.

Painting a Floor

With the country look so popular today, we're seeing more painted floors. Painting a floor can be an inexpensive solution to the problem of what to do with a floor that's already painted or is in such bad shape that even sanding won't cure it. Paint is also a natural over a wide-plank, soft wood floor.

Use a high-gloss, alkyd-based enamel floor or deck paint to paint a wood floor. This paint will produce a hard wear-resistant surface. If you can paint a wall, then you can paint a floor. Here's how:

Dewax and sand. If the floor has many coats of wax, scrub it with medium-coarse #2 steel wool and mineral spirits or a commercial wax remover. Then use a medium-grit sandpaper to remove scratches and create a good surface for the paint to grab on to.

Vacuum the floor. Sweep up excess sawdust and vacuum the floor clean. Then apply a primer coat of paint.

Apply paint with a roller. Use a roller and extension pole to apply the paint, and don't paint yourself into the room! Begin in the far corner and work your way out.

Lighten Up! Whitewashing a Wood Floor

Designers call it the "pickled wood look." We call it plain old whitewash (you know, like Tom's fence). This is a rather simple process that can camouflage damaged or mismatched wood floors. Only a few steps are involved:

Step 1: If the floor has old finish on it, have the floor sanded or remove the finish as already described.

Step 2: Thoroughly vacuum the floor. Make sure you get dust and grit from corners and crevices.

Step 3: Use an alkyd-based white paint, and brush it on with a large, stiff brush. Apply the paint to a small section at a time.

Step 4: Immediately after you apply the paint, remove it with a rag (you'll need lots of them). Burlap works well and it's not very expensive. Wipe the rag across the grain, rubbing the paint into the wood. As you progress through the room, be careful to blend sections.

Step 5: If you want the color to be more intense or deeper, then repeat the process. Otherwise, when the paint has thoroughly dried, apply a polyurethane varnish for top coat protection.

Installing Vinyl Tiles Yourself

Vinyl tile is one of the easiest flooring materials to install. The variety of colors and patterns seems endless, and vinyl tile provides a long-wearing floor that is easy to maintain. Self-stick tiles have adhesive already applied to the backs of the tiles. If your old floor is basically sound and not heavily embossed, you can install vinyl tile directly over the existing floor.

But if the floor is rough or highly embossed, you will get better results if you pull up the old floor. There also is a practical limit to how many floors can be laid over one another. Too many floors will cause problems at the thresholds. You'll trip, passing from one room into another, because of slightly different levels.

Pulling Up an Old Floor

Avoid this job if you possibly can. It's difficult, time-consuming, and tedious. Do you get the idea this is not one of our favorite projects? Sheet goods (seamless flooring) consist of two layers: the top wear layer and the felt layer stuck onto the surface. Tile, on the other hand, unless it is foam backed, is a single layer. Here is how we pull up a seamless floor:

Remove the baseboard. Use a pry bar and remove the baseboard and shoe molding if there is one.

Check for glue. Use a sharp utility knife to cut through the floor in the center. Try to lift the floor. You might find that the old sheet is glued down only around the perimeter. It could also be stapled in place or held down by double-stick tape.

Cut and peel. With the utility knife, cut the flooring into 2-foot-wide strips, and pull each strip up with a jerking motion. You will most likely leave the felt backing layer stuck in place. Work in small, manageable sections.

Scrape. What is left on the floor is the adhesive and a thin layer of felt backing. The best tool we found to scrape this off is a lawn-edging knife. The process is similar to scraping hard ice off the sidewalk in mid-January, and it's about

as much fun. A razor knife scraper also works. Don't sand the felt layer, because it may contain asbestos, which is dangerous to inhale. To help prevent raising dust, wet the backing material before you begin scraping. Also be careful not to gouge the subfloor.

Patching a Tile Floor Before Adding New Flooring

Only a few bad tiles in the existing floor? Then just replace them. Obviously, the tiles don't have to look the same, but they must be the same thickness. Remove the damaged tiles, using a putty knife or scraper. Some adhesives will come up easier if you soften them with a heat gun. Then scrape away the old adhesive, apply new adhesive, and set the tiles in place.

Installing Vinyl Tiles

Like many home improvement projects, installing tile is not difficult, but to get professional-looking results, you must plan carefully and follow the tile manufacturer's directions. Every box of tile comes with complete illustrated instructions. Here are some additional tips:

Check lot and pattern numbers. Tiles are manufactured in batches, so if you purchase more than one box of tiles, check that the batch numbers stamped on the box are the same.

Do a layout. Follow the manufacturer's layout procedures. Remember, your walls are not square. You can't start laying full tiles along one wall and assume everything will come out. A professional-looking job has border tiles that are about the same size along all four walls, and ideally more than half a tile wide.

Allow the adhesive to set. Some

INSTALLING VINYL FLOOR TILE

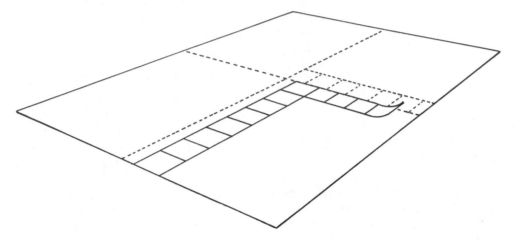

1. Use a chalk line to snap a line parallel to one wall. Then snap another line perpendicular to the first. Lay out the tiles so the border tiles are close to half a tile wide.

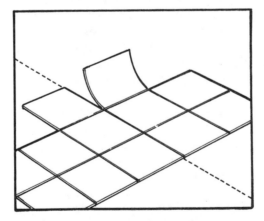

2. Lay the tiles in the center first. Spread the adhesive with a notched trowel over only as much area as you can cover with tiles in the working time recommended by the manufacturer.

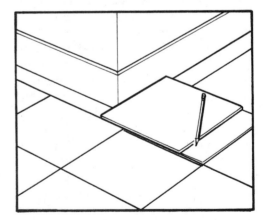

3. To mark a border tile for cutting, place it squarely over the last full tile. Then place another full tile against the wall or molding. Use the edge of the top tile to mark the cutoff line of the border tile.

mastics require time to air before tiles are set in place. All mastics have a certain working time before they "skin over." Read the directions and do not apply adhesive in too large an area. Plan your work so you can set tiles in place before the adhesive's working time expires.

Place tiles at an angle.   Hold a tile at a steep angle and align its edge flush with adjoining tiles, then lower it into place. Don't slide the tiles or wiggle them; that will cause adhesive to pop up between the joints.

Note the arrows.   Tiles are die-cut and the pattern is repeated on each tile exactly. To help you align them, arrows are printed on the back of most tiles. If there are arrows on the tile backs, always install each tile with the arrows pointing in the same direction.

Mark the top.   If you need to make an intricate cut, use a contour gauge to capture the shape of the cut. Use the gauge as a pattern to transfer the shape to the top of the tile. Make sure you don't turn the gauge over, or you will get the wrong shape.

Cut faceup.   Cut through the face of the tile to leave the ragged edge on the bottom of the tile, where it won't be seen. Change utility knife blades frequently to ensure clean cuts.

Dispose of the paper backing immediately. This paper, which comes on the backs of self-adhering tiles, has a slippery coating that will throw you for a loop if you step on it.

Trimming Out the Job

To hide the gap between new flooring and the wall, you should finish off a room with either wooden baseboard or 4-inch vinyl trim cove base. Installing wooden baseboard takes finish carpentry skills and is better left to the pros. But vinyl cove is much easier to install. And, because vinyl will stand up well to moisture from floor cleaning, it is particularly well suited for kitchens and bathrooms.

Vinyl moldings are designed to resemble wooden baseboard. They have a slightly rounded top, that lies flat on the wall, and a flange at the bottom, that rests on the floor. This cove base is sold by building material suppliers and through any retailer specializing in kitchen and bathroom cabinets. It's available in a variety of colors and sold by the running foot or in 4-foot lengths.

Installation is easy, since the vinyl is easy to cut with a sharp utility knife and is glued in place with the same adhesive you use to install floor tiles.

Vinyl cove is flexible, and unlike wooden baseboards, it will wrap around inside and outside corners without the need for mitered or coped cuts. The strips are butted together, and by careful preplanning you can make these joints in inconspicuous places or in corners. Here's how to install vinyl trim:

Prepare the floor.   Prepare the floor and wall by removing all floor shavings, dirt, and dust. A vacuum equipped with a crevice tool makes this prep work easy.

Bend the corners.   Before you put any mastic on a strip of molding that will make a bend, put the molding in place. Force the molding into inside corners, and check that it is still butted tight against the adjoining section. Mark the trim at the corner. Use a sharp knife to lightly score the back of the molding at your mark (where it fits into the corner). This will allow it to flex into the corner. Apply mastic to the back of the trim, and install it.

Score the back of vinyl baseboard to make it fit easily into inside corners. Just bend the baseboard around outside corners. Use a full paint can or other heavy weight at an outside corner to keep the baseboard in place until the mastic sets.

Most vinyl trim will bend around an outside corner without any problems. Just apply adhesive to the back, butt it tight against the adjoining trim, and wrap it around the corner. If one end of the strip is less than a foot or so long, you might have a hard time getting this short side to stick to the wall. The strip will tend to straighten out, and since this side is short, there is less adhesive to grip the wall. Try taping this section to the adjoining piece with a light tape, such as masking tape. Another trick is to place a short piece of wood against the molding and hold it there with a heavy object, such as a full can of paint placed on the floor

in front of the strip. This rig holds the molding against the wall until the mastic sets up.

Apply mastic.   Apply the mastic to the back of the molding only in the area that is ribbed. If the molding has a smooth back, keep the mastic in the flat area; don't put any on the top or bottom flange.

Place the molding.   Put the molding in place so it is in contact with the floor, and then push it against the wall. This will ensure that the mastic will not get on the wall above the molding. If you do get mastic on the wall, wipe it off with a damp rag before it skins over and begins to change color. (Usually it gets darker in color.)

Putting Down Vinyl Sheet Goods

Installing seamless vinyl flooring isn't difficult; it's glued or stapled down. Small areas like bathrooms and small kitchens usually can be covered by a single sheet. Most seamless flooring can be installed directly on old vinyl tile and some seamless floors. With proper underlayment between the old and new floor, it can be installed over any flooring.

If you have a large floor and choose a top-of-the-line material, check into the cost of professional installation. The same reasoning we applied to carpet or high-end ceramic tile installation holds true here. Your hefty investment in costly sheet goods to cover a large area is at risk.

If you're intimidated about cutting the material, consider hiring an installer to do the job. You do the grunt work and prepare the floor for installation. This work could represent a major part of the installation bill.

Choosing Sheet Goods

Besides color and pattern, you have a wide selection of brands and materials to choose from. Before you shop for sheet goods, check out your old floor. Find out what it is made of, its condition, and what's under it. See the section "Search for Your Original Floor" at the beginning of this chapter. The composition and condition of your old floor should be taken into consideration when ordering sheet goods. Some materials can be installed directly on certain old floors, and other materials require underlayment, which is an additional expense.

Your dealer can recommend installation procedures. If you have an old wood or tile floor, find out if the material can be stapled or glued in place around the perimeter. This is the easiest method of installation. When and if you decide to change flooring, the sheet goods will be much easier to remove if the floor is secured only along the edges.

If you are going to cover a large area, find out the type of adhesive required and the method of seaming two sheets together. Some materials can be joined by tape; others require the seam to be glued to the floor.

Using a Paper Pattern to Lay Out New Flooring

Some sheet goods are sold with an installation kit complete with pattern paper, tracing disk, and tape to lay out the job. Here's basically how they work:

Tape the layout paper to the floor. The pattern paper comes in easily handled sheets. Tape the layout paper sheets to the floor, colored side up, about ½ inch away from the wall. (The ½-inch

---

Great Gadgets & Gizmos

☞ **Profile gauge** This device has sliding metal rods that adjust when you push them against a wall, molding, and so forth. Transfer the shape of the gauge to the flooring material, and use it as a pattern for cutting.

☞ **Slamscraper** This tool is designed to remove tough old adhesive from flooring. Its long handle and slide-action design work like a champ to make a dreaded job easier. It's made by Red Devil, Inc., 2400 Vauxhall Road, Union, NJ 07083-1933.

---

space is used later for the tracing disk.) Move along the wall, taping pieces together to the old floor to make a complete pattern of the room.

Cut small paper patterns. Use small pieces of paper to make detailed patterns of moldings, doorjambs, casings, and tricky corners.

Trace the outline. The kit provides a wheel with a hole in it, where you place a pen. Just hold the pen straight and run the wheel along the walls and other obstructions to transfer the exact shape of the room to the pattern.

Transfer the room shape. Unroll the new flooring material on a clean surface, and place the pattern on it. Move the pattern around until you find the best position, so the pattern will look its best. Transfer the layout line on the pat-

USING A PAPER PATTERN
TO INSTALL VINYL SHEET FLOORING

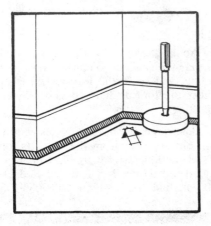

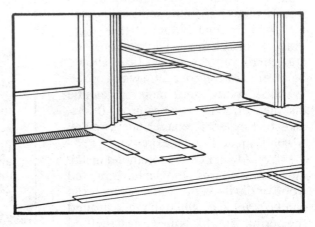

1. Place the paper on the floor so it is at least ½ inch from the wall. Then, using the special tracing wheel, transfer the exact shape of your room to the paper pattern.

2. Copy the shape of the door trim or other intricate patterns to the paper. Then roll it up and carry the pattern to the vinyl sheet.

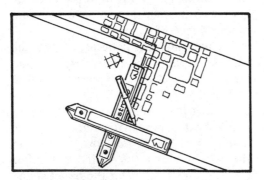

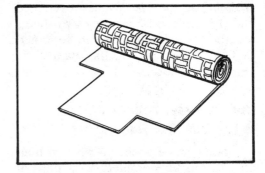

3. Transfer the room outline to the vinyl sheet with the straightedge provided. Then cut the sheet to size.

4. Roll up the vinyl sheet and carry it to the room. Install the flooring with mastic or staples according to the manufacturer's specifications.

tern to the new floor by laying one edge of the transfer guide on the pattern line and running the pen down the other edge.

Installing Vinyl Sheeting

Vinyl seamless flooring should be considered a flooring system. Each manufacturer has a recommended mastic or seaming adhesive. Each flooring material also requires slightly different installation procedures. But all manufacturers provide detailed installation instructions and booklets. Be sure to read these carefully and purchase the recommended adhesives. Follow these tips to make your installation run smoothly:

Ventilate. Seaming adhesives and some floor mastics are flammable and give off explosive fumes. Provide plenty of ventilation, and turn off the pilot lights to the stove and water heater if you are working near them.

Undercut jambs. Place a sheet of new flooring next to the jamb, and mark its thickness on the jamb. Now cut into the jamb about ½ inch deep at the mark, and remove the small slice of jamb. The flooring can then be slipped under the jamb, a much easier approach than trying to trim the flooring to fit the jamb. If after you install the floor, the gap between the jamb and floor is noticeable, fill the cracks with latex caulk. You can paint the caulk the next time you paint the jamb.

Warm the sheeting. When working the sheet into tight corners, we found it helpful to heat the sheet a little with a heat gun to make it more bendable. Be careful not to melt the vinyl, and remember, if you stretch the material, it will eventually return to its original shape.

Use a straightedge. Don't try to cut sheet goods freehand. Use a metal straightedge, such as a carpenter's framing square, to guide your utility knife blade as you trim the flooring flush against walls and counters. Lay a straightedge on the flooring and push it tightly against the wall or other object, then run the blade down the steel edge to cut the flooring.

Don't wipe adhesive. If you get some seam adhesive on the floor where it does not belong, allow it to dry undisturbed. The adhesive melts the flooring, and you will make a worse mess if you try to wipe it up. Don't touch the area for at least 2 hours. With use after time, the shiny spot will dull and not be noticeable.

Installing Prefinished Hardwood Floors

Traditionally, installing hardwood floors has been a job for pros. The solid hardwood strips can shrink and leave gaps after they are installed, and they need to be edge-nailed into place.

But the advent of prefinished laminated wood flooring has made this a feasible do-it-yourself project. This flooring comes in planks of random or uniform length or in parquet tiles. The material consists of several layers of wood with a hardwood veneer on top. This laminating process makes the flooring much more dimensionally stable than solid wood, eliminating the shrinkage problem. It also makes it possible to produce the flooring in thicknesses of ⅜ or ½ inch instead of the ¾-inch standard for solid strip flooring.

The plank flooring has precisely cut tongues on one edge and one end, and grooves milled into the other edge and end. These joints make it possible for the floor to be glued in place or installed on a foam bed in a method called floating the floor.

The parquet tiles come in several sizes and can be made from a wide variety of woods. Installation is not much more involved than laying vinyl floor tile. The wood tiles have to be cut with a saw, but the installation process is similar.

There is one significant disadvantage to laminated flooring, though. Because the hardwood surface is only a thin veneer, you can't refinish the floor by resanding.

Getting Ready for a Professional Installer

If you've decided to hire a professional floor installer to lay a hardwood floor in a room, you can save some of his labor charges by preparing the room. When he arrives, you'll be paying him for his skilled labor, not to do grunt work anyone could perform.

Empty the room of its furnishings. You can leave the pictures on the wall and clothes on hangers in the closet, but everything else should go. If there's wall-to-wall carpeting, pull it up, along with its padding. Use pliers to pull out staples in the floor, and with a pry bar remove the wood strips that the carpeting was attached to. If there were floor tiles, follow the suggestions in "Pulling Up an Old Floor." Use a vacuum cleaner to remove all dirt and debris from the room. The crevice tool is especially handy for getting dust between the wall and flooring.

Preparing the Floor

The preparation for installing a strip or parquet floor is the same for either a no-nail or a floating floor. Before you begin any layout or purchase any materials, you must provide a stable, smooth subfloor. See the previous sections on checking out what's under the old floor.

It's possible to install this type of floor on most solid flooring, but this creates a problem at the doorjambs and thresholds if you are installing the new floor over several old floors. The new floor will be much higher than adjoining rooms. The headroom in your doorway might even begin to get a little tight if you have a tall person in your family.

Your new floor will be easier to install, and you will get a better job, if you remove all old layers of floor right down to the subfloor. If there is adhesive on the subfloor, it must be scraped clean. The subfloor should be completely dry and free of dirt and dust.

Prepare Baseboard and Door Trim

Remove the baseboard. This way you can leave a ⅜ or ½-inch gap between the wall and the flooring. The gap will give you a margin of error to work with and will allow a little room for the floor to expand and contract. Just make sure the baseboard is thicker than the gap, so it will overlap the floor when you reinstall it. To remove baseboard, pry it off the wall and then use the claw of your hammer to pull the nails through the back of the baseboard. Just hook a nail and bend the hammer over sideways. This will avoid marring the face of the baseboard.

Undercut the door casing. Unless you have removed several layers of old flooring, the new floor will be slightly higher than the old one. If this is the case, you have to cut the bottom of the door casing so the flooring can be slipped under it.

The easiest way to do this is to place a scrap of the new flooring next to the door casing, then rest your saw blade on the flooring and cut into the casing. Placing the flooring scrap under the saw raises it off the subfloor the thickness of the new flooring, assuring an accurate cut.

Lay Out the Floor

Here are a few pointers to keep in mind when laying out the floor:

▶ If the room has an odd-shaped doorway or projection, such as a built-in book cabinet or fireplace, begin there. Otherwise, lay out the planks on the longest wall. You should avoid having to cut a thin strip of planking on a prominent wall.

▶ Make a paper template for doorways and around radiators. Cut the shape out of paper, and then transfer it onto the planking, being careful to cut on the correct side of the planking.

▶ Lay out the floor strips in a random pattern. Stagger the end joints so they're not lined up.

▶ Allow for about a ⅜ to ¼-inch gap at the walls, so the planking can expand and contract. This space will be covered with base shoe or baseboard.

▶ Plan ahead before you cut a plank. Each plank needs a tongue on one end and a groove on the other unless it will be installed with its cut end against the wall.

▶ After laying out an area in the room with planks cut to fit, dry fit them for a final test before spreading any adhesive or applying glue to the joints. Make sure all tongue-and-groove joints fit together snugly.

Installing a No-Nail Strip Floor with Adhesive

Use a notched trowel to spread adhesive on the floor. Use an adhesive recommended by the manufacturer. As you lay down sections of flooring, walk over them to press them down.

For a typical 12 × 14-foot bedroom, expect to spend at least a day laying out and installing the flooring. It's important to take your time, especially when cutting and installing the flooring.

Installing a Floating Plank Floor

With this system, the flooring is not nailed or glued to the floor; instead, it floats on top of a foam underlayment. The planks themselves are glued together to form a continuous floor. The foam acts as a cushion between the underlayment and the planks to eliminate squeaks. Here is what's involved in installing this type of floor:

Step 1: After doing the preparatory work already described, sweep the floor and spread out the ⅛-inch-thick foam underlayment. Trim it with scissors or a utility knife to fit the room.

Step 2: Arrange the planks on the subfloor so they are in a random pattern. Maintain ½-inch spacing between the flooring and walls to allow for expansion. Cut short pieces of the flooring, and tape them to the baseboards to act as spacers.

Step 3: After you have loosely laid out several feet of planks in a random pattern, check the fit of each joint. Also

INSTALLING A FLOATING PLANK FLOOR

1. Lay the thin foam sheeting over any sound, smooth, level floor. Use a sharp utility knife or scissors to cut the sheet to fit the room.

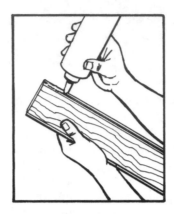

2. Apply carpenter's glue to the groove on each plank before you place it in position.

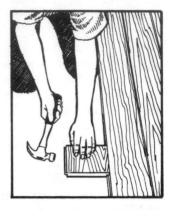

3. Fit a mating piece of scrap against the edge of the flooring, and hit it with a hammer to ensure that all the joints are tight. Check this carefully; you can't redo the joint after the glue has dried.

check the fit of the end joints. You must have a tongue on one side and a groove on the other.

Step 4: Apply carpenter's glue to the tongue and groove of each plank, then join the planks. Make sure the joints are tight by tapping each plank into place with a mallet or hammer. To protect the tongue and groove, fit a mating piece of scrap into the plank you are fitting, and hit the scrap. Use a damp rag to wipe up any glue that squeezes out of the joints.

Step 5: Replace the baseboards.

Installing Parquet Floor Tiles

These floor tiles (usually about ⅜ inch thick and 12 inches square) are installed on a subfloor using adhesive. They are installed exactly the same as a vinyl tile floor except that you have to cut the hardwood tiles with a saw. You should also cut the door casing using a parquet tile as a guide, as already described in the plank flooring section.

Finishing Off with Baseboard

Many of these new flooring systems are sold with matching wood baseboards, which you install with finishing nails or construction adhesive. You can also reuse the original baseboard if you are careful in removing it from the room.

Building a Stove Hearth

When we moved into our present house, we found a cracked wood stove sitting smack dab in the middle of one wall. Unfortunately, the stove was beyond repair. But the chimney was in fairly good shape.

It takes special tools and skills to line a chimney and install a stove, so we hired a professional to do those tasks. But we saved money by building our own tile hearth, a project that proved simple enough for most any do-it-yourselfer to tackle.

While there is nothing difficult about building this hearth, you must make sure its construction and positioning conform with your local building code. Most localities have strict requirements as to the distance a stove can be located from any combustible object. A drywall or plaster wall, furniture, and just about anything not made from concrete or stone are considered combustible. Consult with your stove installer and your local building department before building the hearth.

This hearth should conform to most building codes. Essentially, it consists of a piece of sheet metal placed on the floor, covered by two sheets of ½-inch cement board (Wonder Board). On top of this you can install tile, bricks, or slate. We chose quarry tile set in epoxy. This gave us a noncombustible platform about 1½ inches off of the floor's surface. The exact height will depend on the thickness of the material you use. This thickness probably is more than your code requires, especially if you install a heat shield on the bottom of the stove, but it is better to be conservative.

Here's how to build the hearth:

Do a layout.   Determine the size of the hearth, then pick your tiles and decide how many you will need to cover the area. Use graph paper (or a computer graphic program) to make a rough sketch of the hearth. Then see how the tiles will

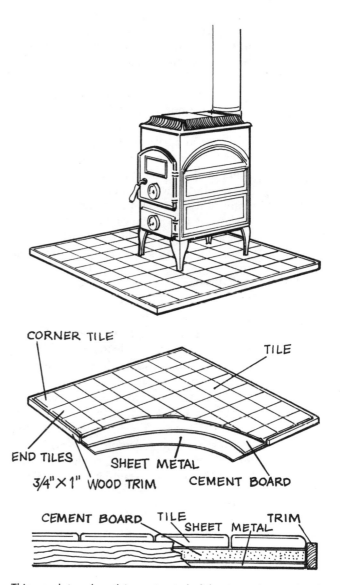

This wood stove hearth is constructed of sheet metal topped with cement board and tile. It is trimmed with wood.

fit. Unless you are restricted by space, it's easier to adjust the dimensions of the hearth to use whole tiles than to cut the tiles to fit.

Order materials.   You'll need bull-nose tiles around the perimeter and bullnose corner tiles at the corners. The bullnose tiles have one rounded edge, while the corner tiles have two perpen-dicular rounded edges. Standard tiles are used in the interior field. In addition, you'll need epoxy mortar, grout, cement board, and a piece of sheet metal. Finally, you'll need $\frac{3}{4} \times 1$-inch wood trim for the perimeter. The wood can be painted or stained to match your decor.

Nail down the edging.   Draw the overall dimensions of the hearth on the floor. Then cut sections of edging to fit inside these layout lines. The edging is installed so the $\frac{3}{4}$-inch side is against the floor. Use 4d finishing nails to hold it in place.

Position the sheet metal.   Cut the sheet metal to fit inside the edging. Place its shiny side up, so it will reflect the heat away from the floor.

Lay the cement board.   Use a cir-cular saw fitted with a masonry blade to cut the cement board to fit inside the edging. Cutting cement board will raise clouds of very fine dust, so do this work outdoors and wear a dust mask. Secure the cement board in place with 2-inch all-purpose screws. Drill pilot holes through the cement board with a masonry drill. Countersink the screw heads so they are flush with the surface.

Install the tile.   Mix epoxy mortar according to the manufacturer's direc-tions. Spread it on the cement board with a trowel that has $\frac{1}{4}$-inch notches. Set the tiles. We found that it's easier on a small job like this to lay the outside bullnose tiles first and then set the field tiles. Clean up any epoxy with a damp rag before it sets, and allow the tiles to set overnight.

Grout the joints.   Prepare the grout and use a short piece of plywood or a rubber float to work the grout into the joints. Work in one small area at a time. Use the float to scrape off as much grout as possible from the tile faces, and then wipe up the rest with a damp rag or sponge. Clean the rag or sponge by rins-ing it in a bucket of water. Be sure to wring out the rag to remove as much water as possible.

When the grout has dried, the hearth is ready for stove installation.

CHAPTER 7

Lighting

Lighting in most houses is inadequate. Older homes often were built with one lonely light fixture in the ceiling of each room and a wall outlet or two for lamps. New houses come with lighting that meets the National Electrical Code, but these are bare minimums.

Moreover, lighting often is overlooked when do-it-yourself remodeling plans are made. Yet there's no more opportune time to upgrade wiring and fixtures than while you are opening or repairing walls or installing new cabinets or other built-ins. When you are planning a project, the lighting scheme deserves as much thought as you give the choice of a floor plan, materials, or colors. It's just as important to the overall success of your project.

Most wiring projects, short of installing new service, can be handled by the homeowner who takes the time to understand exactly what he is doing. But before you begin any wiring project, consult with your local building department. Some building codes require all work be done by a licensed electrician; others will issue homeowner permits and provide an inspection.

Most municipalities adopt the National Electrical Code, but many revise parts of the code to suit their own needs. If you do the work yourself, make sure you find out what materials and techniques are allowed in your community. In many cases wiring, cables, boxes, and devices that do not meet the local electrical codes are sold in local stores. For instance, some cities do not allow nonmetallic (Romex) cable and plastic junction boxes. They require wiring to be run through metal conduit for new work and armored cable (BX) for remodeling work.

This chapter will not attempt to tell you how to rewire your house. Rather, it explains simple lighting improvements you can make to your house—easy-to-do ideas to let you have light where you need it. This will make your home more comfortable, convenient, and safer to live in. But first, a few words about the basics of lighting design.

Basics of Good Lighting

Each room in your house needs three distinct types of lighting—general, task, and accent:

▶ General lighting is for overall illumination. It provides comfortable background brightness, usually in the form of an overhead ceiling fixture.

▶ Task lighting is for a specific function, such as reading a book, chopping vegetables, or putting on makeup.

▶ Accent lighting is to show off a partic-

ular area or object. It can be a floor lamp shining up into plants or a ceiling spotlight highlighting a wall of artwork.

Bathroom Basics

Shaving, applying makeup, and hair styling require both general lighting and task lighting. Many bathrooms have only one source of light—a single overhead fixture or a light over the medicine cabinet. This makes the bathroom a good candidate for upgraded lighting.

Any remodeling plan for the bathroom should take into consideration its basic lighting needs. The bathroom of average size requires three fixtures:

▶ For general lighting there should be a ceiling fixture of at least 120 watts if you are using an incandescent light bulb fixture or 40 watts if you are using a more efficient fluorescent fixture. This fixture should be located over the front edge of the sink. This often is a good place for a vent-and-light combination fixture because rooms often need additional ventilation.

▶ To provide adequate task lighting at the mirror, two side fixtures of at least 75 watts (20 watts fluorescent) should be located at average eye level—about 60 inches above the floor and at least 30 inches apart to keep glare out of your direct line of sight.

▶ You'll probably need a light over the tub. Often there is a soffit over the tub that blocks out some light, and a shower curtain that blocks out even more. So it's a good idea to add a special waterproof tub fixture.

Whenever you add to or change wiring, you'll need to meet the current electrical codes for the municipality in which

All rooms should have general lighting, such as the ceiling fixture in this kitchen, to provide overall illumination. A work area, such as a kitchen sink or range, should also be illuminated with task lighting, which is tailored to the specific needs of the area. Wall texture, ceiling moldings, and works of art can be highlighted with accent lighting. This type of lighting can be recessed in the ceiling, as illustrated, or mounted on tracks.

you live. For bathrooms, this usually means adding a ground fault interrupter (GFI) device on all outlets to prevent shocks. A GFI is a good addition even if it is not required. See the "Installing a GFI" section of chapter 9.

Kitchen Basics

The kitchen is a task-oriented room. When planning any renovation or remodeling, no matter how small, try to work in lighting improvements. Even if

Minimum General Lighting Recommendations

Kitchen Area	Incandescent Light	Fluorescent Light
Small (less than 75 sq. ft.)	2-3 bulbs (total 150 watts)	55-70 watts
Average (75-150 sq. ft.)	2-4 bulbs (total 150-200 watts)	60-80 watts
Large (more than 150 sq. ft.)	2 watts per sq. ft.	¾ watt per sq. ft.

Minimum Task Lighting Recommendations

Sink/Range	Under-Cabinet	Work Island
2 recessed fixtures 15″-18″ apart; 75 watts incandescent or 40 watts fluorescent	8 watts fluorescent per ft. of counter	8 watts fluorescent per ft. of counter

it's a budget face-lift, you will appreciate upgraded lighting for years to come.

A kitchen of average size should have at least 150 to 200 watts of incandescent lighting in a large overhead fixture. A large fixture that contains several bulbs will provide better overall illumination. More efficient lighting of equal brightness can be provided by a fluorescent fixture with at least two 40-watt tubes.

Along with general illumination, kitchen lighting should provide adequate brightness in every work area. Here are the areas in your kitchen that should receive their own task lighting:

Over the sink: A fixture with a strong downlight is needed over the sink for preparing food and cleaning dishes. Recessed can lights are a natural for this application. These are available with standard incandescent lights or with efficient fluorescent tubes.

If the sink is located under a window and there are cabinets on both sides of the window, you can install a fluorescent fixture on the soffit or ceiling above the sink and shield the tubes with a valance.

Over counters: For easy recipe reading and chopping or mixing food, good counter lighting is needed. The easiest way to provide this light is to mount fluorescent fixtures under your wall cabinets. Place the fixtures as close to the fronts of the cabinets as possible, to direct most of the light to your work area. If the tubes are visible, you may have to add a strip of wood to the bottom front edge of the cabinet to act as a valance to shade any tube glare.

Over ranges and cook tops: Preparing food at the range and oven requires light. This is often built into appliances or range hoods. If not, consider adding a hood with a light, or install fluorescent or recessed lighting over the stove area.

Over tables and built-in seating: Eat-in kitchens with tables and chairs also require task lighting. Put a dimmer switch on this lighting, so you can provide the high levels of light needed for family activities, such as playing games or doing homework, and also be able to dim the light for dining.

Dining Room Basics

Most dining rooms have adequate light. But with a few changes you can dramatically change the look and feel of the room. Here are a few tips to consider when planning a dining room face-lift:

Scale the chandelier. The size of a chandelier should be in inches what the diagonal of the room is in feet. But it should be no larger than the width of the table less 12 inches, so people won't bump their heads when rising or passing the table.

Don't hang a chandelier too low. Be sure that diners can see one another across the table unobstructed; 30 to 36 inches above the table is the rule of thumb.

Choose the right fixture. A good dining room fixture provides both general illumination, by reflecting light off the ceiling, and task lighting, by directing light down on the table.

Install a dimmer. For a chandelier to provide adequate general lighting, it must be bright. But when you sit down to the table, a brightly burning chandelier does not set the proper mood. A dimmer will let you create a variety of moods.

Use pendants or wall sconces. Suspend pendant lights over your buffet, or install wall sconces, to provide task lighting there. Recessed can lights are another

MAKE A VALANCE TO SHADE UNDER-CABINET LIGHTING

Cabinets with shallow recesses allow light fixtures to be seen, causing glare to anyone who is seated in the kitchen or who is not standing directly at the counter.

One solution to this problem is to construct a simple valance out of matching wood and screw it to the bottom of the cabinet. In most cases the wood strip has to be no more than 1 to 1½ inches wide. Make the strip from ¾-inch stock, and stain it to match the cabinet. Drill pilot holes for the screws through the edge of the strip. Then attach the strip to the front lip of the cabinet with #8 × 1½-inch flathead wood screws.

alternative. Both these sources should be controlled by dimmer switches.

Light cabinets. Adding lights inside a china cabinet can add just the right amount of light to a dark corner while highlighting your china.

Lighting Dos and Don'ts

▶ If you're remodeling, think about your lighting needs in the planning stages; it's much easier and less costly to run new electrical lines and add circuits when walls are open.

▶ Do not place any lighting directly over people's heads, for example, directly over a sofa or chair. Eyebrows shield the eyes from the light, reducing illumination. At the same time, the shadows create unattractive dark circles under the eyes.

▶ Task lighting should either shine down over your shoulder from slightly behind and above, or come from a wall, desk, or lamp focused directly on the work you're doing. You should never be able to view an exposed bulb while you're working.

▶ Reading lamp placement is important. If you're right-handed, the light source should come over your left shoulder. The reverse is true for you lefties! You tend to move in the direction of the side you use most, thus blocking a badly placed light and creating a shadow on the page you're reading.

▶ Light stairwells with several lights, as opposed to a single light that may cause deep shadows.

▶ A lamp in a child's room should be at a safe height, so there's no danger of it breaking during playtime.

Computer in the House?

Your house might not be an electronic cottage yet, but a home computer will probably be in place somewhere in your house in the not-too-distant future. Whether for a home office or homework, here are a few tips on how you can properly light this area. These points also apply to the TV screen:

General lighting: The room should be bright enough to minimize the contrast between the brightness of the computer screen and that of the work area, yet subdued enough to prevent glare and fixture reflection on the screen.

If the work area is near a window, position the monitor (computer screen) at a right angle to the window to prevent incoming sunlight from shining in either the operator's eyes or onto the screen and causing glare.

Task lighting: Light fixtures in the vicinity of the computer should illuminate the area around the screen while also lighting the keyboard and tabletop work area. To help prevent glare, a neutral-colored matt surface should cover the work surface.

Working with a Lighting Specialist

A lighting specialist works with a client to effectively use daylight and electrical light in a room. Many times, the cost of a lighting specialist can be paid back in reduced energy consumption.

In a kitchen, for example, a lighting specialist can specify energy-efficient fixtures that will replace high-wattage incandescent units and save you money in lower lighting costs and in reduced air-conditioning costs. Since fluorescent lights are more efficient, they don't contribute excess heat to the room.

An alternative to hiring a lighting specialist is to work with a lighting consultant, employed by most large showrooms. These consultants assist you in buying fixtures. Ask for someone certified by the American Home Lighting Institute or someone who has attended classes sponsored by this group. There is usually no charge for their services, since they are selling you fixtures.

Before you consult with a lighting specialist or consultant, do a little homework. Prepare an accurate drawing of the area you want to remodel. Then have answers to the following questions you'll likely be asked:

▶ What is your budget?

▶ What is your time frame for the project?

▶ What is your lifestyle?

Make a list of how you and your family use the area. The list will guide the specialist in analyzing your needs.

How much work do you want a specialist to do? You can hire a lighting specialist just to supply a plan, or you can have him handle the whole project from design through supervising the electricians.

The least expensive way to consult with a lighting specialist is to come prepared with an accurate drawing of your project. This way, it shouldn't require more than a couple of hours of design time to prepare a drawing with clearly marked fixture locations. Also indicated will be the type of light best suited for the job and a basic wiring diagram.

Light Bulb Savvy

Incandescent: The ordinary light bulb we're all familiar with is called an incandescent lamp. It gives off a warm light rich in red and yellow tones. Most people and colors look good under this warm light. Incandescent lamps are the least expensive to purchase but the most expensive to operate. They come in a wide variety of wattages, several shapes, and various coatings.

Fluorescent: Fluorescent tubes cost more than light bulbs, but they last longer and are much cheaper to operate, since they use less electricity to produce the same amount of light as a standard incandescent light bulb. The older tubes produce a source of light that is rich in blue-green tones. This light is considered acceptable for the office, but for years many objected to it in the home. Now newer fluorescent tubes are coated with minerals that let it admit a light richer in red and closer to the incandes-

cent lamp. If you have not replaced a fluorescent tube in several years, try the new warmer tubes.

Compact fluorescent fixtures: These fixtures are now manufactured with tubes that are folded and twisted into small packages not much larger than a standard light bulb. They are now available in recessed fixtures and small units for under cabinets.

Quartz halogen: This is a special-purpose high-intensity source of light. Halogen bulbs produce a bright, white light that is close in color to daylight (halogen bulbs are used as video recorder and movie lights). These lights put out a lot of heat, so they must be used in special fixtures.

Torchère lights, those modern-looking, upward-shining floor lamps, use high-capacity halogen lights to pack a lot of power in a small package. Some track lights, especially spots, use small halogen bulbs. Lighting designers like halogen lights in these fixtures because they give easily controlled, high-intensity light.

Track Lighting

You'll find the wiring systems for track lighting ideal for expanding your lighting without having to completely rewire the room. You can use power from an existing overhead light or from a wall outlet. Instead of running wires behind the walls, which is costly, you can run the wires in tracks mounted on the walls.

The choice of fixtures you can hang from the track system is extensive. Floods, spots, high-intensity lights, even small fans can be plugged into the track.

The track can be powered from an existing overhead box. If that's not possible, the track can be "end-fed" by install-

Spot or flood lights attached to a track that supports the lights and provides power is one way to add accent or task lighting to a room.

switch. Another option is to lead the wire from the track end to a wall receptacle that is already controlled by a switch. Many rooms without overhead lights have one or more of the wall receptacles wired to a switch so lamps can be conveniently turned on and off. There are many manufacturers of these products, and they all have similar, but slightly different, features. Each system comes with complete installation directions that you should follow. Here are some general tips to help you breeze through a typical installation:

Don't overload existing wiring. Most lighting circuits are rated at 15 amps. When you plan your track lighting system, do not include so many devices that you overload the circuit.

Don't overload the track. Check the electrical current capacity of the track. Most are rated for 20 amps. This figure is for the entire section of track that is fed from the same source of power.

If you are planning an extensive layout, say around the perimeter of a room, consider breaking the track into two circuits. You can feed power into the track from only one source. Use insulated end sections to terminate the track, then install the track with the insulated ends butted together. This way each half of the track is insulated from the other, but from the floor it looks like a continuous loop.

Plan the track locations. Plan the track location so the lights will not shine directly into your eyes. Sometimes placing track lighting can be a challenge. Before you finalize your layout, check out how the lighting will look from every location in the room. Have someone standing on a ladder where you plan to install the light shine a flashlight in the direc-

ing an adapter with a cord attached to it at the end of the track. You can then run the cord down the wall to an outlet. Most of these cords have a line switch so the lights on the track can be controlled. This wiring could also be concealed with a surface-mounted wiring system. Then you could install a conventional toggle

tion you plan to aim it. Then walk around the room and sit in various locations to check for glare.

Cut the tracks. Some track systems have special sections that are adjustable in length, but most you need to cut with a hacksaw. Don't forget to allow for the end fitting. Most of the time, you have to cut the track slightly short to compensate for the thickness of this fitting.

Observe polarity marks. All tracks and plug-in devices are marked with positive and neutral sides. Some systems are designed to make it hard to hook them up wrong, but take the time to check that you have observed polarity.

Switches

In the early days of electrical lighting, the most common switch had two big buttons, one for on and one for off. They were sturdy switches that required a healthy push to operate their spring-loaded contacts, and many of them are still in service today. If you have an old house with such switches, you'll probably want to keep them, even if you are rewiring. They are just as easy to replace later if they break, and they have a definite old-house charm. Also, they often are accompanied by heavy brass switch plates that look terrific when you polish them up. Of course, after 50 or 60 years the mechanical contacts on these old switches are bound to break. When this happens, you have a choice. You can install modern switches and switch plates with them. Or you can buy replacement push-button switches, which have shorter buttons and lack the sound and feel of the old-time switches. These replacement switches are no better than other modern switches, but because they are a spe-

HOW TO FIGURE LOAD

Since most circuits are rated to carry 15 to 20 amps of current, you should make a rough estimate of how much of this capacity is in use before you add an additional lighting load to the circuit.

The easiest way to do this is to find the circuit breaker or fuse that services the circuit and check its rating. Then turn on everything that you think is on the circuit. Go back and turn off the circuit breaker or unscrew the fuse; everything on that circuit should now be off.

Add up the watt rating for each bulb or appliance, and divide this figure by 115 to get a rough idea of the load on the circuit. Subtract this figure from the fuse or circuit breaker rating, and you have the amount of additional load you may safely add to the circuit.

cialty item available from reproduction hardware companies, they cost at least five times as much.

There are, of course, reasons to replace switches that still work; you may want to install a dimmer, for example. If you do decide to replace a switch, you'll find it is about the easiest and cheapest remodeling task you'll do. And today, you have a wide variety of switches to choose from.

The cheapest and most common switch is the standard toggle. New toggle switches are silent, have very few moving parts, and should last a long time. A rocker switch that is easy to see and push is another alternative. This switch has a rocker that is about an inch wide and 3 inches long. To turn the light on, all you have to do is push the top half of the rocker. To turn the switch off, press the lower half. Everyone in the family can operate this type of switch. There are also switches that glow when they are off so you can find them in the dark.

Replacing a Switch

First we'll discuss the switching situations you might encounter. Then we'll give you the simple step-by-step procedure for replacing any switch.

Single-pole switch: The most common switch is of the type called single pole; it is the only switch controlling the branch circuit it serves. Older single-pole switches have only two terminals, one connected to a hot wire coming in and the other connected to an outgoing wire that is hot when the switch is on. It doesn't matter which wire is connected to which terminal, because all the switch does, in effect, is touch the wires together when it is on and pull them apart when it is off. Some newer switches have grounding terminals. These are hooked up the same way, but they also have a green terminal attached to the yoke for the ground wire. We'll discuss the ground wire later.

If, when you open the box of a single-pole switch, you find only one cable coming into it, this is a switch loop, a run of wire serving only the switch. One of the wires going to the switch will be black. If the wiring is in shielded cable, such as Romex, the other wire going to the switch will be white, and it should have a bit of black tape or paint on it to identify it as a hot wire. However, if the wiring was done with separate conductors run in conduit, the second wire could be any color. It doesn't matter; just hook one wire to

each brass terminal. Other wires may be connected in the box, probably with wire nuts. Leave those alone unless you'll be grounding the switch as described next.

Three-way switches: Most houses have at least one set of three-way switches. You'll usually find them at the top and bottom of staircases or at each end of a long hallway. These are switches that let you turn a circuit on or off from either switch, regardless of whether the other switch is on or off.

The first step in replacing a three-way switch is finding out which one is faulty. With old push-button switches you can sometimes tell by just taking the switches out of the boxes. The mechanical contact mechanisms are exposed, and you'll probably find a broken contact arm. For other switches, you'll need a continuity tester—an inexpensive battery-operated device with an alligator clip on one end and a probe and light on the other. Turn off the power at the service box and remove the switch. You'll find two brass terminals and a dark terminal marked "common." Put the tester's alligator clip on the common terminal, and touch the probe to either of the brass terminals. The tester light should come on when the switch is in one position, either up or down. Leave the switch in the position that activated the light, and move the probe to the other brass terminal. The light should not come on until you flip the switch to the other position.

The wires coming into a three-way switch could be various colors. Like a single-pole switch, all the wires are hot. But unlike a single pole, it matters which wire is connected to which terminal. Your best bet is to draw a diagram of the switch showing which wires go where before you disconnect them.

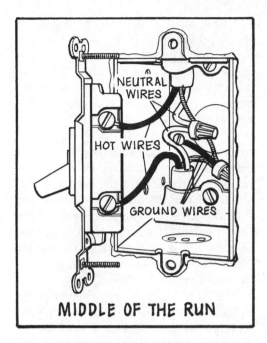

MIDDLE OF THE RUN

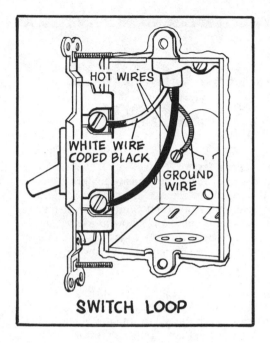

SWITCH LOOP

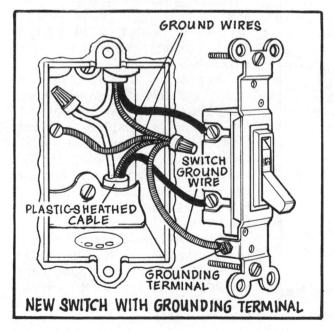

NEW SWITCH WITH GROUNDING TERMINAL

Single-pole switches can be wired in the middle of a run or as a switch loop. Some new switches have grounding terminals that should be connected to the cable ground wire and the grounding screw in the box.

Great Gadgets & Gizmos

☞ **Neon voltage tester** Every home electrician should have one of these inexpensive testers in his toolbox. It's your best defense against shock. The device consists of two contact prongs with a tiny neon light between them. Here's how to use it:

To test whether a receptacle is live, put one prong in each receptacle slot except the ground hole. If the tester glows, there's electricity in the receptacle.

To test a switch, carefully remove the switch plate. Touch one of the probes to the brass screw that the black wire is attached to, and the other lead to the box. If the tube glows, the switch is hot. If you have a plastic box, then the other lead should touch the green or bare ground wire. Be careful until you know the circuit is dead; treat it as if there is power in the box.

☞ **Three-wire circuit analyzer** This inexpensive device can help you pinpoint wiring problems. It has three lights that glow in combinations that tell you whether you have an open ground, open neutral, open hot, reversed ground, reversed neutral, or correct wiring.

☞ **Wire Light** This product is designed to take the difficulty out of working at ceiling level when replacing a fixture. You attach the plate to the box at the ceiling, then wire up the fixture to its jack at your work surface. The jack screws into the ceiling box, and you finish it off with the fixture's canopy. It is made by The Wiremold Company, 60 Woodlawn Street, West Hartford, CT 06110.

One more point before we get into the step-by-step. When you buy a switch, make sure you get one that can carry enough amperage. Most circuits in your house will be 15 amps, but check the marking on the fuse or circuit breaker before you buy a switch.

Step 1: Turn off the juice. This is the most important step. At your electrical service box, turn off the circuit breaker or pull the fuse serving the switch. Check to make sure the switch can no longer provide power to the receptacle or fixture it serves. If, for any reason, you are uncertain that you've turned off the right circuit, turn off all power to the house at the main breaker or fuse.

Step 2: Remove the switch plate and pull the switch. Take off the switch plate by removing the two switch plate screws. Next remove the two screws, at the top and bottom of the switch, that hold it in the wall box, and pull the bad switch out of the box, being careful not to touch the terminals.

Step 3: Test the circuit. To make sure the circuit is off, use a neon voltage tester. This consists of two probes attached to insulated wire, with a small light between. Touch one probe to the side of the electrical box and the other to each switch terminal in succession. If the light comes on at any time, the switch is still hot. Play it safe and turn off all power to the house before going further.

Step 4: Make a diagram if you need to, and when you are sure the power is off, disconnect the wires. Some newer switches and receptacles are not connected by terminals but are back-wired into terminal holes that use internal spring clips instead of screws to hold the wire.

You probably won't encounter this since you are probably replacing an old switch, but if you do, there's a little release slot under each hole. Stick the end of your screwdriver in the slot to release the wire.

If you haven't bought your new switch yet, you can put electrical tape on the ends of the wires, stick them back in the box, replace the switch plate, and turn the power back on until you are ready to replace the switch.

Step 5: Install the new switch. Again, make sure the power is off. Connect the wires to the terminals, making sure the wire loops curl clockwise, the same direction the screw turns when you tighten it.

Step 6: Replace the ground wire. As mentioned, the new switch may have a green grounding terminal screw on the yoke. If the switch you are replacing had a green or bare wire attached to it, attach that wire to this screw. If the old switch didn't have this green screw but there is a green or bare wire running through the box, attach a short piece of 14-gauge green or bare wire to the screw and then use a wire nut to splice the other end of this wire into the green or bare wire running through the box.

Step 7: Reinstall the switch and plate. Push the switch back into the box, install the two screws that hold the switch in the box, and then install the switch plate.

Installing a Dimmer Switch

This is an improvement you'll appreciate every day, and it's so easy you will wonder why you didn't do it sooner! We started installing one over our dining room table an hour before dinner guests were expected. We had plenty of time left over to get dressed.

The dining room chandelier is, in fact, the most likely candidate for a dimmer switch. Even with low-wattage bulbs, most chandeliers are too bright for a comfortable evening dinner. With a dimmer switch you can control the intensity of any permanently installed incandescent light. Dimmers are available for fluorescent fixtures, but they are designed to work only with special fixtures that are designed to be dimmed. Also, dimmers cannot control motors or other appliances. Here are a few tips on shopping for and installing a dimmer switch:

All dimmers are not created equal. The most convenient models have a toggle switch that allows you to turn the light on and off by pushing in on the dial. This allows you to keep the intensity setting. Less-expensive models require that you turn the intensity knob to low and then off.

An even less-expensive variation is the high-low switch that provides only two levels of light: full on and a dimmed setting. The switch looks like a standard wall switch, except the switch toggle moves from off to an intermediate setting, then to high.

Don't overload dimmers. Most full-range dimmer switches are rated for a load of no more than 600 watts. This means you can control about five or six 100-watt bulbs with a single device—no more. This is seldom a problem, since each dimmer usually is connected to a single fixture. Even if your chandelier has multiple bulbs, they are usually less than 50 watts each. High-low dimmers are usually rated at 300 watts.

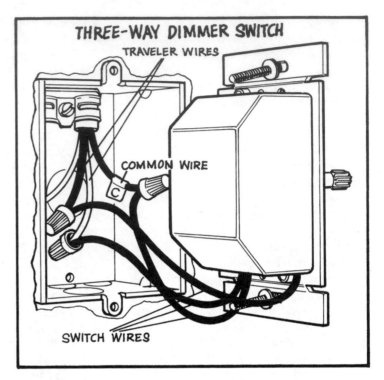

Dimmer switches are hooked up in the same way as other switches, except they usually have wire switch leads instead of terminals.

Use a dimmer for a three-way circuit. If you want to dim a light that is controlled by two switches, purchase a dimmer designed for a three-way circuit.

Whichever type of dimmer you choose, the installation is the same as for any other switch, except that many dimmers have wire leads instead of terminals, so you'll have to use wire nuts to wire the dimmer. Usually, dimmers come with wire nuts. A single-pole dimmer will have two black wires corresponding to the two brass terminals on other single-pole switches. A three-way dimmer will have two red wires and a black wire. The

black wire serves the same purpose as the common terminal on other three-way switches.

Receptacles

Replacing a receptacle takes about 10 minutes and costs less than $2. There are two main reasons you might want to do it. The first is that the receptacle may be damaged; maybe somebody yanked the vacuum cleaner cord and cracked it, or perhaps the slots are so worn with use that plugs don't stay in snugly.

Another reason is to install a grounded receptacle. Many older homes have receptacles with two slots that won't accept the three-pronged plugs on many modern appliances. You should be aware, however, that if your wiring is the oldest "knob-and-tube" type that consists of two wires run separately to each box, then chances are your electrical boxes are not grounded. If the boxes aren't grounded, you can't ground receptacles without rewiring the house. You may still want to install new three-slotted receptacles so you can plug in three-pronged appliances without adapters. The appliances will work, but be aware you won't be getting grounding protection.

In a nutshell, grounding protects against fire and shock by providing a path of least resistance directly to ground. This path usually is a series of wires (the bare wires in Romex cable) that link all boxes to ground. Electricity will take this path before paths of higher resistance, for example, worn insulation or your body. Run through worn insulation, electricity can cause fire. Through your body, of course, it can cause serious shock.

Before the advent of three-pronged appliances, it was considered adequate to ground all the boxes in a house, but not the receptacles. This provided fire protection and eliminated the possibility of getting a shock from a receptacle plate. If, when you remove the old two-slotted receptacle, you find one or more green or bare wires attached to the box at a screw, then the box is grounded and you can ground the new receptacle. If your house was wired with metal-armored cable, you can usually ground the receptacle even though there is no green or bare wire in the box. This is because the metal cable itself often was used as a grounding path for the boxes. You can

use your voltage tester to find out if a receptacle box is grounded. Put one probe on the receptacle cover screw. Put the other probe in each of the two slots. If one of the slots makes the tester light up, the box is grounded. You'll want to do this test after you install a new receptacle too.

Replacing a Receptacle

Before you replace a receptacle, make sure you buy one with the proper maximum amperage rating. Most circuits in your house probably are 15 amps, but check the marking on the circuit breaker or fuse before you buy the receptacle.

Here's the step-by-step for replacing a receptacle (it's the same procedure whether you have a single receptacle or several ganged in a box):

Step 1: Turn off the juice. This is the most important step. At your electrical service box, turn off the circuit breaker or pull the fuse serving the receptacle. Put the prongs of your circuit tester in the receptacle slots to make sure the power is off. If you don't have a tester, plug in a light or appliance that you know is in working order, and make sure it doesn't switch on. If, for any reason, you are uncertain that you've turned off the right circuit, turn off all power to the house at the main breaker or fuse.

Step 2: Remove the receptacle plate and receptacle. Remove the screw that attaches the plate to the box and remove the plate. Then remove the screws that attach the receptacle, and pull the receptacle out. If the receptacle is the last one on the circuit, you'll find a black wire going to a brass terminal and a white wire going to a silver terminal. If the circuit continues past the receptacle, you'll

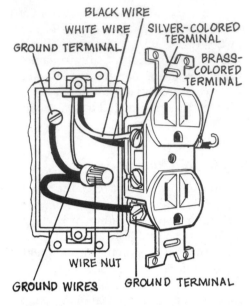

BLACK WIRE
WHITE WIRE
GROUND TERMINAL
SILVER-COLORED TERMINAL
BRASS-COLORED TERMINAL
WIRE NUT
GROUND WIRES
GROUND TERMINAL

Illustrated here is wiring for a receptacle at the end of a circuit run. If the circuit continued past this receptacle, there would be another cable entering the box, with its white wire connected to the empty silver terminal, its black wire connected to the empty brass terminal, and its bare ground wire spliced into the wire nut.

find two black wires, each going to a brass terminal, and two white wires, each going to a silver terminal. If the receptacle is grounded, there will be a green or bare wire attached to a green screw on the metal receptacle yoke. Note where the wires go, and disconnect them.

Step 3: Attach the white wires and black wires to the new receptacle in the same way they were attached to the old, making sure to put the wire loops on the terminal screws in a clockwise direction, the same direction the screws turn when you tighten them. If the old receptacle was grounded, reconnect the bare or green ground wire to the green screw on the receptacle yoke. If the old receptacle was not grounded but the box is, disconnect the green or bare ground wire from the screw attaching it to the box. Cut two 4-inch lengths of green wire. Attach one piece to the screw in the box and the other piece to the green screw on the receptacle. Use a wire nut to attach both wires to the green or bare wire or wires coming out of the cable or cables.

Step 4: Push the receptacle into the box, screw it into place, and replace the receptacle plate.

Surface-Wired Receptacles

Adding surface-wired receptacles is the easiest solution when you just don't have a receptacle in the place you need it. These receptacles are much easier to install than wiring in the wall.

However, adding receptacles, surface mounted or otherwise, is not a solution to inadequate electrical service. If the receptacles around your house are bristling with three-way adapters, you're creating a fire hazard that probably can be solved only by adding new circuits, or perhaps more service to your house. Frequently blown fuses or tripped circuit breakers are further evidence of inadequate wiring. Consult an electrician or get a thorough electrical wiring book.

If, on the other hand, you have an isolated situation where you find yourself using an extension cord without a three-way adapter, you probably don't need more power, you just need a more convenient receptacle. In this case a surface-mounted receptacle can be the most convenient solution. The drawback, of course, is that the metal channel that contains the wire is visible on the wall. This may not be as bad as it seems at first; most of the channel probably will be hidden by drapes, furniture, and other objects in the room.

Another use for surface wiring is to add a light fixture. You can run wire in a channel along walls and ceilings from a receptacle to a new switch to a fixture.

The first step in installing a surface-mounted receptacle or fixture is to decide where you want it and where the closest source of electricity is. Careful planning is the key to a successful job. You can run the channel just about anyplace, but in general, the more direct the path, the better and cheaper. However, the closest receptacle might not always be the best choice. The channel might be easiest to install and most inconspicuous if you run it halfway around the room rather than work it up and over a doorway, where it would require several turns and be highly visible.

Each manufacturer supplies complete instructions for installation and wiring, which should be followed. Also check out the system so you can become familiar with the components. Most systems have several types of channel, inside and outside corners, tees, and boxes. Just looking over the system will give you some ideas about where you can and can't run the wire and how it will look when you are done.

Remember to make sure the power to the source receptacle is off, as described in the section on replacing receptacles. To cut the channel, use a hacksaw with a fine-toothed blade—at least 32 teeth per inch. Here are some general guidelines for installing surface-wired receptacles and fixtures:

Install the extension box. Remove the plate screw and plate from the receptacle that will supply the power. Remove

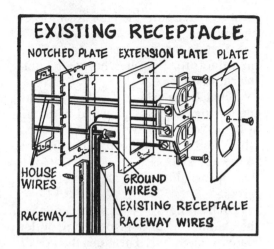

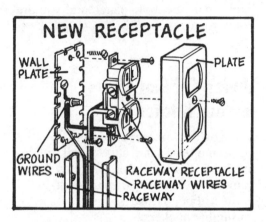

Surface wiring allows you to add receptacles, switches, and overhead lights without the hassle of pulling wires through the walls. Systems vary, but shown here is a typical installation from an existing receptacle to a new receptacle.

the screws holding the receptacle to the box. Put the extension box base plate over the existing box, and attach it with the screws that held the outlet in the box.

Run the channel base. The channel cover will run over a base, which you'll run from the supply receptacle to the new receptacle. Use a carpenter's level to make sure the base is run level and plumb.

Install the new outlet box. The manufacturer supplies hardware and instructions.

Install the cable. Carefully follow the wiring diagrams provided with the system. You will have to run a black, a white, and a green wire from the old box to the new one. Use 12-gauge wire for a 20-amp circuit and 14-gauge for a 15-amp circuit.

When the wire is in place, snap on the channel covers and install the outlet plates at each box. Then turn the power back on at the main panel, and you are ready to go.

Under-Cabinet Lights in Your Kitchen

You'll be amazed at how much easier, not to mention safer, cutting and preparing food is with additional lights under your cabinets. Using them as night lights in the kitchen is also a handy feature for midnight snackers.

Under-cabinet fluorescent fixtures come in two varieties. One type of fixture is equipped with a cord and plug and is meant to be mounted under the cabinet, with the plug running to the nearest outlet. If you have a convenient receptacle, this will, of course, be the easiest fixture to install. Other fixtures do not have cords and are meant to be wired into your house wiring. Both have on-off switches built into the fixtures.

Before you purchase a fixture, measure the width of the recessed area under your cabinet. Also measure the depth of the cavity. Under-cabinet fixtures are sold in standard lengths and must fit in the recess under the cabinet.

Most fixtures are at least 1 to 1¼ inches deep and should be mounted as close to the front of the cabinet as possible. If the depth of the under-cabinet cavity is less than 1 or 1¼ inches, the fixture will be visible and cause glare.

Because under-cabinet lights are usually switched separately, their installation involves bringing power from a junction box that contains a lighting circuit. The most recent National Electrical Code requires that all lighting circuits be separate from receptacle circuits. This way, you won't be left in the dark if the microwave blows a fuse while you are preparing a midnight snack.

You will find that operation of a light will be most convenient if you wire it to its own wall switch. If this presents a problem, you can use the built-in switch in each fixture to turn it on and off.

Once the power is run from the switch to a fixture, it's easy to install additional fixtures wired in series if the upper cabinets are not interrupted by a window, door, or wall space. If they are, cable fishing is required.

If all this sounds too involved, install the under-cabinet lights yourself and hire an electrician to hook them up. Don't worry about getting a shock, because until you plug in the fixtures or the electrician hooks them up to a switch, there is no power in this circuit. If you do wire the fixtures yourself, be sure to turn off the electricity, as described in the section on replacing switches. Here's how to hook up two under-counter fixtures side by side:

Step 1: Determine the least conspicuous place to run cable through the bottom of your cabinet. Then hold the fixtures temporarily in place under the cabinet. Mark on the cabinet the location of the best-situated knock-out hole on the fixture end (some fixtures have them on the back). Then through the cabinet, drill a hole large enough so you can run wire through it. Use "14-2" Romex nonmetallic cable if your local electrical code allows it. (Otherwise, use BX armored cable of the same size.) The "14" refers to the wire gauge — 14-gauge is standard for 15-amp circuits. The "2" means two-wire, although you'll find three wires inside the cable, including the bare ground wire.

Step 2: Following the manufacturer's directions, disassemble the fixtures and mount them below the cabinets; most mount with a couple of short screws. Place the fixtures as close to the front of the cabinets as possible, so maximum light will be shed on the work area.

Step 3: Cut pieces of cable long enough to reach between the fixtures. Be sure the wire is long enough to allow

you to hook it up to the fixture wires at both ends.

Step 4: At each end of the cable, strip off several inches of cable sheathing and remove 1 inch of insulation from the wire ends. Carefully follow the manufacturer's directions and wiring diagrams. Usually, you will find a black and a white wire inside the fixture, but the usually black wire could be another color. Twist the white wires together, then push the pair into a wire nut and tighten it. Do the same with the black wires or the black wire and the colored wire (except green; that's the ground wire). Then connect the bare copper wire to the grounding terminal on the fixture or to the green wire in the fixture. (You should do all this twice, once at each end of the cable, so the two fixtures are wired together in series.)

Step 5: When the fixtures are in place and wired together, you have to run a wire from the last fixture, through the cabinet, to a source of power. If you

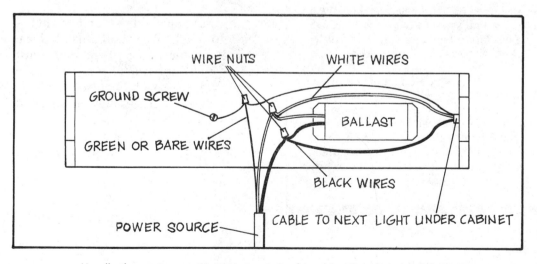

Usually, the most convenient way to wire under-cabinet lights is to hook them up in series with power supplied by one source.

decide to wire the fixtures to a wall switch, then you will have to fish the wires through the wall to the switch and then from the switch to the source of power.

Fishing wires up and down walls is easy, since the wire goes in the same direction as the wall studs, but it's almost impossible to run wires across the studs without having to open the wall at least at every stud.

Chances are you will find it a lot easier to run the wire through the wall into the basement, over to the wall where the switch is located, then up through the wall to the switch.

HOW TO DEAL WITH OLD WIRES

Whenever you open up an old electrical box, you are bound to find a rat's nest of old wires. Through the years the insulation becomes hard and brittle, especially in light fixtures, since they get hot after hours of use.

Bend all the old wires carefully, and before you push everything back into the box, check that none of the insulation has broken off. If you do see bad or missing insulation, purchase rubber insulation tape at an electrical supply store to rewrap the wires. Cracked insulation can be dealt with by wrapping the old insulation with plastic electrical tape before it is pushed back into the box.

Self-Contained Light Fixtures

You really do need light in a closet, but for some reason, builders rarely wire closets for light fixtures.

In most cases, fishing wires through finished walls and ceilings isn't worth the trouble just to get a utility light in the closet. The perfect alternative, we think, is a surface-mounted, battery-powered light. The fixtures are inexpensive and simple to install, and since closet lights are on for only brief periods, the batteries will last a long time. You'll find a good selection of these fixtures in any large home center or hardware store. Some of them have rechargeable batteries, which is a nice feature.

Installation is a simple matter of screwing the mounting bracket to the wall. These lights do not weigh much, so you can use plastic wall anchors to secure the screws in either drywall or plaster walls. (See "Wall Anchors" in chapter 3.)

Mount the light so that the switch is easy to reach. We found a handy location is on the inside of the closet just above the door frame. You can easily reach up to turn the light on, and the upper closet shelf is usually the area that needs light.

Alkaline batteries are the best choice to power this type of light because of their long shelf life.

SURFACE-MOUNTED BATTERY-POWERED FIXTURE

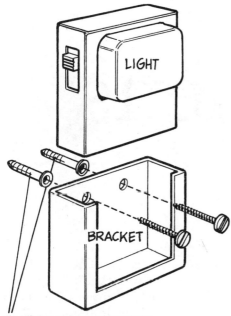

LIGHT

BRACKET

PLASTIC WALL ANCHORS

A surface-mounted battery-powered fixture is an effective, inexpensive alternative to a wired fixture and can be installed in a closet in a matter of minutes.

CHAPTER

8

Kitchens

In most homes, the kitchen plays a much different role than it did just one generation ago. The major difference is that it's no longer "Mom's kitchen." These days, Mom is likely to pick up a briefcase and walk out the door instead of tying on an apron and spending the day taking care of the house and preparing meals.

This modern kitchen needs more storage and counter space to accommodate a host of appliances that make meal preparation quicker and more convenient. The microwave is, of course, king of the new appliances. In many homes, it gets more use than the oven, and has earned prime, easily accessible counter space.

Often, the kitchen no longer is hidden behind doors, and this adds to the design challenge. Many homes have an "open plan" that encourages people to congregate in this room and demands that the kitchen be at least as attractive as the rest of the house. Finally, just as newer homes have gotten smaller, so have kitchens. This increases the need for well-conceived layout and storage design.

Hiring professionals to completely remodel your kitchen is likely to require a second mortgage on your home. But there are many easy ways to make your existing kitchen work harder and smarter without spending a small fortune.

Installing Essentials and Extras

Many of the accessories available on new cabinets can be added to the cabinets you already own simply by drilling a few holes and screwing them into place. For example, you can install a trash container holder or storage racks that are made of coated wire and pull out like drawers. There is also a variety of swing-out shelves that you can install into blind corners of overhead or base cabinets to provide accessible storage in those places that would otherwise be impossible to reach. On a more modest scale, you can customize your cabinets with quick-to-install towel racks, small shelves, and bins. These units are available at home centers. Here are some tips to help the customizing of a cabinet go smoothly.

Paper Towel Racks, Wire Bins, and Racks

Items such as racks and bins are inexpensive and easy to install. Yet they can go a long way toward customizing your kitchen, because you can place them where you really need them. Just think about where you were standing the last time you said to yourself, "Now where did I put those paper towels?" In addition to towel racks, there's a wide assortment of wire and plastic bins and shelves.

These units easily mount on the wall or can be hung on the sides of your cabinets. Most can also be installed on the backs of cabinet doors or even inside the cabinet.

There's nothing at all difficult about installing these items; you just need to know which fasteners to use for the surface to which they'll be mounted. Here are some tips to make the job a snap:

Walls: Most of the rack and shelf units are light enough to mount with the plastic wall anchors that are included with them. If you are going to install a rack on a wall that is covered with ceramic tile, use a carbide-tipped masonry drill to make the mounting hole in the tile. Instead of a wall anchor, use a toggle bolt. Wall anchors grip the tile but might not extend deep enough into the wall to grab hold of the plaster or drywall. That means you are relying on the tile adhesive to hold the tile and rack in place. The toggle bolt goes through the wall and ensures that the rack will not pull the tile off the wall. For more on anchoring things to walls, see the "Hanging Up Your Hang-Ups" section of chapter 3.

Cabinet sides: Wood screws are the best choice when mounting a rack or bin on the side of a cabinet. If possible, plan to position the rack or bin so the mounting screws will hit the cabinet frame. Look inside the cabinet and note where the thick pieces of framing wood are located. There is usually a frame member at the top, bottom, and sides. Some large cabinets have intermediate frame members.

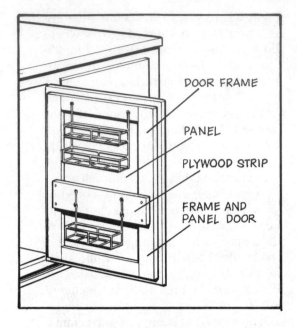

DOOR FRAME

PANEL

PLYWOOD STRIP

FRAME AND
PANEL DOOR

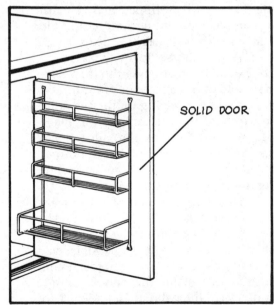

SOLID DOOR

Mount wire brackets on the frame of a frame-and-panel door. If this is not possible, and the panel is ¼ inch or less thick, screw a strip of plywood to the door frame to support the basket and prevent the mounting screws from going completely through the door panel. Screw directly into a solid door.

If mounting the rack so the screws extend into the cabinet frame is not practical, then you must reinforce the cabinet side. Most cabinets have thin plywood sides, and screws do not have enough wood to bite into. The screws provided by the bin or rack manufacturer are usually too long and will extend through the side and protrude into the cabinet.

To solve this problem, glue a small piece of ¼-inch plywood inside the cabinet where the screws penetrate. The plywood will give the screws more wood to bite into and also strengthen the cabinet side. If you are going to put heavy things in the rack, increase the size of the plywood backer piece.

Backs of cabinet doors: Most cabinet doors are either solid panels or frames with panels set in them. In a solid panel door, the entire door is of the same thickness, usually ¾ inch. If you have ¾-inch-thick solid doors, just screw the rack right into the inside of the door. Just make sure the screws are shorter than the thickness of the door.

A frame-and-panel door has a panel set into a frame. The frame usually is about ¾ inch thick, but the panel can be as thin as ¼ inch. If this is the case, use a piece of ¼-inch plywood as a backer where the mounting screws go into the panel.

If the door is very light, and if the panel is flush with the frame in the back, you can extend the backing board to reach the door frame on each side of the panel. Attach the backing board to the back of the door frame with screws or glue. This will stiffen the door and provide a thicker area for the mounting screws to bite into.

A ROLL-OUT PANTRY

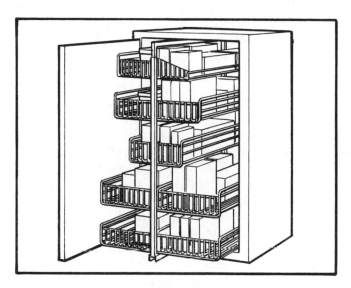

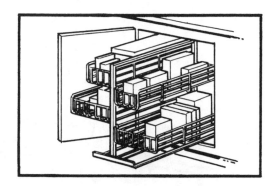

Increase usable under-cabinet storage with this wide roll-out unit with adjustable shelves. Purchase the frame and glider, and then add the size and type of shelves you need; they just snap into the main frame.

Slide-out wire racks can be installed inside any cabinet to increase storage. Remove the standard shelves and replace them with this center-hung unit that eliminates the problem of reaching items in the back of the cabinet.

Inside-Cabinet Storage

Customize the interior storage of your cabinets by installing roll-out pantry units, spice racks, or half-moon-shaped shelves that swing into the unreachable area of a blind cabinet. These nifty items expand your storage and allow you to make full use of every inch of cabinet space. These units are made of epoxy-coated wire. Most are self-contained and need only be bolted on or attached by screws.

The frame mounts to either the base or side walls of the cabinet. Because you're mounting these units inside the cabinet, they must fit into the door open-

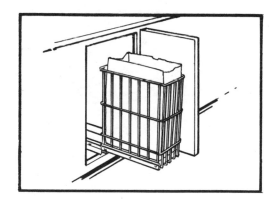

Roll-out waste baskets allow you to use a paper bag or plastic container to collect trash. It's easy to get to and will never tip over or be pushed to the back of the cabinet.

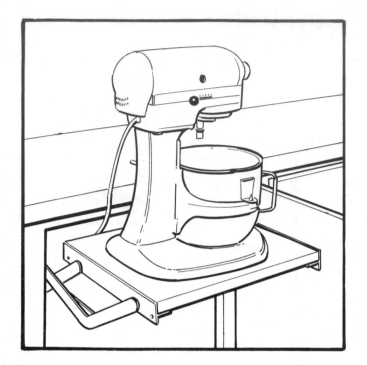

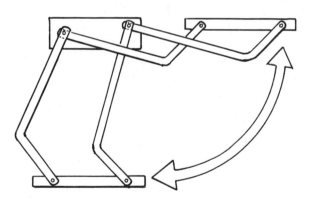

Help relieve counter clutter with a swing-up appliance stand that retracts into an under-counter cabinet when not needed.

ings and not be deeper than the cabinet. Most are designed to fit into standard-size cabinets. Before you purchase a unit, check the overall dimensions of your cabinets.

Under-Cabinet Appliances

Custom cabinets feature built-in storage for small appliances such as food processors, blenders, and mixers. You can add this feature to your existing cabinet by installing a swing-up shelf that hides inside the base cabinet.

This unit uses a system of parallel arms that keep the appliance platform level as it swings up and out of the base cabinet. All these units fit into standard-size base cabinets and will swing closed with an appliance about 13 to 14 inches high. If you have a tall food processor, the top can be removed when you retract the appliance shelf.

The hinge unit mounts on the side of the cabinet. There is considerable load on the mounting plate, so you should use a piece of ¼-inch plywood to reinforce the cabinet side, as already described.

Most of these units include only the hinge mechanism, so you have to make your own appliance platform. The easiest method is to use a ¾-inch-thick piece of maple, which is good to use around the kitchen because it is hardwood, ideal for chopping and cutting food on. You can use the edges of the platform for a chopping block.

Face-Lifting Cabinets

Not only can you customize the storage of your existing cabinets, but with a little work you can completely change the way they look. Through the years a finish can become dark and dull. This is especially true for kitchen cabinets that are subjected to cooking fumes and food splatters.

Many times old cabinets need nothing more than a renewed finish. Refinishing a cabinet isn't difficult, because most of the visible surface consists of doors. Refinishing your doors and replacing the hardware can give your cabinets a whole new style.

Here are some surefire ways to improve your cabinets. We suggest you try the easier remedies first. If you don't like the results, you can try a more involved solution.

Reconditioning Wood Cabinets

As you scrub dirt and grease accumulated on a cabinet finish, you eventually wear down and dull the finish. We have found that a quick reconditioning is sometimes all that is necessary to lighten the finish and give it a new shine. Here's what we do:

Wash with mineral spirits. Remove accumulated grease and dirt by washing the cabinets with a rag dampened with mineral spirits. The mineral spirits also will remove wax buildup. Be careful, because mineral spirits is flammable. Keep the rags away from open flames.

Allow the cabinets to dry for a few minutes or until dull. If the cabinet finish looks lighter and it is not badly cracked, and the wood under the cracks is not black, the finish is ready for the next step. But if you don't like the cleaned finish, you'll need to refinish or paint the cabinets, because the next step will not cover defects; it just restores the shine.

Apply a wipe-on oil finish. An oil finish that wipes on is an easy way to make your cabinets shine again. This type of finish is sold in most hardware and paint stores and home centers. Some brands have tung oil in them, but they are all basically the same. After a couple of applications, they provide a pleasing finish that is easy to maintain.

Follow the manufacturer's directions for application and drying times. We found that the more coats you apply, the deeper the shine gets. Be careful to allow adequate drying time between applications, otherwise the finish gets sticky. For a really high shine, rub the finish with fine steel wool between coats.

Refinishing Wood Cabinets

Here's a project that makes a Cinderella story out of your old wood cabinets. But it works only for wood cabinets that have not been painted and have a lacquer finish. Removing lacquer isn't difficult, but it is messy. Wear old clothes; get a pair of heavy-duty rubber gloves and some plastic goggles. Put the paint stripper away, and try this easy method:

Step 1: Test to see if the finish on your cabinets is lacquer. Put a couple of drops of nail polish remover on the finish in an inside corner or any inconspicuous area of the cabinet. You also can wet a rag with remover and dab it on the finish. If the finish softens and becomes sticky or comes off on the rag, then it is lacquer. If it does not soften, then you probably have a varnish or polyurethane finish, and you will have to use a paint remover to strip this finish off.

Step 2: Buy an antique or furniture refinisher that is designed to remove lacquer finish. This type of product removes only the lacquer finish and leaves the stain in the wood. This process won't lighten stain, but it will completely remove the old, darkened top coat, and many times that is enough to drastically lighten the look of your cabinets.

Step 3: Remove the cabinet doors and all the hardware. Store the hardware in a plastic bag and label the bag. (If you're like us, you might have more than one project going and consequently several mysterious bags of hardware!) Take the doors to the basement or garage if you have one. An ideal work space for this job is anywhere with good ventilation and lighting. Place the doors on a flat surface at a working level that is comfortable for you. Protect the work area with a plastic drop cloth (or several garbage bags) covered with layers of newspaper.

Step 4: Follow the manufacturer's directions for use of the refinisher. We use medium-grade steel wool (shaped into a pad) dipped into refinisher. Change the pads often because they load up with old finish quickly. We also like using a refinishing pad (like the green scouring pad you use for pots and pans).

Step 5: When working on cabinets that are in place, carefully mask surrounding areas so they are not splattered with refinisher. See the "Cover Up to Protect Furnishings" section of chapter 1 for suggestions on masking. You don't need to empty the cabinets, just clear the front half of all the shelves to protect items from refinisher.

Step 6: After removing the old finish, let the wood dry at least overnight. Sand the wood lightly using a fine-grade abrasive paper before applying a top coat.

Step 7: If your cabinets are a light wood and you want to darken the color, apply a penetrating oil stain. The stain contains oil that penetrates the old finish. It is not possible to lighten wood without first applying wood bleach to remove all color and then staining the wood a lighter color. This is a process we don't recommend, because it's difficult to do right and the results are not predictable.

Step 8: You have several options when it comes to choosing a finish top coat. We suggest you use one of the wipe-on oil finishes because of their goofproof application. Follow the manufacturer's directions. If you want to add color to the wood, choose one of the new rubbing oils with stain. It's the same one-step application. For the most heavy-duty protection, apply a polyurethane finish. Be advised, though; these finishes are not as easy to apply as a wipe-on finish. Provide good lighting and use a foam applicator. In order to avoid run and drip marks, remove the doors from the cabinets so you can work on a horizontal surface. Two light applications are better than one heavy one. Between coats, sand lightly with a refinishing pad, then wipe down the surface with a tack rag.

Step 9: Replace all door hardware and rehang the doors on the cabinets. If you're planning to replace the cabinet pulls, choose ones with holes that align with the original holes in the cabinets. Otherwise, choose a style that has a back plate to cover the old holes.

Stripping Cabinets

If testing showed that the finish on your cabinets is not lacquer, then you'll need to strip them before refinishing. The technique is similar to using a refinisher except that you use a paint remover, which contains stronger chemicals. Strippers are designed to eat away many layers of paint or finish. The job can also be messy, depending on how many layers you remove. Strippers come in several consistencies. We prefer gelatinous strippers because they stick to the cabinet and don't run down the surface. Ventilation is a must with strippers. Keep children and pets out of the work area while

Great Gadgets & Gizmos

☞ **Finishing pad**   Save time finishing cabinets and cut the cost of purchasing lots of steel wool pads by using a 3M finishing pad. This pad is similar to a pot scrubber but is not affected by paint removers or other strong chemicals. It is virtually indestructible and can be rinsed out and reused many times. It is made by 3M Do-It-Yourself Division, 3M Center, Building 223-4S-01, St. Paul, MN 55144.

☞ **Groove cleaner**   Make your own groove cleaner by cutting a finishing pad into thin strips. You can also twist steel wool into strands or use a piece of heavy string or twine. Let it soak in the paint remover or refinisher while you work on the flat areas. When you come to the grooves, work the strip, wet with remover, back and forth (like dental floss) in the groove, and it will pull the old finish out of the crevice.

☞ **Antique refinisher**   By using antique refinisher instead of a standard paint remover or stripper, you can skip restaining a cabinet after removing the old finish. This product is designed to remove a lacquer, shellac, or varnish finish and leave the stain behind. Then all you have to do is to apply a new finish to the cabinet; no staining is necessary. It is made by Minwax Company, 102 Chestnut Ridge Plaza, Montvale, NJ 07645.

☞ **Plastic spacers**   Installing large tiles or tiles without spacer tabs on their edges can be a challenge. You have to constantly check tile alignment to keep rows running straight and grout lines consistent. If you are faced with such a project, purchase a set of plastic spacers. These cross-shaped plastic inserts are placed on the corners of the tiles and maintain constant spacing. After you have the tile in place, you can then remove the spacers and reuse them. They come in several thicknesses so they can be used with large quarry tiles or smaller tiles. Be sure to remove all the spacers before the mastic sets.

☞ **Basin wrench**   Before you attempt any plumbing under the sink, go out and purchase a basin wrench. This little gem costs less than $10, but it's worth its weight in gold. It allows you to loosen or tighten those impossible-to-reach nuts at the base of the faucet where standard tools can't be used. This wrench has a long handle with a tee at one end and an automatically adjusting pipe wrench at the other. All you have to do is work the handle up under the sink and place the jaws around the nut. Then tighten or loosen the nut by turning the tee handle. If you use this specialty tool only one time, it will be worth the purchase price. You can always loan it to your neighbor after he gives up trying to tighten the nuts on a faucet under a tiny vanity in his half bath!

using this strong stuff. Use a wide-blade putty knife to remove the heavy top layers. The old finish gums up and clogs steel wool, so use it to wipe down the cabinets just for final removal.

A heat gun is another alternative. Hold the gun in one hand and use a broad knife scraper in the other to lift the finish from the cabinet surface. This technique works well on the large flat surfaces of cabinets. Use steel wool with stripper to remove finish from grooves or crevices and for a final washing down of the cabinet.

GIVE METAL CABINETS A FACE-LIFT AT A BODY SHOP

Spray painting can be tricky unless you have done it before, and painting your kitchen cabinets is not a good practice project. Before you decide to spray the cabinets yourself, get an estimate from an auto painter. They are experts in spray-painting metal. You'll get a hard, high-gloss finish that will last a long time.

Body shops will also spray a custom-mixed enamel that you can have mixed at your local paint store. They might recommend a paint used to paint boats or appliances.

If you have appliances that need a face-lift (a refrigerator, for example), get an estimate on them, as well. Ideally, you can get the painter to come to your kitchen to do the work with cabinets in place. If not, removing and transporting cabinets and appliances to a body shop can be a serious drawback.

After you have stripped off the old finish, you will have to stain the cabinets because the stripper removes most of the stain along with the finish. We recommend a penetrating oil stain used according to the manufacturer's directions. Most recommend that you apply the stain with a brush or rag, allow it to remain, and then wipe it off. Don't skip the wiping-off step, or you will get a blotchy-looking stain job. If you're staining a soft wood such as pine, use a wood conditioner first to seal the porous wood fibers to prevent them from absorbing too much stain and creating a blotchy finish.

Refinishing Metal Cabinets

If your kitchen has good-quality metal cabinets and they show no signs of rusting through or other problems, you can paint them. In fact, with new hardware most metal cabinets can have the clean look of an expensive European laminated cabinet. But getting a paint job that looks good and lasts without chipping takes time and lots of prep work. Here are a few tips we learned when painting cabinets:

Spray, don't brush. Spray-painting the cabinets is by far the best technique to use. We have not been able to get a good finish with a paintbrush. The enamels used to paint cabinets are difficult to apply without lap marks. We have used spray paint in cans for small jobs, but if you have an entire kitchen full of cabinets to paint, this approach gets expensive.

Rent the right equipment. If you don't have spray equipment, rent a small unit. There's more about spray painting in the "Power Painters: Time-Savers?" section of chapter 1.

We've discovered that a small high-speed finishing sander is a big help in sanding the cabinets, since it leaves few if any swirl marks. You can also rent this type of sander.

Remove the cabinets or carefully mask around them. You can probably get a better finish if you take the cabinets down and move them into your basement or garage. If this is not possible, carefully protect all areas around the cabinets with masking tape and newspaper. See the "Cover Up to Protect Furnishings" section of chapter 1 for information about masking.

Clean first, then carefully sand. Wash the cabinets with a strong detergent solution to remove all dirt and grease. Then sand the cabinets with 120-grit abrasive paper. Sand the area around chips smooth, or as the pros say, feather out the edges. You can tell if it is smooth by running your finger over the chipped area. It's good enough when you don't feel a ridge or bump. Sand any rusty areas until they are shiny; also feather the edges of all rust areas. If you skip this step, the rust will bleed through later. Finish sanding the cabinets with 220-grit abrasive paper.

Apply primer. Wipe down the cabinets with a rag dampened with mineral spirits. Then spray on a coat of oil-based primer as soon as possible. If you can't paint all the cabinets, give the bare metal areas a quick shot of primer to prevent new rust from forming. Later, when the spot priming is dry, apply a coat of primer to the whole cabinet. Be sure to choose a paint that is made by the same manufacturer or one that is compatible.

Fill in any imperfections. When the primer is dry, carefully look over the cabinets, especially the doors. Have bright lighting in your work area to help find imperfections. Any dings or dents should be filled with an auto body filler. Apply the filler according to the manufacturer's directions, and when it's hard, sand it smooth. You might have to use several coats of filler to cover a deep scratch.

If you plan to replace the hardware, you can fill in the existing holes. Lightly mark their locations on the inside so you don't mount new hardware close to the edge of an old screw hole. When all imperfections are leveled and the filler is sanded smooth, spray on another coat of primer.

Spray-paint. Before you give the cabinets a coat of paint, check again for any imperfections. Enamel paint will show even the smallest scratch. When you are satisfied with the preparation, give the cabinet a final wipe with mineral spirits to remove all dust.

Provide plenty of ventilation. Make the room a "Do Not Enter" area so no one wanders in. Wear the mask that comes with the spray equipment at all times when using the sprayer. Mix the paint for spraying according to the manufacturer's directions. You will get the best results if you apply several thin coats of paint, as compared with one heavy one. Hold the spray gun about a foot or so away from the cabinet, and move it back and forth parallel to the cabinet surface. Don't swing the gun in an arc, or you will end up with more paint in the center, where the gun is closest to the cabinet. Release the trigger at the end of each pass.

If you do get unwanted paint runs, use a small foam applicator to soak up the excess paint. Do this only when the paint is still wet. If you miss a run and the paint has become tacky, leave it alone. You can sand it out later when the paint is dry. If you try to remove the run after the paint has skinned over, you will create a real mess.

After the first coat is dry, sand lightly with 220-grit abrasive paper, wipe down the cabinet with mineral spirits, and give it a second coat of paint.

Face-Lifting Hardware

One of the easiest ways to change the look of your kitchen cabinets is to change the hardware. An even cheaper way is to clean the hardware. A good cleaning often will brighten the hardware enough to make it look almost new. Here are some tricks we have used to rejuvenate and replace cabinet hardware.

Rejuvenating Hardware

We've used this home brew recipe on kitchen cabinet hardware as well as other metal pieces darkened with tarnish and dirt:

Mix 1 tablespoon of white household vinegar and 1 tablespoon of table salt into 1 cup of hot water in a glass container. Let the hardware soak in the mixture for an hour. Then use an abrasive cleaning pad (the kind sold for scrubbing pots and pans) or an old toothbrush to scrub off the dirt and tarnish. For small narrow grooves, cut the pad into thin strips and work it back and forth like dental floss. You might need to secure the hardware in a clamp or vice to be able to work on it properly.

If the hardware is painted, you can soak it in paint stripper and use a brush or steel wool to remove the paint.

Replacing Hardware

Sometimes all that's needed to change the look of cabinets is to replace their hardware. For example, painted white cabinetry goes country with black iron drawer pulls and hardware. But with bright red or natural wood hardware, the look is more contemporary.

Knobs make for the easiest replacement job—you don't have to worry about lining up two holes, as you do with handles. But if the old stuff has two holes, try to get hardware with holes spaced the same as the old hardware. If the old holes don't line up with new holes, you'll have to patch the holes with a wood filler or patching compound and then repaint or refinish the cabinet fronts.

Another option is to choose new hardware with a large back plate that covers the old holes. You have to buy two pieces for each one that you're replacing, but it spares you from redoing the cabinet fronts.

If you have hidden or inconspicuous hinges, you can, of course, change the handles or knobs without changing the hinges. But sometimes hinges are a decorative element on the outside of the cabinets, and you may want to change them to go along with the other hardware. If you do change hinges, be aware that cabinet hinges vary widely, not only in style but in the way they are designed to work. Some are designed to work with flush-mounted doors—when the doors close flush to the cabinet. Others are for full-overlay doors, in which the doors close against the cabinet. Still others are designed for partial-overlay doors, in which part of the door goes into the cabinet but the face of the cabinet acts as a stop. And for each of these types of doors there are several types of hinges, each with its own mounting system. Your best bet is to take one of your old hinges with you when you shop, to make sure you get hinges that will work for your situation.

If you can't find hardware that you like at home centers or hardware stores, look in the Yellow Pages under the headings "Hardware Distributors" and "Decorative Hardware Manufacturers."

Installing a Tile Backsplash

Besides a fresh coat of paint or wallpaper, there is probably no faster way to dramatically change the look of your kitchen than to install tile between the countertops and cabinets. A tile backsplash provides fashion and function because of its durable, waterproof surface where frequent spills and splashes can discolor an unprotected wall.

This is a good first tiling project because the area between the counter and cabinets is small, usually less than 24 inches high, and is a regular shape without corners that are difficult to tile.

Your first task in this project is to choose the tile. Look for ideas in your favorite decorating and home magazines. Clip treatments you like. You'll find that tile is available in an amazing array of sizes, shapes, colors, and patterns.

Measure the wall area you plan to tile, and draw a rough sketch with detailed measurements. This will allow you to calculate how much tile you need and what it will cost. If you're matching a paint color, wall covering, or flooring material, attach a sample to your sketch, so you can keep all this information in one place. A snapshot of the kitchen also is handy.

As you shop for tiles, you'll find there are various sizes to choose from. You will find that the standard 4×4-inch tile is probably the most economical and widely available. But tiles can range from small mosaic types of about 2 inches square to large tiles of over a foot square.

A medium-priced 4×4 or mosaic tile is a good bet for your first tiling project. If you are going to invest in expensive hand-painted tile, you will have a considerable investment in material, and the cost to have it professionally installed will be a small part of the overall job, so don't do this yourself unless you have some experience.

Unless the distance between the top of your counter and the top of the backsplash is an exact multiple of the tile size, you will have to cut some tiles. Take some time and figure out how much you will have to trim off a tile before you

order any or start the job. You can make a rough estimate by just dividing the size of the tile into the distance between the counter and cabinets. Don't plan to start laying full tiles along the counter, or you might end up having to trim off ¼ inch from the top tiles.

Use a nonflammable mastic to install the tiles. This type has a reasonable working time and can be cleaned up with water before it skins over. Follow the manufacturer's directions. All mastics are workable for a specific amount of time.

We use a latex additive when we mix up the grout. This helps seal the grout from dirt and makes upkeep easier, especially in the kitchen. There are also grout sealers that will do the same job, but we never seem to get around to coating the joints with sealer after the job's done, so we can't say how effective they are.

Once you have a general idea of your needs and a rough layout, take your sketch and calculations with you when shopping. Show this sketch to the tile retailer, and ask for suggestions about tiles. Review your layout so you will be sure to get the right materials and enough adhesive and grout. The tile supplier is also a source for tools. Usually, you can borrow or rent a tile cutter, tile nipper, and notched trowel. You will also need a straightedge, measuring tape, chalk line, carpenter's level, bucket and sponge, rags, squeegee, and caulk gun.

Creating a Standard Tile Backsplash

Here's how to add a decorative and practical tile backdrop behind the busy work centers at the stove and sink:

Prepare the area.   Remove any wallpaper and use a household detergent to thoroughly wash the area where you will

TILING A BACKSPLASH

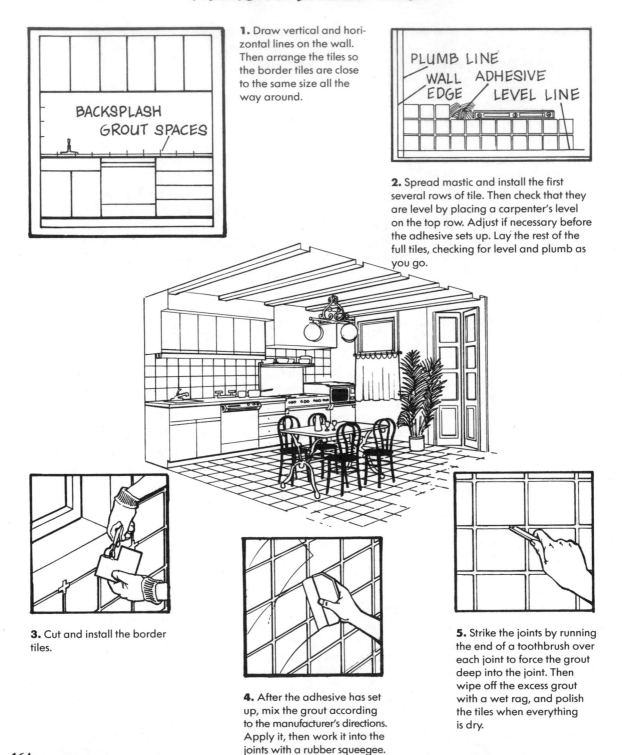

1. Draw vertical and horizontal lines on the wall. Then arrange the tiles so the border tiles are close to the same size all the way around.

BACKSPLASH
GROUT SPACES

PLUMB LINE
WALL ADHESIVE
EDGE LEVEL LINE

2. Spread mastic and install the first several rows of tile. Then check that they are level by placing a carpenter's level on the top row. Adjust if necessary before the adhesive sets up. Lay the rest of the full tiles, checking for level and plumb as you go.

3. Cut and install the border tiles.

4. After the adhesive has set up, mix the grout according to the manufacturer's directions. Apply it, then work it into the joints with a rubber squeegee.

5. Strike the joints by running the end of a toothbrush over each joint to force the grout deep into the joint. Then wipe off the excess grout with a wet rag, and polish the tiles when everything is dry.

install the tiles. Remove any loose or flaking paint, and roughen up glossy painted surfaces with sandpaper. Fill any large holes with spackling compound. Check the adhesive manufacturer's recommendations for any additional prep work that may be needed.

Lay out the job. Use a carpenter's level to strike a plumb line from the top to the bottom of the area you will be tiling. Get someone to help you hold tiles against the line, to see how many full tiles you need in each vertical row. Don't try to do this by just dividing the length of the plumb line by the nominal dimension of the tile. Most tiles have spacer bumps on their sides that automatically leave space for the grout.

Now strike a level line across the area you'll be tiling, and lay out tiles to see how many you need in each horizontal row.

If you end up with less than an inch of tile at the end of a row, either horizontally or vertically, you will get a better-looking job if you trim both tiles at both ends of the row. We found it's difficult to trim off a small section of tile. It is much easier to cut off a 1½-inch chunk than to try to trim off a ½-inch edge. So, for example, if your layout would leave you with ¾ inch of tile at the top, trim 1 inch off the bottom tile and make the top tile 1¾ inches. If your plan includes border tiles, don't forget to include them in your calculations.

Spread adhesive. Use a notched trowel to spread the adhesive on the wall in a small area. If the tiles are thick, spread adhesive on the tile backs as well as on the wall. Use a twisting motion to set each tile in place, but don't slide it into position, or you will cause some adhesive to be pushed up through the joint.

If you do get adhesive in the tile joints, use a toothpick or piece of thin cardboard to remove it. Wipe all the adhesive off the tiles with a damp rag right away, otherwise the adhesive will set hard and prevent the grout from getting into the joints. Then the thin grout will crack and fall out.

Check the layout frequently. As you place tiles on the wall, step back frequently to see that the grout spaces are running plumb and level. Check frequently with your level. You can spread tiles very slightly if you need to compensate for wandering lines, but in a small job such as a backsplash, you shouldn't have much trouble keeping the tiles running true.

When all the tile is set and excess adhesive is cleaned off the tiles, you're finished for the day. Most adhesives should cure for at least 24 hours, but be sure to check the recommendations of the adhesive manufacturer. Don't get the newly tiled area wet—go out to dinner and breakfast!

Grout the tile. Mix the grout with water until it is creamy and without lumps. Some grouts require a short set-up time before use; read and follow the manufacturer's directions. Use a squeegee or rubber trowel to spread the grout diagonally across the joints, forcing it into the joints between the tiles. Wipe away excess grout with a wet sponge.

After you have grouted several square feet but before the grout begins to set, score the joints. Use a craft stick or Popsicle stick or the end of an old toothbrush to force the grout deeply into the joints. Make all the grout joints consistently smooth and the same level.

When the grout has completely dried, use a silicone caulk to seal the joint between the countertop and the bottom row of tiles. If you like, trim out the top and side edges of tile with thin molding and caulk.

Decorating with Tile

You can use tile in other areas of the kitchen. Because it is so easy to clean, tile is an ideal surface for many places around the home:

▶ in a chair rail around the dining table

▶ in a border outlining the range

▶ inserted into the countertop as a hot plate

▶ as a kitchen or bathroom countertop

▶ as a buffet countertop

▶ in wainscoting on walls

▶ for trimming the range hood vent

▶ as a kitchen tabletop

Hanging a Microwave Oven

Microwave ovens are becoming standard equipment in many kitchens. But the time they can save has to be weighed against lost counter space. If you have a kitchen already short of working counters, deciding to give some up to a microwave is a tough decision.

Most manufacturers are aware of the situation and sell hardware that allows their newer units to be suspended from the bottom of a standard kitchen cabinet. By hanging the microwave, you can enjoy its convenience without sacrificing counter space.

If you have an older-model microwave oven or there's no hanging hardware available, consider our alternative, a do-it-yourself microwave shelf.

Using Factory Hardware

The major manufacturers of microwave ovens offer an under-cabinet kit for suspending their units. Often the kit comes with every unit. If not, check with the store where you purchased the microwave to see if this hardware is available for your particular model. Also check that your unit will fit under the cabinets.

A typical hanging kit has hardware that requires drilling holes through the cabinet base. You attach the support hardware and slide the microwave into place. For adequate usage you need about 18 inches between the bottom of the cabinet and the counter. You also need sturdy cabinetry. Before shopping, know the model number of your microwave oven and measure the underside of your cabinet. The specifications on the kit will tell you how much space is required (width and depth) and suggest the appropriate thickness of the cabinet base.

Most standard cabinets will support the unit, but there are several other factors to consider in selecting a location for your microwave. Here are a few we think are important:

Check the microwave's depth. Most wall cabinets are about 12 inches deep. Measure the depth of your microwave to make sure it will fit under the cabinet. Also consult your owner's manual to make sure that the unit can be mounted close to a wall. All units have ventilation requirements, and some need space in the rear. Check that there will be the required clearance between the unit and the wall.

Check that there is adequate room under the microwave. Most standard full-height wall cabinets are installed 18 inches above the counter. Subtract the height of your microwave from this dimension, and you will have an idea of the space between the microwave bottom and the counter. Unless it is more than 6 or 7 inches, you will not gain much usable counter space, but this space can be used to store things. Since the microwave is suspended over the counter, this area also will be easier to clean.

Check that there is a source of power handy.   You need a source of electrical power to run your microwave. Suspending it from a cabinet that is located above an outlet will solve this problem.

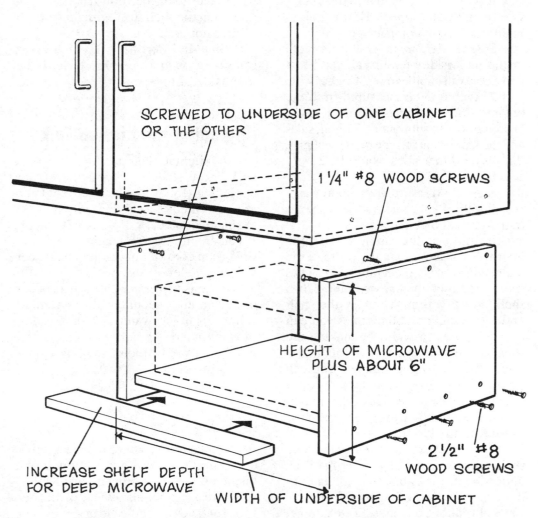

SCREWED TO UNDERSIDE OF ONE CABINET OR THE OTHER

1¼" #8 WOOD SCREWS

HEIGHT OF MICROWAVE PLUS ABOUT 6"

INCREASE SHELF DEPTH FOR DEEP MICROWAVE

2½" #8 WOOD SCREWS

WIDTH OF UNDERSIDE OF CABINET

This simple microwave stand is attached to the underside of a kitchen cabinet. Most cabinets are 12 inches deep, so 1 X 12 lumber (actually ¾ X 11½ inches) will work out. If your microwave is deeper than this, increase the depth of the shelf by gluing an additional piece of wood to the front edge. Allow at least 1 inch of clearance between the shelf and the back wall for ventilation.

Making Your Own Under-Cabinet Microwave Shelf

Older microwave ovens are larger and do not have suspension kits. We found the easiest way to hang these units from a cabinet is to make a simple shelf with side supports that attach it to the underside of the wall cabinet. Here's how to build it, as shown on page 167:

Step 1: Measure the width and depth of the underside of your cabinet. Most two-door wall cabinets are 24 inches wide and 12 inches deep measured from the outside. Most cabinets are made from ¾-inch stock, so subtracting for both sides and the face frame of our example cabinet, the inside dimensions would be 22½ × 11¼ inches.

Step 2: Measure your microwave. It's all right if your microwave is deeper than your cabinets, if you don't mind it sticking out past the cabinets. But if the microwave is more than the width of the underside of the cabinet minus 1½ inches (the combined thicknesses of the two shelf sides), you can't mount the shelf under one cabinet. Sometimes you can get enough extra width by making the shelf so one side attaches to the underside of the adjoining cabinet. You can get even more extra width by screwing a block along the underside of the adjoining cabinet and then attaching the shelf support to the block.

Step 3: Make the shelf parts. The shelf supports must be the depth of the underside of the cabinet (11¼ inches in this example) by the height of the microwave plus about 6 inches. For example, if the microwave is 15 inches tall, make the side pieces 11¼ × 21 inches. If the microwave will fit under the cabinet, make the shelf as wide as the underside of the cabinet. Otherwise, make the shelf as wide as necessary to support the microwave. Draw a line across each support ¾ inch from the bottom. Place the bottom edge of the shelf along these lines when you screw the supports to the shelf with #8 × 2½-inch wood screws. This will make a sturdier construction than attaching the shelf flush with the bottom of the supports.

Step 4: Insert #8 × 1¼-inch wood screws through the supports into the underside of the cabinets.

Upgrading the Kitchen Sink

A kitchen sink used to be just a sink; now it can be considered an appliance. Today new sinks are sold in a rainbow of colors and they are available in single, double, or triple-bowl designs. If you are not up to replacing the whole sink, then consider upgrading the faucet to a single-lever washerless type. You also can easily install a garbage disposer or add an under-counter filter system to supply drinking water. All these additions basically are bolt-on projects and require only basic tools and skills. Here's what's involved.

Replacing a Sink

Replacing a sink can make a big difference in the look and usefulness of a kitchen. This job is straightforward unless you have a custom-installed sink that has been set below ceramic tile or some other custom counter material. In this case we recommend that you don't replace the sink unless you also are going to change the countertops.

Your sink is either a self-rimming or surface-mounted type. Both types are held in place by screws attached to clips hooked to the underside of the sink. Surface-mounted sinks have a metal band that runs around the perimeter of the sink. This stainless rim sits on top of the counter, and the sink bowel is attached to the underside of this rim. A self-rimming sink sits directly on the countertop. We recommend purchasing a self-rimming sink as a replacement. They are easier to install, and there is only one joint to seal between the sink and countertop.

Before you rip out the old sink, measure it. Also look under the sink and see whether your faucet requires one, two, or three holes. The third hole is usually for a sink spray hose. Whatever combination you have, make sure the new sink you purchase not only fits into the old counter hole but that the old faucet and all its attachments are compatible with the new sink.

Unless there is framing around the sink that restricts you to the size of your present sink, there is no reason why you can't enlarge the cutout for the present

sink and install a larger two-bowl or three-bowl type.

In most cases you can reuse the faucet, strainer assembly, P-trap, and other parts of the old sink. We found that the sink strainer assembly usually is reusable, but it is not a good idea to reuse the other parts of the drain system if there are any signs of rust or corrosion. If you replace a single-bowl sink with a two-bowl model, you will need additional drainage plumbing, since the two bowls must be connected together and then connected to the P-trap.

Also purchase new risers (the tubes that run up to the faucet from the supply valves on the wall). We found the flexible plastic risers easiest to install. Purchase them longer than you think you need, because they are easy to bend and cut. You also will need a medium-size container of plumber's putty to use as a bed for your new sink. Roll the putty into a rope, and place it under the lip of the sink flange. After you tighten the sink's locking screws from under the counter, use a screwdriver to scrape away the putty that squeezes out.

SELF-RIMMING SINK

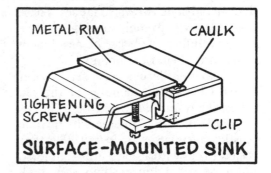

SURFACE-MOUNTED SINK

Most modern sinks are self-rimming. These are easier to install and are less likely to leak than surface-mounted sinks, which have two caulk joints. However, self-rimming sinks protrude above the counter, while surface-mounted sinks are flush with the counter.

Replacing a Faucet

An old, drippy faucet with most of the chrome worn off is a sure sign of an outmoded kitchen. Not only are the new single-lever faucets easier to operate, they also are less prone to leaking. When they eventually do leak, they are easy to repair.

Probably the hardest part of replacing a faucet is choosing a style. There are so many to choose from. The lever mechanism and style are a matter of personal choice. We have found that unless you are willing to spend at least $50 to $70 to purchase a good-quality faucet, you are probably better off rebuilding the one you have. Inexpensive faucets have many plastic parts that do not wear well or stand up to hard kitchen use. The lever on a kitchen faucet takes a lot of abuse. Unless it is well constructed, the faucet will soon begin to leak from the base of the spout and from the ball mechanism.

Before purchasing a faucet, check your old sink to see how many mounting holes there are and how far apart they are. Many of the newer faucets require a center hole. Some older sinks have only two widely spaced holes to accommodate an old-style two-valve faucet. These holes also vary in their spacing, so measure carefully and check the new faucet to be sure it will fit your sink.

Also purchase a new set of riser tubes. Check the diameter of the old tubes. They probably will be either ⅜ inch or ½ inch in diameter. The flexible plastic type is easiest to install. This type is easy to cut with a sharp utility knife, so purchase a set longer than you think necessary and cut them to exact size on the job. You also will need a container of plumber's putty to seal the joint between the faucet and sink. This putty prevents water that accumulates on the sink from seeping under the faucet base and dripping under the sink.

Installing a new faucet is easy. Mounting-hole locations and supply tubes vary, but most faucets require the same basic procedures. All come with complete directions, so follow the specific recommendations of the manufacturer. Generally, here's what's involved in swapping a kitchen faucet:

Remove the old faucet. Turn off the water to the faucet at the stop valves under the sink or at the main shutoff valve. Then remove the riser tubes connecting the faucet to the water lines. Loosen the hold-down bolts under the faucet, and then pry the old faucet off the sink. It might be stuck in the hardened plumber's putty. Then scrape all old putty or caulk off the top of the sink area.

Install the new faucet. Roll new plumber's putty into a thin rope, and stick it around the underside perimeter of the new faucet body. Then place the faucet on the sink and align it. Tighten the hold-down bolts from underneath the sink until the putty is squeezed out between the sink and the faucet base. Run the tip of a screwdriver around the faucet base to cut away the excess putty, then roll it into a ball and return it to the container.

Install the hot and cold riser tubes. Before the advent of flexible plastic risers, this part of the installation was sometimes frustrating. Most of the newer faucets have copper tubes leading out of the valve body that extend below the sink for several inches. This makes reaching the nuts easier, but it creates another problem. Sometimes the ends of the fau-

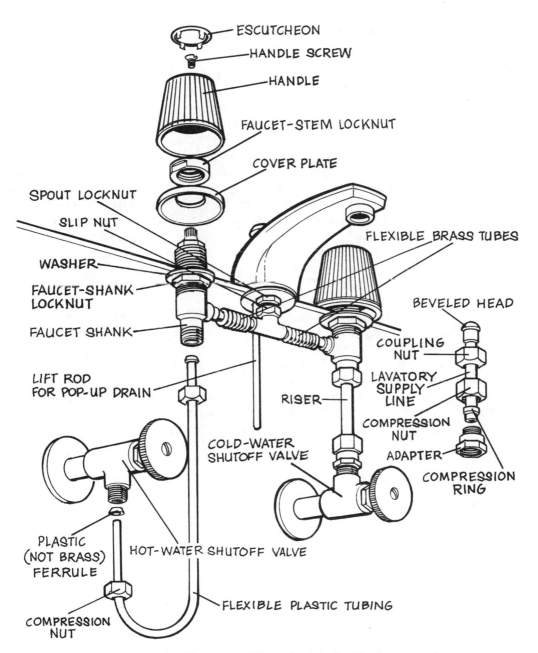

ESCUTCHEON

HANDLE SCREW

HANDLE

FAUCET-STEM LOCKNUT

COVER PLATE

SPOUT LOCKNUT

SLIP NUT

FLEXIBLE BRASS TUBES

WASHER

FAUCET-SHANK LOCKNUT

BEVELED HEAD

FAUCET SHANK

COUPLING NUT

LIFT ROD FOR POP-UP DRAIN

LAVATORY SUPPLY LINE

RISER

COMPRESSION NUT

COLD-WATER SHUTOFF VALVE

ADAPTER

COMPRESSION RING

PLASTIC (NOT BRASS) FERRULE

HOT-WATER SHUTOFF VALVE

COMPRESSION NUT

FLEXIBLE PLASTIC TUBING

Hooking up a kitchen faucet is not difficult, thanks to flexible plastic riser tubes. If the shutoff valves are too close or badly out of alignment, you can turn the shutoff valve over and use a loop of plastic tubing to make the connection.

cet tubes are so close to the stop valves that aligning the risers is almost impossible without getting a leak.

We found that if you shut the water off, remove the shutoff valves, and reinstall them so they are facing down, it becomes a simple matter to run a long flexible riser tube down from the valve and loop it up to the faucet valve. This is easier than trying to make the riser take a sharp bend in the short distance between the stop valve and faucet.

Test the faucet. When the risers are in place, tighten all nuts and remove the aerator from the end of the faucet spigot and turn on the water. Allow it to run so it flushes out any loose particles in the pipes. Then turn the water off and check for leaks.

Fix the leaks. If you find a leak, try tightening the compressing nuts slightly. Most of the time, though, this will just make the leak worse. If the leak persists, remake the joint and try again. The secret to getting a leak-free joint is to have the riser tube straight and fully seated in the compression fitting before you tighten the nuts.

Rejuvenating That Old Faucet

If you have decided to save money by rebuilding your faucet instead of buying a new one, you should be able to find parts at a large hardware store or plumbing supply house. If the faucet is so old that you can't find parts, it's probably a good idea to replace it anyway. If you have removed the faucet to replace the sink, then take the faucet with you so you can be sure to purchase the right parts. Here's what we do to an old faucet to get it working again.

Replacing All Washers and Seals

Replace everything rubber in the faucet, even if it does not leak. Hundreds of faucet designs have been manufactured in the last 20 or 30 years, and finding replacement parts can sometimes be a challenge. Most faucets can be rebuilt with new parts, which will cost a fraction of the price of a new faucet. But sometimes you have to weigh this savings against the time it takes to shop for the parts. Call first and find several stores that claim to have the parts you need, then remove the faucet and take it with you. This is about the only way you are guaranteed to get the right washers, packing, or seals on your first trip.

Cleaning or Replacing an Aerator

The aerator is the device at the end of the faucet that directs the flow of water and catches mineral sediments in its screen. Sometimes the aerator gets clogged with sediment, restricting the flow and making it seem like you've lost water pressure. If all your other faucets work fine, that's good evidence that the aerator needs to be cleaned out. To unscrew it, wrap masking tape around the end of the faucet and use pliers to loosen it. Pay attention to the order of how its parts are assembled, so you can put it back together or replace it. Clean all of its components by washing water through it. Remove mineral deposits and grit with a straight pin. Reassemble it and tighten it with pliers.

A new aerator costs about $2, so if the old one shows any corrosion, replace it. Remove the old one and take it to the store to find a replacement. You'll be amazed at the variety of aerators. (We had five to choose from at our local hardware store.) The important thing to notice is how the screw end is threaded. You can replace a straight aerator with a swivel type or one that has an adjustable flow, just make sure that the threads are the same.

Replacing the Sink's Spray Hose

If you're getting only a trickle from the spray hose, check its nozzle. Some unscrew, others are removed by loosening a screw in the center of the nozzle. Clean the small holes with a straight pin, and remove any grit or dirt from behind the nozzle. Then reassemble and test how it sprays.

If the spray is still slow or erratic, the cause might be in the diverter valve inside the faucet. This valve usually is located inside the base of the spout. There are many design variations. We find it easiest to take the faucet to the store and have the parts man disassemble the faucet and find the right replacement valve.

If the spray head or hose leaks, it's a straightforward replacement job. Unscrew the head from its coupling and remove the coupling from the hose by prying it off with a utility knife or screwdriver.

The tricky part is removing the spray head at the base of the spout under the sink. Use a basin wrench or pliers to unscrew it. Take it with you when you shop for a replacement. If you can't find an exact replacement, purchase an adapter kit that allows the hose to be installed on just about any faucet. To install the new hose, follow the manufacturer's directions, which will be basically the reverse of how you took the old one out.

Installing a Garbage Disposer

Adding a garbage disposer will certainly help modernize any sink. This is a fairly straightforward project, and all manufacturers supply complete installation directions. If there is not an electrical outlet that you can easily tap into under the sink, you will have to run a 20-amp line from the main electrical panel to the disposer. If this is the case, hire an electrician to run the line; then you can install the disposer yourself. If you do the wiring, consult with your local building department before you begin, to make sure your work meets all the building codes.

When shopping for a garbage disposer, you will find two basic types—batch feed and continuous feed. They both grind up the waste in the same way, and installation is the same. The difference is in how they operate. A batch feed unit is first filled with waste, then turned on by replacement of the sink strainer. A continuous feed unit is turned on by a wall switch near the sink and runs continuously while you feed in the garbage. The continuous feed unit can handle more waste quickly, but the batch feed unit is considered safer because it operates only when closed:

Here is what's involved in installing a disposer:

Step 1: Turn off the water supply. Place a bucket below the P-trap to catch the water, then loosen the P-trap nuts, using a pipe wrench or channel pliers. Let the water drain into the bucket, and wipe the pipe dry with a rag. Loosen and remove the slip nut that joins the drain pipe to the plumbing stack behind the wall.

Step 2: Remove the tailpiece (short piece of chrome pipe) from the sink basket assembly, and then loosen the locknut that holds the basket assembly in the sink. If you don't have large pliers to grip this nut, put a screwdriver against one of the flange ears and tap the handle with a

INSTALLING A GARBAGE DISPOSER

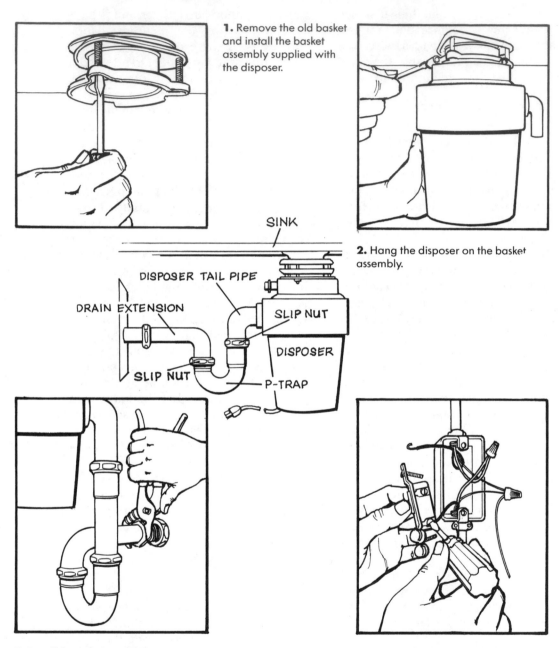

1. Remove the old basket and install the basket assembly supplied with the disposer.

2. Hang the disposer on the basket assembly.

SINK

DISPOSER TAIL PIPE

DRAIN EXTENSION

SLIP NUT

DISPOSER

SLIP NUT

P-TRAP

3. Install the tail pipe and P-trap. You sometimes can use the old one or at least part of it. Otherwise, measure the distance from the disposer to the wall and purchase a trap to fit. Get it a little longer so you can cut it off if necessary.

4. Wire up the disposer according to the diagram supplied by the manufacturer. If the unit is a continuous-run type, install the switch in a convenient place. If the unit is a batch type, the switch is built into the unit and all you have to do is wire it up.

hammer to loosen the locknut, then unscrew it with your hand. Remove the basket from the sink. Don't discard any fittings or gaskets, because you might need them later.

Step 3: Clean the top and bottom of the basket opening in the sink. Make sure that you remove all the old, hardened plumber's putty or caulk.

Step 4: Install the disposer in the sink according to the manufacturer's directions. The usual order of installation is to install the basket assembly first (use plumber's putty between the disposer basket and the sink). Then wire up the motor assembly and install it on the basket assembly. Check to see that the electricity to the disposer is turned off. Finally install the drain line.

CHAPTER
9

Bathrooms

Improving your bathroom is one of the best investments you can make. National surveys on home appraisals indicate that most bathroom improvements increase the value of a house more than the cost of the improvement, and that includes paying someone to do the work. Doing it yourself will give you an even greater equity return on your dollar. Plus, you'll be making improvements every member of your family will enjoy every single day.

Half the battle in improving a bathroom is knowing what to do yourself and when to call the plumber. This chapter provides a wide range of easy projects that can dramatically improve your bathroom. But when plumbing gets more involved than changing faucets or installing a new toilet, most homeowners don't have the skills or the special tools for the job. In addition, plumbing work can bring unhappy surprises. It's no fun to discover on Sunday afternoon that you don't have the right fitting for the shower you'll need first thing Monday morning. And the older your plumbing is, the more you want to leave it to the pros. You may have a very hard time finding fittings for old plumbing, even on Monday.

Complicating things further, new fixtures often don't line up with old supply and waste lines. The key to success in any project involving new fixtures is to take the time to carefully measure the locations of existing supply and drain pipes before you go shopping.

Replacing a Faucet

Does it leak? Is it ugly? Or are you remodeling the entire bathroom? There are many good reasons to change a faucet, and some are much easier than others to replace. Here are some guidelines that will help:

Check the mounting requirements. There are many different faucets on the market, and all do not mount in the same holes. Some of the newer high-style faucets require a single hole, others require two, and those with drain controls require three.

Not only do different faucets need different hole configurations, but they also require different spacing between the holes. Finding a faucet to fit the sink might seem complicated, but it's not that tough, especially if you are buying all new. Just be sure the faucet you choose will fit the sink top. We've laid out what's involved in making a simple faucet swap. The accompanying illustration will help you identify the parts.

Remove the old faucet. Turn the water off and disconnect the risers from both the water supply and the faucet

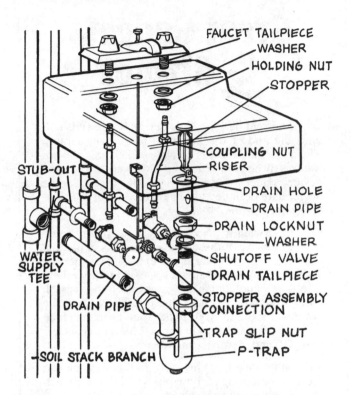

BATHROOM SINK PLUMBING

FAUCET TAILPIECE
WASHER
HOLDING NUT
STOPPER
COUPLING NUT
RISER
DRAIN HOLE
DRAIN PIPE
DRAIN LOCKNUT
WASHER
SHUTOFF VALVE
DRAIN TAILPIECE
STOPPER ASSEMBLY CONNECTION
TRAP SLIP NUT
P-TRAP
STUB-OUT
WATER SUPPLY TEE
DRAIN PIPE
SOIL STACK BRANCH

tailpieces. Remove the hold-down bolts that hold the faucet to the sink. There are many systems for attaching a faucet, but they are all under the sink and it's always obvious how to remove them. Lift the old faucet out. If the plumber's putty around the faucet is old, it may be stuck. You may have to tap the faucet a bit with a hammer to loosen it, or tap the blade of a screwdriver between the faucet and the sink to break the connection. You don't care about damaging the old faucet, but be careful you don't chip or mar the sink porcelain.

Prepare the sink. With the old faucet out, you should clean the top of the sink completely. Remove all traces of

Great Gadgets & Gizmos

☞ **Antiscald device**   This device is screwed right onto the end of the faucet to replace an aerator. The antiscald device is activated when only the hot water is turned on. When the water gets too hot, the device reduces the water flow to a trickle. Some devices are designed to remain at a preset comfortable temperature.

☞ **Basin wrench**   No bathroom remodeler should be without one of these tools. It consists of a metal rod with a pipe wrench at one end. At the other is a T-shaped handle that allows you to twist the wrench. The long handle enables you to place the wrench around the nuts up under the sink. There is usually not much room for your hands, but the skinny handle of the wrench slips in easily. This tool costs less than $10 and is worth every penny.

☞ **Strap wrench**   This nifty tool is designed to prevent scratching chrome pipes and fixtures when you're tightening or loosening them.

eter of the faucet's underside. Also put putty around the holes in the sink.

Set the faucet.   Position the faucet on the sink so the new risers and the drain-stop mechanism are aligned with the holes, then push the faucet down on the sink. Work it back and forth to spread the putty.

Attach the mounting screws.   From underneath the sink top, attach the mounting screws and screw the mounting washers and nuts onto the risers protruding through the holes.

Connect the risers.   Use two wrenches to connect the risers. While you hold a riser with one wrench, use the other to tighten the nut onto the water supply. Use a friction ring from the package that comes with the faucet.

Flush the pipes.   There's a device called an aerator screwed into the end of the water spout. Remove it, then turn on the water supply and let it run for a few minutes to set the seals and flush, and then turn the faucet on to flush any minerals or debris from the lines. Put the aerator back on, and the sink is ready to use.

the old plumber's putty or caulk. This will help ensure that the new faucet will not leak. Also, you won't be left with a brown ring around your new faucet if the base is a little smaller than the old faucet.

Apply plumber's putty.   Apply plumber's putty to the bottom of the new faucet. The easiest way to do this is to knead a ball of putty in your hands until it gets warm and pliable. Then roll it between your fingers into a long snakelike tube. Press the tube around the perim-

Replacing a Wall-Hung Sink

Simple wall-hung sinks with separate hot and cold faucets were standard equipment in many old homes. We replace these sinks not only because we find them unattractive but also to gain the convenience of a single-spout faucet. Replacing a wall-hung with a pedestal sink usually is easier than replacing it with a vanity, because you have more room to work with. But that's not always the case; you can make cuts into the back frame of a vanity, but you can't cut the porcelain of a pedestal. Another reason we like to replace wall-hungs with pedestals is that pedestals tend to look appropriate in old houses.

The main thing is to do a little investigation before you tear the old sink off the wall. First measure the distance between the floor and where the supply pipes come out of the wall. Older wall-hung sinks have their water supply pipes located high up under the sink so they don't show. This becomes a problem if you try to replace the sink with a modern pedestal sink or vanity that requires supply pipes to be located lower on the wall. If the pipes sticking out of the wall are very close to the underside of the top of the new sink, it can become very difficult to hook up the new faucet.

Usually, you can switch to a pedestal sink if the pipes will fit under the sink and allow it to be placed against the wall. If you purchase a pedestal sink that has a back lip that interferes with the existing plumbing, you'll have to have the pipes moved. This is a job for an experienced plumber.

Fortunately, most pedestal sinks are close to the same height as old wall-hung sinks. Some pedestal sinks attach to the wall, others are freestanding. If you are looking at one that attaches to the wall but find a plumbing conflict, take a look at the freestanding models. They tend to be more expensive but might save you from having to call a plumber.

Most pedestal sinks are installed in the same way. About the only difference might be how they are attached to the floor. Check this out along with the roughing-in dimensions for the plumbing, which are supplied by all manufacturers.

Another point to check is whether the style of faucet you like will fit into the sink. Check the dimensions of the mounting holes, and then check these against the faucet you plan to use. After you are sure that everything will fit, making the switch is not hard. Here's what's involved:

Disconnect the plumbing. Most sink plumbing has shutoff valves so you can just shut the water off there before removing the hot-water and cold-water supply lines (risers) to the faucet. But if your plumbing is very old, there may be no shutoffs at the sink and you'll have to find the shutoff for the whole house. (If you don't have shutoffs, consider installing them so you won't have to shut down all your plumbing every time you work on the sink.) Also remove the drainpipe at the P-trap. You might be able to reuse the drainpipe, but it's usually false economy, especially since this hardware is exposed and will look pretty ratty underneath the new sink. The drainpipe probably will require a new Marvel fitting (compression fitting connected to the drainpipe as it emerges from the wall). If you don't replace the whole drainpipe, remove the nut and take the compression ring to the hardware store to find a replacement for that.

Remove the old sink. Remove the sink from the wall by lifting it up and off its mounting bracket. Some sinks are bolted directly to the wall. Either type will come off if you loosen the mounting bolts. Be sure to support the sink so it cannot fall on you while you are working under it.

Patch the wall. After the sink is off the wall, you can survey the patchwork needed. Most of the time, all you will have to do is fill in the bolt holes. If the wall is badly cracked or shows signs of water damage, you will probably be better off cutting away a section of the drywall or plaster and replacing it with a new piece of drywall. In either case the goal is a smooth wall behind the new sink. See the "Patch and Repair" section of chapter 1.

Do a plumbing dry run.   Position the sink where you want it, then check the alignment of the water and drain lines. If the hot and cold supply lines are very close to the underside of the sink, turn the shutoff valves so they face down. You can then lead long, flexible plastic risers from the shutoff valves through a loop to the faucet. A loop works much better than trying to make sharp bends, which may kink the risers.

Check out the alignment between the drain line in the wall and the sink. You can purchase different-length tailpieces (the section of pipe connected to the bottom of the sink). Attached to the tailpiece is the P-trap. This will slide up and down the tailpiece several inches, giving you some leeway in adjustment. The P-trap also allows adjustment in aligning the drain with the pipe in the wall. If all else fails, you can purchase a flexible plastic tailpiece that usually solves most P-trap alignment problems.

Drill hold-down holes.   After everything checks out, mark the floor according to the manufacturer's requirements, so you can drill the holes for the hold-down bolts. If your sink has a wall bracket, mark this also. Then move the sink and do the plumbing and drill the necessary holes (use a masonry bit to drill into ceramic tile) for the hold-down bolts and wall brackets.

Assemble the faucet and drain.   Before you replace the sink, install the faucet and drain assembly. It is a lot easier to work on the sink when you can get

behind it than while lying on your back trying to reach up behind the sink.

Install the sink.   When everything is ready, move the sink into position and bolt it in place. Hook up the hot and cold risers to the faucet, then connect the drain lines. Check that everything is tight and then turn on the water.

Installing a Vanity and Sink

Sprucing up a bathroom with a new vanity is easy if you already have a vanity; just choose one that's exactly the same size, so you don't have to patch walls or replace flooring. But even if you choose a vanity of a different size, this still isn't a big job.

A vanity also is a good replacement for old wall-hung or pedestal sinks, but as mentioned, there is a potential conflict with the plumbing. You'll find vanity cabinets sold in widths of 18 inches and more.

Vanity tops are sold separately. The newest types are one piece, with the sink bowl molded into the countertop. Most are made from synthetic marble, but new materials are arriving on the market all the time. These tops are easy to clean and have no joints to leak.

Another type has a laminated top similar to a kitchen counter. The bowl is an insert. The advantage to this type of top is that it can be custom-made to fit any configuration. This style often is used to top double-sink installations.

Points to Consider When Replacing a Vanity

A new vanity can really spruce up a bathroom and increase the storage, but

INSTALLING A VANITY

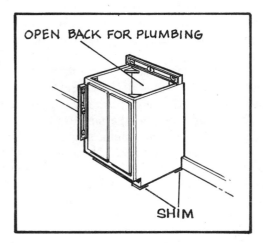

1. Set, level, and attach the vanity.

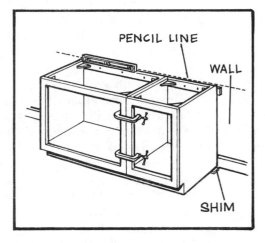

2. You can use two vanity bases together to form a larger cabinet. Before you attach them to the wall, clamp the sides of the cabinets together at the front. Use screws driven through the adjoining sides of the frames to hold them together. Then level them and attach them to the wall.

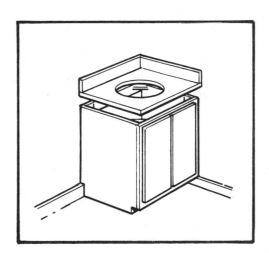

3. Secure the vanity top.

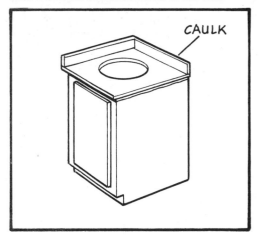

4. Caulk all joints, especially above the backsplash.

there are some things you should consider before you purchase one. Run down this list to get an idea of how involved the installation of a new vanity, sink top, and sink faucet will be:

Check the existing plumbing. Carefully measure the distance from the floor to the hot-water and cold-water supply and drain pipes. Compare these measurements with the rough-in dimensions of the new vanity you plan to purchase. Plumbing that was installed for wall-hung and pedestal sinks is sometimes so high on the wall that the pipes will not fit under the vanity.

Sometimes we have had to drill or cut holes in the back framing of the cabinet for the pipes to pass through. We have found that if you can get the water supply pipes to fit under the vanity so it will fit flush against the wall, you will be able to install it.

Size the vanity correctly. Install a vanity that fits the bathroom. Be sure to allow ample space between the tub and toilet and the vanity. Also remember that narrow spaces are very hard to clean and will harbor moisture and mildew. If you install the vanity too close to the tub or shower, the vanity eventually will be damaged by water.

Check the door swing. Most vanities have doors that can be mounted to open to either the right or left, but check this out. Sometimes the vanity door can conflict with the bathroom door or a shower stall door. You will find it very inconvenient if you have to close one door to open the other.

Install shutoff valves and flexible risers and drains. If there are no shutoff valves on the hot-water and cold-water pipes, install them. This will allow you to turn the water off where you are working

and still have it on in the rest of the house.

Shutoff valves are also the easiest solution for supply pipes mounted high on the wall tight under an old sink. Position the valves so the riser tubes face down, or at an angle away from the sink. Install extralong, flexible riser tubes between the valves and the faucet. These longer tubes are easier to bend into loops and align with the faucet.

If alignment between the tailpiece (attached to the sink bottom) and the trap is a problem, substitute a flexible plastic tailpiece. These are available in different lengths with a flexible section in the middle that allows you to bend the pipe several inches to the right or left for alignment.

Plumbing for a vanity sink is identical to plumbing for a pedestal or wall-hung sink. See the "Replacing a Wall-Hung Sink" section of this chapter for information on how to hook up the pipes. Here's the simple procedure for setting up a vanity:

Install the base. Set the vanity in place and level it carefully. Place shims under the cabinet if necessary, then screw it to the wall. Use long screws driven into the wall studs. If you can't find the studs, then use toggle bolts to secure the base to the wall.

Install the top. Secure the vanity top with screws driven through the vanity frame into the underside of the top. If you use a one-piece cast top, secure it with construction adhesive because synthetic marble or other materials will not take screws.

Caulk the vanity. Use a silicone caulk to seal all joints between the vanity top and wall, especially above the backsplash.

Replacing a Vanity Top

You can replace just the vanity top if you are happy with the base you have. The vanity top you choose depends on your budget and taste. Of course, the size of the vanity base will determine the size of the top, but you can purchase tops with extension arms to extend over the toilet tank. These provide added shelf space. Before you decide, look at all the possibilities.

Check for faucet compatibility. Decide on the type of faucet you will install, or take a good look at the one you have, to make sure it will fit into the new vanity top. Newer faucets are becoming standardized, and unless your old faucet really is something special, you'll probably want to replace it while you are removing the old sink. But if you plan to use your old faucet, check the distance between the hot and cold connections. Vanity tops are not easy to modify.

Adding a Bathroom Vent

The bathroom is a small room with lots of warm moisture, exactly the cozy kind of home mildew loves. Sometimes controlling excessive humidity in the bath can be as simple as opening a window, but most of the time the best solution is to install an exhaust fan. This type of fan will help prevent mildew and other moisture problems, such as peeling wallpaper and the foggy mirror after a shower.

Many times, if you are going to the trouble to install an exhaust fan, you might as well make it a light-fan combination. It won't cost you much more, it's no

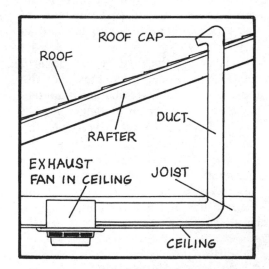
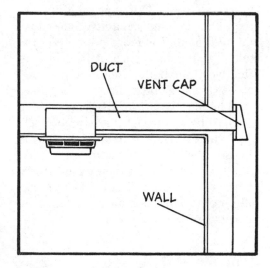

A combination light-fan allows you to improve ventilation and general lighting in the bath. Here's how to vent one through the roof or through the wall.

more work, and you'll improve the lighting in your bathroom.

All combination light-vent units have stickers indicating that Underwriters Laboratory approves them for bathroom ceiling installation. But this doesn't mean they are intended for installation in a shower stall. Shower stall fixtures have special waterproof gaskets. If you install a fixture in your shower, make sure it is designed for that purpose.

Also available are fans combined with heat lamps that allow you to take the chill out of the bathroom while keeping the rest of the house at an energy-efficient temperature.

If you have an existing ceiling light, the easiest job may be to replace it with an overhead light-fan combination; the wiring already is where you want it. But, as we will describe, the tougher part of installing the new fixture will be routing the flexible exhaust duct to the outside.

If you want to avoid snaking the duct through your ceiling, consider installing a wall vent. This type of vent has greater air-moving capacity than most ceiling fans and is more commonly installed in the kitchen, but it is just as effective in the bath. The only disadvantage is you won't be adding a light, just a fan. The big advantage is, of course, that it vents directly through a hole in the wall.

Whatever fan or light-fan unit you choose, it will probably come prewired, so all you have to do is hook up three wires as in any other fixture. All of these units come with complete installation instructions.

Sizing the Vent

The vent you choose must be able to remove the moisture from the bath-room quickly enough so that it does not have a chance to cool and condense on the walls or other objects in the bath. The Home Ventilating Institute recommends that the ventilator for a bathroom be capable of exhausting eight times the volume of the air in the room per hour. A rule of thumb that you can use to size your vent is to multiply the length of the bath by its width in feet and then multiply this figure by 1.1. The answer is the cubic-feet-per-minute (cfm) rating of the vent.

For example, if you have a bath that is 5 feet wide and 7 feet long, you should multiply 5 by 7 and get 35, and then multiply this figure by 1.1 to get 38.5. Round it off to 39. You should shop for a vent with at least a 40-cfm rating. Use the chart on the opposite page to quickly find the size vent you need.

When you are deciding on vent capacity, don't get carried away. High volume is good to a point, but an oversized vent will do more than remove the moisture fast. It will pull out more of that expensive warmed or cooled air than is necessary.

Most suppliers stock vent fans in the 70-cfm range, since these are the most popular sizes. Fans are manufactured with smaller and larger ratings in 10-cfm increments. Before you order the fan, check the size of the duct it requires. The larger-capacity fans require larger-diameter ducts. Check that you have the room to install the required duct. If you use ducting that is too small, you'll be wasting a lot of electricity.

Installing
a Light-Vent Combination

Each bathroom presents its own set of circumstances that must be dealt with

Bath Vent Capacity Sizing
(CFM)

WIDTH											
16	88	123	158	194	229	264	299	334	370	405	440
15	83	116	149	182	215	248	281	314	347	380	413
14	77	108	139	169	200	231	262	293	323	354	385
13	72	100	129	157	186	215	243	272	300	329	358
12	66	92	119	145	172	198	224	251	277	304	330
11	61	85	109	133	157	182	206	230	254	278	303
10	55	77	99	121	143	165	187	209	231	253	275
9	50	69	89	109	129	149	168	188	208	228	248
8	44	62	79	97	114	132	150	167	185	202	220
7	39	54	69	85	100	116	131	146	162	177	193
6	33	46	59	73	86	99	112	125	139	152	165
5	28	39	50	61	72	83	94	105	116	127	138
	5	7	9	11	13	15	17	19	21	23	25

LENGTH

Note: *Bathroom width and length are in feet. CFM stands for cubic feet per minute.*

when installing a vent fan. We have found the key to doing a job like this is careful planning before you do any purchasing or wall cutting. The actual installation of the vent is easy if you know what to expect when you cut into the ceiling and have planned exactly how you are going to route the duct to the outside. Also figure out where the electricity to power the fan will come from. Here is a list of areas you should check before you begin this project; then, when you have everything together and your attack planned, all you have to do is follow the manufacturer's installation directions:

Sketch the bathroom. Your sketch can be rough but should accurately indicate locations of the door, windows, tub/shower, sink, and toilet. Also mark the location of any overhead light or wall lights and where the switches are located.

Determine the joist direction. This is important because it's much easier to run ducting along ceiling joists than through them. If the bathroom is below the attic, you can go up there to check out the joists. Or, because ceiling joists usually run in the same direction as floor joists, you can check the joists in your basement. If either of the above approaches is impossible, you can use a stud finder that detects the drywall or lath nails or screws. These fasteners run in the same direction as the joists. Mark the direction of the ceiling joists on your plan.

If the joists run perpendicular to the outside wall, you can usually push the flexible ducting between joists to the outside wall. Just make sure there are no pipes or wires in your way. If your bathroom is under the attic, it's often easiest to run the duct into the attic and then through the eaves or the roof.

If the joists run parallel to the exterior wall and the bathroom is under the attic, then the attic route is almost definitely your best choice. The only alternative is to drill through the joists. This requires removing part of the ceiling to get to the joists, and we've never thought it was worth the trouble unless we were going to replace the ceiling anyway. If you do decide to drill through joists, check with your local building department. Some codes allow holes to be drilled through joists but do not allow the joists to be notched. In any case, you should not make a 3-inch hole in a 2×6 joist. Most joists are made from 2×8, 2×10, or 2×12 stock. You can drill through these joists without much concern if the area of the hole is not in the center of the joist span. Talk to your building inspector before you cut any joist that is supporting a floor above.

There are special fittings for each type of installation, so you should know whether you will be going through the roof, through the wall, or down through the eaves when you buy the vent.

If the joists run parallel to the exterior wall and the bathroom is not under the attic, we suggest that you shop for a wall vent.

Match the fan to the wiring capacity. Most of the time you can swap a vent fan for the overhead light in the bath. If there is no overhead light, the closest electricity usually is located at the lights around the mirror. Most older and all newer branch circuits are rated for at least 15 amps. Since the fan motor in the vent is small, it usually can be added to an existing circuit without fear of overloading.

Recaulking the Tub and Sink

Another source of moisture damage is leaks around the tub and between the sink and faucet. These small leaks can cause a lot of damage if left unchecked. Most repairs for leaks will go a long way toward improving the look of either the kitchen or bath, too. Leaking usually causes unsightly stains around fixtures, and the water can discolor the sink vanity or base. A worn caulk joint between the tub and the tile looks dirty and is usually discolored. Bad grout

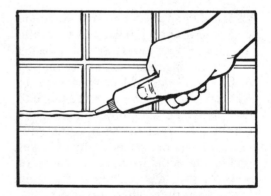

If you've just got one tub to caulk, purchase a small squeeze tube of silicone caulk. Whether you use a squeeze tube or a caulk gun, remove loose and crumbling caulk and grout, fill the joint, smooth with your finger, and let it dry overnight before using the tub.

between bathroom or kitchen tile also usually is discolored and filled with dirt. All of these areas are breeding places for mildew.

Caulking a Tub

Caulking a tub probably is one of the easiest jobs you can do around the house, but that doesn't mean you want to do it frequently. So use a high-quality silicone caulk. Other products will seal the joint and keep out the water, but eventually they will shrink and crack and look terrible.

Silicone caulk is available three ways: standard caulk cartridges in full or half tubes, squeeze tubes, and strip caulk that you press into place. The cheapest way to buy caulk is in the standard caulk tube, but unless you have several other areas to caulk, most of the caulk will probably go to waste. For a single job, purchase a squeeze tube sized for a single tub or buy a roll of caulk.

With any type of caulk, the key to a lasting professional job is in the preparation of the joint. Here is all there is to it:

Clean the joint.   Use a putty knife, utility knife, or beverage can opener to scrape out all the old caulk and grout. Chip out as much grout as possible, then vacuum the crack. The easiest method we have found to remove old, hard caulk from a porcelain tub is to scrape it off with a sharp razor. This will not work with a fiberglass or plastic tub, because the razor can cut into the tub surface.

Dry the joint.   Allow the joint and the area behind the joint to dry thoroughly. This might take several days if the weather is hot and humid and the joint has been leaking for a long time. You can usually tell when the wall behind the tile is dry if the plaster or drywall produces a dust when you scrape it with a screwdriver. If you get damp, crumbly grains, then the area is still wet. To speed the drying process, direct a hair dryer at the joint. A fan directed at the joint also will help.

Fill the tub.   Just before you're ready to caulk, fill the tub full with water so it's at its heaviest. This causes the tub to settle and open the gap between the tub and tile. Then fill the gap with caulk, and allow the caulk to set up for a couple of hours before you drain the water. The tub will then rise and squeeze the caulk bead in the joint. This trick allows you to use the movement of the tub to help keep the joint tight rather than pull the joint apart.

Caulk the joint.   Fill the joint with caulk. If you are using a caulk gun or squeeze tube, see "Doing the Prep Work" in chapter 2 for caulking tips. If you are using place-and-press caulk, unroll the caulk tape and start by cutting a length about 2 inches longer than you need for the back of the tub or sink. At the end of the tape, peel back the liner a few inches, and then position one end in a corner. The tape is undercut and designed to wedge itself into the joint. As you work your way along and around the tub, continue peeling back the liner as you tap the caulk into place. Don't worry if you goof; just reposition the tape and press it firmly into place. Miter corners by cutting the tape at a 45-degree angle.

Rejuvenating Grout in Ceramic Tile

Renewing tile grout is the next best thing to installing new tile. Most ceramic tile usually holds up pretty well. All it usually needs is a good scrubbing, but old grout is another story. Grout that has

REGROUTING TILE

1. Remove the loose and crumbling grout with a putty knife or the pointed end of a beverage can opener.

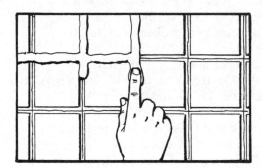
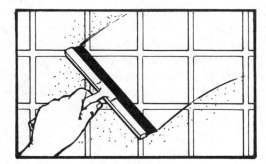

2. Mix up grout of a matching color, then apply it to the joints with your fingers, or use a rubber squeegee to cover a large area.

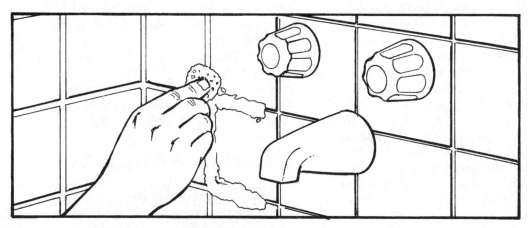

3. Wipe off the excess grout with a wet sponge, and then polish the tiles when the grout has set up and turns hazy white on the tile.

not been cared for collects dirt and stains and is a breeding ground for mildew. If it is cracked, water can get behind the tile and cause damage in the wall. Regrouting might be all that's needed to give a fresh new look to the old tile. New grout will also help secure any slightly loose tiles and fill all open joints.

You can buy grout specifically designed for regrouting, or you can use standard grout that is epoxy or portland cement based. Tools are simple; your index finger is the most important one. In addition, you'll need a beverage can opener, a Popsicle stick or craft stick, and two large sponges. A window squeegee can be helpful if you have one.

As in recaulking, the most time-consuming but important job is preparing the joints by removing all the old, loose grout. We like to use a beverage can opener and an old screwdriver, but use whatever works for you. Don't be afraid to experiment. You'll find that after working at it for a few minutes, you'll come up with your own tricks for removing the grout. Here are the basic steps for regrouting tile:

Chip out the grout.   Remove all loose or badly discolored grout from the joints. You don't have to chip out all the grout if it is solidly in the joint. Scrape these joints to remove all surface dirt and to rough up the old grout so the new material will have something to attach itself to. Remove enough grout to create a groove at least ⅛ inch deep in each joint.

Wet the joints.   Use a sponge or a spray bottle to wet all the tile joints with water. This prevents the dry tiles from absorbing too much moisture from the grout.

Apply the grout.   Mix the new grout according to its directions, and apply it to the joints with a squeegee. Spread the grout on the tile with your hand, and then work it into the joints with the squeegee. If it's a small job, use your index finger to spread the grout and work it into the joints. Work in a small area so the grout does not set up before you have worked it into all the joints. The working time should be specified by the manufacturer.

Strike the joints.   With a clean, wet sponge, wipe off the excess grout, working across the tile joints. Then use a craft stick, the end of an old toothbrush handle, the end of a wooden paint-stirring paddle, or anything else that fits into the tile joints to push the grout deep into the joint. This is called striking the joint. Use the sponge to remove the excess grout pushed aside by the tool. You should be able to clearly see the edges of each tile after the joints are struck. Go back over the joints with the stick after sponging; some grout will probably be pushed back into the joints.

Polish the tiles.   After you have removed as much of the grout as possible with the sponge, allow the grout to dry. As the grout dries, a film will form on the tile. Remove it with a clean, dry, soft rag. Let the grout cure for as long as the manufacturer specifies, then apply a grout sealer to retard staining and mildew.

Installing the Essentials

Many basic bathrooms can be improved with the addition of simple bolt-on convenience items. Color-coordinated towel bars, toilet paper holders, and toilet seats can go a long way to changing the look and function in a simple bathroom. The installation of strategically placed grab rails goes a long way in improving safety in the bathroom. All these bolt-on accessories are inexpensive and easy to install. Teamed with a coat of paint or new wallpaper, you will be pleasantly surprised at how an ordinary bathroom can be improved, both in appearance and function. Here are some basic items every bathroom should have.

Installing a Towel Bar

Even the most basic bathroom probably has a towel rack. If it is ceramic and built into the tile, you can't do much about it. But if it's the bolt-on type, it is probably easy to remove and relocate.

If you have the wall space, consider using several racks full of colorful towels to help decorate the bathroom. Everyone in the family can have his own towel and a place to put it. Designer towel bars are available in every imaginable shape and size and made of various materials, but most use the same mounting system.

The most common two-end bar-type towel rack is held to the wall by a hidden plate behind each end support. The plate is attached to the wall with either screws, toggle bolts, or wall anchors. Most other wall-hung accessories, such as soap dishes and toilet paper holders, are installed the same way. Here's how to make a switch:

Remove the old accessory.   A surface-mounted accessory is easy to remove. Just loosen the setscrew, which usually is located at the bottom of the fixture. Then swing the fixture bottom away from the wall as you lift it up to unhook its top edge from the wall plate. You now can get at the mounting screws.

Install the new accessory.   To install a surface-mounted accessory, first decide where you want it. Most accessories come with mounting hardware and screws, but the screws are useful only if you can mount the supports directly over a wall stud. The screws will not hold for long in plaster or drywall. Instead, use wall anchors. See the "Wall Anchors" section of chapter 3.

We follow the specific directions supplied by the manufacturer but have found that it is easier to get towel racks level if you mount one of the wall plates first at the desired height (according to the directions). Then put the second plate on the wall where you think it should go but don't mount it. Place a carpenter's level between the two plates, and adjust the height of the second plate until it is perfectly level with the first. Then drill pilot holes for the wall anchors. It is easier to level the light mounting plates than to try to hold the whole towel rack level and mark the wall.

Installing a Toilet Paper Holder

A toilet paper holder is installed basically the same way as a towel bar. The surface-mounted type sticks out rather far from the wall, so be sure to mount it far enough from the toilet so it will not be hit by your knee or interfere with sitting. To solve this problem, some styles of holders have short mounting arms and store the paper roll in a wall recess. These units require cutting a rectangular hole in the wall. They are designed to be put in a wall that is at least 3 inches deep. Before you cut up your wall, check that you have room in the wall cavity and that there is not a water pipe or electrical line running through the wall behind the area you want to cut into. To check, look directly

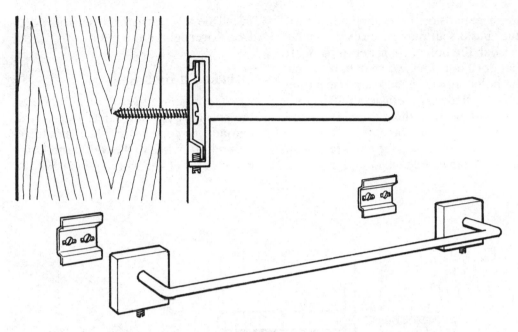

To mount a towel rack, screw one of the mounting brackets to the wall, and level across for the height of the second bracket. Temporarily hang the rack on the first bracket, and use the rack to mark the horizontal position of the second bracket. Secure the second bracket, mount the bar, and tighten the setscrews at the bottom of the bracket covers.

above and below the area to see if there's an electrical receptacle. Then turn off the electricity in case you do hit a wire, and probe the wall by slowly and carefully drilling a small hole in the plaster or drywall. Stop drilling if you feel unusual resistance; it's very easy to drill into a copper or plastic pipe. Drill only most of the way through the drywall or plaster lath, then poke through with a screwdriver to make sure you won't be hitting a water pipe. Insert a section of coat hanger wire through the hole and wiggle the wire around to feel for wall studs or pipes.

Replacing a Toilet Seat

It's easy to replace an old toilet seat. Because toilets now come in several styles, it's important to have a rough sketch with dimensions of the seat you're replacing. Better yet, bring the old seat and its bolts with you when you shop for a new seat, to guarantee you'll buy a new one that will fit. The distance between the holes for the mounting bolt differs on some older toilets, as does the length of the bowl.

Modern toilet seats are sold with plastic or nylon nuts and bolts or neoprene expansion bolts that don't rust. But an old seat may have rusty bolts. If so, soak the bolts with penetrating oil. If that does not work, you will have to saw the bolts off with a hacksaw. Use a fine-toothed blade (32 teeth per inch) in your saw, and protect the underside of the bowl with masking tape.

Before installing the new seat, clean the toilet bowl and tank thoroughly, then install the new seat with the bolts provided. Don't overtighten the bolts.

Installing a Grab Rail

Grab rails in the tub or shower area are probably the best safety feature you can add to your bath. They should be securely attached to the wall studs. Don't install a towel bar where people will be

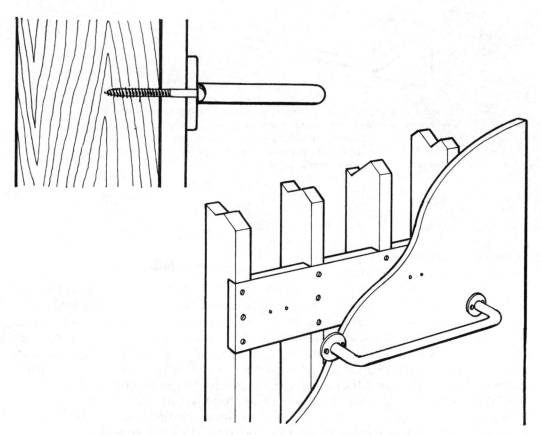

A grab bar must be attached directly to wood; plaster and drywall are not strong enough. Screw the bar directly into the wall stud, or if the wall is open, "let in" a piece of plywood so it is flush with the wall surface of the studs. This will give you more choice of where to install the grab bar.

tempted to use it as a grab bar. This can cause someone to fall, because towel bars are not designed or installed to carry the weight of a person.

A grab bar should be capable of supporting at least 250 pounds of force, more if there are heavyweights in your house. It should be installed directly into the wall studs with screws that are long enough to penetrate the studs at least 1½ inches. Wall anchors or toggle bolts are not strong enough.

If you are into a major bathroom remodeling and have removed the plaster or drywall around the tub, consider installing a band of ¾-inch exterior-grade plywood around the tub or shower stall area wherever you might want to mount a grab bar. The wood plies in exterior plywood are held together with waterproof glue. This grade of plywood stands up well to the moisture in the bathroom. Then after the walls are replaced, you will have more latitude in mounting the grab bar, since it can be screwed directly to the plywood-backed walls.

Installing a Sliding Tub Door

A sliding tub door is a surefire way to contain shower splash. These doors are not difficult to install, and if you choose one with a mirror, they can go a long way to visually opening up a small bath.

Some of the first sliding tub doors were more of a nuisance than a convenience because it was difficult to clean the tracks and the accordion-type fiberglass or plastic doors. The doors on the market today are well designed and come in a variety of colorful trim finishes,

SAVING WATER IN THE BATHROOM

As fresh water becomes increasingly scarce and expensive in many parts of the country, there's good reason to be more frugal in how we use it. Here are ways to cut down use of this precious resource many of us take for granted:

▶ A water-saving, low-flow shower head helps decrease the amount of water used to take a shower. Choose one with a built-in shutoff that lets you turn the water off at the shower head while soaping up and turn it back on for rinsing. Because of the shutoff valve, there's no need to readjust the hot and cold water. These shower heads are inexpensive and easy to install; usually that means that it is just a simple screw-in device. They can reduce water usage by 25 to 40 percent.

▶ Use a gallon plastic jug to make a displacement bottle for the toilet tank. Cut the top off the jug and weigh it down with a few stones. Put it along one side of the tank where it won't interfere with the flushing mechanism. The jug will fill with water, so every time the toilet is flushed, it will require less water to refill its tank. You have to experiment with this idea, customizing it to the inside of your tank. (Two quart bottles might work better in some instances.)

truly a high-style improvement for any bathroom.

Shower doors fit a standard 5-foot tub and have either two or three panels. The two-panel style allows a 30-inch opening space, while three panels allow a 40-inch opening. The three-panel doors are great if you have to bathe children, since they open wide enough to give

INSTALLING A SHOWER DOOR

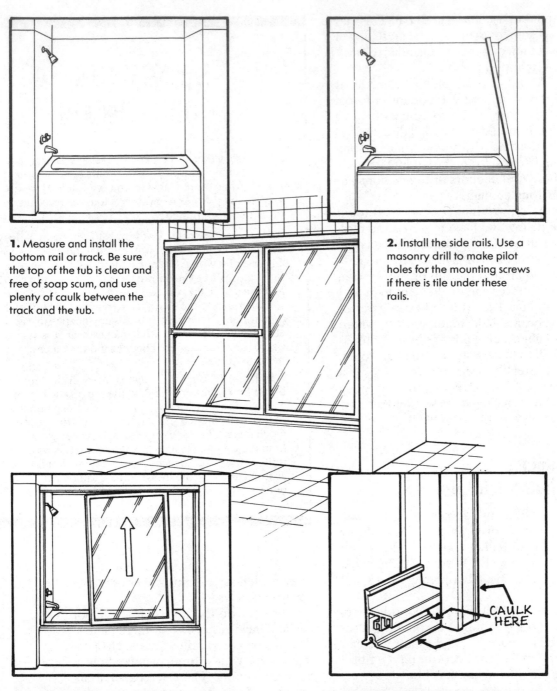

1. Measure and install the bottom rail or track. Be sure the top of the tub is clean and free of soap scum, and use plenty of caulk between the track and the tub.

2. Install the side rails. Use a masonry drill to make pilot holes for the mounting screws if there is tile under these rails.

3. Install the top rail. Then hang the doors and adjust the top roller mechanism.

4. Caulk all joints between the bottom and side rails and the tub and bottom rail. Allow the caulk to set for 24 hours before using the tub.

CAULK HERE

you plenty of elbow room to reach into the tub area. Both styles have optional towel bars.

We have installed several types of sliding doors, and the only problem we have encountered is that eventually the U-shaped bottom track begins to leak when the caulk dries out. This track also collects soap film and dirt and eventually looks bad. There are several doors now available with bottom tracks that are not U-shaped. Before you purchase a door, check out the bottom track and try to visualize if water can collect in the track. The U-shaped tracks have drain slots to let out the water they collect, but other designs don't even allow water to collect in the lower track. You can check out these doors at most larger home centers.

You'll receive detailed instructions with the sliding door that will help you install it properly. But here are some tips to prepare you for the job:

▶ If the area around the tub is covered with ceramic tile, check the installation instructions for the size of the jamb mounting screws. Then purchase a masonry bit this size so you can drill through the tough tile.

▶ Use a fine-toothed (32 teeth per inch) hacksaw blade to cut the aluminum top, bottom, and side jambs of the door to size. Always wear safety glasses when cutting metal, and measure twice before cutting anything.

▶ Check the caulk supplied by the manufacturer. If it is not a silicone type, purchase some that is. It will last much longer and will act as a strong adhesive to help hold bottom and side jambs in place.

▶ Thoroughly clean the tub and wall surfaces before installation.

Installing a Tub Surround

We have found ceramic tile usually can be saved, but other surfaces such as plaster or plastic tile are not worth the effort to rejuvenate. The quickest, most economical solution to bad walls around a tub or shower is to install a fiberglass or plastic tub or shower surround.

These are sold in kits and are available in many colors and styles. The prices of these kits also vary, and you generally get what you pay for. The more expensive kits are made from heavy-gauge materials and have superior finishes. This is an important consideration because fiberglass and plastic, while strong and rotproof, are not very scratch resistant. They are easy to keep clean, but you have to use cleaners designed for them; otherwise, the coarse abrasives in standard cleaners can dull their shiny finish.

Units made with heavy-gauge materials can be installed over old walls that are not perfectly smooth, but check with the supplier if you plan to do this. The walls must be structurally sound, because the panels are not strong enough to go directly on the studs. They are designed to be glued in place, so the mastic has to have something solid to adhere to. These panels should be considered a waterproof wall covering, not a structural surface. Their big advantage is quick and easy installation.

All these surrounds have at least three panels—one for each end of the tub and one for the back. Most have corner pieces that can contain soap dishes or just provide a gentle radius to the corners so they are easy to clean. More elaborate models have built-in storage and handrails.

Whatever type appeals to you, look carefully at how the joints are made.

INSTALLING A PREFORMED TUB SURROUND

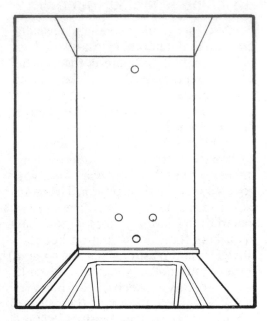

1. Carefully measure and lay out the position of the faucets and shower head. Then cut these holes with a saber or hole saw.

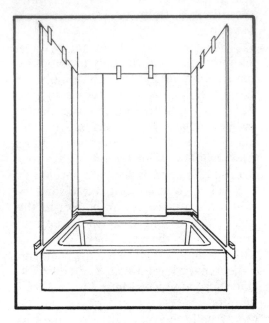

2. Install the large panels. Most are glued in place and can be installed over any sound, smooth surface.

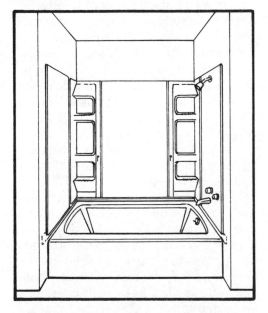

3. Install the corner panels; most have molded-in storage. If required, carefully caulk all joints with a caulk that is approved or supplied by the manufacturer.

The panels should overlap or join in tongue-and-groove joints. Butt joints rely on the caulk alone to remain watertight, and sooner or later the caulk will dry out. Exposed caulk also will collect dirt.

Each manufacturer supplies do-it-yourself instructions with the kits, and you should follow them exactly. Here are a few tips that should help you make a hassle-free installation:

Gather the right tools. Most kits come with all parts and adhesive, but you will need the following tools: tape measure, carpenter's square, straightedge, utility knife, drill, hole saw or saber saw to make openings for plumbing controls, screwdriver, hacksaw, masking tape, pencil, and caulk gun (used to apply the adhesive).

Protect the tub. Lay an old blanket, drop cloth, or heavy cardboard (use the carton the kit comes in) in the bottom of the tub to protect its finish.

Test fit the panels. Use masking tape to temporarily hold panels in place after trimming them to size. Some panels can be cut with a sharp knife; all you have to do is score the face and snap the panel off like a piece of drywall. Other panels require a saw. If you are cutting this type of panel with a saber or circular saw, place the good side of the panel down, since the saws cut in the up stroke of the blade. If you are using a hand saw, then place the panel face up; a hand saw cuts on the down stroke. Tape everything in place to be sure it all goes together before you apply the mastic.

Drill from the finished side. Lay out the location of the plumbing controls, and drill their holes from the good side of the panel. If you are using a saber saw to cut the holes, work on the back side. This will give you the smoothest edge on the finished side.

Use proper adhesive. Use only adhesive supplied or recommended by the manufacturer. If you run out of adhesive, take the tube with you when you get more. The acrylonitrile-butadiene-styrene (ABS) plastic panels are especially sensitive to the type of adhesive used. Some will buckle or bubble if you use an adhesive that contains a solvent that is contained in the plastic.

Replacing a Medicine Cabinet

We have found the following to be generally true: the older the bathroom, the smaller the medicine cabinet. And sometimes the cabinets are in the most inconvenient places. This is another area in the bathroom that can be upgraded inexpensively.

In a small, old bathroom you are likely to find a small, custom-built, wooden recessed cabinet. Some have mirrors, others don't. If it is located over the sink, you can remove the old cabinet and find a new one that fits into the existing opening. If the cabinet is surface mounted, you have much more leeway in choosing a replacement.

Swapping Cabinets

If you swap an old, worn-out recessed cabinet for a replacement of the same size or smaller, you won't need to make changes to the wall framing. Before you tear out the old cabinet, measure it to be sure you can find a replacement. The cabinet probably has trim covering the joint between the cabinet and the wall. Remove this trim so you can see the true size of the wall opening.

Compare the new cabinet with this measurement, to be certain it will fit into the old hole. If you purchase a cabinet that is smaller than the original, nail shims or thin strips of wood to the old framing to make the opening smaller to fit the size of your new cabinet. Strips of plywood are handy for this.

Cover the gap around the cabinet with trim molding, or fill it with spackling compound. If the gaps are more than a couple of inches, you will have to cut and fit pieces of drywall to fill the gaps. You must plan ahead to make sure the drywall fits flush with the existing wall. In houses with plaster walls, the carpenter would build a light frame for the cabinet. This frame would be installed

MOUNTING A MEDICINE CABINET

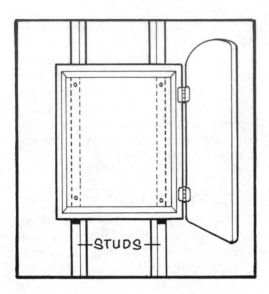

Surface-mounted cabinets are screwed directly to the wall studs.

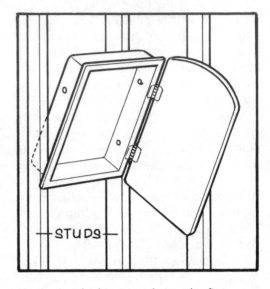

Most recessed cabinets are designed to fit between studs and are screwed directly to the studs.

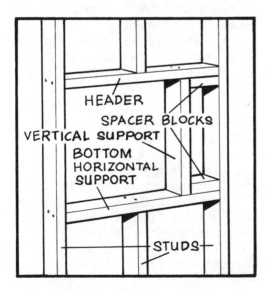

For larger cabinets, you have to cut away a stud, and frame around all sides of the cabinet.

so that it protrudes far enough from the studs to allow the lath and plaster to be built up flush to it. You'll have to cut this frame back equal to the thickness of the drywall patches.

If you require a cabinet that is larger than the opening, the easiest solution is to choose a surface-mounted model that is large enough to cover the existing opening. You might want to cut a short piece of 2 × 4 to fit vertically in the center of the opening. You can toenail 8d common nails into the bottom and top edges of this short stud so they go through both the short stud and the top and bottom horizontal pieces you are nailing it to. Do this on both sides of the top and bottom of the stud. Note that the face of this stud should be flush with the wall surface. This new, short stud will give you additional support behind the cabinet.

If you are changing the location of the medicine cabinet or installing a new one, make it about 8 inches above the sink.

Recessing a Cabinet

The advantage of a recessed medicine cabinet is, of course, that it does not stick out from the wall as far as a surface-mounted cabinet. But since most walls are only 3½ inches deep, this advantage might not be worth the effort, especially if you are planning to install a large cabinet. Most cabinets designed for surface mounting can be recessed into a wall cavity. Just check to see that hinged doors open properly.

Most houses are built with 14½ inches between studs (16 inches on-center), and so it's easy to find medicine cabinets that are 14 inches wide. If you buy a cabinet that will fit between two existing studs, you can install it in any wall in your house. But if you use a wider cabinet, you'll have to cut a stud. This is no problem if the wall does not bear the load of a second floor or roof. But you don't want to cut a stud in a bearing wall unless you are prepared to build a structural header to take the load of the severed stud. We don't think it's worth getting involved with retrofitting a structural header just to recess a medicine cabinet.

All exterior walls are bearing walls. You can tell other bearing walls by going up to the attic or down to the basement to check the direction of joists in your house. If the wall runs perpendicular to the joists, it's probably a bearing wall. If the wall runs parallel to the joists, it's not a bearing wall and you can remove a stud without causing the ceiling to sag.

Checking the Wall Cavity

Before you cut a big hole in your wall to recess a cabinet, you must make sure there are no pipes or electrical lines where the cabinet will go. Unless there is another bathroom directly above on the next floor, water pipes probably do not run up the wall behind the sink area. But there might be a vent line for the sink, especially if it is more than a couple of feet from the toilet. There usually is a large pipe (vent stack) running up the wall behind the toilet, so think twice before you decide to recess a cabinet over a toilet.

The only sure way to check the area behind the wall for pipes and wires is to cut a small hole and look, as described in the "Installing a Toilet Paper Holder" section of this chapter. Turn off the electricity before you do any cutting, just in case you "discover" a wire with your saw. Make this hole in the center of where the new cabinet will be located. Then if you find the wall full of stuff, surface-mount the cabinet and it will cover the inspection hole.

Mounting a Cabinet between Studs

Most medicine cabinets made for recessing come with installation directions including rough opening dimensions. Follow these directions closely. Here's how we install a cabinet between studs, in case you don't have manufacturer's directions (by the way, while you have the wall open is the time to do any wiring for lighting fixtures or receptacles):

Scribe the opening. Locate the inside edges of the two studs that will flank the cabinet. Position the cabinet between the studs, and use a carpenter's level to make sure it is plumb and level. Now scribe a pencil mark where the cabinet meets the wall.

Cut the opening.   If the wall is drywall, the cut will be neatest if you use a metal straightedge and a sharp utility knife to cut the hole. Just keep scoring all around the perimeter until you've cut through. If the wall is plaster, the best method is careful plunge cuts with a circular saw. You can also use a saber saw or a short hand saw.

Install the cabinet.   Slip the cabinet into the opening, and screw through the mounting holes in the sides of the cabinet into the studs. If the cabinet is a loose fit, you may have to put some shims between the studs and the cabinet.

Mounting a Wider Recessed Cabinet

As mentioned, if your cabinet is wider than the distance between two studs, it's only practical to recess it into a nonbearing wall. Here's how to do that:

Lay out the opening.   Start by scribing the perimeter of the cabinet on the wall as already described. Now draw two more level lines, one at $1\frac{1}{2}$ inches above the top of the cabinet and one at $1\frac{1}{2}$ inches below the bottom of the cabinet. You'll have to make the opening at these lines so you can cut away enough stud to allow for the thickness of horizontal and vertical support pieces.

Cut the opening.   This is done in the same way as described for mounting a cabinet between studs. The only difference is, you don't want to use a saber saw to cut the wall in front of the stud. The saw will bounce dangerously, probably breaking the blade and surrounding plaster.

Cut the stud.   After you remove the plaster or drywall, you will see a stud running through the opening. Removing this stud is the trickiest part of the job, especially if you have plaster walls, because the motion of your saw can easily crack plaster above, below, and behind the opening. Use a circular saw to cut out the stud flush with the top and bottom of the opening. Check the maximum depth of cut of your circular saw. Most won't quite make it through the $3\frac{1}{2}$-inch dimension of a 2×4, and you'll have to finish the cut with a hand saw. Also make sure you don't cut so deep you go through the wall behind the stud. If you don't have a circular saw, you can do the whole job with a hand saw.

Remove the stud.   If the wall behind the stud is lath and plaster, you can usually pull the piece of stud away from the lath nails without cracking the plaster. If drywall is on the other side, you have no choice but to pull the nails or screws through the drywall when you remove the stud. You'll have to patch these holes later.

Install header and bottom supports. These are the horizontal pieces that support the cabinet at top and bottom. They span the distance between the studs to either side of the one you cut away. In most houses this distance should be $30\frac{1}{2}$ inches, but studs are rarely placed exactly, so measure and cut for a snug fit. Use 10d common nails to face-nail these pieces at top and bottom where you cut away the stud. Then use 8d common nails to toenail the supports into the full studs on either side. Make sure the supports are level.

Install vertical supports. How you do this step depends on the width of your cabinet and where it will be placed between the studs. If your cabinet is 30 inches wide, the existing studs are your vertical supports, and all you have to do is screw the cabinet to them. If the cabinet is only slightly less than 30 inches, you may just have to shim the studs or "pack them out" with strips of plywood, a piece of 2 × 4, or both. If the cabinet falls more than 2 inches short of one or both studs, your best bet is to make spacer blocks. For example, let's say your cabinet is 28 inches wide and the opening is oriented so that the left side can be nailed directly into the stud. That leaves a 2½-inch gap between the right stud and the cabinet. Make two 2 × 4 spacers, each 1 inch long. Nail a spacer at the top and bottom of the stud. Cut a vertical support to fit between the horizontal supports. Place the vertical support behind the wall against the spacers, and toenail it to the horizontal supports. The spacers will keep the vertical piece in position while you toenail.

Screw the wall to the frame. Use drywall screws to fasten the wall to the new framing.

Repair the wall. If the wall is drywall, cut 1½-inch-wide strips of drywall to cover the horizontal supports. If the wall is plaster, use patching plaster or drywall. If you use drywall, you'll have to shim behind it to bring it flush with the rest of a plaster wall. Cover the repair with joint compound.

Install the cabinet. After the joint compound has dried and you've sanded it smooth, position the cabinet in the hole, making sure it fits snugly against the wall. Make sure no chunks of plaster behind the cabinet are pushing it out of plumb. Screw the cabinet to the frame. Caulk the joint between the cabinet and the wall. Otherwise, the joint will open up as the cabinet expands and contracts at a different rate than the wall. Now you can paint the repair.

Fixing or Replacing a Toilet

Most of the time we try to work around the existing toilet. But an old toilet with a wall-hung tank certainly can date a bathroom. Toilets can also look terrible if badly stained from hard water or water that contains high concentrations of iron.

Sometimes we have had to remove the toilet to lay a new floor or to repair the floor under a leaking toilet. This can be a messy job but it's not hard. If you don't want to buy a new toilet, it's usually easy enough to bring an old toilet up to snuff.

If you decide to keep the old toilet, check to see if there is any leaking between the large cast-iron, copper, or plastic pipe, sometimes called the soil pipe, and the toilet. Check for rust stains on the soil stack (you usually can see the soil stack from the basement if the toilet is on the first floor). Also, look for the inspection door (these usually are located in a closet in the wall behind the sink and toilet). Sometimes you can see the soil stack and other drains from here. If not, check the pipe in the basement. Rust stains running down the pipe are a good indication of a toilet leak, although these stains can come from other sources, such as a leak at the roof collar or from a leaky supply pipe.

A leaky toilet isn't as tough to fix as you might think. Just follow these steps and you will have it back on the floor in a couple of hours (the same steps apply if you are replacing a toilet):

Step 1: Collect supplies from your local home center before you tackle the toilet: Purchase a new wax ring to go between the toilet and soil stack, 10 pounds of plumber's putty to seal between the toilet base and floor, and a set of brass hold-down bolts and nuts to fasten the toilet to the soil stack flange. You should also pick up a flexible water supply tube (most toilets use a ⅜-inch tube, but check yours) and a new gasket to seal between the tank and the bowl.

Step 2: Turn off the water supply valve. (It's close to the floor under the tank.) Flush the toilet to drain the water from the tank and bowl. Sponge out as much as you can from the tank to prevent water from spilling out when you remove it. If you have a wall-mounted tank, it does not have to be removed. If the tank is attached to the toilet, remove it by loosening the hold-down bolts, using a screwdriver to keep the bolts from turning inside the tank.

Step 3: Bale as much water from the toilet bowl as possible. Use a wrench to remove the hold-down bolts located at the toilet base. You might have to clean old, hard plumber's putty from the bolt threads. If the bolts are corroded, cut through them with a hacksaw blade between the nut and the washer. These brass bolts are not too hard to cut.

Step 4: Rock the toilet back and forth to break its seal with the floor. Then lift it up and off the soil stack.

Dump the remaining water into the tub, then place the bowl upside down on a piece of cardboard or blanket to protect the porcelain finish. Stuff newspapers or an old rag into the drainpipe to contain odor.

Step 5: Use a putty knife to scrape old wax and putty from the bottom of the bowl. Also scrape the top of the soil stack flange. It is important to remove all the old, hard putty from both surfaces.

Step 6: Unwrap the new wax ring and place it on the bowl. Push it back and forth so it will stick in place. If it is cold, allow the wax ring to warm up to room temperature. Or if you are in a hurry, set it in some hot water for a couple of minutes so it will soften and be more pliable. It is hard to get the toilet to sit right in the soil stack flange if the wax ring is hard and will not compress.

Step 7: Pack plumber's putty around the wax ring. Then twist putty into a ½-inch-diameter rope, and put the rope around the bottom edge of the toilet. This will provide a tight water seal at the floor.

Step 8: Pack plumber's putty around the bolt slots in the soil pipe flange, to hold the toilet hold-down bolts upright. Place these bolts in the slots, and use more putty if needed to hold them in place.

Step 9: Turn the bowl over and carefully align it so the hold-down bolts pass through the holes in the base of the toilet. Then push it down onto the soil stack flange with a slight twisting motion. Use a level to assure that the bowl is level.

Step 10: Apply petroleum jelly to the tank bolts to prevent corrosion. Then tighten the hold-down bolts. Make them snug but don't overtighten or you can

INSTALLING A TOILET

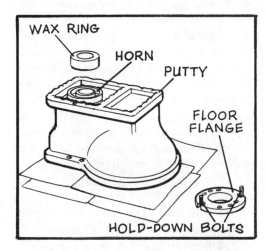

1. Apply putty around the bottom edge of the bowl, and install a new wax ring. Clean the floor flange and make sure it is screwed securely to the subfloor.

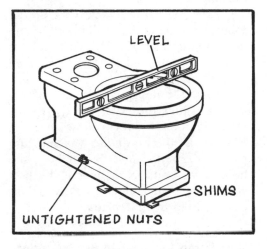

2. Set and level the bowl, using shims if necessary. Tighten the flange nuts, but not so much that you crack the bowl.

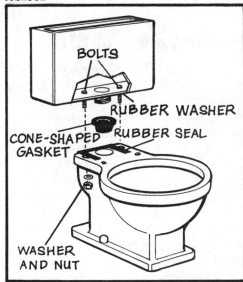

3. Put the rubber seal on the bowl so it lines up with the bolt holes. Push the cone-shaped rubber gasket over the flush outlet, and set the tank in place. Bolt the tank to the bowl; again, don't tighten the bolts too much.

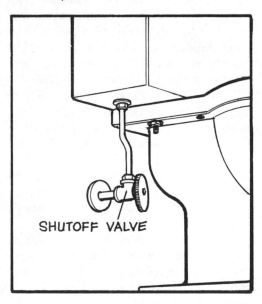

4. Reconnect the water supply.

crack the china. Use the edge of a putty knife to remove excess putty that squeezes out onto the floor.

Step 11: Put the tank back on the toilet, or if the tank is wall hung, reconnect the water supply pipe. If the rubber seal between the tank and bowl is cracked or hardened, replace it.

Step 12: Replace the water supply tube and turn the water on. Check for leaks. Wait a few days to allow the toilet to settle a little bit on the wax ring and plumber's putty, and then tighten the hold-down bolts. Next, install the bolt covers by placing plumber's putty in their base to hold them in place.

Measuring for a Replacement Toilet

Before you can go shopping for a new toilet, you need a few vital statistics about your old one. Manufacturers supply the critical dimensions required to install their toilets. These measurements, called rough-in dimensions, tell the plumber where to install the pipes.

You can find the rough-in dimensions of your toilet by measuring the distance from the wall (not the baseboard) to the hold-down bolts. Use the bolts nearest the wall if there are two sets. Most new toilets require that the center of the soil stack flange be 12 inches from the wall. The hold-down bolts fit into slots on this center line.

If your house is 20 years or older, you may have a toilet with a wall-hung tank that has a 13-inch rough-in dimension. You might also encounter an old toilet with a rough-in dimension of 10 inches. In newer homes you will most likely find a 12 or 14-inch dimension.

If the walls have been tiled, the rough-in dimension probably is ½ inch less. If you have an 11½-inch measurement, choose a 12-inch-rough-in toilet. Manufacturers allow for this by making the toilet slightly short of the true rough-in dimension. Remember you cannot install a new toilet with a rough-in dimension larger than your old toilet. You can, however, use a toilet if its rough-in is less; the toilet will stand away from the wall slightly. Most new toilets have the tank mounted on or built into the toilet and require a 12-inch rough-in dimension.

Another critical dimension is the location of the water supply pipe. Older toilets with wall-hung tanks have supply lines that come out high on the wall. If you plan to install a one-piece low-profile toilet, check the rough-in requirements for the supply; there probably will be a conflict.

Installing a GFI (or GFCI)

If you modify any electrical outlets or lights in the bathroom, the National Electrical Code and most local building codes require you to provide a ground fault circuit interrupter (GFI or GFCI). A GFI is much more sensitive to circuit overloads than is a circuit breaker or fuse. It cuts power when it detects a tiny imbalance in the current between the hot and neutral conductors of an electrical appliance. The imbalance means there could be a current leakage that could deliver a dangerous, even fatal, shock to any person in contact with ground. A GFI usually is required for receptacles near water because water is an excellent conductor of electricity. Contact with water increases the likelihood that your body will become the path of least resistance that electrical current is seeking.

A GFI receptacle has a test button that simulates a ground fault and a reset button that restores power. You can replace a standard receptacle outlet with a GFI. Other options are to change the circuit breaker in the main electrical box so that all the outlets on that circuit are protected or to get a portable GFI that requires no installation except plugging it into a receptacle. If you use a GFI receptacle for the first receptacle on a circuit—the one closest to the fuse or breaker box—all other receptacles on that circuit will be protected.

GFI protection is not exclusive to the bathroom. These safety devices should be installed wherever water and electricity are used near each other. The kitchen, workshop, garage, and backyard are other places where protection is needed.

Installing a Receptacle GFI

All GFI receptacle devices are wired in the same way and come with complete wiring instructions. The pass-through type is designed to be wired into a circuit and provides GFI protection to receptacles wired to the device. This type has an additional set of black and white wires labeled "load" coming out of the back. Unless you want to wire additional receptacles to the device so they are also protected by the GFI, tape the end of these wires and fold them behind the device in the box.

Before doing any electrical modifications, always turn off the power at the service panel. Prepare the GFI for wiring by stripping off ½ inch of insulation from the ends of the green wire and the black and the white wires. Then join each wire to the matching-color wire in the box (follow the manufacturer's directions). Push the GFI device into the box, and secure it in place with the mounting screws provided. Most of these devices need special receptacle plates (box covers), so be sure to purchase one when you get the GFI.

Installing a Circuit Breaker GFI

The GFI breaker has an on/off toggle switch just like a standard circuit breaker. In addition to this toggle, the GFI breaker is equipped with a test button that, when pressed, will trip the breaker toggle. This button tests the ground fault system in the breaker.

This device is designed to give ground fault protection to the whole circuit. The protection is desirable, but some old houses have wiring with poor insulation that allows small amounts of current to leak to ground. While this condition does not affect the operation of the house, it will trip the sensitive GFI. If you have an old house that has the original wiring, you will probably be better served with the individual GFI-type devices. If you add a circuit to the bath, kitchen, or outside that requires GFI protection, then install the breaker.

CHAPTER 10

Storage Strategies and Solutions

The typical American household is facing a storage crunch. We all seem to have more stuff than our parents did. At the same time, new housing goes up with less storage space. The cavernous attic under grandma's rafters has given way to low-pitched roofs constructed of prefabricated trusses that divide the space into near uselessness. Houses and condos are built on slabs without basements, which in most cases means no storage at all except for closets. Even those of us lucky enough to have big attics, basements, or garages never seem to have enough storage space.

One way to solve this problem is to join the growing legions who plunk down an extra $80 or $90 a month for an inconvenient "U-Store-It" along the highway somewhere. But we think there are better ways to spend our time and money. To make this possible, you have to make the most of the storage space you have. That's the topic of this chapter.

Building More Storage

Free enterprise has responded to the storage crunch by creating businesses to help solve your storage problems. Look in the home section of your newspaper and you'll find ads for shops that specialize in designing storage space and selling various storage systems and components. Mail-order catalogs are another good source for specialty storage products. And of course you'll find shelving systems and storage components in home centers and hardware stores.

Quick Open Shelving

We've added shelving in many of our houses for a variety of storage needs —such as over the washer and dryer for laundry products, alongside a desk to hold additional supplies, and under kitchen cabinets for cookbooks.

Slotted metal standards that mount on the wall are probably the easiest and most flexible way to install shelving. Shelf brackets snap into slots that run the entire length of the standard, allowing you to change and adjust the height of each shelf to suit your needs. This system can also be mounted inside furniture or with the standards facing each other in a bookcase.

The most common colors for the standards and brackets are white, gold, and aluminum. The brackets come in depths of 6, 8, 12, 15, and 18 inches. There are also adjustable angle brackets for shelves with a lip that can hold magazines at an angle.

Installing shelving with standards is

easy. For all but the heaviest loads, plastic wall anchors are strong enough to attach the standards to any wall surface. Shelves that are to support heavy loads, such as stereo equipment or books, are best screwed directly to the wall studs. Here are a couple of tips we found helpful to ensure *level* shelves:

Spread the load. Don't space the upright standards more than 24 inches apart, even for light loads, or the shelves will droop. Place the standards even closer—16 inches—if the load is heavy.

Plumb the standards. Install the top screw of the standard first. Hang the standard from this screw but don't tighten it. The standard is free to swing back and forth and will act as a plumb bob hanging straight down. Swing it back and forth several times until you are sure the standard is hanging straight down. You can check it with a level. Hold it in place while you mark the location of the other screws with a pencil point through the screw holes.

Install standards in the same direction. Once you have installed the first standard, use a level to horizontally align the other standards. Make sure that all the standards are installed with the same end facing up. Usually the top and bottom of each standard have a little extra space without a slot. If you have cut the standards from longer pieces, it's best to use the top of the first slot on each standard as a guide when aligning, instead of the top of the standard.

Particleboard or Plywood Shelves

Using ready-made shelf brackets makes a lot of sense, but buying prefinished shelving can get expensive. We have found that making shelves is easy

INSTALLING METAL STANDARDS

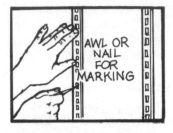

1. Place one standard in position, and install the top screw only.

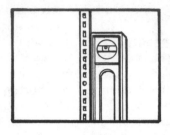

2. Plumb up the standard with a level.

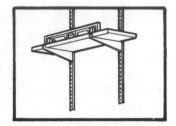

3. Use a level to horizontally align the other standards. Put the shelf on and check that it's level before installing all the screws.

INSTALLING METAL SHELF BRACKETS

1. Install the first bracket on the wall at the desired height.

2. Screw the second bracket to the bottom of the shelf.

3. Place the shelf in position on the first bracket, level, and mark the position of the mounting screws for the second bracket on the wall. Then install the second bracket, and screw the shelf to the first bracket.

and much less expensive. The cheapest shelving material around is particleboard.

Particleboard (also called chip board or flake board) is made of chips of wood impregnated with resins and formed into sheets like plywood. Particleboard is heavier than plywood and more prone to sagging. But it's cheaper than all but the crummiest plywood; it's dimensionally stable and suitable for shelving, as long as spans do not exceed 24 inches and loads are not heavy. If the shelves will have to carry heavy loads, such as big books or your record collection, you'll probably want to use plywood.

The cheapest way to buy particleboard is in 4 × 8-foot sheets. But the sheets are heavy, and unless you have some way to transport them and a circular saw to cut them, you'll want to purchase material that has been precut into shelves.

These precut ¾-inch-thick particleboard shelves are available in various widths and lengths unfinished or prefinished with a white surface. Some pieces have the edges filled or rounded over, but the more finished the strips are, the more they cost. We found that unfinished precut strips are the most economical, since filling the edges and painting doesn't take much time.

Finishing Particleboard Shelves

Painting the shelves is easy, but making them look good takes a little more doing. The edge of standard particleboard is fairly smooth, but it does have some imperfections that are highlighted when you apply paint. Filling in the front edge or covering it with a solid strip of wood is the best solution we have found. Both processes are easy and work just as well for plywood shelves. Here's how to do them:

Filling edges: The easiest way to finish a shelf edge is to fill the minor depressions with wood filler. We found a two-part polyester-based filler is what the doctor ordered. The stuff sets up hard and sticks to just about anything. All we do is apply the filler to the edge of the shelf. When it hardens in about 15 minutes, we sand it smooth and it's ready to paint.

Covering edges: Trying to avoid mak-

ing this a project for a cabinetmaker, we nail and glue a piece of 1 × 2 pine to the front of the shelving. This material is actually 1½ inches wide and ¾ inch thick, and it is inexpensive.

Cut the pine strips to length, and then glue and nail them in place with carpenter's glue and 6d finishing nails. Carefully clean up any dripping glue with a damp rag before it sets. Then use a nail set to drive the nail heads slightly below the surface of the pine. Fill in the nail heads with a wood filler, and then sand. The shelves are ready to paint. These edges will also help keep the shelves from sagging under heavy loads.

Wood veneer tape is another option. You'll find tape sold in ¾-inch-wide rolls at most large home centers or lumber yards. Some tapes have to be glued to the shelf edge, but we like the kind that has heat-sensitive adhesive already applied to the back. All you have to do is hold the tape in position and heat it with a clothes iron. The glue melts and then sets as soon as the strip cools.

An Easy Coatrack

In many homes, the first storage problem confronts us the moment we walk through the door. Where do you put the coats? Here's a simple wall-hung coatrack we've installed in the mudroom of several houses. Nicely finished, it could be perfectly suited to the front entrance hallway as well. The rack is made from a piece of 1 × 4 pine and ready-made shaker-style pegs we find at large home centers or lumberyards.

All you have to do is lay out the location of the pegs on the board; usually a foot spacing between the pegs works well. The pegs require a ½-inch hole, so

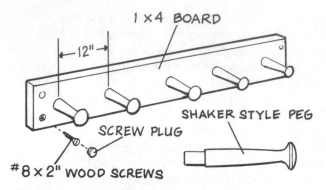

This coatrack is a snap to make and will find plenty of use in any mudroom or front hall.

the easiest bit to use is an inexpensive spade bit in an electric drill. After you drill the holes, sand the 1 × 4 and glue the pegs in place.

We finished the rack with a light coat of oak stain followed by a couple of coats of polyurethane varnish. Mounting the rack on the wall isn't hard; just screw it to the wall studs. The board is long enough to span at least two studs no matter where you mount it.

Window Seat Storage

All the unused nooks, crannies, and corners in your house are likely candidates for built-in storage. For instance, there's nothing more charming (and comfortable) than a window seat below a bay window. Designed with either cabinet or sliding doors or a lift-top seat lid, a window seat provides accessible storage where you can always use it.

Constructing this type of storage unit isn't hard, since the bay window provides most of the structure. The front of the unit is the only thing visible, since the walls and the cushion cover the rest of the unit.

The seats we have constructed have fronts covered with drywall, because this is the least expensive and easiest material to work with. The seat front can also be covered with a piece of hardwood-veneered plywood. The plywood can also be used for the seat. Add hardwood trim to the unit, and it will look like a piece of built-in furniture.

Whatever material you decide to use for the front of the seat, the frame is constructed from 2 × 4 stock attached to the walls of the bay window. The top framing should be about 16 inches from the floor. This will make the finished seat between 18 and 19 inches from the floor, since you will have a ¾-inch plywood seat top and a cushion. Adjust the height to suit your needs, but don't make it too high (especially in the kids' room), or your feet will not be able to touch the ground.

After you have made some initial design decisions, here is how a window seat takes shape:

Remove the molding. Carefully remove baseboard and shoe from the bay. Put them aside to reuse at the front of the window seat.

Strike a line. Use a 4-foot carpenter's level to draw a level line around the three sides of the bay at the seat height minus ¾ inch to allow for the plywood seat. If your floor isn't level, pick a point and make the line level. You can custom-fit the vertical supports and you'll have a level window seat.

Install the cleats. Cut a piece of 2 × 4 to the length of the window wall. Align the top of this cleat with the line, and nail it in place through the wall to each stud with 12d common nails. If your walls are plaster, substitute 3-inch drywall screws to avoid cracking the wall.

BUILDING A WINDOW SEAT

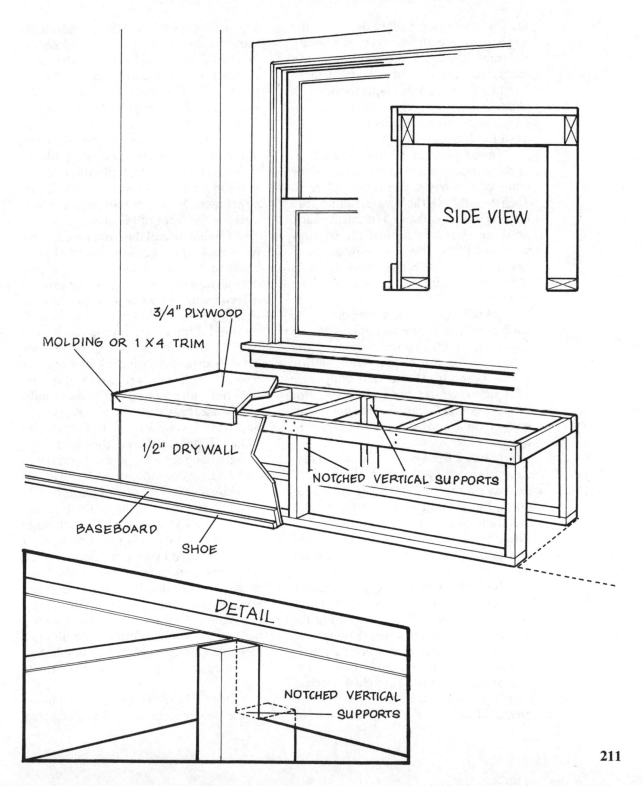

SIDE VIEW

3/4" PLYWOOD

MOLDING OR 1 X 4 TRIM

1/2" DRYWALL

NOTCHED VERTICAL SUPPORTS

BASEBOARD

SHOE

DETAIL

NOTCHED VERTICAL SUPPORTS

211

Measure both side walls of the bay (if the bay isn't square, they won't be the same). Subtract 3½ inches from each measurement, and cut the side cleats to these lengths. Butt the side cleats to the back cleat, and nail or screw them to the line. The cleats should be recessed 2 inches from the front of the bay.

Install plates.   Measure the length of the window wall and the width of the front of the bay, and cut one plate to each length. (If the bay is square, the lengths will be the same.) Install the back plate on the floor against the window wall. Install the front plate on the floor between the side walls, recessed in ½ inch to allow for the thickness of the drywall.

Install vertical wall supports.   At each corner, measure and cut a piece of 2 × 4 to fit between the bottom of the cleat and the top of the plate. Nail or screw these into the corners with their wide sides against the wall. The front supports should align with the plate with half of their top edges under the side cleats.

Install a front beam.   Measure and cut a piece of 2 × 4 to span the front of the bay on top of the front vertical supports. Place them on the verticals, and nail them to the ends of the side cleats. All the front surfaces of your frame should now be flush and recessed ½ inch from the front of the bay.

Install horizontal braces.   Measure and cut braces to fit between the front beam and the rear cleat, centered at 16-inch intervals. Face-nail them through the beam with 10d common nails; then toenail them to the cleat with 8d commons.

Make and install notched vertical supports.   Measure from the top of the rear cleat to the rear plate. Cut a piece of

2 × 4 to this length. Make a notch 3½ inches long and 1½ inches deep on the end of the piece, to fit around the cleat. If the centermost horizontal brace is no more than 24 inches from either side wall, face-nail the notched piece to that, plumb the piece, and toenail it into the plate. If the span is more than 24 inches, add a horizontal brace in the middle of the seat; then face-nail, plumb, and toenail the notched vertical support at the new brace. Make another notched support for the front of the seat.

Cut and install the front piece.   We like to make this piece from ½-inch drywall because it is cheap and takes only a little drywall tape and joint compound to make it blend with the walls on either side of the bay. You could also use ½-inch plywood. Either way, cut the piece to fit over the front of the seat. If the piece is drywall, attach it with drywall screws or nails. If the piece is plywood, use construction adhesive and 6d finishing nails.

Make the seat.   Chances are, you've discovered your bay is not perfectly square. If this is the case, the flip-up seat will get caught on the walls if you try to make it fit against the walls. To solve this problem, cut a piece of ¾-inch-thick plywood so it will fit ⅛ shy of flush to the front of the drywall and end ½ inch short of the rear and side walls. This ½ inch will be covered by seat cushions. Check the fit and then cut 4 inches off the back of the plywood. Install a continuous piano hinge between these pieces. Put the top in place, and nail the 4-inch piece to the back of the frame. Drill a hole about 1 inch in diameter near the front of the top so you can stick your finger into it to lift the top.

Install the trim board.   Cut a piece of 1 × 4 or a piece of molding to cover the joint between the top plywood and the drywall. Nail this piece through the drywall, not to the plywood.

Finish the drywall joints. If you used drywall, use drywall tape and joint compound to finish the joints between the walls and the front of the seat.

Install the baseboard and molding. The baseboard and molding on the walls flanking the bay should end with a 45-degree-angle cut to receive the pieces you removed. Using the pieces you removed, measure for length and cut 45-degree angles so you can create a continuous run of baseboard and molding across the front of the window seat. If you are lucky, the piece from the window wall will be enough to do the job.

A Corner Cabinet

Corner cabinets are usually seen in dining rooms, but they're equally at home in a den or study—anywhere you want to display pottery, porcelain, or a favored collection. These cabinets are sold ready-made, and installation requires minimum carpentry skill and tools. The biggest challenge in their installation is to get the unit to fit tightly into the corner of your room, which is probably not square. You might also have a floor that is sloped. These factors add up to make it almost impossible to fit a cabinet squarely against both walls while resting squarely on the floor.

You will also have to cut either the base of the cabinet or the wall molding in order for the cabinet to fit into the corner. We have found it is usually easier to remove the molding if it is a single piece. If you have a wide, complex molding, then it is probably easier to leave the molding in place and cut the cabinet to

fit around the molding. If you do cut the molding, then you have made a commitment to leave the cabinet in place, because removing it means purchasing new molding.

We have also found it easier and a lot quicker to finish or paint the cabinet before we install it permanently. Here is what is involved in securing a corner cabinet:

Check the fit. Push the cabinet as tightly into the corner as possible. The floor molding will prevent you from getting the cabinet all the way into the corner. Level the cabinet by putting shims under it. Then check the gaps between it and the walls. If the gap is equal all the way around, you are unusually lucky and the cabinet will fit against the wall. Otherwise, your best bet will be to get the cabinet as close to the wall as possible and cover gaps at the side with molding.

Decide on whether to remove the base molding. You will have to either remove the base molding or cut the cabinet to fit around it, otherwise the molding will keep the cabinet from butting the wall. Most often, we trim the cabinet to fit around the molding. It's tough to cut the molding in place to the right angle, and there is a good chance that the floor molding will be damaged when you try to remove it.

The easiest method uses a compass to transfer the shape of the molding to a piece of cardboard. Open the compass about ½ inch, and then hold the steel, pointed edge of the compass against the molding. Move the compass along the molding, keeping the point against the molding while the pencil side of the compass scribes the contour of the molding onto a piece of cardboard.

Cut out the contour on the card-

Great Gadgets & Gizmos

☞ **Home respacing design kit**   This kit will help you visualize your closet's potential. It includes a reusable peel-and-stick vinyl floor plan grid and storage component pieces. You arrange the pieces to get a three-dimensional layout of your design. It is made by Clairson International/Closet Maid and Design Works Inc., 720 South West 17th Street, Ocala, FL 32674.

☞ **Hammer-all hooks**   To hang bicycles or heavy sports gear, use large, square, bent hooks that you hammer into wall studs or 2 × 4s in a basement or garage. These plastic-coated hooks are made by Acme Metal Goods Manufacturing Company, 2 Orange Street, Newark, NJ 07102. You'll find other variations and configurations that screw into the wall and hold large items.

☞ **Teddy Bed**   The menagerie of stuffed animals in a kid's room can take over the room. To get the gang of furry critters up off the floor and bed, use a Teddy Bed, a hammocklike shelf that fits in a corner of a room. It comes with hardware and is easily installed wherever "soft" storage space is needed. It is sold by Premarq, P.O. Box 840, Astoria, OR 97103.

☞ **Z brackets**   You'll find these brackets in most home centers. Each set of brackets is designed to hold three shelves, and they are ideal for light to medium-weight loads. Brackets are screwed to wall studs, and the bottoms of the shelves are screwed to the brackets to hold them securely in place.

☞ **Closet Carousel**   This device is a scaled-down version of the conveyor you see at the dry cleaner. It is not cheap but there's no better way to make every inch of a big closet accessible. Here's where to find the ultimate in a push-button closet system: White Home Products, Inc., 2401 Lake Park Drive, Atlanta, GA 30080.

☞ **Hinge-It**   No space at all for hanging a clothes hook? Try a new device designed to mount on existing door hinge pins. It doesn't damage your wall or door and mounts easily with a hammer and screwdriver. The hinges of the door and the strength of the steel tubing hold bulky coats, towels, whatever you have. It swings independently of the door and comes in several different styles made of oak, brass, and white epoxy. Contact Hinge-It Corporation, 2233 South West Street, P.O. Box 1544, Indianapolis, IN 46206.

---

board, check the fit, and then scribe it onto the cabinet. Use a coping saw to cut it to shape. If all this sounds too hard, then you can just notch the cabinet to fit around the molding. Measure how far the molding protrudes from the wall. It's usually under ¾ of an inch. Cut the base of the cabinet to fit around the projection.

Find the studs.   Usually, it is best to attach the cabinet to the wall studs. You should find the studs about 16 inches from the corner, although sometimes they are closer. When you find a stud on each side of the corner, measure the same distance on the back of the cabinet. Drill small pilot holes through the cabinet at these marks. After you have leveled the cabinet and pushed it into place, you can attach it from the inside through these holes with 3-inch drywall screws.

Another alternative is to use toggle bolts and attach the cabinet directly to the wall. This works fine because the cabinet supports its own weight and the bolts only have to hold it against the wall.

Level the cabinet. Place the cabinet in the corner. Place shims under it if necessary to level it. Check that it is level to both the right and left and also that the cabinet is sitting straight.

Attach the cabinet to the wall. When the cabinet is level and as tight against the wall as possible, attach it to the walls with 3-inch drywall screws or toggle bolts.

Install the trim. Unless your walls are unusually straight, there will be some gaps between the cabinet and the wall. The easiest way to cover these gaps is with molding. You can use cove or quarter-round moldings, which come in widths from ½ inch to 1½ inches. If the gaps are small, you could fill them with caulk.

Putting Up Metal Shelves

One of the quickest and most economical ways to convert found space into usable storage is to install metal shelves. Ready-to-assemble metal shelving units can be used freestanding or bolted to the wall for added strength and durability. Originally, these units were sold only in gray or black, but now you'll see them in bright primary colors, nicely suited for high-tech or contemporary furnishings.

Metal shelves should not be considered heavy-duty shelving, but they are amazingly strong for being so light. We found that the secret to getting these lightweight units to hold heavy loads is

to attach them to the wall. The unit is very strong as long as it does not tilt or twist. If you set it on a level surface with the top screwed to the wall, it provides very stable storage.

The upright standards are punched full of holes, so it is an easy matter to screw the units to the wall. Use a toggle bolt or a plastic wall anchor.

If there is a base molding along the wall where you are going to secure the shelving, the screws pulling the standards tight against the wall will cause the shelving to tip back. Prevent this by making wooden spacers. Cut the spacers about 1 inch long, and slip them between the shelf standards and the wall over the anchors. Then install the mounting screws. You may have to get longer screws. The spacers will hold the top of the standards securely 1 inch from the wall.

Installing Plastic-Coated Wire Storage Units

Solving storage problems is big business—just look at all the storage systems that are now available at local stores. Plastic-coated wire storage bins, baskets, and racks are not inexpensive but are easy to install. Visit a home center and you will find a bin or basket to hold whatever you want. The wall-hung units come equipped with wall anchors and screws, so no other hardware is needed. The only tools you need are a drill, screwdriver, and carpenter's level.

Closet Storage Systems

Most closets are underused. Many manufacturers claim that if your closet has only a clothes pole and maybe a

TABLECLOTH CLOSET

In some large older homes we have found small closets tucked beneath stairways, or in the pantries, that were designed to hold linen tablecloths. The closets have round poles or dowels to hold tablecloths to prevent wrinkling.

If you have several large tablecloths and nowhere to store them, consider converting a corner of a closet into a table linen storage. Install closet pole dowels across the back of the closet. Hold them in place with pole hardware at each end. Stagger the poles in descending order, allowing about 12 inches in between. At the bottom or top, add shelving to hold napkins and table decorations.

shelf, you can almost double the capacity with a storage system. The system components we have used certainly bear this out. By using careful design to take advantage of the tremendous variety of bins, shelves, racks, and hooks available, you can create a tremendous amount of organized storage.

Closet Space

We found graph paper a great help in redesigning a closet. Make each square represent 6 inches. Then carefully make a scale drawing of the closet. Be sure to note the location and how the door swings or if it is sliding or bifold.

You can pick up a free storage system brochure wherever storage components are sold. The brochure will give exact dimensions and clearances for each

component. Be sure to note the manufacturer's specifications for load capacity, so you can provide adequate support for heavy items.

Use your closet diagram along with the brochure to check that all baskets and drawers you plan to install have the required clearance from doors, door jambs, and walls.

Wire System Components

We've redone several closets using these systems. While it hasn't changed our lives (we are still basically unorganized), our stuff is easier to locate. You can raise the status of your closet from household dumping ground to orderly and useful storage with a plastic-coated wire shelving system.

Here is a rundown of the major components:

Shelving: Most wire shelving systems offer shelves that range from 12 to 16 inches wide and come in 2 to 5-foot lengths. The wide shelving is designed to store blankets, linens, and bulky items.

Racks: One component you will not have trouble finding is the rack. Some are made for wall mounting or can be hung from the backs of doors. Other racks are designed to be installed on or suspended from the shelving. These can hold ties, shoes, hats, scarves, belts, and anything else that can be hung up.

Some systems allow you to make shoe racks from sections of wire shelving mounted close to the floor. These racks are attached to the wall and angled downward, with short feet that attach to the front of the shelf. They can be lifted for cleaning under the racks easily.

Baskets and bins: These units can be mounted on walls or the backs of doors. Some are designed to mount under existing shelves. There are also basket units that come in their own freestanding roll-around cart. The cart can be rolled in or out of the closet or storage area.

Design Tips

You'll find wire systems by several manufacturers sold in retail stores, home centers, and through mail-order catalogs. Pick up a brochure for planning purposes. You don't have to invest a fortune initially. You can begin with a basic shelf installation and add on baskets and so forth as your time and budget permit.

Here are some tricks we have used to customize our closets:

▶ Combine short sections of shelving with longer pieces to create custom lengths to fit your closet. The wire shelves are easy to cut with a hacksaw, and spacers link sections together. Plastic end caps install quickly and give a finished appearance.

▶ Since a clothes-hanging rod is usually built into the front of the shelves, mount one level of shelving low, for kids to reach. Then mount another set of shelves above, to create a double-deck system. Place everyday clothes on the bottom for easy access, and hang dress-up clothes and out-of-season outfits above them.

Installation

All these systems are installed in the same manner. Some have wall brackets that have built-in anchors; others use separate wall anchors. If you have installed a plastic wall anchor, you will have no problem with either type. Here is a gen-

eral rundown on installing the basic shelf; after you see how easy it is, you can get creative:

Step 1: Measure up from the floor and make a light pencil or chalk line at the height of each shelf.

Step 2: Place a carpenter's level at each shelf height, and use it to lay out a level line across the back wall of the closet. A 4-foot level is best, but you can use a straight board or wooden yardstick to extend the reach of a short level.

Step 3: Mark the position of the shelf anchors along this layout line. Place one 2 inches from each end wall and every 12 inches along the layout line.

Step 4: Drill a pilot hole for the shelf anchors through each mark.

Step 5: Tap the plastic anchors supplied with the unit into the holes. These anchors are specially designed to wrap around the shelving wire. Hold the anchors straight, and tighten the screws to spread the anchors and lock them in place.

Step 6: Mark the locations of the end brackets on the side walls by putting the brackets on the shelf and holding the shelf level. Remove the brackets, drill the holes, and install the anchors.

Step 7: Snap the shelf into place in the wall brackets. Then lower it into the end brackets on the side walls.

Step 8: Install support braces and use joiner clamps wherever two sections of shelving are joined together or to support the end of a shelf that does not run wall to wall.

Adding a Closet in a Room

Sometimes our search for more storage space has led us to the conclusion that there just is not enough closet space.

We find ourselves with no choice but to build a new closet.

Building a closet is not as complicated as it might sound. In fact, it is the perfect project for getting your feet wet as a carpenter. It involves simple carpentry and drywalling. For a door you can use a regular swinging door, sliding door, or bifold. All are easily installed. This job is easy, but not particularly quick. It involves waiting periods (drywall compound needs time to dry), so expect to spend a month of weekends to complete the job. And plan to have half of the room set up as a work station where you can leave tools and building materials without having to clean up.

A corner of a room is the ideal location for a closet because two walls of your closet are already built. If a bedroom needs a closet and the room has a window centered on one wall, you might consider adding two closets on either side of the window and tying them together with a window seat or dressing table centered on the window.

You'll be limited by the size and shape of the room in laying out the closet. Allow a good 2 feet for its depth, and unless you are using sliding or bifold doors, leave space for the closet doors to swing open without hitting the room door or other obstacles. To save money, incorporate standard-size doors in your design, to avoid paying extra for custom-cut doors. To make the closet look like it's always been there, match the casings and trim work with what's already in the room. Here's how to build a closet with 2 × 4 lumber:

Lay out the closet on the floor.   Starting in the corner, measure and mark the width of the closet on the wall, then measure and mark the length of the closet on the adjacent wall. Try to make the closet width and length lines align with studs in the wall you will be attaching to. If you can't, use construction adhesive on the closet studs that will be against the wall. Remember, you are marking the outside of the closet on the wall. For example, if you want a closet to be 24 inches deep, then the mark should be 28 inches from the corner. You must add 3½ inches for the studs and ½ inch for the drywall inside the closet. This will give you the position of the outside face of your stud wall.

Use the wall marks as reference points when you draw the outline of the closet on the floor. A chalk line is a handy tool to do this. It makes straight lines if you hold the line tight. Check that the layout lines are parallel to the room walls.

Mark the rough door opening.   Now mark the rough opening required for the door you are using. For a single swinging door, this opening should be 2½ inches more than the door width, to allow for the doorjamb, leveling shims, and a little space around the door. If you'll be using a bifold, prehung, or sliding door, the manufacturer will provide rough-opening dimensions.

Remove the carpet and moldings. Remove any carpeting by carefully cutting it away. (When the closet walls are in place, you can reinstall it inside the closet.) Carefully remove all moldings from the ceiling, wall, and base shoe, and save them to reinstall later.

Cut the plates. Retrofitting stud walls into a finished room presents a problem the carpenters didn't have when they framed your house. Normally, stud wall partitions are built on the ground with a top plate, a bottom plate, and

FRAMING A CLOSET

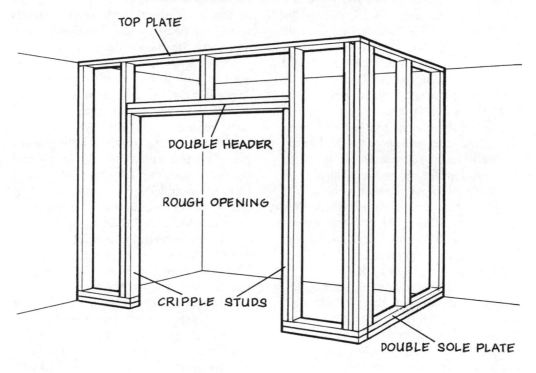

TOP PLATE

DOUBLE HEADER

ROUGH OPENING

CRIPPLE STUDS

DOUBLE SOLE PLATE

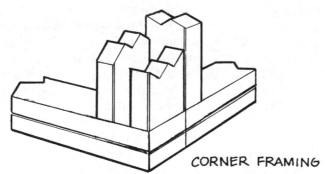

CORNER FRAMING

studs in between. Then the walls are raised as a unit and nailed to the floor. Ceiling joists are laid on top later. If you were to measure the distance between your finished ceiling and floor and then build a stud wall to fit, you'd find it would

jam into the ceiling before you could get it plumb. The way around this problem is called the double-sole plate method.

First, cut three sets of plates. Two of these sets are identical sole plate sets and cover the perimeter of the closet except for the rough opening for the door. The third is for the top plate set. It's the same except that it covers the rough opening. Nail one set of these sole plates to the floor.

Lay out the stud locations. Use a carpenter's square to strike lines on the other sole plate set, indicating where the right side of each stud will go. Draw an "X" to the left of each line so you'll know to put the stud on top of the X. Extend each line to the narrow side of the plate. Put a stud at the end of each wall and 1½ inches from where the plates end for the rough door opening. You'll need three studs at outside corners to provide nailing for drywall on both sides of the closet. The illustration on page 219 shows how these studs are positioned.

When the studs are laid out on the second sole plate set, align the top plate set over it. Extend the stud marks from the sole plates onto the sides of the top plates. Flip the top plates over, and extend the lines onto the bottoms of the top plates. Make an X where each stud will meet the top plate.

Cut the studs.   Measure from the first sole plate to the ceiling. Subtract 3 inches and cut the studs to this length.

Assemble the walls.   Working on the floor, face-nail the plates to the studs according to the layout.

Raise the walls.   Your walls are 1½ inches shorter than your ceiling height, so you'll have no trouble raising them to a vertical position. When you have each wall straight up, slip it onto the first sole plate set and nail the two sets of sole plates together. Have a helper put a 4-foot level on the outside of each wall to tell you when it's plumb. When it is, nail the top plate set to the ceiling, making sure you nail into joists.

Frame the door.   For a single swinging door, cut two studs to the same height as the door, usually 80 inches. Here's why: You need to add 3 inches for the jamb and the space under the door, but you need to subtract three inches for the doubled sole plate. Place one of these "cripple studs" against the stud on either side of the rough door opening and nail each in place.

Measure the distance between the two studs you nailed the cripples to, and cut two pieces to that length. These will form the doubled header, which will sit on top of the cripples and be nailed to the studs the cripples are nailed to.

Measure and cut a block to fit between the top of the header and the bottom of the top plate. Toenail it in place, centered over the header.

Install and finish the drywall.   See the "Budget Face-Lifting a Ceiling" section of chapter 5 for tips on cutting, installing, and finishing drywall. Here are two more tips that pertain specifically to walls:

Cut the drywall to fit exactly around the inside and outside of the closet, but make it about ½ inch short of the ceiling. Put the drywall against the wall and the blade of a flat bar under the bottom edge of the drywall. Using a scrap of 2 × 4 laid flat as a fulcrum and the flat bar as a lever, push down on the bar with your foot while pushing the drywall against the wall. This will force the drywall up tight against the ceiling. Now you can put a few screws or nails into the drywall before releasing the flat bar. Baseboard will cover the ½-inch gap.

Install corner bead at the outside corners. This is a metal bead you nail to the corner to provide your drywall knife with a smooth surface to ride on and make finishing corners very easy.

Install the doorjamb. If you are not using a prehung, bifold, or sliding door, buy a standard interior doorjamb set at the lumberyard. Tell the lumberyard it is for $\frac{1}{2}$-inch drywall, and you'll get the right width. The head jamb will fit into dado notches in the side jambs. Assemble the parts, then measure the inside dimension of the top jamb. This measurement should be $\frac{1}{8}$ inch more than the width of the door. If it's not, cut the head jamb to length.

Measure from the inside surface of the top jamb to the bottom of each side jamb. This dimension should be $1\frac{1}{16}$ inch more than the height of the door, assuming your finished floor is in place. If the finished floor is not in place, add in its thickness. Cut the side jambs to the right length.

Reassemble the jamb and drive three 8d casing nails through the outside of each side jamb into the edges of the head jamb. Center the jamb in the rough opening.

Cut a 1 × 6 spreader to a length exactly equal to the distance between the side jambs measured at the top. Place it between the side jambs at floor level. Measuring from the side the door will swing into, draw a vertical line down each side jamb at a distance equal to the thickness of the door plus $\frac{7}{8}$ inch. All your nailing will be along this line, so it can be covered by the door stop.

Center the jamb in the rough opening. Check that the top jamb is level. If it's not, shim under one of the side jambs to adjust it. When the top jamb is level, wedge it into place with tapered shims. Use the shims in pairs, putting one in from each side of the jamb so they overlap. By adjusting the shims together, you'll be able to wedge the jamb into place without twisting the jamb. Use two or three sets on the head jamb. Now wedge the side jambs into place using three or four sets of shims on each side. On the hinge jamb, place one set of shims 7 inches up from the bottom and another 11 inches from the top and a third set halfway between the two. Adjust the shims until the side jambs are plumb and at right angles with the top jamb.

Nail the jamb in place with 8d common nails staggered $\frac{1}{2}$ inch on either side of the line. But don't drive the nails home yet. After all the nails are in place, check again that the jamb is plumb and level. Then drive all the nails home. Now you can trim off the shims with a utility knife so that they're flush with the jamb.

Hang the door and install the hardware. See the "Working with Interior Doors" section of chapter 4 for instructions on hanging a standard swinging door. Make sure the door closes so that it is flush with the jamb. If you are using a prehung, bifold, or sliding door, follow the manufacturer's directions.

Install the stop. The stop consists of strips of wood, usually a little wider than the door, that run around the jamb and absorb the impact when the door closes. Cut three pieces to fit around the inside of the jamb. Step into the closet and close the door. Scribe the edge of the door lightly on the jamb, and then use this as a guide to install the stop.

Install the casing. Casings can be mitered at the corner or butted, or corner blocks may be used. Again, try to match what you have in the rest of the room. Whatever type of casing you use, use 8d finishing nails to attach it to the edge of the jamb and through the drywall to the rough-opening studs.

INSTALLING A DOORJAMB

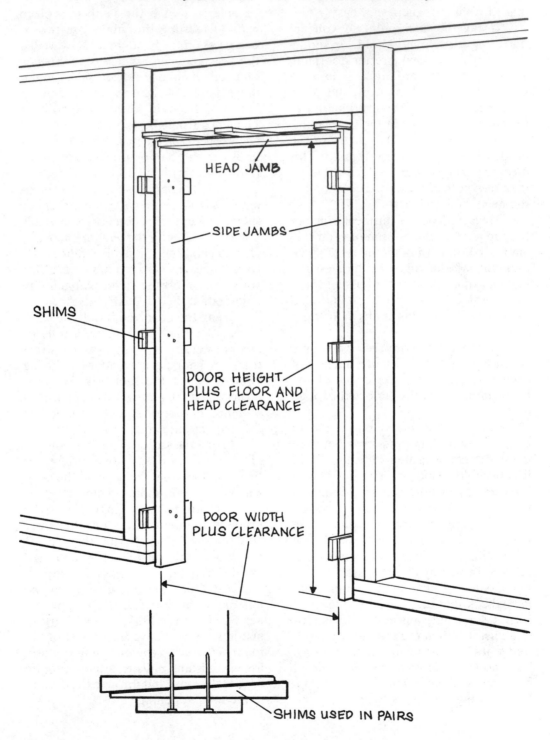

HEAD JAMB

SIDE JAMBS

SHIMS

DOOR HEIGHT
PLUS FLOOR AND
HEAD CLEARANCE

DOOR WIDTH
PLUS CLEARANCE

SHIMS USED IN PAIRS

Installing Disappearing Attic Stairs

Unless there is convenient access to the attic, this storage area goes virtually unused. Instead of a stairway, many houses just have a small access hatch or trapdoor. In order to store stuff in the attic, you have to get a ladder and then try to squeeze through a small opening.

Your attic will be a much more useful storage space if you make it easy to get up there. The best way we have found to do this is to install pull-down attic stairs. These disappearing stairs are not expensive and come preassembled. If you have done any carpentry work, you will find these stairs easy to install.

Not all homes have the space or floor plan for pull-down stairs. It's best to locate the stairs directly under the roof ridge so there will be maximum attic headroom above the stairs. This is particularly important if your roof has a low pitch. Note the location of doors and the traffic pattern, so the unfolded stairs don't interfere with doors or passageways you'll need access to on your way to the attic. It will be very inconvenient if you have to close a door in order to lower the stairs. Several trips to the attic then become a long series of raising the stairs and opening doors.

Usually, if access to the attic is limited, the attic won't have flooring over the ceiling joists. If this is the case, you'll need to put down some ⅝-inch plywood to make the attic useful for storage. Install the sheets down the middle of the attic. Some homes have ceiling joists below the attic that are not beefy enough to support concentrated heavy loads. But you will not have trouble if you store the

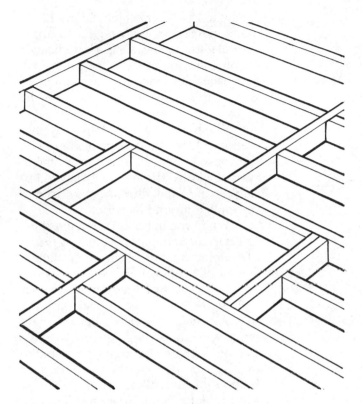

You have to cut at least one ceiling joist, and add headers, to install disappearing attic stairs.

heavy objects in the center of the attic on sheets of plywood, which help spread the load over several joists.

Before you shop for the stair unit, carefully measure the area where you plan to install it. Check in the attic to be sure there are no heating/cooling ducts running over this area. Also, look at the ceiling joists. If possible, install the unit so its long dimension runs parallel with the joists. With this type of installation, only one joist has to be cut. If you can't find a convenient location that allows for this type of installation, consult with a qualified contractor because this is no longer a do-it-yourself job. To install the stairs across the joists requires cutting several joists and installing a large header. If you don't do this right, the ceiling will sag, especially since it is human nature to pile things in the attic close to the stairs.

When shopping for a fold-away unit, compare its required rough opening with the space you have. The stairs come in several widths. Choose a set that will fit into the area and allow room for trim to be applied around its perimeter.

When you purchase the stairs, don't forget to get a couple of 8-foot-long pieces of framing lumber of the same dimensions as the ceiling joists. These will usually be 2 × 6s, or larger lumber. If your ceiling has 2 × 4 joists, check with the installation instructions, because you might have to use larger pieces to make the rough opening. Also purchase molding to cover the space between the stair frame and the ceiling. You might also want to get a can of foam insulation to seal any air leaks around the stairs after they are installed.

The manufacturer provides a specification sheet on the stairs, stating the exact opening size to cut in the ceiling. Installing stairs is definitely a two-person project; you'll need somebody to hold the unit while you screw it in place. Here are the steps for installing the stairs (but be prepared to modify any of these suggestions to fit your particular situation):

Lay out the opening. Draw the rough opening on the ceiling where you want the stairs. Then drill a hole through each of the four corners, and stick some-thing through each hole so you can find it in the attic. Crawl up into the attic, find the holes, and check that there will be no conflicts with ducts, wiring, or other structures.

Cut out the ceiling. Following the layout lines, cut through the plaster or drywall on the ceiling. You can use a coping or saber saw. Remove the cut-out piece. Wear eye protection because there is plenty of falling dust.

Cut the joist flush with the opening. Make the cut as square as possible so the headers will be straight.

Measure the opening. Measure the exact distance between the joists on either side of the joist you just cut. Take the measurement at the edge of the rough opening. Do this at both ends. The joists may not be exactly parallel, and the distance could be different.

Cut the headers and nail them to the existing joists. Follow the manufacturer's directions on whether or not they should be placed flush with the opening in the plaster or drywall.

Install the trim joists. Measure, cut, and install the trim joists on either side of the opening.

Check the fit. Check the fit of the stair assembly in the rough opening. Then install it according to the manufacturer's directions. Some are nailed in place; others use screws. Place shims between the stair frame and the rough opening to hold the frame square while you install it.

Trim the opening. Cut and fit trim around the perimeter of the stairs. Then insulate any cracks where air could leak through from the attic.

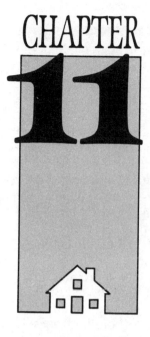

CHAPTER 11

Laundry, Workshop, and Garage

They are the workhorse areas of our home. We don't much care if they are pretty, but we often spend more time in them than we do in the living room. They are the laundry, the workshop, and the garage.

Of these three areas, the home laundry, if it doesn't already exist, is a top improvement priority for most people. In an era in which Mom and Dad both work outside the home, most people can't imagine spending time at a Laundromat.

Many people seem to get along fine without a work area. But if you are reading this book, you are not one of them. More likely, you are like us and consider a work area, however humble, to be a necessity. You need a space where you can patch, repair, and assemble things for the rest of the house. The simplest project can become a major hassle if you don't have a place to work and store tools—even if it's just a corner of the basement or garage or an empty closet.

The garage, if you have one, is a popular place for the work area. But without careful organization, your work space can force your car out into the cold. In this chapter we offer ways to make the most of the utilitarian spaces in your home.

The Laundry/Utility Room

Not everyone has the luxury of having a laundry room, or a space designated specifically for washer, dryer, and ironing board. In some houses the laundry is a corner of the basement. In others, it's in the utility room where the water heater, water conditioner, and furnace are located. Sometimes you'll find it partitioned off in a section of an attached garage. Condominiums and apartments short on space often tuck a stacked washer-dryer unit into a narrow closet. Laundries are even finding their way upstairs near the bedrooms, which is a great way to save hauling dirty laundry down and clean laundry up.

Wherever the laundry is situated, it's bound to be well used because we are a nation of squeaky-clean people. Working with the laundry space you have, no matter how small, is the challenge.

The laundry should be well ventilated and have a water hookup for the washing machine. You need room for an ironing board, storage for cleaning supplies, and elbow room for sorting and folding things. A hanging rack for clothing fresh out of the dryer or newly ironed items is another essential. Here are some ideas to make your laundry more efficient, both spacewise and energywise.

A Foldaway Ironing Board

If you have ever remodeled an old kitchen, you may have removed a long, narrow cupboard that housed an ironing board. Many times these cupboards are nicely converted to spice cabinets, but usually they're cast aside. Today you can buy a new version of the original, a pre-fab ironing cupboard designed to fit between the wall studs. The hinged door front opens to a narrow cabinet that houses a fold-down board. The cupboard is designed to fit between typical 2×4 wall studs built 16 inches on-center.

These units are available as bare-bones styles with a basic ironing board or with an electrical outlet and shelf for the iron. Some even have a shutoff timer, work light, and sleeve board. All are sold with the necessary hardware, wire, solder-less connectors, and fasteners. The cupboard door can be stained or painted and is sold in several styles.

The installation of the basic space-saving board is straightforward. Here's how to do it:

Step 1: Lightly lay out the rough opening (see the manufacturer's directions for exact measurements) on the wall with pencil in the general area you want to install the board. Consider the space needed for the board to fold out into the room (typically about 50 inches), as well as the space you need to move around it in its extended position. Mount it so the board unfolds at a convenient work height, possibly at the same level as a nearby counter. You can then lay a large tablecloth or another cumbersome ironing job on the counter as you work on it.

If the board has a light or electrical outlet, install it in a wall with an existing

INSTALLING A FOLDAWAY IRONING BOARD

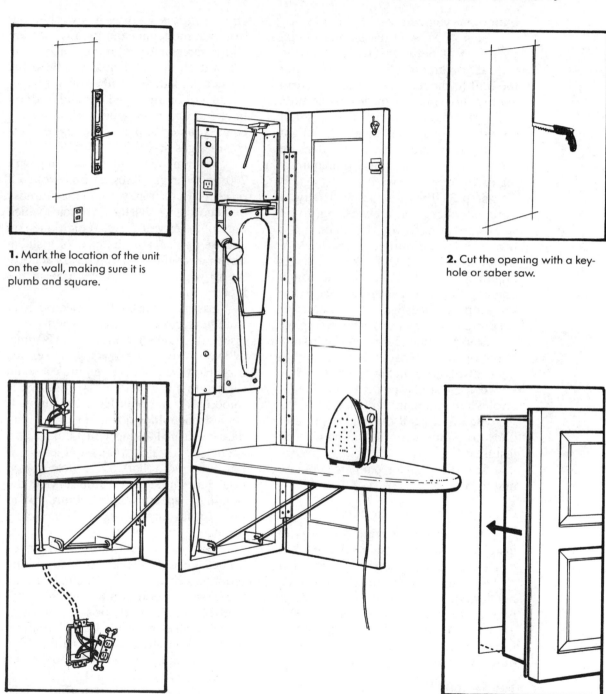

1. Mark the location of the unit on the wall, making sure it is plumb and square.

2. Cut the opening with a keyhole or saber saw.

3. If required, run the power cable through the wall to the nearest outlet.

4. Install the unit between the studs.

outlet that you can wire the unit into.

Step 2: Most of these units are designed to fit between two studs in the wall. If you hit a stud, you'll have to put the unit to the left or right of it, so drill another hole about 8 inches to one side. Make the hole big enough so you can fit a hand mirror inside. Shine a flashlight on the mirror and move it around inside the hole to make sure there is no plumbing or wiring in the way.

Step 3: Turn off the electricity to the area where you are working, to be safe—just in case you do encounter a wire. Scribe the outline of the back of the unit on the wall, checking that it is plumb and level. Then cut the rough opening. If you feel any resistance to the saw, stop and investigate. It is too easy to cut through a copper or plastic water pipe.

Step 4: Install the ironing-board unit in the opening. Most units are nailed to the studs. You might have to insert shims between the studs and the unit to hold it level when you nail it in place.

Step 5: Install the trim if the unit does not come with the casing already installed.

Step 6: Stain or paint the unit to match your room.

Cabinet Drawer Ironing Board

Another space-saving option is to install an ironing board in a drawer. You can purchase specialty hardware that replaces the drawer with a metal slide-out fold-up unit. All you have to do is remove the drawer and install the mechanism. You can use the existing drawer front, so the closed unit looks like all the other drawers.

The Clothes Washer and Dryer

The core of every laundry room is, of course, the washer and dryer. You can choose various features in a washer, but from a remodeling standpoint, they are all the same. They all require a 20-amp, 120-volt circuit dedicated solely to the washer, and they all need a hot-water and a cold-water hookup and a drain line. But dryers are another matter because you can choose between an electric or a gas dryer.

We don't recommend working with 240 volts or gas lines as do-it-yourself projects. But before you call the plumber or electrician, you'll have to decide which kind of dryer you'll use. Which one you choose depends on the ease of installation and cost factors, which vary according to your situation. Let's look at the factors:

Ease of installation: An electric dryer usually is easier and less expensive to install. It requires just one cable, a 30-amp, 240-volt circuit run from your service box. However, it also requires a main service that is wired for 240 volts and is rated for a total of at least 100 amps. If your service does not meet these standards, you are looking at installing a new service box, which will cost at least several hundred dollars. Of course, if you don't have modern 100-amp service, the building inspector might require you to install it for any significant remodeling project.

Gas service can be natural gas or bottled liquid petroleum gas (LPG). Either requires a 20-amp, 120-volt circuit to run the blower, in addition to a gas hookup. Bottled gas becomes most attractive if you are already using it for cooking, because you already have a tank. The cost of hooking up the line depends on how far the dryer is from the tank. Also, with bottled gas, you have to find a place for the tank that is accessible to the delivery truck.

If you already have natural gas coming into your house for heating and/or cooking, the cost of having a plumber run a line to the dryer won't be much more than the cost of an electrician to hook up an electric dryer. Usually, if you already have natural gas coming into the house, it pays to go this route, because natural gas is significantly cheaper than electricity in almost all locales.

Cost: Electric dryers are simpler machines than gas dryers, and this makes them a little cheaper to buy. But, as mentioned, you'll usually spend more operating an electric dryer than if you use natural gas. LPG usually is sold on a sliding scale; the more you use, the less the per-unit cost. This means if you install bottled gas just for a dryer, it may cost you more to operate than an electric dryer. But if you are using LPG for a stove and/or heating, the cost may be less than electric.

Whatever power source you choose, locate the dryer next to the washer, and try to put the pair near existing plumbing, to save the cost of installing long plumbing lines.

Venting the Dryer

Since moisture can do so much damage to a house, getting rid of excess humidity is important. It is surprising to us that many of the houses we have remodeled have no provisions for venting a clothes dryer. The clothesline must have been the mainstay for these households.

Ducting the hot, humid air from the clothes dryer to outside the house will keep air-conditioning bills down. In the winter it reduces condensation on windows.

In most cases, installing a dryer vent is easy. Ideally, the duct should go directly outside through the wall. The shorter

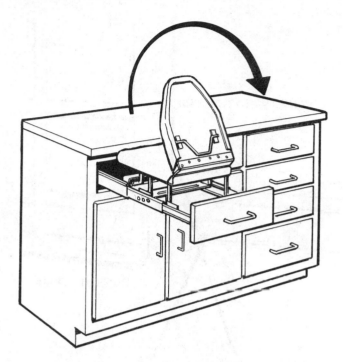

This ironing board is designed to replace a drawer, using the original drawer front.

the path, the better, since any restriction in the airflow out of the dryer will decrease its efficiency.

Sometimes, it's not possible to go directly through the wall. Other duct routes can be found through the ceiling and then out the roof or over to the eaves. You can also route the duct from a dryer on the first floor through the floor into the basement and then out through a wall or window.

Using a Prepackaged Kit

You can purchase the ducting, duct clamps, and vent hood (the part that leads through the wall) separately, or more conveniently, the components come in a vent kit. Most kits come with flexible ducting that is easy to use. This ducting

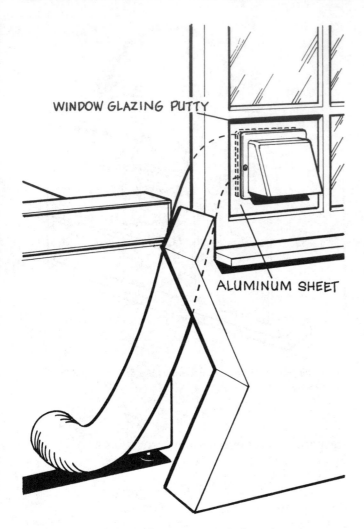

WINDOW GLAZING PUTTY

ALUMINUM SHEET

The easiest way to vent a dryer is to route the hose through a window. This involves replacing a pane of glass with an aluminum panel. The vent hood is mounted on the panel.

is okay for runs of about 10 feet or less.

If you need a longer duct, use aluminum ducting because the flexible duct has more internal air resistance. The aluminum ducting also collects less of the lint and dust that tends to clog a long run of dryer duct. To make the installation as easy as possible, use a section of flexible ducting to connect the dryer to the aluminum duct and another piece to connect the other end to the vent hood. You can use clamps or duct tape to make the connections.

Support the ducting well, especially the flexible type. Every time it droops, the small bends create additional resistance and cut its air-handling capacity.

Venting through the Window

Running a vent through a frame wall isn't hard, but it can be a real challenge in a brick wall. If you are faced with this obstacle, the easiest way to vent your dryer is to run the duct through a window. Install the vent hood in an aluminum sheet cut to replace a glass windowpane. You can also use a piece of plywood, which is more energy efficient because wood is a better insulator than aluminum. However, the plywood will need to be painted.

Purchase a vent kit and a sheet of aluminum at least as large as the glass pane it will replace. You will find sheet aluminum in 2 × 4-foot pieces in racks that also hold tubing, bar stock, and rectangular stock. These are heavy enough to stand up in a windowpane of up to about 12 × 14 inches. If your window is larger, use a sheet of ⅛-inch hardboard behind the aluminum to stiffen it. The aluminum should be on the outside to protect the hardboard from the weather.

Follow these steps to install your dryer vent:

Step 1: Remove the pane of glass by chipping out the putty around it. Wear heavy work gloves and safety glasses as you loosen the old putty and remove the glass.

Step 2: If you can get the glass out in one piece, use it as a pattern to cut the aluminum. Otherwise, measure and cut a piece of the aluminum to fit into the open pane.

Step 3: Trace an outline of the vent hose mounting ring in the center of the aluminum, and cut out the hole with tin snips. Install the vent hood over the hole on the outside of the aluminum, using the mounting screws.

Step 4: Install the aluminum replacement pane from the outside of the window. Hold it in place with glazier points (small triangular-shaped pieces of steel) pushed into the window frame. Then apply glazing putty.

Step 5: Attach the end of the duct hose to the end of the vent hood with a clamp or duct tape. Then run the duct (supporting it every foot or so) to the dryer. Attach the free end of the duct to the dryer exhaust, and you are in business.

Installing a Dryer Vent through the Wall

Venting a dryer through a frame wall is a little more involved than through a window, but not much. Inside the house the ducting is the same. Cutting the hole in the wall is the only tricky part. Here's how to do it:

Step 1: Mark on the inside where you want the vent to penetrate the wall. Then check that there are no conflicts on the outside of the house, such as an oil-fill pipe running through the wall. On the inside, make a small exploratory hole to make sure you won't run into a stud, wiring, or pipes.

Step 2: Use a keyhole or saber saw to cut the hole for the vent in the inside wall. Remove the insulation and push the duct part of the vent hood into the

wall until it lies flush with the inside of the outer wall. Work it back and forth, pushing against the unit to mark the outer wall. If this does not mark the wall, put some chalk or lipstick on the edge of the duct and try again.

Step 3: Drill a hole through the center of the layout circle on the outside wall. Then take the duct hood outside, center it over the hole you just drilled, and trace around it with a pencil.

Step 4: Cut the hole in the outside wall from the outside with a keyhole or saber saw.

Step 5: Apply caulk to the back of the hood flange, and then push the duct part into the wall. Use the screws provided to hold the hood flange tight against the siding. Apply extra caulk to any cracks or openings.

Step 6: Caulk up the inside opening. Some units come with a trim ring for the inside. If not, you can use spackling compound to repair any chipped plaster if the walls are finished.

Step 7: Connect the flexible ducting to the duct hood and to the dryer.

A Heat Recovery System for the Laundry Room

The dryer is a source of excess heat and humidity in the summer, but that might be just what your house needs in the winter. If your house has radiators or does not have a central humidifying system, recovering moist air from the dryer will not cause problems in your dry house. The heat is always welcome in the winter.

The easiest way to do this is to unhook the duct leading outside. But this brute-force approach allows the clothes lint to be blown around your

HOMEMADE DRYER EXHAUST FILTER

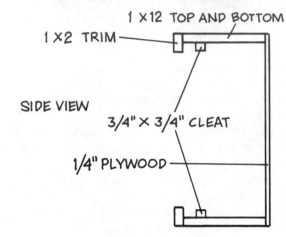

1 X 12 TOP AND BOTTOM

1 X 2 TRIM

SIDE VIEW

3/4" X 3/4" CLEAT

1/4" PLYWOOD

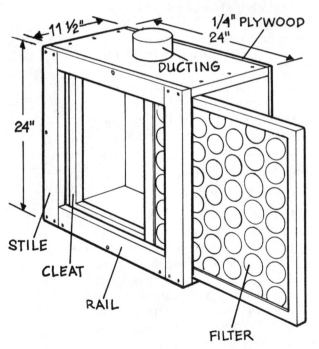

11 ½"

1/4" PLYWOOD

24"

DUCTING

24"

STILE

CLEAT

RAIL

FILTER

house. You can solve this by putting a nylon stocking over the vent opening.

A more convenient method is to install a heat recovery kit that has a two-way valve that is installed in the duct. If the valve lever is turned one way, the dryer air is directed outside; if turned the other, the air is diverted to an inside lint trap.

The lint trap varies from model to model. It can be as simple as a nylon stocking clamped to the end of the duct valve, or it might be a housing holding a furnace filter. Valves with stockings on the end are the cheapest, but the stocking fills up quickly, restricting air flow and cutting efficiency. The furnace filter models are much more efficient but more expensive. We enjoy the best of both worlds by removing the stocking from a cheap valve and hooking up a homemade furnace filter vent. The unrestricted air goes outside in the summer and into the house through the homemade vent in the winter. The unit uses a 2-foot-square filter and a 5-inch-long piece of aluminum duct of a diameter to fit the flexible ducting you are using. If you do any carpentry or woodworking, you can probably build it out of scrap. Even with all new material it won't cost more than $15. Here's how to build the vent:

Step 1: To make the top and bottom, cut two pieces of ¾-inch plywood to 24 × 10 inches. You could also use 24-inch lengths of 1 × 8, 1 × 10, or 1 × 12—or even particleboard if that's what you have handy. The material and width of the box is not important, as long as it is wide enough to hold the aluminum duct. Center the piece of aluminum duct on one of the pieces, and trace its circumference. Cut the hole with a jigsaw.

Step 2: Use tin snips to make cuts about 1 inch deep about every inch around one end of the aluminum duct. Bend each of these tabs out to form a flange. Insert the duct in the hole, and tack the tabs down with ½-inch nails. Roofing nails work great because they won't punch through the wood. If you don't have ½-inch nails handy, you could use longer ones driven part way in and bent over.

Step 3: Cut two side pieces of plywood, each 22½ inches long. Make one piece as wide as the top and bottom. The other should be that width less the thickness of the filter plus $\frac{1}{16}$ inch so the filter can slide in and out. For example, if your filter is 1 inch thick and your top and bottom 10 inches wide, one side should be 10 inches wide and the other $8^{15}/_{16}$ inches wide. Nail the top and bottom of the sides with 8d common nails.

Step 4: Cut two pieces of 1×2 stock (actual dimension $\frac{3}{4} \times 1\frac{1}{2}$ inches) to 24 inches for stiles and two pieces to 21 inches for rails. Nail the stiles and rails to the front of the frame. You can nail three of the pieces all around, but the stile next to the narrower side piece can be nailed only to the top and bottom.

Step 5: Cut a 24-inch-square piece of ¼-inch plywood or particleboard, and nail it to the back of the unit. Mount the unit on the wall, clamp the flexible duct to the aluminum duct, insert the filter, and you're ready to go.

The Workshop

Friends have laughingly said that our workshop is nicer than our house. Admittedly, in some houses, we have spent more time and money outfitting our work space than furnishing the living room. Our present house has virtually no shop space, so we rent a corner of an old mill that suits our needs just fine. One of our workshop mainstays that didn't make it out of the house has become somewhat of a conversation piece. We use our massive, handmade maple workbench as a buffet in the dining room, and it's difficult to imagine the room without it. Someday we envision it in a large kitchen as an island; it's doubtful it will ever find its way back to a workshop!

We're making do at the shop with another one, far less attractive, but certainly as serviceable. A workbench is the key ingredient in a shop and should have a sturdy surface to work on and organized storage for the tools and gadgets needed to make repairs around your house. Even with limited space, you can create an efficient workshop on just 4 feet of wall.

Lumberyards have everything you need to build your own workbench. Or you can buy an unassembled kit. Whichever you choose, an ideal home workbench and shop incorporate these features:

▶ a sturdy work surface at a comfortable height—about 35 inches for most people

▶ storage for bulky tools

▶ hanging storage for tools

▶ containers for small hardware

▶ grounded electrical outlets

▶ a vise for securing work objects

▶ good lighting

▶ comfortable and cleanable flooring

A Quick and Easy Workbench

An inexpensive and very durable workbench top can be made with particleboard. This material is very dense and holds up well. You should seal the top with varnish or paint, because if you spill a lot of water on this material, it swells up and starts to crumble. One bench we made that worked out well had a top of particleboard with a sheet of ¼-inch hardboard laid over it. Hardboard is inexpensive and has a nice, smooth finish. Whenever the hardboard got too beat up or had too many holes in it from careless drilling, we just replaced it with a new sheet.

Here's a plan for a basic workbench that we've made and used. It's easy to build using readily available lumber. The legs are made of sturdy 2 × 3s, and the top is 24-inch flake board, which can stand up to hard use and be replaced when too many holes are drilled through it.

We made the top from a 24-inch-wide piece of shelving stock, which has a finished front edge. If the lumberyard does not stock this material, have them cut a full sheet in half. Then rip the half down the center to form the 2 × 4 foot piece. All the remaining pieces are cut from dimension lumber (nominal dimensions, not actual dimensions, are provided here). Cut the pieces to size as you go. It's always a good idea to check the actual dimensions of your project before you cut a piece. This way, you'll adjust for small measuring variations as you go, instead of accumulating them. Use the dimensions provided below as a guide. We used 2½-inch drywall screws wherever we were attaching a 2 × 3 to a 2 × 3. For attaching the 1 × 4 stock to 2 × 3 stock, we used 1½-inch drywall screws. We also used yellow carpenter's glue at all the connections except for the top to the frame, in case we want to take the top off to replace it.

Cutting List for the Workbench

Name	Quantity	Size	Material
Top	1	¾″ × 24″ × 48″	flake board
Top stretcher	3	¾″ × 3½″ × 40″	1″ × 4″ pine
Side/brace	5	¾″ × 3½″ × 19½″	1″ × 4″ pine
Bottom stretcher	1	¾″ × 3½″ × 38½″	1″ × 4″ pine
Leg	4	1½″ × 2½″ × 29¼″	2″ × 3″ pine
End	2	¾″ × 3½″ × 12″	1″ × 4″ pine
Backsplash	1	¾″ × 3½″ × 48″	1″ × 4″ pine
Cleat	2	1½″ × 2½″ × 14½″	2″ × 3″ pine

QUICK AND EASY WORKBENCH

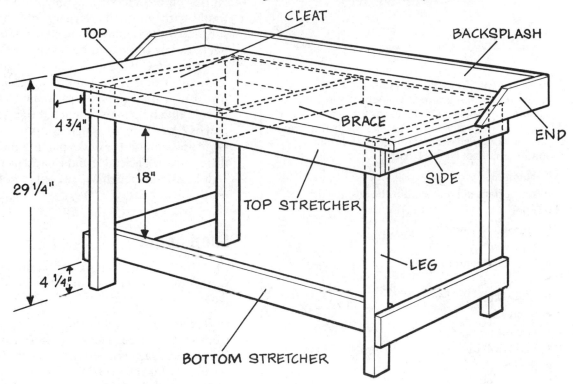

Step 1: Cut and assemble the legs and stretchers. Note that three of the stretchers are the same length, while the bottom stretcher is 1½ inches shorter. This is because the longer stretchers are positioned to go ¾ inch past the outsides of the legs to make butt joints with the side pieces. Butt the front stretcher ends flush with the outsides of the legs so the side pieces can go past. Position the top stretchers flush with the tops of the legs. Position the bottom stretchers 4¼ inches from the bottoms of the legs. Check that your joints are square, and glue and screw them in place.

Step 2: Cut and attach the side pieces and the center brace. All of these pieces are the same size. The top side pieces butt into the rear stretchers and are positioned flush with the fronts of the front legs. The brace is centered between the side pieces with its top flush with the tops of the top stretchers. Its ends are glued and screwed to the stretchers. Place the frame on a flat surface while the glue is drying, and check that all legs are on the ground, because it is impossible to straighten the frame after the glue sets.

Step 3: Install the cleats. The dis-

INDISPENSABLE TOOLS

Few of us can afford to completely outfit a work-shop in one shopping spree. A practical approach is to accumulate tools and gadgets as you need them. There are, however, some essentials, tools that you need to accomplish general repairs and installations around the house. Here's a list:

▶ hammer
▶ set of flathead and Phillips head screwdrivers
▶ pliers
▶ adjustable wrench
▶ tape rule
▶ 2-foot carpenter's level
▶ try square
▶ utility knife
▶ hand saw
▶ nail set
▶ hand drill or ⅜-inch electric drill
▶ drill bits
▶ ¾-inch chisel
▶ vise
▶ wire brush
▶ safety goggles
▶ all-purpose oil
▶ C-clamps
▶ assorted nails, screws, abrasive paper, and adhesive

Step 4: Cut and install the top. After cutting the top to size, center it on the frame with a 4-inch overhang on each side and a 1½-inch overhang at front and back. Screw the top to the cleats.

Step 5: Cut the backsplash and glue and nail it along the back edge of the top, flush with the ends of the bench top. Use 4d finishing nails. Then cut the side pieces (the 45-degree angle is optional). Glue and nail on the ends, placing them flush with the back edge of the backsplash.

Finish the bench with a coat of poly-urethane varnish.

Shop Space

Here are suggestions for planning a workshop area within the confines of a garage or basement:

▶ Because of dust and the difficulty of transporting large pieces of material and lumber, a garage is a better choice than a basement for a workshop. This is especially true if the basement doesn't have an outside entrance.

▶ If your job transfers you from one location to another every few years, consider using shelving and benches that are freestanding and consequently portable.

▶ When a table saw is in use, locate it in the center so there's plenty of room for ripping large pieces of material.

▶ Workshop necessities include good lighting over work surfaces and good ventilation. A shop vacuum is another must-have item.

The Garage

A garage is many things to many people, including protected shelter for

tance between the front leg and the back leg on each side should be 14½ inches, but measure to make sure, and cut the two cleats for a snug fit. Screw the cleats to the insides of the side pieces, flush with the tops of the side pieces.

automobiles, bicycles, and other family vehicles and possessions. A thorough sorting out and cleaning a couple of times a year is the minimum attention needed for a garage. Beyond that, here are some ideas to create more usable space in your garage, no matter how small.

Storing the Extras in the Garage

Over the years, we have used a number of methods to pack a little bit more into an already overstuffed garage. Most of these ideas use inexpensive off-the-shelf hooks and gadgets that you can pick up at any home center:

▶ Hang a wire bicycle basket on the wall to hold sports equipment like balls, mitts, and helmets. Another place to store athletic equipment is in a net hammock strung from wall to wall over the hood of your car.

▶ To hang tools and odd-shaped items, install ¼-inch-thick pegboard on the back wall of the garage. Use the heavyweight hanging attachments designed for ¼-inch-thick pegboard to keep things accessible and visible. But don't store anything with sharp edges or cutting blades that are exposed. It is easy to bump into one of these tools and get cut or have it fall off the hook and damage its cutting edge or, worse, your foot.

▶ Nail a piece of 1 × 4 to the garage wall studs, then mount spring-loaded clips designed to hold the handles of brooms, shovels, and digging garden equipment to this wood strip.

▶ When bicycles and tricycles are out of season, get them off the floor by hanging them from the ceiling or wall. You'll find special vinyl-coated hooks that screw into the ceiling joists to hang a bike upside-down by its tires. There are also hooks designed to screw into the wall studs that hold a bike away from the wall. You might have to loosen and turn the handle bars of some bikes so they will fit against the wall.

▶ If you have wall-mounted shelves in the garage and want to conceal all the clutter they're holding, mount inexpensive bamboo shades from the ceiling in front of them. The shades hide the paraphernalia, yet provide easy access to what's behind them.

▶ Probably the easiest way to hang long-handled garden equipment is to drive a 12d galvanized nail into the wall stud and use it as a hook. To make a rack, use a section of 1 × 4 nailed to the studs with a row of 12d nails as hooks.

Sealing a Garage Floor

Cement floors in garages seem to attract dust and dirt, but there's an easy way to seal them with a protective coating. A concrete sealer prevents surface dust and spilled liquids from soaking into the concrete. Emptying the garage is the most difficult and time-consuming part of this job, but it's worth the effort. We've used both water sealer and concrete sealer with the same good results.

First do a thorough job of sweeping the floor, then use a paint roller with a handle and pan to liberally apply the sealer. Use an old roller if you have one; you'll never get the sealer out of the roller, so you'll have to throw it away. Provide good ventilation while you're making the application and while the sealer dries. Let it dry overnight and then give it a second coat. Every time you clean out the garage, give the floor another single application for continued good maintenance.

Repairing a Garage Floor

If your garage floor is damaged by cracks and crevices and stained by car oil, it needs more than a good sealing. What's required is a thorough cleaning followed by surface repairs to prevent further cracking.

Begin by broom sweeping, or using a shop vacuum to remove dust and dirt. Use a scraper and then the crevice tool of the vacuum to remove particles in holes and cracks. If you have oil or grease stains on the floor, use one of the many degreasing products designed to remove oil and other stains on the concrete. Then wash the entire floor with a heavy-duty cleaning solution of trisodium phosphate or Spic and Span. Rinse the floor after washing and let it dry.

Small cracks or pits in the floor are not hard to repair. Kits are sold at your local home center that contain patching cement and a latex bonding agent. If you already have some cement around the house, you can purchase the bonding agent separately. Follow the manufacturer's directions for mixing these products. If you are filling large holes or cracks, include a gravel aggregate. But if you are filling small cracks, leave out the gravel because it won't fit into the cracks.

The latex bonding agent provides a good bond between the old concrete and the patch. This bond can be improved in a large patch if you use a cold chisel (a chisel with an all-metal handle) to undercut the perimeter of the patch. This gives the patch more surface to adhere to and keys it into the slab.

Hold the chisel so its handle slants toward the center of the patch so when you hit it with a hammer (wear safety glasses), you will undercut the concrete. Don't get carried away; if the hole starts to open up, chisel straight down. What you want to accomplish with the chisel is to enlarge the area of the joint around the edge of the patch.

After you have undercut the patch, clean out all dust and chips from the area. If the bonding agent's manufacturer recommends, use a spray bottle of water to wet the cracks or holes. This will keep the old concrete from absorbing the water from the patch, causing a poor cure.

Weather-Stripping the Garage Door

Stopping the wind from blowing through the garage not only makes it a better place to store things, it cuts down your energy bills. Unless the garage is detached from your house, there is at least one exterior wall shared by the garage and your warm house. Even though this wall is insulated, stopping air infiltration through the garage will help cut the heat transfer through this wall. Weather stripping, especially at the bottom of the door, helps stop rain and snow from blowing under the door, too.

You can purchase heavy vinyl garage door weather stripping kits for the bottom of a garage door. These are sold in lengths of 9 or 16 feet. You also can purchase weather stripping by the foot.

Before you install or replace weather stripping, seal the bottom of the door with paint or varnish. This area of the door is exposed to water and, if left unprotected, can absorb the moisture, causing it to rot and delaminate.

Scrape off any loose or flaking paint. Then apply a thinned coat of exterior primer to the raw wood. Oil-based paint can be thinned with 20 percent mineral spirits. For latex-based paints, add a little water. When that is dry, recoat with full-strength primer.

After the primer has thoroughly dried, apply a coat of exterior house paint that matches the door. If you don't have paint in the matching color, you can use any color if you are careful, because the rubber weatherstrip will cover the entire door bottom. This might be a good time to paint the entire garage door.

Weather stripping can be installed with roofing nails or with aluminum nails provided with most of the kits. Weather stripping can get stiff if it gets below about 40°F. Keep the roll inside until you are ready to install it, if it's cold outside.

Troubleshooting the Garage Door

Sooner or later the garage door will stick or become difficult to open, especially in an old garage that has settled. Adjusting the door's basic mechanism isn't hard, and replacement hinges, rollers, pulleys, and springs can be purchased at most home centers. There are many types and styles of door hardware, so take the old parts with you when shopping for replacement parts.

As soon as your overhead garage door binds or drags, you should find out why. As it gets harder to open, more wear and stress occur to all the moving parts. When you force a door that is hard to operate, you can bend the track or rollers. Most of the time, all that's needed to get a door back in the swing is to lubricate the moving parts or realign the track.

Don't tamper with the garage door springs when the door is down. These springs are under extreme tension, and it can be dangerous if they are allowed to spring loose. Adjust them only when the door is firmly wedged in the up position with a long 2 × 4.

Be extremely careful if you decide to lower the door without the counterweight action of these springs. Raising the door is a one-hand operation with the help of the springs, but the door actually weighs several hundred pounds and will come crashing down without the restraint of the counterweight springs. Here are several easy steps you can take to tune up your door:

Locate the area where the door sticks. Open and close the door. Look to see if the door sticks at a specific spot; the track could be out of alignment or bent. If the door is difficult to open but does not stick in any particular spot, the rollers most likely need oil.

Oil the rollers and clean the track. Use light machine or multipurpose household oil to lubricate each door roller. Silicone spray lubricant and products like WD-40 also are good for unsticking your door. Lubricate the rollers; also oil all spring cable pulleys or shafts.

Dirt also will accumulate in the track. After lubricating the roller wheels, clean the track by wiping it with a rag soaked in mineral spirits. Don't oil the track, though. That will cause dirt to accumulate faster.

Tighten loose lag screws, nuts, and bolts. Look for any loose lag bolts where the track is attached to the garage door frame and overhead rafters or braces. If you find loose bolts, check that the track is plumb before you tighten any bolts. If the door track is out of alignment, loosen the screws or lag bolts and pound the track back into alignment with a hammer. Put a piece of wood on the track to protect it when you hit it. Check the

OVERHEAD GARAGE DOOR

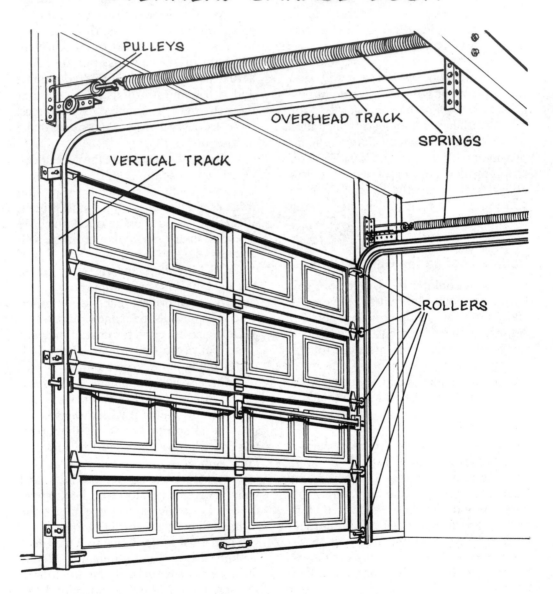

PULLEYS

OVERHEAD TRACK

SPRINGS

VERTICAL TRACK

ROLLERS

track again with a level, and tighten the screws or lag bolts.

If the door continues to malfunction after you have tried these simple repairs, seek help from a garage door installer.

Installing an Automatic Garage Door Opener

An automatic garage door opener is one of those conveniences that make you wonder how you ever did without them. Not only do they make life more convenient, they add to your security. On a rainy, dark night you'll really appreciate pulling your car into an opened and lighted garage.

You'll find several automatic openers that are available in the $100 range. These do-it-yourself kits include complete installation instructions, all the mounting hardware, and a remote control transmitter.

Before shopping, make a sketch of your door, noting its dimensions and the clearance between the door and the garage ceiling when the door is up. Choose a unit that is designed for your door (swing up or roll up) and powerful enough to handle the weight.

While you are at the store, figure out how you will suspend the motor unit. Consult with the salesperson where you purchase the unit. They sell metal angle iron, which has holes punched in it so that it is easy to cut with a hacksaw and allows great flexibility in installation. Also purchase any lag bolts, wall anchors, or other hardware you might need. You will need to connect the opener to a power source, so purchase the necessary wiring supplies.

Great Gadgets & Gizmos

☞ **Polder folding clothes dryer**   This little unit has seven plastic-coated steel rods for drying hand washables in a small laundry. It comes with two sets of mounting brackets, so you can use it in the bathroom, too. It is sold by Polder Inc., 200 Central Park Avenue, Hartsdale, NY 10530.

☞ **Frontiersman's tool**   This is a multiuse tool that you'll use for many jobs in and out of the workshop. Use it to pull nails, as a pry bar, or on a camping trip to pitch your tent. It's also called a five-way handy tool. It hammers and chops, and once you have one, you can't imagine what you did without it. It is sold in Brookstone stores and through their catalog at Brookstone, Inc., 127 Vose Farm Road, Peterborough, NH 03458.

☞ **Ultra Code remote system**   This is a garage door opener that fits on your key ring. It's compatible with all of the electric garage door openers now on the market and has four billion electronic codes to deter even the most serious burglars. It is sold by Clifford Electronics, 20750 Lassen, Chatsworth, CA 91311.

☞ **Workmate**   This is the classic portable, yet sturdy, workbench. Ours has stood up to years of abuse. The Workmate 400 has vertical and vise jaws for clamping, and it knocks down and sets up quickly and easily. It is made by Black & Decker, 626 Hanover Pike, Hampstead, MD 21074.

☞ **Foldaway ironing boards**   One source for built-in ironing board units for cabinets is The Woodworkers' Store catalog, 21801 Industrial Boulevard, Rogers, MN 55374-9514.

The transmitter is part of the package, but other features you might want to consider are a vacation switch that turns off the garage control so that it is not triggered by someone else's transmitter, a manual control, an automatic light delay that turns off the light after a few minutes, and a garage work light.

You'll need about half a day to do the job. If you can get the help of a friend, it will save you countless trips up and down the ladder. To install the opener, you need only basic tools, including a hammer, screwdriver, adjustable wrench, hacksaw, drill, and measuring tape. A pair of work gloves will make handling the greasy chain less messy.

Read the directions included with the unit, and spread out all of its parts on the garage floor to check the inventory before you begin. Most openers are installed in the same general way. Here is what's involved:

Install the header bracket. All units are installed with their tracks aligned with the center of the door. Check the installation instructions for the exact height that the track should be mounted above the door. Then install the header bracket on the door wall at the center line of the door at the prescribed height above the doorjamb.

Assemble the track. Put the track and chain or screw drive assembly together. Install the motor drive unit, and then attach the track end to the header bracket.

Secure the drive unit to the ceiling. Raise the drive-unit end of the track into position. Hold it temporarily in place by propping it with a ladder or other temporary support. Then install the ceiling supports according to the recommendations of the manufacturer.

Connect the drive unit. Turn off the electricity to the garage, and then wire up the motor. Screw in the light bulb, turn the power on, and it's ready to use. Cycle the unit up and down several times. You might have to adjust the track or limit switches for smooth operation.

After the unit is operational, make sure all members of the family know and understand how to operate the opener. Kids will have to know how to raise the door to get their bikes out, unless there is another door to your garage.

CHAPTER 12

Outdoors

The exterior of your house is the perfect example of the old saying "First impressions are lasting." Many factors, from the condition of the gutters on your home to the shrubbery and landscaping, contribute to what real estate agents like to call "curb appeal."

These days, many people think of their yard as more than just a place to mow. It's an outdoor room. A well-designed deck on a typical subdivision rancher can be the added architectural feature needed to set it apart from its neighbors. Exterior lighting, walkways, and fences are other improvements that encourage family and friends to spend time in the backyard.

Remodeling surveys by *Practical Homeowner* and *Homeowner* magazines show that when houses are sold, decks and landscaping are among improvements that usually pay back more than half of the amount paid to the contractor who installed them. Of course, the payback is even bigger if you do the work yourself.

In this chapter we'll suggest improvement ideas. Also, we'll talk about some of the most commonly needed maintenance and repairs around the outside of your house.

Outdoor Lighting

Adding exterior lighting to the yard or patio makes it a safer, more enjoyable place to spend evenings. It also helps deter crime. Outdoor lighting systems can be 120 volt or 12 volt. Each system has its advantages and pitfalls. Here is what we have learned working with both systems.

120-Volt Systems

If you are looking for bright light, for example to light up the patio or for security lighting, then a 120-volt system is the best choice. With 120 volts you can use mercury vapor, metal halide, or high-pressure sodium lamps, all of which cast extremely bright light and are very efficient. The major drawback is that everything looks strange under the yellow or blue light that these lamps cast. They are the same types used in street lamps and to light up parking lots. Of course, 120 volts can be used for outdoor versions of the standard incandescent fixtures used inside.

Installing 120-volt exterior lights is not much different from working with a standard inside fixture. You should be sure that you use only components that are approved for outside use and that seal properly against the weather. Wiring for 120 volts must also be buried deep in a trench to protect it from being cut by a shovel or other digging tool. Before you do any exterior wiring, check your local electrical codes. Some areas allow you to bury exterior cable directly in the ground, while others require the cable to be placed in a plastic or metal conduit.

For these reasons, running 120-volt exterior lines around your property is not a task for the beginning electrician. You will be better off if you have a professional contractor handle this job.

12-Volt DIY Systems

The major advantage of 12-volt do-it-yourself systems is that they are easier and generally safer to install than 120-volt systems. A 12-volt shock can't kill you. These systems are particularly well suited for garden accent lighting or to light a pathway. They cast a limited pool of light, often just what you need for pathway or garden lighting.

Energy-efficient 12-volt systems are sold in kits that include transformers to convert your 120-volt household current into 12 volts. The transformer can be plugged into a standard 120-volt receptacle or be wired directly. Because there is no danger of electrocution, cables for a 12-volt system may be laid directly on the ground, although you'll probably want to bury them a few inches deep to get them out of the way.

You can augment a basic 12-volt kit with additional fixtures and wire. Wiring is simple; usually the fixtures just clamp right to the cable with little prongs that pierce the plastic wire insulation and make the connections.

Most manufacturers offer several types of fixtures, including spots, floodlights, and accent lights. Some also have lights on posts and hanging fixtures. During the planning stages of this project, you should check out the options offered by the manufacturer.

Transformers are rated for limited numbers of fixtures, so check the one you buy to make sure it will fill your lighting needs. Electrical cable offers resistance to electricity, so very long wire runs can affect the performance of even a 120-volt system. But low-voltage systems are affected by this voltage drop over relatively short distances, causing the lamps to dim. Keep this in mind when you buy and install a 12-volt system.

Tips about Where to Put Lights

The possibilities for outdoor lighting are endless, so use your imagination. Just remember to consider how lighting at your house will affect neighboring houses. Here are some areas that usually can benefit from exterior lighting:

▶ Lighting in the soffit overhang near the door increases the visibility at the entrance.

▶ Low path lights help direct foot traffic to the door or through a yard.

▶ Emphasize a shapely tree with an uplight that focuses light upward through its branches.

▶ Shine a light down from high in a tree to create a moonlight effect.

▶ Low "mushroom" or 'bollard' fixtures provide lighting on steps, making them safer to navigate in the dark.

▶ Never aim floodlights directly at driveways or walkways, where they will obscure people's vision.

▶ For convenience, install photocell controls that automatically turn lights on at dusk and off at daylight.

▶ If you want to illuminate a pond, light the surrounding area to create a reflection.

Instant Edges, Planter Boxes, and More

Wood that has been pressure treated with cromated copper arsenate has become very popular for projects around the garden. Before pressure-treated wood was available, the only woods that would stand up to direct contact with the ground were more expensive, naturally rot-resistant woods, such as redwood or cedar, or wood that had been treated with creosote. Pressure-treated wood is more expensive than untreated pine, but cheaper and even more rot resistant than redwood or cedar.

We use pressure-treated wood to construct border and driveway edging. We find that 2×4 stock is ideal for edging stone or gravel walks and driveways, while 2×6 stock can be partially buried in the ground and still be high enough to hold a raised bed of flowers or vegetables. Both these materials should be held in place with 2×2 stakes.

Larger pieces of 4×4 stock make planters and large raised beds and are a lot easier to work with than the old oil-soaked or creosote-soaked 6×10 railroad ties we have struggled with in the past.

Relatively new to the marketplace are wood module kits of precut sections of 4×4 pressure-treated wood. The pieces are designed to fit together in various configurations, so even a first-timer can easily make landscape edging, a sandbox for the kids, a raised planting box for

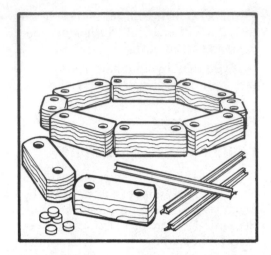

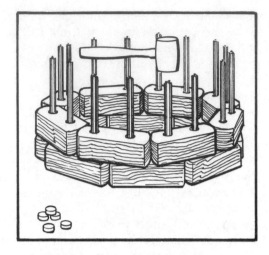

WoodScapes is a product that simplifies using wood in the garden. All you have to do is lay out your design, pound in the plastic stakes, and tap on the wooden caps.

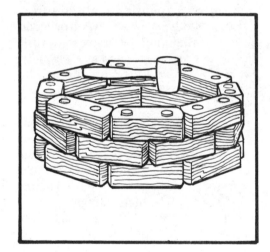

perennials, and even a walkway. The kits are assembled with high-impact plastic stakes, and each piece of wood is predrilled for the stakes. The ends are slightly rounded, to allow the pieces to be configured in a circle or strung together to form curved edging or beds.

Several manufacturers offer these landscape building product kits. For example, one of the manufacturers' kits can be made into any number of configurations. It contains 12 running feet of precut 4 × 4 wood in 7½-inch, 15-inch, and 22½-inch lengths with the needed pegs and caps. You can use the long components for a small box of raised perennials or to surround a tree. Use the three lengths to create a random bricklike pattern. The smaller-size components give the appearance of brick lining a stone walkway or edging a garden. Other kits contain components to make a 2-foot-square mailbox planter or a 4-foot hexagonal planter.

When shopping for one of these kits, know the area you plan to cover. No matter what the project, carefully measure the distance to know how many feet of material you need. Little or no excavation is needed, because the wood components are designed to sit on the ground and are held in place with the pegs pounded into the ground. However, if you are building on uneven ground, it's necessary to level it first before laying them. The easiest way to do this is to lay out the first layer of wood pieces. If they do not lie level and are off an inch or so, soak the ground under the high pieces until it is soft. Protect the high piece with a scrap of lumber, and give it a couple of good blows with a sledgehammer to drive it into the ground.

If the difference between the low and high pieces is more than a couple of inches, mark the edge of the high pieces with a spade. Remove the piece and dig away the high spot. You have to remove at least the sod, which can be several inches thick.

In-Ground Irrigation

Maintaining your lawn, garden, and shrubbery is an important part of landscaping. Proper watering is one of the most important aspects of this maintenance program. Water is also getting a little more scarce in many areas, so efficient use of water is becoming more important.

Proper watering of your lawn can mean dragging out the old hose, but there are much better and more convenient methods. We're talking about automation —subsurface watering systems that drip, soak, and sprinkle water in prescribed doses on your lawn, flower garden, or vegetable plot. Since these systems can be turned on and off easily or set on a timer, a more exact watering schedule can be effortlessly maintained with a substantial savings in water. Subsurface systems save even more water because none is lost to evaporation, as with sprinkling.

Thanks to the advent of inexpensive plastic plumbing components, automatic sprinkler systems are now sold in kit form for do-it-yourself installation. All the necessary underground piping and fittings are included, along with a selection of sprinkler heads. You can also purchase the heads separately.

Choose from a vast array of plastic spray, drip, or soaking heads that can cover areas of just about any shape. There are also a rotary shooter lawn spray head and a misty gentle sprayer for flowers.

In addition to the sprinkler heads, you can add a soaker system that consists of a thin water line buried about 8 or 10 inches below the lawn surface. This type of system soaks the soil underneath the lawn so the grass roots get all the water and none can evaporate.

In addition to in-ground systems, there are surface irrigation systems. A drip system can be laid on the surface of the soil. It has an emitter placed at the base of a plant that drips a small stream of water at a precise rate.

A soaker system can also be installed on the surface or buried underground. Through a network of rotproof pipe or hose made from materials like polyethylene, vinyl, and rubber, soaker hoses can be put in place permanently and controlled at one spigot.

With one of these systems, you can irrigate a raised flower bed, or install a bubbler head and flood a vegetable garden with a gentle flow of water. Soaker, bubbler, and drip systems can also be added to an in-ground sprinkler system.

Planning Tips

Do-it-yourself sprinkler and irrigation systems are sold at gardening centers,

INSTALLING A SPRINKLER SYSTEM

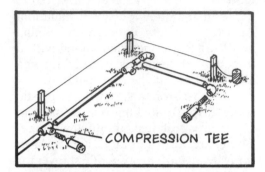

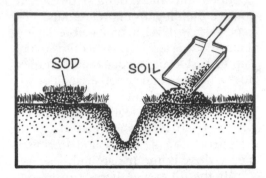

1. Lay out the system on the lawn with stakes and string. Then place all needed components next to the layout lines. Check that you have all the parts before you dig up the lawn.

2. Remove about a 6-inch strip of sod along the layout line and set it aside. Then dig a trench for the pipes. Follow your local codes on how deep the pipes should be buried.

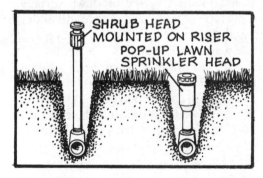

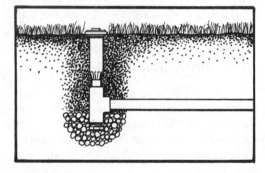

3. Install the piping and sprinkler heads according to your plan. When finished with the hookup, test the system for leaks, then fill the trench and replace the sod.

4. If the ground freezes solid in your area, install drain-down valves at the low points in the system. Also provide a drainage point in the main supply system.

home centers, and through various garden mail-order suppliers. You also can have them professionally installed.

Installation isn't hard, so the main advantage in having your system designed and installed by a professional is you will probably get a better-designed system. We have found there is more to laying out a watering system than just drawing overlapping circles on a grid of paper. Here are the main considerations in designing a home irrigation system:

Make a rough sketch. To determine your exact needs, you'll have to make an accurate drawing of your property. A 100 or 200-foot tape measure is handy here. Begin by mapping out the perimeter of your yard, recording the dimensions on a rough sketch. Then plot out the major features of your yard, including gardens, driveway, walkways, and the location of your house. Also indicate any unusual areas, such as low, wet spots and shady areas where little will grow.

Make a scale drawing.   Consult the manufacturer's literature to learn the type of sprinkler head and coverage pattern needed in each area. Most manufacturers offer planning booklets that explain how to lay out your system using their specific products. Spend a good deal of time designing the system.

Use the planning sheet in the instruction or layout booklet or make your own. All you need is a sheet of ¼-inch-square graph paper. Set up the sheet so that you make each square equal to 1 foot. If you have a large yard, you might not be able to fit the whole area on one sheet. This is a standard scale used for most house plans. If your yard is large, then you might have to tape several sheets together.

Start your plan by drawing the basic shape of your lot on the plan. Mark off the lot, house, and other features on the graph paper. After you have a basic sketch, refer to the manufacturer's booklet to see what is available to fill the watering needs of each particular area.

Plan the system.   Go through the booklet and plan a system to fit your watering needs and your pocketbook. Remember, you don't have to install it all at one time, but the system has to have the capacity to allow for future expansion. You cannot keep adding sprinkler heads to a run of pipe without eventually causing the water pressure to drop. The basic piping system has to be large enough to handle future capacity.

Check your water pressure.   To properly size the system, you have to know your water pressure. There are gauges that fit the spigot of your house outlet that you can borrow from the dealer, or you can call the city water department. After you determine the water pressure, consult the manufacturer's literature and determine the size of the piping needed to supply water to the number of sprinkler heads you plan to install. The more sprinkler heads, the larger the pipe needed to supply the volume of water and still keep the pressure up so it will sprinkle properly.

If you plan to add sprinkler heads to the system, size the pipe for the ultimate number of heads you will eventually install. Another approach is to plan to add another branch line instead of adding to the existing set of pipes. Adding on to the system is easy if you have planned for it in the initial installation. Pick a system that has all the accessories and options you might want someday. For example, you might want a fertilizer injector that is plumbed right into the water line to feed liquid fertilizer to the sprinkler heads, soaker hoses, or drip system.

Consider your climate in the design. If you live in an area that has freezing temperatures and a deep ground frost, take this into consideration in your design. The system should be designed so it can be drained or have air forced through the pipes to eliminate the water during winter.

Get a bid from a professional.   Contact several professional lawn services or irrigation specialists, and get a bid on your planned system. This will be valuable information because it will give you a realistic idea of just what your savings will be if you decide to do it yourself.

The professionals also may offer valuable advice as they explain what you need and how their systems work. Ask if there will be a charge for the estimate before making an appointment with a specialist.

A typical home watering system installed by a professional can cost more than $1,000, depending on the size and complexity of your system. One advantage the pro has is that his equipment does not dig wide trenches in a lawn. Most of them use a machine that cuts a narrow, 1-foot-deep trench for the piping.

Rent equipment. A lawn irrigation system requires a trench for the water pipe. You can dig this by hand, but it's a lot easier to rent and use a power trencher. If you do opt to rent a trencher, then check with your telephone, electric, and gas companies and the water utility. Usually, they will stake out the locations of their buried lines without charge.

Renting a trencher will also allow you to spend your energy checking that everything is laid out right, and you won't be tempted to cut corners because you don't want to dig another trench. Be sure to add the cost of the trencher rental to the cost of the do-it-yourself job when you compare it against the cost of a professional installation.

Asphalt Driveways and Walkways

Asphalt is an easy material to keep looking good if you perform simple but regular maintenance. Most problems can be prevented if you keep a driveway or walkway sealed. Asphalt sealers are inexpensive and easy to apply. If you have

asphalt in need of repair and don't have the time to fix it, it's probably money well spent to have a sealing company do the job. Putting it off for a couple of years until you get around to it will probably cost you more in repairs than the money you can save by doing it yourself.

Resealing an Asphalt Driveway

Every few years you should give a face-lift to your asphalt driveway, which will extend its life considerably. By filling the small hairline cracks and shallow holes, you'll prevent these imperfections from enlarging and becoming a major problem. A word of warning—this is a sticky, messy job often resulting in shoes and pant legs permanently covered with asphalt. So dress accordingly.

All you need is some asphalt cleaner, sealer, and an old long-handled push broom or roller. Sweep the driveway clean and then remove any weeds or grass growing in the cracks or alongside the driveway. Then follow directions with the asphalt cleaner to prepare the driveway for the sealer.

Begin at the top of the driveway or where it meets the garage, and work from the center out to the sides. Spill the sealer onto the driveway, and work it into the driveway in an area that you can comfortably cover. Continue working your way down the driveway until it is completely resurfaced. Use the empty cans to form a barricade to prevent traffic on the wet surface.

Patching a Hole in an Asphalt Path or Driveway

A blacktop or paved asphalt path shows signs of damage when cracks appear or it breaks away on the edges. This is weather related because as water enters a crack, it erodes the soil beneath it; then when it freezes, the the soil expands and the crack becomes larger.

This is one of those maintenance chores that you can't afford not to do, because the patch material is inexpensive and this project requires minimal time and skill. Here are the basics; you will probably develop a few tricks of your own after a few patch jobs:

Take note of the season.   This project is best done in the summer months, when patching material can be kept warm.

Remove loose particles.   Chip out the loose asphalt in the hole with a cold chisel (a chisel with an all-metal handle) or a pry bar and hammer, being careful to remove all the loose material, even the fine particles.

Fill the hole.   Patching blacktop is sold in large ready-to-use bags that cost less than $10. Pour it into the crack and mound it slightly higher than the driveway or walkway surface.

Compact the patch.   You can use your car to drive back and forth over the patch, to firm up the patching material. You can also compact the patching material with the end of a 4 × 4. Whatever you use, pack the patching material as hard as you can.

Fill the entire patch area. It's better to have a slight bump than a depression that will collect water. Feather the edges of the patch evenly out from the center.

Concrete Patchwork

Repairing concrete requires different steps than repairing asphalt, but the job is just as easy and important to do. Cracked or pitted concrete will only get

---

SAND AND SEALER MIX TO PATCH SMALL CRACKS

Patch small cracks in your driveway with a mixture of sand and driveway sealer. Mix the two together in an old gallon milk carton or some other disposable container. Make the mixture thick at first, for the large cracks, then add more sealer to make it soupy to fill the small cracks.

---

worse. Here again, water is the main problem, especially in cold climates where the freeze-thaw cycle tends to widen cracks. The frost heave lifts the broken pieces to cause uneven walks and lumpy driveways.

To repair concrete, you'll need a cold chisel, a wire brush, and a trowel. Purchase a concrete repair kit or use premixed cement and sand, which you mix with a latex concrete patching liquid according to the directions on the products. Mix up only what you can use in half an hour or so.

This patching is the same as repairing a garage floor, and it's just as important to get the area clean. Use a broom to sweep up any debris, or use a shop vacuum. Use a scraper to remove particles in holes and cracks. If you have oil or grease stains on the drive in the patch area, use a degreasing product designed to remove oil and other stains from concrete. Wash the patch area with a heavy-duty cleaning solution of trisodium phosphate or Spic and Span. Then rinse the patch with your hose.

Small cracks or pits in the concrete are easy to fix. Kits are sold at your local home center that contain patching cement and a latex bonding agent. You can purchase the bonding agent separately if you have some cement around the house. Follow the manufacturer's directions for mixing these products.

The latex bonding agent provides a good bond between the old concrete and the patch. This bond can be improved if you use a cold chisel to undercut the perimeter of the patch. This makes the edge of the patch thicker, and it will not crack as easily as the thin edge formed when you smooth the patch level with the original surface.

To do this, hold the chisel so its handle slants toward the center of the patch so when you hit it with a hammer (wear safety glasses), you will undercut the concrete. Don't get carried away—if the hole starts to open up, chisel straight down. What you want to accomplish with the chisel is to enlarge the area of the joint around the edge of the patch.

After you have undercut the patch, clean all dust and chips from the area. If the bonding agent's manufacturer recommends, use a spray bottle of water to wet the cracks or holes. This keeps the old concrete from absorbing the water from the patch, causing a poor cure.

If you are filling large holes or cracks, include a gravel aggregate, but if you are filling small cracks, leave out the gravel because it won't fit into the cracks.

Fences

Fence building takes no special skills, but it is not usually quick and easy. You do have to know what you are doing. If you do decide to tackle fence building yourself, we recommend you purchase a book devoted to the topic. There are many types of fences and building techniques to consider. Whether you decide to build a fence yourself or hire someone to do it, you'll need to do some careful planning before the first posthole is dug. Laying out and constructing a simple fence on level, rock-free ground isn't hard, but such ideal conditions are rare. So much depends on the property itself. Rocky soil is extremely difficult to dig; a sloping lot can be another challenge. You might be faced with a hedge of indestructible forsythia that requires removal. A tree that is sitting half on your property and half on your neighbor's might make your fence-building project a community affair.

Here's what we've learned about fence planning:

Locate the boundaries. Get out the survey plot of your property to know exactly where your property line begins and ends. Positively locate the boundary stakes, pipes, notches in the sidewalk, or other marks that identify your property. If you can't find these marks, seek help in locating them. You may be able to get some help from the firm that prepared the survey of your house or from the local building department or recorder of deeds in your local municipal or county office. The tax department might also be of some help because they usually have tax maps showing each lot with its tax numbers. Sometimes they will give you a photocopy. If you live in a town or city, you may have to get a permit, so the building inspector may help you locate these marks.

The main thing to remember is that

it is your responsibility to see that the fence is on your property. Your neighbor may not care if it's a little off, but when you sell your house or he sells his, a misplaced fence can cause all sorts of problems.

If there already is a fence running along part of your property line, find out who it belongs to. Traditionally, the post side of a fence faces the fence's owners, but not all fences are built this way. Check all this out with neighboring property owners.

Check the codes. Find out what the building code restrictions are in your neighborhood, as well as any community restrictions that might affect the design of your fence. There may be restrictions pertaining to height, material, and proximity to a building or driveway or proximity to power, water, and gas lines.

Determine the function. The reasons for building a fence are many: privacy, protection for kids and pets, wind protection, and to block out an unattractive view or noise. Let function follow fashion in determining the style of fence for your home. Once the function is determined, clip pictures from magazines or snap photos of fences that you like. Consider whether you want to combine materials, for example, use brick pillars with lattice frames.

Do you want to use a kit? Look at the many fence kits or preassembled sections available at your local lumberyard. These usually are sold in 10-foot sections with a post on each end. They make erecting a wooden fence a lot easier. When you are looking at these preassembled sections, check them out carefully. They are attractively priced and will save you a lot of labor, but many are made from thin stock and stapled together.

You have to weigh the savings against purchasing the materials and assembling the fence from scratch.

Use the right wood for the job. Even though they are considerably more expensive, use only rot-resistant woods, like redwood or cedar or pressure-treated wood, to construct the frame of your fence. Standard construction-grade lumber will not last long and will soon become an eyesore or begin to rot.

Since cedar, redwood, and pressure-treated woods are expensive, the cost of a fence built entirely from these materials will add up fast. You can save money and build a perfectly functional, long-lasting fence by using pressure-treated wood for the posts and stringers. Use pine for the rest of the fence. The slats, battens, or boards attached to the frame of the fence are usually not as susceptible to rot and insect damage as wood that comes into direct contact with the ground. Pine that is treated with a wood preservative, then stained or sealed with a water repellent, has a long service life and is considerably cheaper.

Use a water repellent. All of these woods need some protection from the elements if they are to keep looking good. Even rot-resistant and pressure-treated woods will become dirty and discolored if neglected. Whatever material you build your fence from, you will have to apply some sort of protective coating.

The easiest to apply and least expensive coating is a water repellent. These are clear and will not change the color of the wood, although most will darken and highlight the grain slightly. Their main advantage is that they seal the wood cells and help stabilize the moisture content of the wood. This prevents excessive expansion and contraction, which is the major cause of splitting, checking, and twisting. We recommend that you apply a water repellent sealer to the fence even if you plan to stain or paint the fence.

Use stain, not paint.   A house surrounded by an impeccably painted fence is a sure sign of wealth. Either the owner pays somebody to paint it every couple of years, or he's got plenty of free time on his hands. Since we are not in a position to dedicate our lives or pocketbooks to fence painting, we use solid stain instead. Solid stains come in white and many other colors and look very much like paint. But they won't peel like paint, so you can recoat them for many years without having to scrape flaking paint off the fence. You can also use semitransparent stains, which add color without totally obscuring the grain of the wood.

The Fence Gate, or First Impression

Whatever type of fence you have, the gate is the part that people come into contact with most. Often, the gate will be part of a visitor's first impression of your property.

A sagging and wobbly gate does not put its best foot forward. Here are a couple of simple repairs you can do to improve an old, tired gate:

Tighten loose hinges.   If your hinges are not recessed into mortises, the easiest way to tighten them up is to remove one at a time, reposition it slightly, and drill new screw holes in solid wood.

Remove the lower hinge first. Mark the position of each screw with a pencil, and then drill pilot holes for the screws. Install the hinge, and then repeat the process on the upper hinge.

Repair hinge screw holes.   If the gate hinges are mortised, remove the

hinges; then dip the end of a wooden match into carpenter's glue, and push it into each screw hole. Break the matches off, and then reinstall the hinges.

Support a sagging gate.   Use a diagonal wire brace to correct the sag. If your gate sags, install a large galvanized-steel T-bracket in the sagging corner with the base of the T pointing to the opposite corner. Install another T in the opposite corner, with its base pointing to the first T. Attach a piece of wire to each T-bracket. Then open a galvanized turnbuckle about ¾ inch, and attach the wires from the Ts to it. Correct the sag by propping up the low corner of the gate until it's level, and then tighten the turnbuckle to hold it there.

Decks

A deck added to your house is much more than an outdoor extension. Properly conceived and designed, a deck can complement a house by adding architectural interest. It can unify ground levels and tie different elements of a yard together while acting as part porch and part patio.

A deck should be in scale with the house, not a tiny postage stamp tacked on the back of the house nor an overbuilt aircraft carrier. Let form follow function in determining the design and scale of your deck. To do this takes a lot of thoughtful consideration on your part. Here are some details to consider when you are planning your deck:

▶ Who uses the deck? And how do they use it? are the first questions. Do you want a deck for entertaining, sunning, or a place for little kids to play?

▶ Do you want a deck to incorporate

seating or storage? What about garden boxes for flowers or trees or a fire pit or a spa?

▶ Do you want a deck open, or built with railings? Codes require railings for decks more than a step or so off the ground.

▶ Will the deck need electricity? Outdoor lighting is an important element of a well-designed deck. Incorporate it in the design if night use is part of your plan. Will you need power to operate electrical equipment, a barbecue perhaps?

Make sure you know your property boundaries before planning a deck. Check with your local building department to find out about minimum setbacks required from your neighbors' properties.

You can build a deck attached to the house or make it freestanding. A deck can be designed to spread across the back of a house or wrap around its sides. Its design can be as unique as your house or even make a typical house something special.

Once you have a wish list and can pinpoint the primary use and users of your deck, you need to assess the site. Note the effects the changes of season will play on where you plan to build a deck. Check the track of the sun. Determine how light it will be at different times during the year. Your first choice of a location might be too sunny or too shady during the months you'll use a deck.

Choose only wood that can combat the effects of the weather. The most common rot-resistant materials are pressure-treated lumber and redwood and cedar. The price of redwood and cedar varies according to your region, so investigate their cost relative to pressure-treated wood before you get your heart set on a redwood or cedar deck.

If you live in the east, where redwood is expensive, and you want a redwood deck, consider using pressure-treated material for the foundation joists and framing, which are not visible. Use the more expensive redwood or cedar for the decking, which you do see.

The next step is to find out about the local building codes and zoning regulations regarding decks in your area. A building permit is required, and restrictions can limit you to things such as the deck's height, size, and depth of footing. Code probably requires rails for a deck more than one step above the ground. Zoning may address such issues as required setbacks, requiring that your deck be a certain minimum distance from your neighbor's property line.

Check out the drainage characteristics of your yard and the location of underground utility lines.

You can design the deck yourself, get a design from a book, purchase plans, or buy a precut deck kit. You can also commission a designer to create plans, or have a builder come up with the plan after you tell him what you want.

And when it comes to building the deck, you have the options of building it yourself, hiring a contractor to do the whole job, or working with the contractor. Unless you have considerable building experience, anything but the simplest deck is probably best left to the professionals. The best method we have come up with is to work with a contractor on the project.

We hire him to dig and pour the footing and set the posts and build the frame. Then we install the decking as described later. This part of the job basically involves driving thousands of nails. Since nailing the decking in place is so labor intensive, if you do it, you can save a bundle. We found that when working with professionals, we could build a more complex deck than we ever would have attempted ourselves.

Using Deck Kits

Many lumberyards and home centers offer deck kits. These kits contain all the materials necessary to build the deck and a set of plans. Some kits also include full-size templates that you can lay on the joists or decking to guide you when cutting any joints or angles.

The main advantage to these kits is that the lumberyard has assembled all the materials together and you are assured that you have enough wood, concrete, nails, and other materials to actually build the deck. Also, the kits can be cheaper than purchasing the components.

The main disadvantages to using kits are that they usually are rather basic and most lumberyards have only two or three designs to choose from. The wood is not precut, so you are not saving on labor, and the same skills are needed to build from the pile of lumber that makes up the kit as are needed to build a custom-designed deck.

If you do choose to purchase a kit and it seems to be priced far lower than the cost of the individual components, check with the lumberyard to be certain they will supply first-quality lumber and not a pile of split, twisted boards that have been rejected from other jobs. Just because the wood is of construction-grade pressure-treated lumber is no guarantee that the wood is usable.

Working with Pressure-Treated Wood

We seldom use anything other than pressure-treated wood for outdoor proj-ects. This building material is impregnated with waterborne preservatives to make it resist decay caused by fungi and insects. The same chemicals that protect the wood can be harmful to you if not handled properly.

The biggest danger comes from inhaling the sawdust as you cut the wood or from absorbing some of the toxins through direct contact with wood that is still wet with preservative. When working with treated wood, wear gloves and a mask, and wash your work clothes separately from other clothes.

When purchasing pressure-treated lumber, be just as fussy as you would when selecting any lumber. Just because it has been treated and is more expensive does not mean it is free from imperfections. If possible, hand-pick the decking boards, which will be visible.

Reject boards that have split ends, even though the split is small. Chances are that the split will grow when the board dries out and is installed on your deck. Also, save yourself a lot of hassles by choosing boards that are straight and not twisted. You can muscle crooked or twisted boards into place, and every board is not going to be perfect, but why set yourself up for more work than necessary?

Boards with large knots that go completely through the board should also be suspect. Small knots usually do not dry out enough to fall out, but a large knot always has the potential to fall out. Also check out the edges of the board, especially at the ends. Sometimes the edges of the boards are rounded, with traces of bark on them. This is because the board was slightly smaller than the cutting head that forms the edge in the lumber mill. These bad edges are not visible if you use the lumber for beams or joists, but the edge will show if the board ends up as decking.

If you're having the material delivered, order a few extra joists and decking boards, because some will be warped or have other problems. You can return the ones you don't use.

Installing Decking

If you can drive a nail straight without bending it (this is not as easy as it sounds), you can install decking. This is a very labor-intensive part of the project, and carpenters sometimes use nail guns for some of the job, which speeds things up quite a bit.

If you are using 2 × 4 decking, use two nails to hold the decking to each joist. For 2 × 6 decking, use three nails. The nails should be 12d or 16d galvanized or spiral shank for extra holding power. To help prevent splitting, use blunt-nosed nails when nailing the end of the decking in place, or better yet, predrill a pilot hole for each nail.

Install the decking with the curve of the growth rings facing down. Look at the end of a board, and you will see the arc of its growth rings. To reduce the chance of a board cupping, shrinking, or twisting and to keep water from puddling on the board, install the boards so the convex sides of all growth ring arcs are facing up.

To help maintain proper spacing between the deck boards, some builders use the head of a 16d nail; others use a ⅛-inch-thick piece of wood. Whatever spacing you decide on, make at least two spacers to insert between the decking board that is nailed in place and the board you are installing, to maintain even, precise spacing.

Even if you handpick the decking

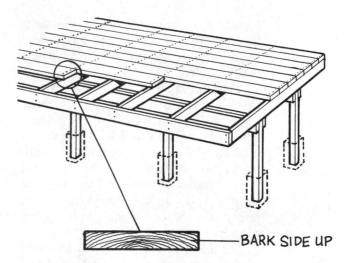

BARK SIDE UP

When installing decking, place the boards with the bark side up. Stagger the joints. For 2 × 4 decking use two nails in each joist. For 2 × 6s use three nails.

material, some of it is bound to be slightly warped. Use a pry bar to push these stubborn planks into position. We find it is easier to install the board with the ends arcing away from the decking we've already installed. Then we start nailing the board at one end and allow the other to arc out. We place the spacer shims at the next joist and have a helper push the end of the board toward the decking until it is tight against the spacer. Then we nail the board to the joist and move on to the next joist. This way you have leverage the full length of the board when you push on its end. As you near the other end of the board, you might have to use a pry bar to force it into position.

Maintaining Outdoor Wood

The two greatest threats to outdoor wood are sunlight and water. If you have a deck that's been fighting the elements successfully but is dark and dirty, there are rejuvenator products to give it a new lease on life.

If your deck is made of pressure-treated lumber, look for a deck cleaner or brightener that removes dirt or mildew. This solution is mixed with water and applied with a spray container. Depending on how dark the deck is, use a stiff bristle brush to remove the gray and grime residue. If the deck is only slightly dirty, apply the cleaner with a paint roller or mop.

Once the wood is clean and dry, apply a wood sealer to protect it and help stabilize its moisture content. Even though pressure-treated wood is protected against rot, it is not protected against checking or splitting caused by changes in moisture content. So a water repellent is an important treatment.

Repellents help to stabilize the moisture content in wood by reducing the swelling and shrinking that cause it to warp, twist, and split. These repellents contain wax or resins mixed with mineral spirits. When applied, the spirits evaporate and the waterproofing remains on the surface of the wood.

Some water repellents have wood-preserving additives that help prevent mildew from forming on the decking. These are especially helpful if your deck is in a damp, shady area of your yard.

To apply water repellent, we use a paint roller with an extension handle. If you wash down and seal your deck once a season (or however often it's needed), you'll be able to keep your deck looking almost as good as it was the day after it was built. We have found that this yearly maintenance is a better strategy than to wait until the deck is really looking dingy and then give it a major cleanup.

Tree Stumps

If your yard is cluttered with the remains of a nasty old tree stump, it's not as difficult as it might seem to permanently remove it. Before getting the stump out of the ground, consider how you'll remove it from the site. If it's extremely large and difficult to handle, you'll probably have to make arrangements (and pay extra) for your local trash hauler to make a special pickup.

You don't have to remove the whole stump. It can be cut below grade level, covered with earth, and allowed to decay.

You can rent a stump grinder to remove the stump, or you can dig it up by hand. Here is what's involved in both methods. After you read this, we are sure you'll agree that renting a stump grinder is the way to go.

Stump grinder: Stump-grinding machines have a carbide-toothed cutter that can grind most stumps to fine chips and sawdust. Try to have the machine delivered, because it's a brute to move around. If you take it home, you will need a trailer hitch to pull it behind your car.

These machines are big and clumsy but not too hard to operate. You align the machine over the stump and then lower it until the blade cuts into the stump. It uses a sideways motion to chew up the stump in 5-inch-wide swaths. The real muscle work is repositioning the machine when you're working on a large-diameter tree.

Hand-digging: Hand-digging the stump is the other alternative. We've used this technique on small stumps and shrubs. We found the trick to hand-digging a stump is to dig as much dirt as possible away from the roots before trying to cut them. Dig a deep trench around the stump, cutting away any roots in your path.

We have found a sharp spade, an ax, and a Come-a-Long (also called a Power-Pull) are necessary to uproot even a medium-size stump. These are two brand names for a racheting tool with great pulling power.

After digging for a while, you will expose most of the roots, but the stump still won't budge. Attach the cable of the Come-a-Long to the center of the root system by weaving it throughout and around the stump. Secure the other end to a stationary object such as a nearby tree or pickup truck, and pull the lever tight. You then can see exactly which roots are still holding the stump in place. Cut them and pull some more; eventually you'll cut away the maze of tree roots, and the stump will come out of its hole.

Fascia Boards, Gutters, and Downspouts

Even if you have beautiful landscaping, the curb appeal of your house can be spoiled by a few feet of rusty, drooping gutters. Likewise, a missing or leaking downspout signals neglect. Any improvements you make in this area or effort you put into keeping the gutters, downspouts, and fascia looking good is time and money well invested.

Wood Fascia Repairs

The board nailed to the end of roof rafters where gutters are attached is called the fascia. You can use exterior wood filler, as we will describe, to repair small sections of board that have rotted because of leaky gutters and downspouts, but if the board has long sections of soft, rot-

ted wood, you'll want to replace the entire piece. For one thing, good wood filler is not cheap. If you use it for anything more than small holes, it may be cheaper to replace the whole board. It is possible to cut out a section of fascia between two rafters and fit in a replacement, but we don't recommend it. The extra butt joints don't look good and may collect water that will cause further rot.

Peeling paint is a sure sign of a rotten area. Also, fascia boards get rot in their ends at butt joints and corners. While painting or doing gutter repairs, check out any suspicious-looking spots. Poke a screwdriver into the area. If the blade sinks in, there is rot. When making the repair, try to determine why the area rotted in the first place. If the rotten area is under a leak in the gutter or downspout, fix the leak, or the rot will keep spreading.

When the exterior wood around your house splits or begins to rot, no amount of paint will cure the problem. We have used a two-part exterior wood filler to repair damaged wood rather than replace it. Choose a two-part filler with a polyester or epoxy base that cures chemically, instead of one that is water based. Once bonded to the wood, it won't shrink, crack, or fall out. Here is how we repair a small area of bad wood in fascias or other outside wood:

Remove the rotten wood. Scrape away all the old flaking and loose paint and all of the rotten wood. It is important that you remove all the rot because the filler needs solid wood to adhere to. Use a beverage can opener, grapefruit knife, or old chisel as a scraper to get into tight areas. If you find the wood is rotted through, don't try to fill it. Replace it.

Fill the area with wood filler. Use a two-part exterior wood filler, and mix it according to the manufacturer's directions. Apply the filler with a putty knife, putting it on as thick as needed to build up a little higher than the surface of the wood. When it dries, you can sand the repair flat.

If there is a large gap or gouge, the filler needs an anchor. Drive several nails or screws into the gouge at an angle. Make sure their heads are below the level of the finished patch so the filler will cover them. Then pack the filler into the gap, and work it around and behind the anchor nails or screws. This will work for a small area that is larger than just a crack, but if the whole board is involved with rot or badly split, then the cost of the filler to repair the board will be more than a new board. The only time we fill in large areas is when it would be difficult to replace the board, like behind a long run of gutter or in the middle of a perfectly good fascia board.

Sand it smooth, and prime. Sand the patch smooth with a sanding block and 80-grit sandpaper. Check the contour of the patched area, and apply more filler if it is needed to build up to its original shape.

Paint the entire fascia for protection. Complete the repair by coating with an exterior primer. Then give the whole fascia a coat of good-quality exterior paint. We paint the whole fascia because we find it impossible to match the old paint.

Gutters and Downspouts

Clean Out Gutter Day rolls around on two Saturdays, one each spring and fall, at our house, and admittedly it's not something we look forward to. But with our system now well established, we can get the main event over and done with before lunch. The event, of course, is cleaning and flushing out gutters and downspouts.

By removing leaves and dirt from the gutters, you allow the drainage system attached to your house to work smoothly and effectively, which in turn keeps moisture from damaging the siding and foundation. Decaying leaves lying in the gutters also abet the rusting process by keeping the gutters damp.

Ours is a one-story ranch, so the job is not one for high-level heroes. If you have a two-story house, cleaning out the gutters can be a considerable chore, since it's going to be a long climb up and down the ladder. Plan on doing a section of gutter at a time. Then you will not be tempted to lean out to stretch your reach to save a couple of trips up and down the ladder.

We use a bucket and wear rubber gloves to scoop out the debris. The most strenuous part of the operation is repeated trips up and down the ladder to dump bucketfuls into the trash.

The second and final phase is flushing out the gutters and downspouts with the garden hose. First, use the spray attachment to clean out the gutters, directing the water flow to the downspout. Look for water leaks in the gutters that will need repair. Then, force the hose down the downspout so the water pressure will dislodge any clogs in the downspout.

As long as the ladder is up, it's a good time to trim any tree branches overhanging roof or gutters.

Sagging Gutter Repairs

The last things you notice about a well-groomed house are the rain gutters and downspouts if they're in good condition. But if they're drooping, rust stained, and worn, they shout for attention and damage the home's appearance. Of course, they can also damage the house, because water will be leaking into fascias, along foundations, and into other places water can cause trouble.

Check to see that gutters and downspouts are securely fastened to the house and not loose or sagging. These conditions are especially common in areas of heavy snowfall. Pull against the gutters where they attach to the fascias. If you find loose spots, check the gutters for slope and then reattach them. We found a few shortcuts in rehanging gutters:

Check the pitch.   Place a straight piece of 8 foot long lumber on the gutter, and use a carpenter's level on top of that to check that the gutter is sloping toward the downspout. Or check that the ends of roof shingles are level, and use them as a reference point when checking the gutter slope. If the gutter is set so that the fascia is exposed above the top of the gutter, you can snap a properly sloped chalk line (½ inch per 10 feet of gutter length) on the fascia and then set the gutter top even with the chalk line.

On very long runs, gutters usually are set high in the middle and slope both ways to downspouts at the two opposite corners of the house. On runs of 25 feet or less, the gutter runs to a single downspout at one corner of the house.

Rehang the gutter.   To raise sagging sections, you may have to first pull out the old spikes or cut the metal hangers with snips. Raise the gutters, check their alignment with a straightedge or chalk line, and then reattach with new spikes and sleeves. The more slope the better is not the case here. Too much slope will cause the water to run down the gutter too fast and spill over the end.

Aluminum or galvanized gutters can be rehung easily with a spreader sleeve and a long hanging spike. Place the spreader inside the trough, and drive the spike through the front of the gutter and into the sleeve. Then drive the spike through the rear of the gutter and into the fascia or rafter tail. If the gutter is galvanized steel, drill a ¼-inch pilot hole through the front of the gutter; insert the spike and drive it home.

If the fascia will not hold the spikes adequately, use a strap-type metal hanger. Lift the front edge of the first row of shingles, and slip the hanger straps underneath. Then nail the straps to the sheathing with galvanized roofing nails. Do this on a warm day so the shingles will be soft and flexible. If you have to nail through the shingles to secure the straps, coat the nail heads with roofing cement.

Gutter Patchwork

In galvanized gutters, leaking seams or holes usually occur where the metal has rusted through. For any repair to last, you have to remove and stop the rust. Any repair will last only a couple of years, since it is all but impossible to completely stop the rust from recurring. But getting 5 or 6 more years out of leaking gutters is sure worth a try. Replacing them can get expensive. Here is how we made our longest-lasting repairs:

Step 1: Remove heavy rust and chip away any metal that is rusted through. A round wire brush wheel that fits on an electric drill is the best tool for this job. Use sandpaper on areas where the wire brush can't reach. You don't have to get the metal shiny, just remove all the loose rust and thin crumbly metal.

Step 2: Spot-prime the area with a rusty-metal primer. These primers completely displace moisture and seal the metal. When the primer has dried completely (24 hours), give the whole area another coat of primer. Extend the coverage a couple of feet past the hole, and don't forget the underside of the gutter.

Step 3: Patch the area with roofing cement or with one of the many easy-to-apply patch kits available. The cheapest patch we have found that lasts about as long as the more expensive systems is roofing cement and fiberglass drywall tape. Remember, it's the metal that rusts and causes the patch to fail, not the patching material itself. Spread the roofing cement around the hole; then place a piece of tape on the cement. Next, put more cement on the tape. Do the same on the bottom.

Allow the cement to set for a week or so if you want to paint the gutter. Give the patch a coat of pigmented shellac, such as Kilz or Bin, to kill the stain. Don't paint the patch with oil or latex paints before you prime the area, or the roofing cement will bleed through the paint. Aluminum paint also prevents roofing cement from bleeding through.

Leaky Downspouts

Since your gutters collect the runoff from the roof and direct it to the downspout, a leak in the downspout can be a disaster. A downspout leak will damage the fascia, siding, and foundation of your house. Here's how we handle a leaking downspout:

Check the downspout joints and gutter spout. Inspect the downspout where it is attached to the gutter. Its top usually is held to the spout sticking out of the underside of the gutter with a couple of sheet-metal screws or rivets. Otherwise, push the end of the downspout up over the spout, and secure it with a couple of ¾-inch #10 sheet-metal screws. Drill ⅛-inch pilot holes for these screws if there are not already holes in the spout and downspout. Check all other joints and refasten them with sheet-metal screws as needed.

Inspect the downspout hangers. The most important one is located at the top of the downspout, close to where it turns out toward the gutter. Use galvanized nails or screws to replace any missing or loose fasteners. If there is a missing strap, purchase a new one at a hardware store or home center.

Check for split downspouts. Splits can be caused by ice and rusted-through areas that leak. Older houses with galvanized gutters have round downspouts; newer ones have rectangular aluminum downspouts.

If you have a bad section of downspout, replace it. Downspouts are available in curved sections called "elbows" and 10-foot straight sections. If you have to cut the downspout to length with a hacksaw, measure from the crimped end and cut off the open end. When fitting the pieces together, remember the open end faces up, and the crimped end slips inside to prevent leaks.

Vinyl Gutters

If your house is in need of gutters, we have found installing vinyl gutter systems an easy do-it-yourself project. In less than a day you can install a gutter system on a two-car garage. A long weekend should cover a typical house.

These vinyl systems are lightweight and engineered to snap together, forming a leakproof joint without soldering, sealers, or pop rivets. This is a big advantage over the aluminum systems. No matter how we caulk the joints in aluminum gutters, sooner or later they leak. Jointless aluminum gutters are great, but you can't install them yourself, since you need a big machine to extrude the gutter channel. The vinyl systems are the perfect compromise; they come in 10-foot sections that are light and leak free.

The vinyl systems also come with an array of gadgets to keep leaves out and prevent the downspouts from clogging. There is really not much that can go wrong with this job; just follow the manufacturer's directions. Here is how most systems are installed:

Step 1: Make sure the fascia boards are in good condition. If not, make repairs or replace them and paint. Also check to see that roof shingles project at least ¼ inch beyond the fascia boards. If not, an aluminum drip edge should be installed under the edge of the shingles so water will drip into the gutter.

Step 2: Make a rough sketch of the roof and fascias with overall dimensions to help determine the amount of materials required. You need gutter corners, one for each inside or outside corner (they are both the same). You need gutter connectors, one for each 10-foot section of gutter, and support brackets, three for each section of gutter. If you cannot hang the brackets on the fascia board, you also will need roof strap hangers.

In addition, you'll need at least one downspout outlet. In general, plan a downspout for every 35 to 40 running feet of gutter. Order enough gutter sections. They come in 10-foot lengths to run around

Great Gadgets & Gizmos

☞ **WoodScapes** This system consists of 4 × 4-inch treated wood components designed to make outdoor projects. You can make a garden edging, planter box, and much more with it. It is made by Weyerhaeuser Company, 3601 Minnesota Drive, Suite 750, Bloomington, MN 55435, or call 1-800-548-5767.

☞ **Underground downspout** This is a product that directs rain water away from the house without an unsightly downspout. It's designed to be buried 8 to 10 inches beneath the ground with its 30-inch PVC pipe connected to the existing downspout. An elbow attaches to two 4-foot lengths of PVC that attach to a bubbler pot with a lid that flips open for easy cleaning. For more information, contact Beaver Industries, 890 Hersey Street, St. Paul, MN 55114.

☞ **Leaf strainers, gutter guards, and downspout diverters** Here are three gutter and downspout gadgets designed to keep damaging water from your house. If your house is surrounded by trees, get a leaf strainer, a round wire strainer that fits over the downspout to trap leaves. You'll also find gutter guards, which are metal or plastic mesh screening designed to fit over the edge of the gutter. Both of these gadgets simply clip into place and are sold in home centers and hardware stores. A downspout diverter is an important addition to every house, no matter where it's located. Made of cement, plastic, or fiberglass, one of these troughs is placed at the end of each downspout and directs the water flow out and away from the house and its foundation.

the perimeter. Don't forget connectors and end caps.

Step 3: After checking that you have all the necessary parts, begin the installation by finding the highest point (usually right under the roof shingles) where the gutter will be attached. This point usually will be in the center of the longest gutter run. Hold a bracket close to the shingles, and mark the location of the mounting hole.

Step 4: Remove the bracket and tap a small nail into the mark. Stretch a chalk line from the nail to the nearest corner or downspout opening, allowing for a pitch of at least ¼ inch per 10-foot gutter section. Install the downspout outlet, or install a gutter corner and continue with the chalk line to the next corner or outlet. Remember, the low points must be attached at the downspout outlets.

Step 5: When all the corners and downspout outlets are in place, mark the placement of the gutter connectors. We found we could make it an easy one-man job by placing a nail next to one connector and hooking the end of a tape measure over it to measure out 10 feet to the next connector. Back up 2¼ inches to allow for the portion of the gutter that extends into the connector, and mark that location on the fascia's chalk line. Use a nail set to make pilot holes.

Step 6: Install the support brackets. They should be installed at least every 30 inches. Mark the position of the center bracket, make a pilot hole with the nail set, and install it. Mark and install the other two brackets equidistant between the center bracket and the connectors.

Step 7: Snap a gutter section into the brackets, and proceed to install the next connector, to save ladder climbing. Install all the sections and connectors, working from connector to connector or from connector to corner or downspout opening. The plastic gutter sections are easily cut with a fine-toothed saw.

Step 8: The downspouts are installed next. If you have a wide fascia, cut a short section of downspout as a spacer so the elbow will clear the fascia bottom. Slip an elbow into a downspout wall support bracket, and hold it in position where the downspout will run down the wall.

Measure the distance between the elbows, add to this the section of downspout in the fittings, and cut the angled section of downspout to this measurement.

At the bottom of the downspout, install another elbow and support bracket. Cut a length of downspout to carry the water away from the foundation. We like the swing-up type of outlet that is hinged to allow for easy grass cutting.

13 Ventilation and Insulation

Good ventilation in a house is something you don't see or hear, you just enjoy it. Most of the effects of poor ventilation don't become evident until considerable damage has already occurred. Peeling paint, excessive moisture, and mildew are common ventilation-related problems.

Most old and many new homes have undersized vents serving the attic and crawl space; some have no ventilation in these areas. Much has been written about stopping cold drafts and air infiltration into the house for comfort and energy conservation, but this tightening up increases the need for adequate ventilation in other areas of the house. In the quest to cut heating and cooling costs, attic and foundation vents are sometimes closed off.

Some of the houses we have renovated have had all sorts of things stuffed into the crawl space vents—old newspapers, plastic garbage bags, and insulation. The result is excess moisture collecting there. In some cases the only problem was a musty damp smell in the crawl space. In others, the dampness was the perfect environment to promote termites, carpenter ants, and wood rot.

The doors and windows in your house are built-in ventilators, but they're not enough. A continuous air exchange throughout the house keeps air from becoming stagnant. In addition to your doors and windows, vents in the attic allow hot air to escape in the summer and help remove excess moisture in the winter, thus increasing the efficiency of your insulation.

If your house has a crawl space, proper ventilation will go a long way toward removing excess moisture that is the chief cause of rot and insect infestation. A dry crawl space will also help your floor insulation work more efficiently in the winter.

Rooms such as the kitchen and bathroom, where water and heat are present, require local fans and vents. See the chapters on kitchens and bathrooms for ideas on how to vent these areas. The ventilation improvements we suggest in this chapter deal with increasing the efficiency of your house's attic and crawl space ventilation.

Ventilating an Attic

A poorly vented attic is a potential problem in both the summer and winter. In the summer the stagnant air can be heated to 150°F or more on a hot day. This hot spot above your ceiling reduces the effectiveness of your insulation.

The amount of energy transmitted through insulation is determined by the temperature difference on each side of the insulation. The greater the temperature difference, the more energy passes through the insulation. No matter what the R-value of your attic insulation, the amount of heat that is transferred through it into the rooms below is directly related to the difference between the air masses on each side of the insulation. The hotter the air is in the attic, the faster the room below will heat up. Unvented attics get unbearably hot, even on cool, sunny days.

Excessively hot roofs cause premature failure of shingles. The hot air also dries out roof framing and plywood sheathing. No building materials benefit from being exposed to extreme heat.

During the winter, poor ventilation causes a buildup of moisture in the attic space. This moisture can come from many sources, but the major one is moisture passing through the walls and ceilings from living spaces below. If the relative humidity in the attic builds up too high, the cold attic air cannot hold the moisture. The moisture then comes out of the air in the form of condensation.

Condensation settles in the attic insulation, severely reducing its effectiveness. Condensation can get so bad in a poorly vented space that it actually runs down the rafters and may make you think you have a roof leak. This water does your house no good, and it costs you money in lost heat.

Another side effect of poor attic ventilation is snow-melt problems and ice dams. These potentially damaging ice dams are caused when snow melts at the warm roof peak. The water then refreezes near the eaves, where the roof is cooler. Proper attic insulation placed either in the floor of an unheated attic or in the rafters of a heated attic will help this problem, but it is still important to provide ventilation. The insulation along with the circulation of air under the roof will equalize the roof temperature and prevent rapid melting of the snow at the warm roof peak.

Vent Systems

In most newer homes you'll find a minimal attic vent system. Some older homes have attic vents, but they often are undersized and were installed to meet inadequate standards. Increasing your attic ventilation can be done quite easily. There is a wide variety of products on the market designed for do-it-yourself installation. Some systems are easier to install than others. Following is a run-down on the vent systems that we think are easiest to install.

Passive Vent Systems

Most older homes have some form of passive vent system that relies on the fact that warm air rises. If you cut a hole in the top of the roof and a few in the eaves, the hot air can rise and flow up and out the hole. New, cooler air will flow into the lower holes to replace it. The same principle works to draw smoke up a chimney.

Since there are no moving parts, the system does not consume any energy and is very efficient. A passive system is the least expensive ventilation scheme, but there is a catch. For the system to work properly, it has to be installed correctly and the size of the vents has to be sufficient to allow an adequate flow of air.

Homes equipped with passive vent systems have rectangular or round roof vents designed to be located in the upper portion of the roof. Triangular or rectangular vents also can be installed in gable ends or through the attic walls as close to the roof as possible. Newer houses might have ridge-line vents that are installed along the ridge of the roof.

These roof vents should be teamed with under-eaves or soffit vents. Without these vents, the air cannot get into the lower part of the attic to allow the hot air out through the upper vents.

Active Vent Systems

Vent schemes that use some form of external energy are active systems and can move larger volumes of air through the attic with smaller vents. These vents can be either wind driven or electrical.

A rooftop wind turbine ventilator uses wind power to rotate a fan to create suction that moves attic air up and outside. A motor-driven vent uses electricity to run the fan.

Active systems are more compact for a given capacity. This type of vent is a sensible replacement for an undersized passive system in an older home, because you don't have to cut additional holes in your roof.

Sizing Up Your Attic Vent Needs

A little calculation will help you determine what size ventilator and vent is needed for your house. Attic vents are rated according to their net free area. This is the amount of vent area free of obstructions, such as insect screens, louvers, rain baffles, or turbine blades. These restrictions make the net free area considerably smaller than the actual size of the vent opening.

Sizing a Passive Vent System

Today's standards for passive vent systems call for 1 square foot of net free vent area for every 150 square feet of attic floor space. For example, if your attic measures 30 feet wide by 50 feet long, the vent area is calculated like this: $30 \times 50 = 1,500$ square feet. Dividing this 1,500 square feet by 150 tells you that you need 10 square feet of net free vent area.

If your house has a vapor barrier applied to the warm side of the ceiling and half of the vent area is installed under the eaves or soffits, you need only 1 square foot of net free vent area for every 300 square feet of attic space, or about half the net free vent area.

Most vents are rated in square inches. To convert square feet to square inches, multiply by 144. For example, our 1,500-square-foot attic requires 10 square feet net free area, which is equal to 1,440 square inches of net free vent area. One half of this—720 square inches of vents—should be placed in the upper third of the roof area to exhaust air out. The remaining vents are needed in the lower third or under the eaves to allow air to enter the attic. Use the table on the opposite page to find the vent area requirements for your attic.

Sizing an Active Vent System

Active attic vent systems need considerably less net free vent area since the air is forced through the opening by a fan. The Home Ventilating Institute recommends that a powered attic ventilator should provide at least ten air exchanges per hour to the attic.

This type of vent also must work in conjunction with gable or soffit louvered vents, since fresh air must enter the attic in order for the old air to escape. To find the proper cfm (cubic feet per minute) rating for a power roof ventilator, multiply the total square footage of your attic by 0.7. Using our 1,500-square-foot attic as an example, $1,500 \times 0.7 = 1,050$ cfm. Add 15 percent to this figure if you have a dark-colored roof or if your attic has a very steep or very shallow pitched roof. Both types of extreme pitches lower the ratio of attic volume to roof surface, requiring a higher cfm rate.

You'll find standard ventilators ranging in capacity from 1,100 to 1,200 cfm. Some are designed to be gable mounted; others mount on the roof between rafters that are 16 inches on-center.

The vent intake area required can be calculated by dividing the cfm rating of the powered ventilator by 300 and multiplying the answer by 144. If we divide our 1,050 cfm by 300 and then multiply by 144, we get 504 square inches.

Vents for under soffits or eaves are made of aluminum and are sold in various sizes and shapes. The net free area is noted on the package.

Improving Your Attic Ventilation

Now that you know why it's important to get the air moving through the attic and how much you have to move, here are some ways to do it. We have found that if you already have some openings in your roof, installing an electric ventilator usually is the easiest way to upgrade attic ventilation. The fan can

Attic Ventilation Passive System
Net Free Vent Area
(square inches)

	20	25	30	35	40	45	50	55	60	65	70	75
100	1,920	2,400	2,880	3,360	3,840	4,320	4,800	5,280	5,760	6,240	6,720	7,200
95	1,824	2,280	2,736	3,192	3,648	4,104	4,560	5,016	5,472	5,928	6,384	6,840
90	1,728	2,160	2,592	3,024	3,456	3,888	4,320	4,752	5,184	5,616	6,048	6,480
85	1,632	2,040	2,448	2,856	3,264	3,672	4,080	4,488	4,896	5,304	5,712	6,120
80	1,536	1,920	2,304	2,688	3,072	3,456	3,840	4,224	4,608	4,992	5,376	5,760
75	1,440	1,800	2,160	2,520	2,880	3,240	3,600	3,960	4,320	4,680	5,040	5,400
70	1,344	1,680	2,016	2,352	2,688	3,024	3,360	3,696	4,032	4,368	4,704	5,040
65	1,248	1,560	1,872	2,184	2,496	2,808	3,120	3,432	3,744	4,056	4,368	4,680
60	1,152	1,440	1,728	2,016	2,304	2,592	2,880	3,168	3,456	3,744	4,032	4,320
55	1,056	1,320	1,584	1,848	2,112	2,376	2,640	2,904	3,168	3,432	3,696	3,960
50	960	1,200	1,440	1,680	1,920	2,160	2,400	2,640	2,880	3,120	3,360	3,600
45	864	1,080	1,296	1,512	1,728	1,944	2,160	2,376	2,592	2,808	3,024	3,240
40	768	960	1,152	1,344	1,536	1,728	1,920	2,112	2,304	2,496	2,688	2,880
35	672	840	1,008	1,176	1,344	1,512	1,680	1,848	2,016	2,184	2,352	2,520
30	576	720	864	1,008	1,152	1,296	1,440	1,584	1,728	1,872	2,016	2,160
25	480	600	720	840	960	1,080	1,200	1,320	1,440	1,560	1,680	1,800
20	384	480	576	672	768	864	960	1,056	1,152	1,248	1,344	1,440

ATTIC LENGTH (vertical axis) / **ATTIC WIDTH** (horizontal axis)

Note: *Attic length and width are in feet.*

move more air, and often the increased capacity is all that is needed.

If your house does have adequate roof vents, then all you need to do is increase the vents in the lower part of the roof, mainly under the soffits or eaves. Increasing the number and total net free area of these vents will improve the attic ventilation.

Installing a Louvered Gable Vent

We also have installed gable vents that can be made to look as if they are part of the architectural detail of the house. An adjustable-pitch louver is an effective, easy-to-install vent that can be mounted in a roof gable. This type of vent is not as effective as a roof-mounted

Power Attic Vent
(CFM)

ATTIC LENGTH	30	35	40	45	50	55	60	65	70	75	80	85
100	2,100	2,450	2,800	3,150	3,500	3,850	4,200	4,550	4,900	5,250	5,600	5,950
95	1,995	2,328	2,660	2,993	3,325	3,658	3,990	4,323	4,655	4,988	5,320	5,653
90	1,890	2,205	2,520	2,835	3,150	3,465	3,780	4,095	4,410	4,725	5,040	5,355
85	1,785	2,083	2,380	2,678	2,975	3,273	3,570	3,868	4,165	4,463	4,760	5,058
80	1,680	1,960	2,240	2,520	2,800	3,080	3,360	3,640	3,920	4,200	4,480	4,760
75	1,575	1,838	2,100	2,363	2,625	2,888	3,150	3,413	3,675	3,938	4,200	4,463
70	1,470	1,715	1,960	2,205	2,450	2,695	2,940	3,185	3,430	3,675	3,920	4,165
65	1,365	1,593	1,820	2,048	2,275	2,503	2,730	2,958	3,185	3,413	3,640	3,868
60	1,260	1,470	1,680	1,890	2,100	2,310	2,520	2,730	2,940	3,150	3,360	3,570
55	1,155	1,348	1,540	1,733	1,925	2,118	2,310	2,503	2,695	2,888	3,080	3,273
50	1,050	1,225	1,400	1,575	1,750	1,925	2,100	2,275	2,450	2,625	2,800	2,975
45	945	1,103	1,260	1,418	1,575	1,733	1,890	2,048	2,205	2,363	2,520	2,678
40	840	980	1,120	1,260	1,400	1,540	1,680	1,820	1,960	2,100	2,240	2,380
35	735	858	980	1,103	1,225	1,348	1,470	1,593	1,715	1,838	1,960	2,083
30	630	735	840	945	1,050	1,155	1,260	1,365	1,470	1,575	1,680	1,785
25	525	613	700	788	875	963	1,050	1,138	1,225	1,313	1,400	1,488
20	420	490	560	630	700	770	840	910	980	1,050	1,120	1,190
ATTIC WIDTH	30	35	40	45	50	55	60	65	70	75	80	85

Note: *Attic length and width are in feet. CFM stands for cubic feet per minute.*

vent, which can gather all the hottest air that gathers at the peak. But a big advantage of a gable vent is you don't have to cut a hole in the roof to install it. For best ventilation, install matching louvers in both gable ends.

This type of vent can be made from aluminum, galvanized steel, or plastic. You also can make a custom wood version. The vents are sold in various colors, or you can paint them to match your siding.

Since you'll be doing a good part of this work on a ladder, make sure you place it on firm ground.

Calculate how much additional net free area you need, then choose a vent that is close to this value. Of course, check that it will fit into the planned area.

Look at the back of the vent and note that it is smaller than the front, which has a wide flange. The hole you cut in the siding should fit the back of

Active Attic Ventilators
Gable/Soffit Net Free Area
(square inches)

ATTIC LENGTH	20	25	30	35	40	45	50	55	60	65	70	75
100	672	840	1,008	1,176	1,344	1,512	1,680	1,848	2,016	2,184	2,352	2,520
95	638	798	958	1,117	1,277	1,436	1,596	1,756	1,915	2,075	2,234	2,394
90	605	756	907	1,058	1,210	1,361	1,512	1,663	1,814	1,966	2,117	2,268
85	571	714	857	1,000	1,142	1,285	1,428	1,571	1,714	1,856	1,999	2,142
80	538	672	806	941	1,075	1,210	1,344	1,478	1,613	1,747	1,882	2,016
75	504	630	756	882	1,008	1,134	1,260	1,386	1,512	1,638	1,764	1,890
70	470	588	706	823	941	1,058	1,176	1,294	1,411	1,529	1,646	1,764
65	437	546	655	764	874	983	1,092	1,201	1,310	1,420	1,529	1,638
60	403	504	605	706	806	907	1,008	1,109	1,210	1,310	1,411	1,512
55	370	462	554	647	739	832	924	1,016	1,109	1,201	1,294	1,386
50	336	420	504	588	672	756	840	924	1,008	1,092	1,176	1,260
45	302	378	454	529	605	680	756	832	907	983	1,058	1,134
40	269	336	403	470	538	605	672	739	806	874	941	1,008
35	235	294	353	412	470	529	588	647	706	764	823	882
30	202	252	302	353	403	454	504	554	605	655	706	756
25	168	210	252	294	336	378	420	462	504	546	588	630
20	134	168	202	235	269	302	336	370	403	437	470	504

ATTIC WIDTH

Note: *Attic length and width are in feet.*

the vent; the flange prevents the vent from passing through the hole. Here's basically how to install a gable vent:

Step 1: Adjust the pitch of the vent to match that of your roof. Then position the vent on the siding, and trace around its back (not the flange) to transfer its outline to the siding.

Step 2: Use a saber saw or keyhole saw to cut the opening in the siding. You can get a start for the blade by drilling 1-inch holes in the corners of the triangular layout. Cut through the siding only from hole to hole, then remove the siding and sheathing from the opening to expose the attic wall studs. After the

TYPES OF ATTIC VENTILATORS

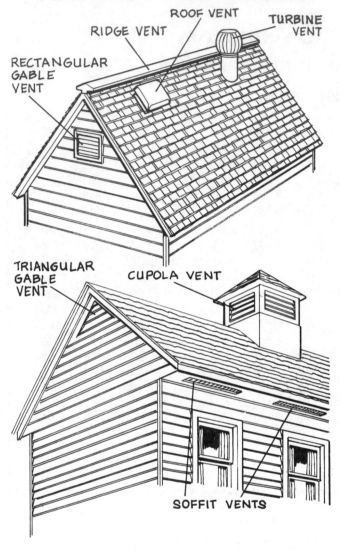

RIDGE VENT

ROOF VENT

TURBINE VENT

RECTANGULAR GABLE VENT

TRIANGULAR GABLE VENT

CUPOLA VENT

SOFFIT VENTS

siding is removed, cut any wall studs that will be in the way of the vent.

Step 3: Check the fit of the vent. If you had to cut more than one stud, install a header for support. To do this, cut the studs back 1½ inches below the bottom of the opening, and then measure and cut a 2 × 4 header to fit across the severed joists and flush with the bottom of the opening.

Step 4: Apply caulk to the back of the vent flange, and then push it into place. Check that the caulk seals all the gaps between the siding and flange. You might have to add more caulk if you have narrow clapboard siding. Use rustproof aluminum or galvanized nails to hold the vent in place.

Step 5: If you plan to paint the vent, apply a metal primer formulated for either aluminum or galvanized steel. When the primer is dry, follow up with several coats of house paint. You can save yourself a little ladder work by priming and painting the vent before you install it.

Installing a Vent in an Attic Window

One of our houses had no attic vents but had a dormer at each end of the attic, with a set of double-hung windows in each. We found several of those portable window screens that can be inserted into the open window and are held in place by lowering the window onto the screen. The problem with these is that they're not leakproof—wind, rain, and snow blow inside. We found that a better solution is to replace one of the window sash with a plywood panel holding a louvered vent. With this easy-to-make setup you can vent the attic without having to cut any holes in your house:

Step 1: Remove the window stop (the strip that holds the inner sash in place), and remove the lower sash. Cut a piece of ¾-inch exterior plywood the same size as the lower sash. Nail pieces of ⅝-inch-thick furring to the back (inside)

INSTALLING A GABLE VENT

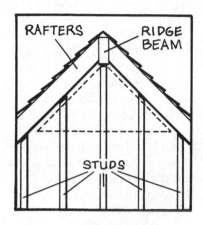

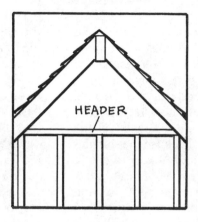

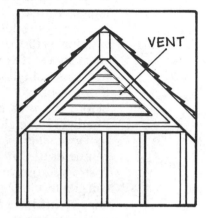

1. Scribe the shape of the vent on the outside of the gable, and cut away the siding and sheathing. Go inside the attic and cut the studs off 1½ inches below the opening.

2. Install a 2 × 4 header.

3. Caulk, and install the vent.

of the plywood to thicken the panel so it fits into the window track.

Step 2: Cut an opening in the plywood panel for the vent. Then paint the plywood panel, making sure to prime and seal the edges.

Step 3: Apply caulk to the back of the vent flange and put it into the opening in the plywood panel. Hold it in place with ½-inch-long sheet-metal screws driven through the flange into the plywood panel. You can drill pilot holes for the screws or use a nail set to make the holes in the soft aluminum.

Step 4: Install the plywood panel in the window with screws driven through the furring into the frame. Then replace the stop.

Installing a Turbine Vent

Wind-driven turbines are more efficient than passive vents because they use wind energy to help eject air from the attic. You can increase the ventilation in an attic by replacing a standard vent with a wind turbine type because the same-size turbine vent will move more air.

If you don't have any vents in your roof, the wind turbine is a good choice. The only objection might be that they are rather industrial looking. If you mount them on the back side of the roof, they can't be seen from the street.

Most passive, turbine, and electric-powered vents install the same way. The main difference is how the flashing (sheet metal that fits under the roof shingles to keep out the rain) is installed. All come with complete directions from the manufacturer.

The most difficult part of this job is working on the roof. Wear sturdy rubber-soled shoes. If your roof has asphalt or fiberglass shingles, pick a day that is not too hot, or work early in the morning before the roof gets hot. If you have weathered shingles, don't walk on the roof when it is cold, because the shingles will be brittle and more likely to crack. A stroll across your roof on a cold day can greatly damage an old roof. To minimize your trips, gather tools together in a bucket or canvas sack so you will have everything handy. Here's what you do:

Step 1: Follow the guidelines from the manufacturer for the location of the vent. You want it close to the ridge and between the roof rafters. Some manufacturers tell you to use the base ring as a guide to mark the hole on the shingles, while others provide a template.

The instructions usually specify how far down from the ridge the vent should be installed. The easiest way to ensure that the vent is located between rafters is to lay out the vent opening from inside the attic. Mark the hole location on the roof sheathing, and then drill a hole through the center. Poke a wire or nail through the hole so you can find it from the outside. Go up on the roof and place the center of the template or vent base on the hole and lay out the cut.

Step 2: Close to the perimeter of the vent hole, drill a hole large enough to start your saw and then use a keyhole or saber saw to cut the hole. If you have several vent holes to cut, rent a reciprocating saw that makes cutting these holes easy.

Step 3: Remove the material in the cutout (it will probably fall into the attic below), and place the base so the upper part of the flange can be slipped under the shingles around the vent hole. Test the fit and use a sharp utility knife to cut away any shingles necessary for the vent base to align with the hole. When everything checks out, coat the bottom of the base with roofing cement and slide it into place. To prevent rust stains, nail it down with aluminum or galvanized roofing nails. Also seal the lower edge with adhesive and then with roofing nails.

Step 4: Attach the neck (or center section) of the turbine to the base according to the manufacturer's directions with the screws provided. Twist the collar around until the top is level. There are usually two movable sections. By twisting them back and forth, you can adjust the angle of the top edge. This must be level so the turbine sits square and the wind-driven rotor can spin freely. Check that the top collar is level by placing a carpenter's level on it while you twist things around.

Step 5: Install the turbine according to the directions. Then check that it spins freely. Any binding will stop it in a light breeze and cause noise during a blow. Take the time to adjust everything; otherwise you will be back up on the roof later. Also, if the metal parts rub together, the galvanizing will rub away, allowing rust to form.

Installing a Power Vent

Adding a power vent or replacing a passive vent with one is the quickest way to pull more air through the attic. This type of vent is installed in the same way as the turbine vent. The base is mounted

INSTALLING A TURBINE VENT

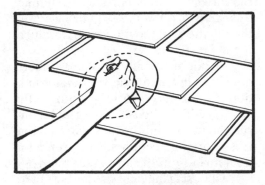

1. Lay out a hole for the vent base, making sure it is centered between the rafters. Use a saber saw to cut through the shingles, underlayment, and roof sheathing.

2. Put caulk or roofing cement on the bottom of the vent base flange. Slip the flange under the up-slope shingles and center the base on the hole.

3. Lift the up-slope shingles and nail the flange underneath them. For down-slope shingles, nail through the flange and shingles underneath. Nail the flange in place. Caulk nail heads and the edges of the flange.

4. Set, level, and attach the turbine.

under the shingles, then sealed up with roofing cement. But instead of installing the turbine, you have to install the fan unit.

Most of these units come prewired, that is, the wiring from the motor is already run to a junction box. You have to run a line from the junction to a source of power. Unless the vent is exceptionally large, you can usually wire the fan to an existing circuit without overloading it.

Check your local electrical codes. If you have no experience with electrical work, call in an electrician for this part of the job. Most fans have built-in thermostats that turn them on when the attic gets hot. They also should have fire shutoffs that turn the fans off if the temperature gets very hot from a fire, say 250°F or so. This prevents a fan from making a fire worse.

Along with the thermostat, consider installing a humidistat. This device senses the humidity level in the attic and turns on the fan when the humidity gets too high. This is basically useful in the winter since it allows the fan to remove the excess moisture from the attic.

Considering a Whole-House Fan

Moving air through the attic is important, but most of us will appreciate a little air movement through the house on a hot day. In many climates a whole-house fan can provide all the cooling power that is needed. In other areas the fan is usable in the spring and fall.

The whole-house fan is not an air conditioner, rather it removes the hot air and replaces it with fresh air from outdoors. This is especially useful in the evening, when the air outside has cooled faster than the hot house. However, if the air outdoors is particularly humid, this fan is less than ideal, because even though the air is moving, the humidity in it can be stifling.

In hot summer months, use a whole-house fan in conjunction with air conditioning. Use air conditioning during the day to keep the house comfortable, and run the fan at night with windows open. It is a lot more economical to run a fan than it is to run the air conditioner.

Choosing the right size fan isn't hard. We have found that the units designed to be installed over the joists in the attic floor are much easier to install, since you do not have to cut the joists and install headers. If you purchase a ceiling louver kit designed for the fan, cutting a hole in the ceiling is the only carpentry work you have to do.

Sizing a Whole-House Fan

The Home Ventilating Institute suggests an easy rule of thumb that should guide you when you calculate the capacity of the whole-house fan you plan to purchase. All you have to do is multiply the total square footage of your living area by 3. This calculation gives you the minimum air delivery needed as measured in cubic feet per minute (cfm). If you live in a warmer, more humid area, such as the southern states, multiply by 4 because greater capacity may be needed.

To determine the total square footage, multiply the overall exterior dimensions (length × width) of each floor, not including the basement, garage, or attic. For example, if you have a 1,500-square-foot house, you need a fan with a capacity of at least 4,500 cfm (1,500 × 3).

When you go shopping, you'll find

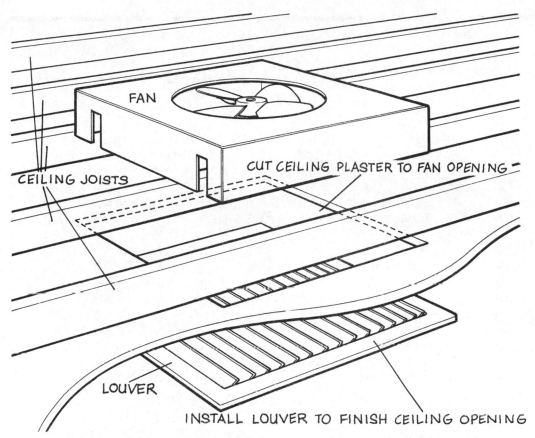

FAN

CUT CEILING PLASTER TO FAN OPENING

CEILING JOISTS

LOUVER

INSTALL LOUVER TO FINISH CEILING OPENING

Easiest to install are whole-house fans with housings that fit over ceiling joists so the joists don't have to be cut.

fans packaged with this information: "30-inch fan vents up to 1,630 sq. ft. at 4,500 cfm." This is the correct fan to buy for our 1,500-square-foot house.

Another important calculation is the "net free vent area," or unobstructed attic vent openings for air to be properly exhausted. To find this, divide the cfm rating of the whole-house fan by 750: $4,500 \div 750 = 6$ square feet of unobstructed attic vent openings. So 6 square feet of vents or louvers will provide ade-

quate venting for the fan's exhaust in the attic.

Installing a Whole-House Fan in the Attic

Cutting a large hole in your ceiling and muscling this brute into position is, we admit, an intimidating task. But it's one of those projects that you'll appreciate for years to come, and it's well worth the effort.

Whole-House Fan Capacity
(CFM)

HOUSE WIDTH	20	25	30	35	40	45	50	55	60	65
100	6,000	7,500	9,000	10,500	12,000	13,500	15,000	16,500	18,000	19,500
95	5,700	7,125	8,550	9,975	11,400	12,825	14,250	15,675	17,100	18,525
90	5,400	6,750	8,100	9,450	10,800	12,150	13,500	14,850	16,200	17,550
85	5,100	6,375	7,650	8,925	10,200	11,475	12,750	14,025	15,300	16,575
80	4,800	6,000	7,200	8,400	9,600	10,800	12,000	13,200	14,400	15,600
75	4,500	5,625	6,750	7,875	9,000	10,125	11,250	12,375	13,500	14,625
70	4,200	5,250	6,300	7,350	8,400	9,450	10,500	11,550	12,600	13,650
65	3,900	4,875	5,850	6,825	7,800	8,775	9,750	10,725	11,700	12,675
60	3,600	4,500	5,400	6,300	7,200	8,100	9,000	9,900	10,800	11,700
55	3,300	4,125	4,950	5,775	6,600	7,425	8,250	9,075	9,900	10,725
50	3,000	3,750	4,500	5,250	6,000	6,750	7,500	8,250	9,000	9,750
45	2,700	3,375	4,050	4,725	5,400	6,075	6,750	7,425	8,100	8,775
40	2,400	3,000	3,600	4,200	4,800	5,400	6,000	6,600	7,200	7,800
35	2,100	2,625	3,150	3,675	4,200	4,725	5,250	5,775	6,300	6,825
30	1,800	2,250	2,700	3,150	3,600	4,050	4,500	4,950	5,400	5,850
25	1,500	1,875	2,250	2,625	3,000	3,375	3,750	4,125	4,500	4,875
20	1,200	1,500	1,800	2,100	2,400	2,700	3,000	3,300	3,600	3,900
	20	25	30	35	40	45	50	55	60	65

HOUSE LENGTH

Note: *House width and length are in feet. CFM stands for cubic feet per minute.*

An attic fan costs about $200 and works very effectively, with the windows open, to suck hot air out of the house and push it through attic vents.

The most efficient location for the fan is in the attic floor in a central location, such as the top of the stairs in a two-story house or in the center hallway in a rancher. This is the most efficient location for pulling air through the house and pushing it out through the attic.

One person can install the fan, but it's a lot easier if you have a helper. Here are some things to consider before you shop for a whole-house fan:

▶ Check the clearance between attic joists and between attic floor and roof

Whole-House Fan
Attic Net Free Vent Area
(square inches)

HOUSE WIDTH	20	25	30	35	40	45	50	55	60	65	70	75
100	1,152	1,440	1,728	2,016	2,304	2,592	2,880	3,168	3,456	3,744	4,032	4,320
95	1,094	1,368	1,642	1,915	2,189	2,462	2,736	3,010	3,283	3,557	3,830	4,104
90	1,037	1,296	1,555	1,814	2,074	2,333	2,592	2,851	3,110	3,370	3,629	3,888
85	979	1,224	1,469	1,714	1,958	2,203	2,448	2,693	2,938	3,182	3,427	3,672
80	922	1,152	1,382	1,613	1,843	2,074	2,304	2,534	2,765	2,995	3,226	3,456
75	864	1,080	1,296	1,512	1,728	1,944	2,160	2,376	2,592	2,808	3,024	3,240
70	806	1,008	1,210	1,411	1,613	1,814	2,016	2,218	2,419	2,621	2,822	3,024
65	749	936	1,123	1,310	1,498	1,685	1,872	2,059	2,246	2,434	2,621	2,808
60	691	864	1,037	1,210	1,382	1,555	1,728	1,901	2,074	2,246	2,419	2,592
55	634	792	950	1,109	1,267	1,426	1,584	1,742	1,901	2,059	2,218	2,376
50	576	720	864	1,008	1,152	1,296	1,440	1,584	1,728	1,872	2,016	2,160
45	518	648	778	907	1,037	1,166	1,296	1,426	1,555	1,685	1,814	1,944
40	461	576	691	806	922	1,037	1,152	1,267	1,382	1,498	1,613	1,728
35	403	504	605	706	806	907	1,008	1,109	1,210	1,310	1,411	1,512
30	346	432	518	605	691	778	864	950	1,037	1,123	1,210	1,296
25	288	360	432	504	576	648	720	792	864	936	1,008	1,080
20	230	288	346	403	461	518	576	634	691	749	806	864
	20	25	30	35	40	45	50	55	60	65	70	75

HOUSE LENGTH

Note: *House width and length are in feet.*

rafters. The fan requires only a couple of feet, but there has to be room for you to work.

▶ Locate a source of electricity for the fan. A ceiling light might be a source, since you can get to the junction box from the attic. Remember, the circuit you tap into has to be on all the time, not a switch leg. Check with your local electrical codes. You can also make arrangements to have an electrician wire up the fan.

▶ Check that there are sufficient vents to allow the air to get out of the attic. See the table "Active Attic Ventilators, Gable/Soffit Net Free Area" on page 271 for requirements. The efficiency of the fan is severely restricted if the exhaust air is restricted. Both the soffit and roof vents count as exhaust vents.

▶ Check that there are no heating/cooling ducts or electrical lines in the area where you plan to install the fan. If there are, you should consider relocating the fan or relocating these obstructions before installing the fan.

After you have checked the feasibility of the installation and calculated the size of the fan, you're ready to go shopping. Be sure to purchase the type that installs on top of the ceiling joists and does not require them to be cut. Also purchase a ready-made louvered vent opening made to fit the fan; it will make installation much easier.

After you have the fan home, read the instructions. This type of fan is designed to sit on the joists with a heavy cardboard box built around it to close off the space between the joists. This makes the installation very easy, but lay out everything carefully before you cut any holes in the ceiling.

All manufacturers provide the dimensions of the rough opening to cut through the ceiling. Many provide a template. If not, make one by drawing the fan's rough opening on the cardboard box that it was packaged in and cut it out.

We have found it is a good idea to tape the template to the ceiling and drill a small hole in each of the four corners. Then remove the template and take it up into the attic. Place it over the holes and check out any potential conflicts. Now is the time to discover that a heating duct is too close to the fan or a plumbing vent pipe is in the way.

If everything looks all right, cut the opening in the ceiling and proceed with the installation according to the manu-facturer's directions. After everything is in place, take the time to seal all the corners and joints with duct tape. Any air leaks will decrease the efficiency of the fan.

Ventilating a Crawl Space

Ventilating a crawl space helps prevent musty odors and damage to your house from moisture condensation. If you have a crawl space, you should find foundation ventilators around its lower perimeter. These vents are designed to create a cross flow of air through the crawl space so that outside air can replace damp, musty air.

If your floor is uninsulated, the temptation is to close off these vents to stop cold air from blowing through the crawl space. You might keep the floor a little warmer, but you also trap moisture and create a potential condensation problem. In any event, the vents should be open in the warmer months.

Your house probably has the minimum standard amount of vent area, since most local building codes are pretty strict about installing crawl space vents. These vents are probably adequate, but if your crawl space is damp and musty and does not have a vapor barrier installed over the bare ground, you can probably cure the problem by spreading heavy plastic sheeting over the entire crawl space. Overlap any joints in the sheets by at least a foot or so, and use bricks to weight it down around the perimeter so it stays in place.

If you suspect that your crawl space could benefit from additional vents, here's how to check if you have enough crawl space ventilation. The crawl space vents should have a net free area equal to $\frac{1}{150}$

Crawl Space
Net Free Vent Area
(square feet)

FOUNDATION LENGTH	20	25	30	35	40	45	50	55	60	65	70	75
100	13	17	20	23	27	30	33	37	40	43	47	50
95	13	16	19	22	25	29	32	35	38	41	44	48
90	12	15	18	21	24	27	30	33	36	39	42	45
85	11	14	17	20	23	26	28	31	34	37	40	43
80	11	13	16	19	21	24	27	29	32	35	37	40
75	10	13	15	18	20	23	25	28	30	33	35	38
70	9	12	14	16	19	21	23	26	28	30	33	35
65	9	11	13	15	17	20	22	24	26	28	30	33
60	8	10	12	14	16	18	20	22	24	26	28	30
55	7	9	11	13	15	17	18	20	22	24	26	28
50	7	8	10	12	13	15	17	18	20	22	23	25
45	6	8	9	11	12	14	15	17	18	20	21	23
40	5	7	8	9	11	12	13	15	16	17	19	20
35	5	6	7	8	9	11	12	13	14	15	16	18
30	4	5	6	7	8	9	10	11	12	13	14	15
25	3	4	5	6	7	8	8	9	10	11	12	13
20	3	3	4	5	5	6	7	7	8	9	9	10

FOUNDATION WIDTH

Note: *Foundation length and width are in feet.*

of the ground area in the crawl space. If you have a vapor barrier installed in the crawl space, then you need vents equal to $\frac{1}{1,500}$ of the crawl space area. The vents should be installed within 3 feet of each corner of the building.

For example, if you have a 1,700-square-foot crawl space, the vent area you need is 11.33 square feet of net free vent area for a crawl space without a vapor barrier, and 1.13 square feet of net free vent area for a crawl space that has the ground covered with plastic.

Insulating

Without exception, every old house that we have worked on has had substandard insulation. Energy cost a lot less 30 or 40 years ago, and consequently most houses were built with little insulation. Some of our houses have had insulation added, but even then it was usually not up to current standards.

Energy audit experts from the local power company tell us that caulking and weather stripping should be on the top of the list and completed before upgrading the insulation. We have experienced this ourselves. Most of the old houses that we have worked on showed noticeable improvement in comfort and energy use as soon as we weather-stripped the doors and windows.

It's been our experience that, unless there is no insulation at all in the ceiling, an old house will lose more energy through ill-fitting windows, doors, and other air leaks in the structure than through the walls and ceiling. We have found it makes good sense to plug up the air infiltration before you add insulation. See the weather-stripping sections of chapter 4, "Doors and Windows." Tightening up your house will do more to cut your energy bill than an extra 6 inches of insulation in the attic, but as soon as the house is reasonably tight, consider adding insulation.

Adding insulation to a house is not one of our favorite jobs. Insulation is itchy, dirty stuff. No matter how we dress for this job, we are ready to hit the shower as soon as the last piece of it is in place. As far as we're concerned, insulation contractors earn their money.

We insulate open attics and other easy-to-reach areas but leave filling wall cavities and insulating floors to the contractors. Whether you plan to do this job yourself or not, get a bid from a contractor. The cost of the labor is low compared with the cost of the materials, especially for a big, easy job. After you have gotten a bid, compare the price with the cost of materials. Many times we were surprised that we could have the insulation installed for little more than we could purchase the materials.

Choosing the Type of Insulation

There are five general types of commonly used insulation materials. Some types lend themselves to do-it-yourself installation better than others. Here are the basic types and our experiences with each type:

Loose Fill

This is the easiest type of insulation to install. It can be poured or blown into place between the attic floor joists. Loose-fill insulation can be made from vermiculite or rock wool, but today the most popular loose-fill materials are cellulose, fiberglass, and polystyrene. All of these materials tend to settle through the years, especially rock wool. We have had many old houses with what seems like an inch of rock wool insulation in the attic that probably started out as 5 or 6 inches when it was installed.

We have installed loose-fill fiberglass, polystyrene, and cellulose insulation with good success. In one house we blew polystyrene insulation into the walls. In another we blew fiberglass and cellulose insulation into open attics. Cellulose insulation is basically ground-up paper, so check the label and be sure that it is treated with a fire-retardant chemical and that the insulation meets all your local building codes. This type of insulation is easy to apply but does not have its own vapor barrier, so it is best applied over existing insulation that already has a vapor barrier in place.

Fiberglass Rolls or Batts

Fiberglass rolls come in long lengths either 16 or 24 inches wide so they will fit between wall studs or attic rafters. The rolls have a built-in vapor barrier in the backing that is either tar paper or aluminum foil. This backing has flanges at each side that are stapled to the rafters or studs to hold the insulation in place and seal the vapor barrier.

Fiberglass roll insulation is probably the most popular in new construction, and we have used it in additions and in areas that have not been insulated. Because of its built in vapor barrier, this type of insulation should not be used to add insulation to an already insulated area.

You can purchase roll or blanket insulation without the vapor barrier, and this type of insulation is your best choice to install on top of existing insulation to bring it up to modern specs.

Fiberglass batts are basically the same as rolls and blankets but cut to lengths of 4 to 8 feet. Unfaced batts are a good choice for upgrading insulation in attics.

Rigid Boards and Plastic Foam

Rigid insulation comes in thicknesses from ½ inch to over 1 inch, in small sheets of about 3 square feet to large sheets over 12 feet long. This type of insulation is best suited for use outside the house along foundations and on the exterior of walls under siding.

Plastic foam is very efficient but is not a do-it-yourself product. Successful installation of foam is difficult, and unless the product is mixed and handled with expertise, the foam usually causes more problems than it solves.

Whatever type of insulation you use (especially rigid boards made from anything but fiberglass), check that it will pass your local building and fire codes. One house we renovated had bad siding, so we removed it and planned to add a layer of ¾-inch-thick rigid polystyrene insulation to the walls before the new siding went back on. But after checking, we found that rigid insulation was not allowed by our local fire and building codes. If we had gone ahead and installed it, they would have made us remove it even though it met national building codes.

Check with your building department before you purchase large quantities of any type of insulation, even though it is sold in local stores. Insulation materials that your local building inspectors or fire department will not approve are sometimes sold and installed on small jobs that don't require a building permit. Just because your neighbor put up some insulation last year does not mean it meets the local codes.

Estimating Your Insulation Needs

Whatever climate you live in, insulation is important and will save you money. If your home is air-conditioned, insulation will pay off even more by cutting your cooling bills as well as your heating costs. The more insulation you have the better, is true up to a point. After that point, the cost of installing additional insulation exceeds the savings in energy costs.

The Department of Energy has published recommended R-values for different locations throughout the country. It has divided the country into similar climate zones. For each zone it has recom-

HEATING ZONE MAP

Recommended R-Values

Heating Zone	Attic Floors*	Exterior Walls	Ceilings over Unheated Crawl Space or Basement
1	R-26	R-value of full wall	R-11
2	R-26	insulation, which is	R-13
3	R-30	3½″ thick, will depend	R-19
4	R-33	on material used.	R-22
5	R-38	Range is R-11 to R-13.	R-22

If you already have R-11 or R-19 insulation on your attic floor, carefully evaluate the cost and potential energy savings of added insulation, to determine whether it will be cost-effective.

mended R-values for ceiling, floor, and wall insulation.

The R-value of insulation represents its ability to resist heat transfer. The higher the R-value, the better the insulating power. Since some insulation is more efficient than others, you need a varying amount of each to achieve the same R-value. For example, a 6-inch-thick piece of fiberglass batt insulation is rated R-19, while the same R-value can be obtained with 2 inches of a rigid isocyanate foam panel.

All insulation works best when it is teamed with an effective vapor barrier. The vapor barrier can be built into the insulation as a backing or installed separately. A plastic sheet at least 2 mils thick makes an inexpensive, effective vapor barrier.

The function of this vapor barrier is to prevent water vapor from entering the insulation. To do this effectively, the vapor barrier must be installed on the warm side of the insulation. This is usually the inside of the house.

Picture the insulation as a wall between the cool outside air and the warm inside air. Some place inside the insulation these two temperature extremes become equal. The house side of the insulation is at room temperature, but as you go into the insulation, the temperature drops until it is equal to the outside air temperature.

Warm air can hold more water vapor than cold air, so as the warm, damp inside air goes into the insulation, it begins to cool. The colder it gets, the less moisture it can hold, until it reaches a temperature called the dew point, where the air cannot hold the moisture and it condenses into water droplets. This water

decreases the effectiveness of the insulation and in severe cases can cause structural damage and rot.

Whenever you are installing insulation, don't ignore the vapor barrier. If your house has to weather a hard winter, installing insulation without a proper barrier can cause you a lot more problems than it's worth. Insulating an old house can be a lot more complicated than just piling on insulation. You can probably get easy access to the inside of a ceiling, but insulating walls is not a project for the do-it-yourselfer. If you live in a cold climate and have an old house with no wall insulation, consult an insulation contractor.

As we said earlier, insulation contractors earn their money. Here are some tips we have found about working with fiberglass insulation. If you pretend you are going into space and dress accordingly, you can emerge from the attic relatively intact.

When you're working with insulation, always be prepared:

▶ Wear safety glasses.

▶ Wear a dust mask, or better yet, a respirator.

▶ Wear protective gloves.

▶ Wear a long-sleeved shirt and wrap rubber bands around the cuffs to seal out the irritating fiberglass particles.

▶ Wear long pants and seal the pant legs with rubber bands.

▶ Toss the clothes into the washing machine immediately after the job, and wash them separately from other laundry. If you let then lie around or put them in a clothes hamper, the fiberglass particles will get all over the place.

Installing insulation requires only a few basic tools, including a measuring tape, utility knife, straightedge, heavy-duty scissors, and staple gun. Consider renting an electric staple gun if you have a lot of wall or ceiling insulation to staple in place. After a couple of hours, squeezing the trigger of a heavy-duty staple gun becomes quite a chore. Trade off the stapling job with a helper if possible.

Insulation is very bulky and takes up a lot of storage space. Don't make the mistake of opening a bundle of fiberglass rolls or bats until you are ready to use them. The insulation material is very compressed, and it will fluff up to several times its original size as soon as you break the package. Don't open the packages in a living area, or you risk getting fiberglass particles over everything.

Insulating an Unfinished Attic

The easiest area to insulate is an unfinished attic. You can do the job yourself in a few hours, and it will pay you back in energy savings for years to come. Unless you plan to finish the attic, your best bet is to insulate the attic floor, not the ceiling. If you insulate the ceiling, you'll still be heating space you don't need to heat, plus you'll have to make sure the insulation doesn't interfere with ventilation of the rafters. Here's what's involved:

Choose a cool day.   The attic gets very hot, even on a cool day, so this is not a project for the middle of August. Start in the morning before the sun has had a chance to warm the roof. Working at night is also another good time. Not much light gets into an attic, so you will probably have to rig a few lights anyway.

Protect the ceiling below.   If your attic has no floor, purchase a couple of sheets of ¾-inch plywood and rip them down the center to form 2 × 8-foot pieces. Lay these over the floor joists for easy walking. Don't try to navigate on the ceiling joists. You will end up with sore knees or slip off a narrow joist and step through the ceiling.

Rig lights.   If there's no light in the attic, use a couple of work lights hung from the rafters in the area where you're working. You need to see what you are doing, so bring in plenty of light.

Use the proper insulation.   If there's no insulation in the attic, use a kraft paper-faced or foil-faced insulation with the vapor barrier laid down, or toward the warm side. If you're adding to existing insulation, use an unfaced insulation.

Don't block eaves vents.   Start installing the insulation at the outside wall. The insulation should extend beyond the top plate of the outside wall but not block the flow of air from eaves vents. Staple the flaps or flanges of the blankets on the sides of the floor joists.

Remember, the vapor barrier goes down toward the warm area of the house.

Use full lengths of insulation.   Use long runs first and save cutoffs for installing in shorter spaces. Make sure that you butt each roll of insulation tightly against the roll next to it. Cut away sections to fit around cross bracing.

Don't insulate light boxes.   Place insulation everywhere you can, but do not put it over light boxes or recessed light cans. Cut the insulation so there are several inches of clearance between the fixture and the insulation.

Add insulation across the joists.   Additional insulation should be placed across the floor joists. The rolls should be unbacked and placed tightly together.

Insulating Floors above an Unheated Vented Crawl Space

Insulating floors is another project that you should consider doing yourself.

Working in the crawl space can be dirty, but the area is usually easy to get into, and placing the insulation isn't tricky. Here's basically what's involved:

Install insulation vapor barrier up.   Use fiberglass rolls or bats with a foil or kraft paper vapor barrier. Install it with this vapor barrier facing up or against the subfloor above.

Push the rolls into position.   Install blankets or batts between the floor joists. Friction will hold them temporarily in place.

Secure the insulation with wire.   Because the vapor barrier is facing up, you won't be able to use the stapling flanges. So hold the insulation in place with galvanized chicken wire or hardware cloth nailed to the joists. You can also use special spring-metal strips that are forced between the joists. Their sharp tips dig into the wood and hold the insulation up.

CHAPTER 14 Home Security

The bad news is that nothing you can do, short of an electric fence topped with razor wire, can keep a really determined professional burglar from entering your home. The good news is that most burglars are not highly skilled break-in artists. And even those that are, most likely, are not all that determined to get into your house. Put some well-planned obstacles in a burglar's way, and he'll move on down the street in search of an easier mark.

Your first line of defense is obvious —a sturdy door and strong locks on all windows and doors. Another important and relatively inexpensive element of home security is outdoor lighting; burglars don't like to be on display when they work. In this chapter we'll discuss locks and lights. We'll also tell you how to install some basic alarms and security systems, just in case someone does get through your locks.

Upgrading Your Locks

Upgrading the lock on your door with a dead bolt is a relatively easy way to greatly increase your protection against thieves. Most older homes have mortise locks, while newly built homes usually have cylinder locks with a key in the doorknob. Many of the cheaper cylinder locks leave a lot to be desired. Some of them have short bolts (the steel rods that protrude into the frame) that allow the intruder to use a pry bar to spread the frame and pop the door open. Inexpensive cylinder locks can be wrenched open with a large pipe wrench or with a special tool designed to pull out the tumbler mechanism.

Installing a good-quality dead-bolt lock will make opening the door without the key much more difficult and time consuming. No lock is burglarproof, but making it difficult for an intruder may deter him from your house and send him looking for an easier mark.

Think heavy metal when looking for a dead-bolt lock. Its working parts should be made of a high-quality steel, and the lock cylinder should have a reinforced protective casing. Most important, the bolt (or latch throw) should be at least 1 inch long, and preferably longer. That means the latch should extend an inch out of the lock and into the doorjamb. A shorter one can be jimmied or pried out of the space between the door and frame. Buy the best-quality lock you can afford.

Dead bolts are easy to install, since they come with templates that locate all holes. Most locks require that you bore a 2⅛-inch hole through the door for the lock mechanism and a ⅞-inch hole in the door edge for the bolt. This is done with a hole saw, which chucks into your drill. If you don't have a hole saw this size, check with the installation instructions before you purchase one, because some locks might require a slightly larger hole. Most hole saws come in two parts, a mandrel that chucks into the drill and the saw itself that threads onto the mandrel. So, if you have a hole saw that's the wrong size, you may be able to just buy a saw and use the mandrel you have.

If you don't have a hole saw or a spade bit to make the holes, purchase a lock installation kit. These kits have both types of bits necessary to install the dead bolt and most other locksets, but check that the sizes of the drill bit and hole saw are what you need. Here's a rundown of the basic steps for installing a dead-bolt lock:

Step 1: Locate the dead bolt 6 inches or more above the existing lock. The template has several lines, representing different door thicknesses, that you can crease it on. Measure the thickness of your door, and crease the template accordingly. Tape the template to the door.

Step 2: Drive nails or pins through the center marks on the template. You have to mark the center of the lock mechanism hole on the face of the door, and the bolt hole on the door edge.

Step 3: Remove the template, then use the nail or pin holes to center the hole saw and drill bit so you can make holes through the face of the door and on the door edge. For the large hole, drill halfway through one side and then complete the hole from the other side, to prevent splintering the surface of the door.

Step 4: Insert the latch in the edge of the door, and then trace around it with a sharp utility knife. Remove the

INSTALLING A DEAD BOLT

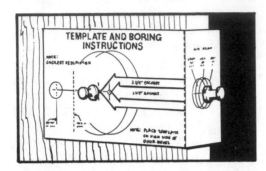

1. The dead bolt should be installed about 44 inches from the floor and at least 6 inches from the key lock. Pin the template in place, remove it, and use the pin holes to locate where the center of each hole should be when you drill into the edge and face of the door.

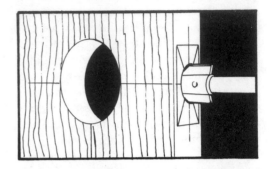

2. Drill a ⅛-inch pilot hole through the face of the door. Then, use a hole saw to cut a 2⅛-inch hole halfway through from both directions. Now drill a hole in the edge of the door, through to the larger hole.

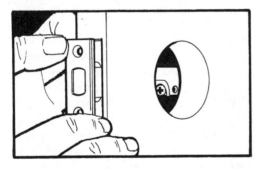

3. Insert the latch, and scribe around it with a utility knife. Remove the latch, and cut the mortise with a wood chisel.

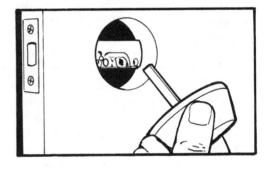

4. Assemble the lock according to the manufacturer's instructions.

latch and use a ¾-inch wood chisel to cut the mortise for the latch plate. The easiest way to do this is start at one end of the latch plate outline and make a series of closely spaced cuts with the chisel. Then go back and remove the small pieces. Try to make the cuts the same depth, so smoothing the mortise will be

easier. Check that the latch is flush with the edge of the door, and secure it in place with the screws provided.

Step 5: Assemble the lock mechanism according to the manufacturer's directions. Test its movement. Slight adjustment might be necessary. Also note that the key should be inserted into the lock with the ragged, cut edge facing up. If the key faces the other direction, then reverse the tumbler mechanism according to the instructions.

Step 6: Mark the location of the striker plate, and cut the mortise on the doorjamb in the same way as the latch plate. Install the striker plate with the screws provided. They should be long enough to go through the jamb and into the surrounding framing.

Making a Sliding Glass Patio Door More Secure

In a pinch, use a cutoff broomstick or piece of 2 × 2 to wedge in the floor track. But a better idea is to use a lock specifically designed for a sliding glass door. There are various types. One is installed in the outside frame at the top, preventing the sliding panel from being lifted out and removed. You can also install a plunger-type window lock on the movable door. It's easy to install— usually involving only drilling a few mounting holes to screw the lock into place.

The body of the plunger-type lock houses the tumblers and locking plunger. When you push in on the key, a steel plunger comes out the back of the lock and protrudes into a hole in the adjoining fixed door. The movable door cannot be opened as long as the plunger is extended, because it is secure in the fixed door. To release the plunger, all you have to do is turn the key. Here's all there is to installing one:

Step 1: Close and lock the sliding door. Make sure that the plunger is retracted into the body of the lock. Hold the lock in position on the edge of the

movable door toward the top, according to the manufacturer's directions. Mark the locations of the mounting screws by using the lock body as a template. Then drill pilot holes for the mounting screws.

Step 2: Some manufacturers provide a template to locate the plunger hole in the fixed door. If not, temporarily secure the lock to the movable door and extend the lock plunger until it touches the fixed door. Mark the location of the plunger on the fixed door, then remove the lock and drill the hole for the plunger.

Step 3: Install the lock on the movable door with the screws provided. Test the lock by pushing the key into the lock body until you hear a click and the key stays in. Then unlock the main lock on the door and try to open it. The plunger will prevent the door from moving. If you drill another plunger hole about 6 inches from the first, you will be able to lock the sliding door when it is 6 inches open. This will allow for ventilation, but an intruder can't squeeze through the 6-inch opening.

Do-It-Yourself Sliding Door Lock

Here's a quick and easy lock that you can make using a 16d nail. First check that the sliding door is fully closed. At the top of the movable panel, drill a ⅛-inch hole at a downward angle through the sliding panel and into the fixed one. All you have to do is insert the nail into the hole, and it will keep the doors from moving.

Make sure everyone knows how to remove the nail, because in case of fire you cannot get the door open with the nail in place.

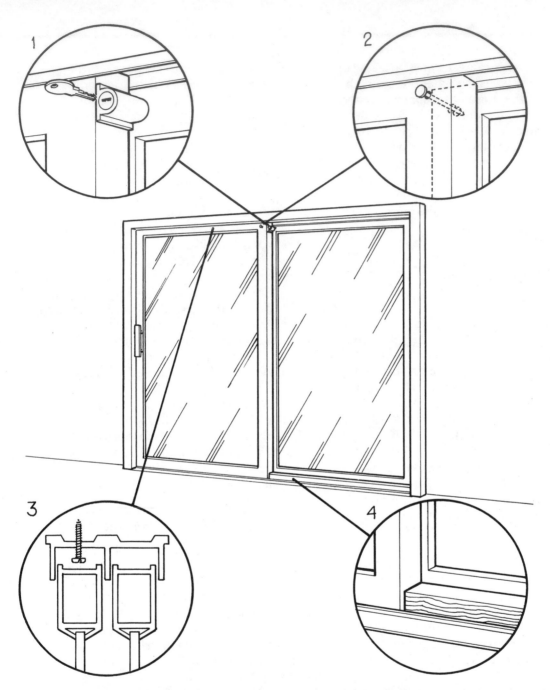

Here are some ideas for increasing the security of your sliding glass doors:
(1) A plunger lock on a movable door prevents it from being pried open or lifted off the track. (2) A large nail inserted into a hole through the movable frame and part way through the fixed frame will lock the doors together. (3) Prevent a movable door from being lifted out of its track by installing several large sheet-metal screws in the overhead track. Tighten the screws just enough to allow the door to slide freely. (4) Reinforce a standard door lock with a piece of 2 × 2 stock, cut to fit between the movable door and jamb.

Adding Window Locks

Take a walk around your house and appraise it as a potential intruder would. Look at each window and decide if you would attempt to break in through it. Windows hidden from view of neighbors or passing traffic are ideal for breaking and entering. Basement and ground level windows are also prime targets for getting into a house.

To help guard against this problem, you'll find a good selection of window locks at home centers and hardware stores. All are designed to be bolted on or screwed in and require just a hole or two drilled into the window casing or frame.

Most windows already have locks, but usually they can be opened if the glass is broken. Keyed window locks keep the window from being opened even if the glass is broken. This is a factor with windows with small panes. It is an easy matter for a intruder to break a small pane near the lock and then reach inside and open the window. A keyed lock prevents this.

Another advantage to a keyed lock is that most are designed so the window can be locked in a partially open position. With this arrangement the window can be left open just wide enough to allow air in but not wide enough to allow someone to crawl through.

If you install keyed window locks, make sure everyone in the house knows where the key or keys are and how to work the lock in case of a fire. You might consider hanging the key near the window but out of reach of anyone trying to reach in through the window. Also, mark the keys so you will not get them mixed up, or be sure that all the window locks can be opened with the same key. This usually can be arranged with locks from the same manufacturer.

You can also purchase window locks designed to replace conventional locks. Consider this if you have windows with hardware that has many coats of paint.

When shopping for window locks, know the type of window you have. Some locks, such as the keyed plunger type, can be mounted on just about any type of window with a little ingenuity. The body of the lock can be mounted on the window sash, and a hole for the plunger can be drilled into the frame. When the plunger is locked in the extended position, the window can't be opened. You can drill several holes in the frame so the window can be locked in different positions. If you remove the existing lock, it's possible that you'll want to repaint the window before installing a new lock.

Taking Simple Steps to Burglarproof Your House

An intruder wants to go unnoticed, so it's very likely that he'll try a side or back entrance to your house. Of course, the word *entrance* doesn't have to refer to doors alone. Windows also are likely entry points. Get a friend or neighbor to survey your house, and then you do the same for him. Imagine that you are the thief sizing up the house for a job. Check these points out carefully:

▶ Look for easy entry points at windows where there's no exterior lighting and where shrubbery is overgrown. Dark, concealed windows, especially in a basement or on the first floor, are easy targets. Second-story windows are likely candidates if there are good climbing trees nearby.

▶ Obviously, a locked door is the first line of defense. Is there a garage with access to the house? Often it's a weak lock (or none at all) on the garage that will allow a burglar to get inside.

▶ Most intruders don't pick the lock on a door. They break down the door with a pry bar or they kick it in. Seriously look at the construction of the doors. Is there a dead bolt and lock plate reinforcement to make it more difficult for the intruder?

Installing a Perimeter Security System

A perimeter system protects your home by activating alarms at entry points. The basic components are sensors placed on doors and windows, with additional components such as an alarm horn or siren and smoke detectors. These systems are controlled by master panels for monitoring and programming.

Home security systems can be wired or wireless. The wired systems use light, concealed wires to connect the sensors to the master panel. The wiring is not difficult. It is low voltage and safe to work with, but concealing the wires can be a real hassle. Installing a wired system is a major project best left to professionals with the skills and tools necessary to do a neat job of concealing the wires.

Wireless systems, on the other hand, use small radio transmitters, infrared light, or high-pitched sound to connect the sensors to the central control unit. These systems have come a long way and are now almost as dependable as the wired type. Their major advantage is that they do not require long wires leading back to the control unit.

Unless you require some special feature only a sophisticated wired system can offer, we think the wireless units are the best systems for the do-it-yourselfer to install. They are sold in kits offering a master panel, transmitters, and magnetic sensors. The basic kits will get you started, but it's likely that you'll need to buy additional sensors and accessories.

When shopping, pick up brochures about various systems. Compare the protection offered and installation techniques needed, to help determine which is best for you. Compare the different accessory sensors and the cost of additional transmitters and sensors. Some basic kits are very inexpensive, but when you purchase the necessary additional components to round out your system, the cost jumps considerably.

Also check out the capacity of the central control unit. Make sure it has the capacity to handle the system you plan. Also keep your basic objectives in mind when you design the system. A simple perimeter alarm system can grow into an elaborate home security system after you discover all the additional sensors that are available. If your system adds up to over $1,000 or so, get a bid from a professional security company. You might be pleasantly surprised that you can have a basic system professionally installed for a very reasonable cost. But it's still cheaper for you to install a basic wireless system. Here are some tips to help you plan and install a basic system:

Make a plan. Before you shop for a system, decide what you want in a security system. For example, you might want to install detectors on all doors and windows to activate the alarm if any are opened. Another option might be to install a motion detector in a large room with several windows and doors. This single unit then will do the job of several individual ones. A pressure-sensitive mat could be installed at the base of the stairs under a rug to warn of anyone coming up the stairs. Motion detectors can also be installed outside. They can be tied to the security system or made to activate outside lights.

Shop for features. After you have a basic plan, go look at systems. When you see a feature or accessory that you didn't know existed (for example, an expensive infrared motion detector), go back to your original plan and see how it fits in. It's possible that this unit placed outside a bay window or on the patio will give you the protection you want in these areas. Don't purchase accessories just because they are available.

Check out how many sensors can be connected to a single transmitter. The transmitters are expensive compared with the sensors. You can save if you can connect several sensors to a single transmitter. Also check that the manufacturer offers the combination of sensors that you plan to use. If not, check to see if another brand of sensor will work with the transmitter. Most sensors are no more than smart switches that are activated by the movement of a magnet, breaking of glass, or pressure from footsteps.

Finalize your plan. Once you have the specifications from the manufacturer and your basic plan, decide exactly which sensors you need and where you will place them. Initially, you'll want to have magnetic sensors on all windows that are covered by shrubs or otherwise hidden from view, and also on all doors, including the garage and basement doors.

Installing a Wireless Security System

The basic devices used in any system are door and window sensors. These are two-part devices: The sensor mounts on the door or window frame, and the magnet is secured to the movable door or window sash. If the door or window is opened, the magnet is moved away from the sensor and it signals the system.

Manufacturers include detailed installation instructions with every system and sensors. The magnetic sensors used in a wireless system are installed in basically the same way on either doors or windows. The easiest place to install a door sensor is on the inside face of the frame casing. Follow the specific manufacturer's directions. Here's what's involved in protecting a door or window with a magnetic sensor:

Step 1: The sensor is installed on the top part of the door frame. Use the template supplied by the manufacturer, or hold the sensor in position so it is flush with the opening of the door frame.

Step 2: Mount the transmitter in the wall above the door frame over the sensor. Lead the wires from the sensor to the transmitter, and hook them up according to the wiring diagram furnished by the manufacturer.

Step 3: Mount the magnet on the face of the door below the sensor. Adjust the placement of the magnet so that it is close enough to the sensor to activate it but does not interfere with the movement of the door.

Step 4: Test the unit by turning on the system and arming the door sensor according to the operating instructions. Open the door and the alarm should sound. Some systems have a test procedure so you can test each device without setting off the alarm bell or siren.

Installing Smoke/Fire Detectors

The easiest type of home smoke alarm to install is a battery-powered unit. You can also get a version that is wired into the electrical system of your house.

Whichever type you choose, an important feature is an emergency light that (operating on its own battery) turns on when the detector is activated. This light is independent of the house wiring and will work during a power failure. Even if the light is small, a dimly lighted hall is better than total darkness.

Where to Put a Smoke Detector

Smoke detectors are more efficient if you install them where the smoke can get to them and the alarm can be heard. If you have a multilevel house, it is important that a detector be installed on every level. Here are the best locations:

▶ in the hallway outside all bedroom areas (or where people sleep)

▶ inside every bedroom where there is a person who smokes

▶ inside every bedroom where a portable heater, humidifier, or other appliance operates

▶ inside every bedroom where someone sleeps with the door closed

▶ at both ends of a hallway with bedrooms when the hallway is more than 40 feet long

▶ at the bottom of a basement stairwell

Where Not to Put a Smoke Detector

There are some areas where the experts recommend that you not install a smoke detector. Mounting a smoke detector in these areas usually results in the unit going off so often that you begin to ignore it—like the boy who cried wolf. Smoke detectors are meant to startle people into reacting. Don't place them in the following locations:

▶ in or near the kitchen or in airstreams passing by it

▶ in or near the garage

▶ near a furnace, water heater, or gas space heater

▶ in very dusty or dirty areas

▶ near a fluorescent light fixture

How to Install a Smoke Detector

Read through this section and then go out and get a smoke detector. We guarantee it will take you less than 30 minutes to install it.

After you decide the best location in your house to install one or more detectors, it is important that you mount them properly. If you plan to install one on the ceiling, mount it as close to the center of the ceiling as possible, but no closer than 4 inches to a wall or corner. For a sloped ceiling, mount a detector about 3 feet (measured horizontally) from the highest point of the ceiling.

If you plan to mount the detector on a wall, check your local building code to see if wall mounting is permitted. If so, mount a detector on the wall between 4 and 6 inches from the ceiling.

Read the directions that come with the detector you purchase, so you install the proper batteries and know how to test it after you have it mounted. Here is what's involved, to give you an idea how easy it is to install:

Step 1: Dismantle the detector and use the base mounting plate, or a template supplied by the manufacturer, to locate the mounting screw holes. Hold the base in position and mark through the holes or slots in the base with a pencil.

Step 2: Drill pilot holes for the wall anchors, using a ¼ or ³⁄₁₆-inch bit, whichever is required for the wall anchors. Push the wall anchors (usually mounting hardware is included) into the holes, and tap them flat against the ceiling or wall with a hammer.

Step 3: Thread the screws into the anchors and tighten them about three-quarters of the way. Then position the base plate on the wall or ceiling so the slots fit over the screw heads. Tighten the screws down.

Step 4: Put the batteries in the detector, being careful to observe the polarity of the batteries. Most use a 9-volt transistor battery with a snap-on fitting that can be installed only one way.

Step 5: Press the test switch and follow the directions provided, to make sure it is working properly.

Great Gadgets & Gizmos

☞ **Outdoor control light** Never before have there been so many automatic lighting products that turn themselves on when triggered by motion or sound. These safety devices offer the homeowner added protection using passive infrared technology. A new First Alert Outdoor Control Light converts existing outdoor light fixtures into automatic lighting that turns the light on as someone approaches the house. This is a handy feature for when guests arrive, as well as a deterrent to burglars. It is made by First Alert, 780 McClure Road, Aurora, IL 60504.

☞ **Keepsafer Plus Pro** This is a wireless security system designed specifically for do-it-yourself installation. It's the deluxe version of the Keepsafer Plus system from Schlage Lock Company, 2401 Bayshore Boulevard, San Francisco, CA 94119.

Index

Page references in *italic* indicate illustrations.
Boldface references indicate tables.